PRAISE FOR *Black Detroit*

"Detroit has found its griot in Herb Boyd. Griots, traditional West African storytellers, carry their people's traditions from generation to generation, and are renowned for their encyclopedic knowledge, their wit, and their ability to bridge the past and present. In the tradition of the griot, Boyd's purpose is to celebrate the black men and women, the city's 'fearless freedom fighters,' who would otherwise remain on history's margins. The characters who walk across Boyd's pages are fascinating."

—*New York Times Book Review*

"Comprehensive and compelling. . . . We owe [Boyd] a debt of gratitude." —*Washington Post*

"Every now and then, a lecture, a moment, or a book comes along that is necessary. Mayor Mike Duggan's history lesson at Mackinac Island, where he recounted how decades of redlining and government housing discrimination helped create some of Detroit's greatest challenges, was necessary. Herb Boyd's book on the history of black Detroit is another. Perhaps 'necessary' isn't the right word. The right word should be 'required.'"

—*Detroit Free Press*

"*Black Detroit* celebrates the resilience of black people in Detroit from the city's birth three centuries ago until the present. [It is] an indispensable study of the Motor City's black church, media, labor struggles, politics, and culture both yesterday and today."

—*Pittsburgh Courier*

"Boyd . . . breathes new life into the history of Detroit through stories of the city's black residents from its earliest days to its bittersweet present. . . . He leaves no stone unturned, making his work an invaluable repository of all that is black Detroit."

—*Publishers Weekly* (starred review)

"An inspiring, illuminating book that will interest students of urban history and the black experience." —*Kirkus Reviews*

"The extensive coverage demonstrates the full range and influence of black citizens in Detroit. . . . Recommended for anyone interested in Detroit or in urban history." —*Library Journal*

"Detroit has become a code for urban failure, which is to say black failure. Herb Boyd's riveting new history, *Black Detroit*, turns an oft caricatured community into a world of actual, struggling human beings. This is not easy work. But Boyd, with his Detroit roots and lucid prose, performs the labor as though he were born to do so." —Ta-Nehisi Coates, author of *Between the World and Me*

"In *Black Detroit*, Herb Boyd does a captivating job of writing, compression, and interpretation. The personal spine of his narrative makes it special. Readers will appreciate Boyd's comprehensive grasp of one of America's most important cities. It's a superb read with vital lessons on a people's struggle for self-determination."

—David Levering Lewis, professor emeritus of history at New York University, and two-time winner of the Pulitzer Prize for biography

"With extraordinary passion, and with truly beautiful prose, Herb Boyd captures all that is the Motor City. Through the pages of this book readers actually feel Detroit—they not only experience a city that has always been at the very epicenter of this nation's most important freedom struggles, but they also come to know a city that has always, *always*, been anchored by a most powerful and determined black community. As Boyd reminds us all: Black Detroit is the place where dreams of justice never, ever die." —Heather Ann Thompson, author of *Blood in the Water: The Attica Prison Uprising of 1971 and Its Legacy*

"As a lifelong resident of Detroit, I was exposed from a young age to the city's political and social history through my father's activism in the UAW. It imbued me with a deep awareness of and love for its black culture, history, and resilience. Herb Boyd's exhaustive research is compelling and extensive—it quickened my knowledge of the city's black history. Beginning in 1701, Boyd guides his readers through the long journey of black Detroiters as they struggle for their place. The depth and breadth of this magnum opus make for a profound and richly informative history of the city. Every Detroiter should read this book." —Representative John Conyers Jr.

"Herb Boyd has done it again. *Black Detroit* is a powerful, timely, and important history of an iconic city whose hopes and dreams, triumphs and tragedies, continue to both challenge and shape the African-American experience and American democracy. This brilliant history is a must-read for students, scholars, and all those interested in the history of the civil rights movement and black freedom struggle." —Peniel E. Joseph, author of *Stokely: A Life*

BLACK DETROIT

ALSO BY HERB BOYD

Brotherman—The Odyssey of Black Men in America
(Co-edited with Robert Allen)

Autobiography of a People—Three Centuries of African
American History as Told by Those Who Lived It (Editor)

The Diary of Malcolm X: El-Hajj Malik El-Shabazz
(Co-edited with Ilyasah Shabazz)

We Shall Overcome—The History of the Civil Rights
Movement as It Happened

Civil Rights—Yesterday & Today
(With Todd Steven Burroughs)

Baldwin's Harlem: A Biography of James Baldwin

Pound for Pound: A Biography of Sugar Ray Robinson

Heroes of America: Martin Luther King, Jr.

Down the Glory Road: Contributions of African Americans
in United States History and Culture

Black Panthers for Beginners (Illustrated by Lance Tooks)

African History for Beginners (Illustrated by
Shey Wolvek Phister)

The Harlem Reader (Editor)

Race and Resistance (Editor)

The Former Portuguese Colonies: Angola, Mozambique,
Guinea-Bissau, Cape Verde, São Tomé, and Principe

Black Detroit

A PEOPLE'S HISTORY OF
SELF-DETERMINATION

Herb Boyd

Amistad

An Imprint of HarperCollins*Publishers*

FIRST AMISTAD PAPERBACK EDITION PUBLISHED 2018.

Designed by Paula Russell Szafranski

Library of Congress Cataloging-in-Publication Data has been applied for.

ISBN 978-0-06-234663-6 (pbk.)

24 25 26 27 28 LBC 10 9 8 7 6

To my mother, Katherine Brown, and the countless other Detroiters who made me feel at home, no matter where I was

CONTENTS

FOREWORD

By Rev. Dr. JoAnn Watson

Detroit was barely a century old when African American fugitives fleeing bondage began arriving from the South. By the 1830s, a considerable number had settled in Detroit.

Thornton and Ruthie Blackburn had ingeniously freed themselves from captivity in Louisville, Kentucky. The attempts to capture them and return them to their slave owners was met with serious resistance by the city's growing abolitionist movement. At the forefront of this movement were black stalwarts such as William Lambert, George DeBaptiste, and William Webb, joined by a coterie of white supporters.

Securing the safety of the Blackburns and facilitating their flight to Canada was not done without violence and turmoil, sparking the city's first racial disturbance. Herb probes this incident with precision, noting in the aftermath of the riot the stabilizing forces that would be a beacon to others seeking refuge from bondage.

From this antislavery foundation, the fight for black self-determination remained evident during the Civil War when African American soldiers from the city were among the first to be deployed as units against the Confederates. A plaque in downtown Detroit commemorates the members of the First Colored Regiment, many of whom died bravely on the battlefield in South Carolina. Other returning veterans would be among the formidable civic leaders fomenting an emerging black middle class after the war.

In its treatment of the Gilded Age, *Black Detroit* shows how such social and cultural mavens as Azalia Hackley, Fannie Richards, and members of the Pelham family placed their stamp on other aspects of self-determination, whether in the arts, education, or journalism. Gaining a foothold in business, as the Pelham family did, cannot be excluded in a discussion of black Detroiters and their push for self-reliance and independence. *Black Detroit* also showcases that same striving for self-determination in the world of entertainment, as well as through the remarkable accomplishments of such inventors as Elijah McCoy, the "real McCoy."

The vitality of that age is extended into the new century, and we witness the role of the city's African American population in the shaping of manufacturing, working as stevedores on the waterfront, in the foundries, or on the assembly line of the nascent automobile industry. When the Great Migration gathered steam, Detroit was a focal point, and the arrival of countless numbers of migrants was the social engine that gave rise to the National Urban League. *Black Detroit* astutely recounts the pivotal role played by such social engineers of that organization as John Dancy and Forrester Washington. It was instructive to learn that they were also key figures in the anti-discrimination quest in employment and during the housing turbulence of the 1920s, being particularly forthright in their defense of Ossian Sweet and his family in the trials and tribulation they endured integrating a neighborhood on the city's east side. The Sweet family's insurgency was indicative of the black residents' determination to break the chain of the restrictive covenant that bound them in Black Bottom and Paradise Valley.

Black resilience in Detroit was never more decisive than during the Great Depression, and *Black Detroit* charts the rise of black workers during this time when they emerged as more than just rank-and-file members of the automotive unions. Horace Sheffield, Buddy Battle, Marc Stepp, and Chris Alston are just a few of the union activists highlighted in the book. They would be the nucleus of the next generation of labor leaders, with none more prominent and unforgettable than Coleman Young. Black workers were at the point of production when Detroit was known globally as the "arsenal of democracy," and some of that same leadership before World War II was instrumental in the political breakthroughs that occurred in the fifties and sixties.

Although the civil rights movement is best noted for the marches in the South, Detroit and its activist community are not ignored here, and Boyd cites the march in the city in 1963 as a precursor of the March on Washington weeks later. The hue and cry for jobs and justice during that historic march found its first iteration in Detroit, with the Rev. C. L. Franklin among the drum majors.

I was impressed to see that my mentor "Reparations Ray" Jenkins was mentioned because he was among the prime movers and indomitable forces in the struggle for reparations.

Throughout Detroit's history, black Detroiters have been ever vigilant when it comes to overzealous police, and the successful fight against STRESS (Stop the Robberies and Enjoy Safe Streets) was emblematic of that resolve. Coleman Young's election as the city's first black mayor was exemplary of the ongoing efforts of black self-determination. At the same time the brutal excessiveness of the police was being stifled, activists on the campuses and in the factories came together and created a critical mass that evolved into the League of Revolutionary Black Workers; this story is one that *Black Detroit* discusses with unique insight.

In fact, from this moment on, whether describing the music of Motown, the political formations of the late sixties, advocacy for reparations, or analyzing the subsequent setbacks of the seventies, *Black Detroit* is an unswerving witness. This tome is impeccably researched and shows that Herb Boyd "knows where all the bodies are buried." *Black Detroit* is a unique blend of social, political, and economic urban history. Many of the work's recollections are similar to my own. As such, in many ways, this is my story, and I am sure that many Detroiters, black and white, will feel the same.

Rev. Dr. JoAnn Watson
Professor, Wayne County Community College District
Associate Pastor, West Side Unity Church
Radio-TV Host, Wake Up Detroit!

BLACK DETROIT

INTRODUCTION

At four years old and only a few hours removed from a peanut farm and cotton patch outside of Tuskegee, Alabama, I was terrified riding a train for the first time. I clutched my mother's hand and shook with fear, not knowing what to make of the huge metallic beast with steam shooting from the engine, making a noise like a bull elephant. My anxiety began the moment a man in a blue uniform yelled, "All aboard." The train gradually gained momentum, and my nerves settled down as I watched the Alabama landscape riffle by like a deck of cards. When my eyes weren't following the passing scenes outside the train's window, they were locked on my new traveling shoes, still somewhat uncomfortable for someone accustomed to being barefoot. My mother told my brother and me that the train would be taking us to our new home.

We were part of a great migration of African Americans leaving the South. We were representative of those who were fleeing the multitude of Jim Crow restrictions, the inequality of sharecropping, and the terror of the Ku Klux Klan and other night riders. There was chatter and excitement from the other black travelers. The buzz overheard was no more comprehensible than the evening sounds of the crickets and cicadas that I heard back home.

"We're in Detroit," my mother exclaimed as she awakened us, wiped our faces, and collected and packed away a few items in our cardboard suitcase.

It was 1943. Michigan Central Station was a grand room with chandeliers suspended from the ceiling. The light from the morning sun beaming through the big windows was almost blinding. There were more people moving about than I had ever seen in one place. In the station were men and women dressed in military uniforms. Charles, my brother, was particularly fascinated by them and repeatedly had to be pulled away from the attraction.

After Mother found a scrap of paper in her purse with some numbers scribbled on it, we boarded a bus that took us through downtown Detroit. With my face pressed against the window, I saw tall buildings and lights that seemed to be everywhere. The Fox Theatre glistened with blinking incandescent bulbs that encircled the marquee like a brilliant necklace, and around the corner a Camel cigarette advertising billboard puffed smoke rings from a man's mouth. In the streets were trolleys, buses, and all kinds of automobiles. We were a long way from the life I had known in Cotton Valley, a very long way.

As in many cities, Detroit's black community was quartered near the river, which in the past had been a point of departure for fugitive slaves hoping to cross into Canada. Our first real residence in Detroit was near the storied section called Black Bottom. There we joined many of our neighbors who also had migrated from Alabama. All newcomers had at least one relative who had previously moved to the Bottom, someone they could call on, much like the Iraqi Chaldean Christian community that would later settle on the upper east side of the city. The main thoroughfare in the Bottom was Hastings Street, where blacks patronized the primarily Jewish businesses.

We moved to the north end of the city before we had an opportunity to meet many of the notables from the neighborhood, such as Joe Louis and his onetime manager, John Roxborough; Coleman Young, the first African American mayor of Detroit; Sunnie Wilson, businessman, nightclub owner, and host extraordinaire; and Ben Turpin, the city's first black police officer. The North End, as it was called, wasn't as congested as the Bottom. Oakland and Russell streets had their bars, pawnshops, beauty parlors and barbershops, funeral homes, and nightclubs. From the standpoint of music, particularly the blues, there was no comparison to Hastings Street or Saint Antoine. The blues that emanated from every keyhole and peephole on Hastings was rather muted on the North End; only from Lee's Sensation, Phelps Lounge, Champion Bar, or the Chesterfield Lounge was there a similar beat. During my youth in this neighborhood, I was in close proximity to the city's most richly endowed African Americans on Chicago and Boston boulevards. The flamboyant Prophet Jones, Congressman Charles Diggs, Motown mogul Berry Gordy Jr., tap dancer extraordinaire Lloyd Story, and several doctors, including Remus Robinson and David Northcross, were among the neighborhood's black notables. This neighborhood, with its lavish homes built by the legendary Detroiters Henry Ford, Walter O. Briggs, and James Couzens, was later named the Boston-Edison Historic District.

Every two or three years, we moved to one of the other neighborhoods of the 139-square-mile city. From North End, we moved to the far west side, near Eight Mile Road. At one time, the six-foot-high concrete wall a block away separated the white and black communities. We were the second black family to live on our block. Across the street from us was an Irish family, on both sides were Italian families, and the remainder of families on the block were Jewish and members of other ethnic groups. I would be among the first black students to attend Edgar Albert Guest School. I also enrolled in Mumford High School for one year, where there were racially insensitive students. For the most part, whether on the block or in school, our blackness was for our neighbors an object of derision and insult.

After my mother and stepfather separated, the house that they had purchased became too much for my mother to handle alone. We returned to the North End and then the Bottom and bounced from one basement apartment to another, always a move or two ahead of the landlords or bill collectors—even though, like other hardworking Detroiters, my mother left home at the break of day and returned after sundown. In addition to various other positions, she worked in Detroit's suburbs as a domestic every day of the week. My mother ran the kitchen at Hall's Department Store on the city's west side, where she got me my first job. I also worked there running back and forth for stock from the sales floor to the warehouse. At MOPAR, a company owned by the Chrysler Motor Company that made small electrical automotive parts—very similar to Ex-Cell-O, where my mother had worked—I did a little bit of everything. The variety of tasks I performed there prepared me for the versatility required when later I was hired at the Dodge Main automobile factory in Hamtramck. There I was a "swing man," which meant that whenever someone didn't show up for work, I was the replacement. From the assembly line to the wet deck, where I worked a buffer taking the shine off the cars' first primer coat, to guiding cars off the final ramp, I had to be ready for practically every job in the plant. Thankfully, the veterans there often rescued me whenever I was less than ready.

Eventually we landed in the Jeffries Projects, which were

near the Brewster Projects. It was there that I met many of the creative musicians who would later populate the blues and jazz world, who would be the performers and producers at Motown Records, as well as those who would become star athletes, political activists, and budding intellectuals.

Long before Motown Records was founded by Berry Gordy Jr., the groups and individuals who would be the mother lode to his empire were my playmates or schoolmates. We lived across the hall from Smokey Robinson's cousins and were privileged to hear the Miracles creating and rehearsing the songs that would bring them international fame. When we weren't invited to their rehearsals, our doors were wide open, and we experienced the seminal notes of "Shop Around," "Got a Job," and "She's Not a Bad Girl." The prolific songwriter Lamont Dozier also lived in the projects, and the Supremes were in the Brewster bricks, as we called them. Demonstrating a mind-set of determination, all of these talented individuals worked their way from the projects to respectable superstardom.

The many luminaries from Motown are but a small number of the city's significant individuals whose contributions have had a global impact in industry, government, international diplomacy, education, entertainment, literary and performing arts, and sports. Less-well-known Detroiters also deserve recognition. William Lambert and George DeBaptiste dedicated themselves to the abolitionist movement and provided peerless leadership as conductors on the Underground Railroad. The great inventor Elijah McCoy at one time called Detroit his home. Heavyweight boxing champion Joe Louis and his good friend and boxing immortal Sugar Ray Robinson spent their early years in the city. Poet and publisher Dudley Randall's Broadside Press provided a forum for such prominent writer/poets as Gwendolyn Brooks, Don L. Lee (Haki Madhubuti), Nikki Giovanni, and Sonia Sanchez. After serving more than six years in prison, Malcolm X joined members of his family in Detroit and subsequently became the national spokesperson for the Nation of Islam. The late track star Henry Carr won two gold medals at the 1964 Olympics in Tokyo.

Almost from the city's inception, African Americans were vitally involved in its growth and development. However, early on, the majority of African Americans were in bondage, and the impact of their unpaid labor was either minimized or denied. Without compensation they tilled the soil, helped to construct the first buildings, labored as blacksmiths, drove the wagons, fired the ovens, forged the steel, built the stoves, hauled the ashes, cleaned the chimneys, and were among the crews of stevedores on the docks. Black Detroiters cleared the land, broke the rocks, poured the cement, paved the streets, and laid the rails, basically turning a wilderness into the foundation of a city.

At the turn of the last century, emancipated black workers were the very vortex of the industrial age. Having migrated from the plantations of the South, many of them took on the most onerous tasks in the automobile plants, often being consigned to the most dangerous and lowest-paying jobs.

When presented with an opportunity, they became teachers, lawyers, inventors, doctors, nurses, and businesspeople. They also became artists and artisans, making considerable contributions to the city's prominent place in the nation's cultural pantheon.

PROMINENT FAMILIES

It is not possible to discuss Detroit's history, particularly the contributions it has made to world culture, without a thorough, comprehensive analysis of the city's black residents. In this volume, I touch on every aspect of the city's glorious history, from its promising beginnings in the early eighteenth century to the latest issues of solvency. Members of notable black families—the Lamberts, Pelhams, Barthwells, Diggses, Hoods, Keiths, Wrights, et al.—have maintained a continual connection to the city, honoring the provenance that has enriched their lives. We recall the forthright and unwavering commitment of the Lambert family during the early stages of the abolitionist movement in the city and elsewhere. We remember how instrumental the Pelhams were in several walks of life, none more crucial than their newspaper the *Detroit Plaindealer*. Barthwell family members were also successful entrepreneurs, with a chain of drugstores, and the Hoods were notable for their political and legal leadership for generations. They are featured among the fearless freedom fighters highlighted in *Black Detroit*. The city's pedigree of struggle has been annealed in the fires of resistance that began in the 1830s with the Blackburn case, and it found resonance a hundred or so years later in the resolve of the Sweet family and in subsequent civic disturbances. The struggle for self-determination was tempered by the race riots in 1863 and 1943 and crested in the rebellion in 1967. When the vicious arm of the police force, through Stop the Robberies and Enjoy Safe Streets (STRESS), sought to impose its will on young black men in particular, that fight-back spirit once again surfaced and halted a burgeoning retrenchment.

BLACK STUDIES AT WAYNE STATE UNIVERSITY

In the late 1960s, Wayne State University became a rallying point for the nascent black nationalist movement. Still an undergraduate, I was now in a classroom *teaching* black history. Many great minds were attracted to Wayne State, such as Malcolm X and his mentors, including Dr. John Henrik Clarke, John Oliver Killens, Dr. Yosef Ben-Jochannan, and a host of other preeminent scholars of African and African American history and culture.

The professors and student body benefited from their presence and willingness to share information.

From 1968 to 1974, Wayne State was a hotbed of activism. It wasn't unusual to have members of practically every political stripe, with sharp ideological differences among them. In the same classroom, one could find communists, socialists, black nationalists (members of the Shrine of the Black Madonna, the Republic of New Afrika, the Nation of Islam, or the Moorish Science Temple), Black Panthers, and members of the League of Revolutionary Black Workers. These political organizations, each of which gained national and international traction, are the bedrock of the institutions that have given Detroit such a distinct reputation. Not only are these social, cultural, and political entities critical to Detroit's history, but also many of them have carved a seminal niche in the evolution of black America. These activities at Wayne State were vital to the addition of black studies to college curricula. Along with San Francisco State, Cornell, and Howard University, Wayne State was at the forefront of that development.

Many of the students who were educated both in the classroom and in the city's dynamic political precincts went on to become the civic leaders, lawyers, judges, doctors, teachers, and entrepreneurs who were so important to the city's growth and development. Moreover, a considerable number remained true to the militancy they cultivated at Wayne State and now are among the professors and administrators whose dedication and vision are responsible for the young people on campus who today embody the spirit and integrity of their predecessors.

COLEMAN YOUNG

An aura of optimism wafted across the black community during the 1970s when Coleman Young was elected Detroit's first

African American mayor. For a score of years from his perch in the City County Building, he challenged the traditional second-class designation of his constituents, empowering them both economically and spiritually. As noted activist Mary Frances Berry observed, "Coleman Young is unabashedly what an earlier generation called a race man, fighting for his black constituents . . . through decades of public life. His is the story of modern urban America with its ills and opportunities graphically displayed. If we are to implement a positive urban agenda, his voice must be heard"—and it was heard with powerful effect as he galvanized the city's business elite and forged an economic plan to rebuild Detroit, beginning with the riverfront, where the Renaissance Center stands as a symbol of his aspirations. His combative, take-no-prisoners style was honed during his days as a labor activist, and it was the hallmark of his tenure in office, right down to his standoff with the city's suburbs. He was emblematic of a Detroit toughness, a self-determinative disposition that continues to resonate from those who experienced his furious passage.

AT THE POINT OF PRODUCTION

Black labor has been indispensable to Detroit's growth and development. From the moment the first fugitive slaves were safely secured in the city, they were put to work. Nearly all of the early buildings—homes, churches, businesses, schools, and other edifices—benefited from the craftsmanship of black workers. In *Black Detroit* you will witness from generation to generation the handiwork of black labor, and it will be more than apparent when the automobile industry is at full throttle. At first they were consigned to custodial and janitorial jobs before being shuttled off to the blast furnaces and the more hazardous workstations. It would be in the factories and auto plants, however, where black sweat and toil would become inseparably connected to production. By the 1960s, black workers, having gathered organizing skills through the various unions, began to assert their independence and make demands on the corporate bosses and the union leaders. The League of Revolutionary Black Workers was a formidable organization that, despite its short existence, had a lasting effect on the workplace. There is an extensive discussion of its influence and some of the key activists whose reputations would exceed the boundaries of the plants and go beyond the point of production.

FROM BEBOP TO HIP-HOP

Any mention of music in Detroit invariably begins with Motown, and while it may seem that any discussion of this empire has been exhausted, there are still significant elements that have been overlooked. Raynoma Gordy Singleton, Berry Gordy Jr.'s second wife, has rarely been more than a footnote in discussions of Motown. She deserves more than a passing nod for her contributions during the early days of the company. But beyond Motown—and it receives more than a glimpse in these pages—Detroit has produced a compendium of sounds—the blues, rock 'n' roll, gospel, classical, jazz, and techno.

In the realm of jazz, black innovators from Detroit have figured prominently in most of the major orchestras, bands, and ensembles, from McKinney's Cotton Pickers in the 1920s down to the bebop era, with such giants as Yusef Lateef, and on to the current groups led by guitarist A. Spencer Barefield and the new music at Palmer Park. Shahida Mausi and her family and colleagues have kept the beat and the flame bright and bouncy at Chene Park, providing a platform for a variety of musical expressions. Black musicians from the city have always been pacesetters, a tradition that's true and evident in the techno wave led by Juan Atkins, Derrick May, and Kevin Saunderson. The underground techno phase put Detroit in the mix of this new sonic development, accentuating the contributions of producer-rapper J Dilla and producer Nick Speed. And we look to writers, such as Charles Latimer and Larry Gabriel, to keep us up to date on the city's bustling music scene, no matter the genre.

BREWSTER, JEFFRIES, AND SOJOURNER TRUTH

Since the 1920s, when thousands of black migrants began arriving in Detroit, housing has always been a troubling issue. The majority of them had few options and settled on the city's lower east side, where they were basically confined by restrictive covenants. In the forties, black residents slowly began to venture to other parts of the city. With the creation of the Sojourner Truth Projects, despite the racial problems and the attendant violence, African Americans took advantage of the federally supplied living space. There were even greater opportunities for better housing when the Brewster-Douglass Projects and the nearby Jeffries Projects were erected in the fifties. Much more will be said about these units and some of the renowned residents who once made "the bricks" their home.

CULTURAL HERITAGE

A community thrives when its cultural institutions are firmly established, well financed, and ably staffed. Detroit has had its share of major institutions, several of which have received national acclaim, including Broadside Press, Lotus Press, Boone House, N'Namdi Gallery, Strata Concert Gallery, the Concept East Theater, and the Charles H. Wright Museum of African American History. Each in its own way has blazed an inimitable path, whether in publishing, exhibition, curating, performance, or archiving treasured memorabilia. These institutions are bolstered by the schools and churches, and together they form the matrix of a city and are guided by a coterie of forward-thinking visionaries. The current success of the Northwest Activities Center, which could serve as a model neighborhood development, is exemplary of black Detroit in recovery mode, a center that wisely combines financial institutions and cultural programming.

BRIGHT HORIZONS

Throughout the history of Detroit, no matter the political strife, economic despair, and racial oppression, the city's black citizens have never lost sight of the prize, as they have been steadfast in their resolve and optimistic about the future. Black Detroiters survived enslavement, white mobs, housing and job discrimination, and municipal indifference, and with each endeavor they chipped away at the age-old misery index. This unwillingness to settle for defeat is manifested in the Detroit Black Community Food Security Network led by cofounder Malik Yakini. Promising too is JP Morgan Chase's Entrepreneur of Color Fund and the Motor City Match program, which provide job opportunities for minority participants. Black-owned restaurants, bookstores, and mixed endeavors like those launched by Bert Dearing must be supported in order to help stabilize the community and put black Detroit back on an even keel.

Black Detroit offers expansive discussions of black studies at Wayne State University and other educational facilities, of a treasury of prominent families, of the life and legacy of Coleman Young, of the city's incomparable musical and cultural heritage, and of a plethora of urban issues—housing, labor, business, and the day-to-day fight for self-determination. It chronicles the milestones without losing sight of the ordinary lives who are the city's lifeblood.

In *Black Detroit* I have gathered the previously underreported stories and the suppressed voices of hundreds of Detroiters, many of whom have been linked to national headlines, and woven them together in a historical and cultural narrative that captures both their individual journeys and the city's. Let us hope that new enterprises, like Shinola, Shake Shack, and Bedrock, and efforts by Mayor Mike Duggan and the Detroit Economic Growth Corporation to stimulate jobs have a far-reaching impact for those suffering from low or no employment. These new ventures and businesses, although not owned by black Detroiters, are nonetheless providing minimum-wage opportunities. These workers, whether employed at the concession stands, as parking lot attendants, valets, or security guards at the stadiums, exemplify a long tradition of service, a vigorous working-class pulse that built the backbone of the city and for many decades kept many industries thriving.

THE LONG VIEW

Black Detroit illuminates the city's rich history, from the French explorer Antoine de Lamothe Cadillac's first habitation at Fort Pontchartrain to the once luxurious Pontchartrain Hotel, located near that historical site, from the meadows "fringed with long and broad avenues of fruit trees" to the pothole-pocked streets like Woodward Avenue, from the waves of fugitives from bondage via the Underground Railroad to today's passengers on the People Mover circling downtown. What was once a little village of "bounding roebuck" and indigenous Pawnees is now a city with a majority African American population. The terminus for runaway slaves soon became a promising beginning for black workers, whose sweat and ingenuity were so essential to the building of the city.

Black Detroit is an amalgam of personal experience, collective research, and the stories gathered from the city's griots. This is the first book to consider black Detroit from a long view, in a full historical tableau.

Despite a long separation of more than a quarter of a century, Detroit will forever be my home—a forever home, because it was here where I witnessed my mother's indomitable, independent spirit as she nurtured and provided for her children. No matter where we lived, it was a city that had a host of sharing neighbors, all of them willing to guide and watch over us. More than anything, it was a city that I explored with wonder, from Black Bottom to Eight Mile Road, from the projects to the beautiful neighborhoods on the far west side. It has taken a long separation for me to understand how crucial the city was to my development, to renew those yesterdays, and to realize how much of the past is still with me. You *can't* go home again, as Thomas Wolfe asserted in his classic novel, but what if in spirit you've never really left?

1

CADILLAC, "THE BLACK PRINCE"

Detroit is a dynamic city, recognized the world over for its innovations in automobile manufacturing. One of its most prized creations was the luxury vehicle produced by the Cadillac Motor Company. The enterprise's name was inspired by the city's founder. In 1700, Antoine de Lamothe Cadillac (*né* Antoine Laumet) sent a letter to Count Pontchartrain, Minister of the French Colonies, presenting his vision for the settlement that would become Detroit. In order to manifest it, he put forth his proposal for dealing with the Indian population, mainly the Iroquois. Cadillac wrote,

> It would be absolutely necessary . . . to allow the soldiers and Canadians to marry the savage [as he called Native

Americans] maidens when they have been instructed in religion and know the French language which they will learn all the more eagerly (provided we labor carefully to that end) because they always prefer a Frenchman for a husband to any savage whatever, though I know no other reason for it than the most ordinary one, namely that strangers are preferred, or, it were better to say, it is a secret of the Almighty Power.[1]

Cadillac's Francophone sense of superiority and his ethnocentricity are fully evinced in his statements to Count Pontchartrain. The central purpose of his precept of interracial marriage was twofold: build a friendship with the Native Americans and replace their "deplorable sacrifices" with Christianity through the Jesuit missionaries. Sanctioning the mixing of races, however, is not to imply that Cadillac regarded the Indians as equals. "He would never smoke a peace pipe with them and would not give his full attention to their powwows." Because of his swarthy complexion he was jokingly called the Black Prince, and that dark skin may have been inherited through the Spanish blood that flowed in his veins.[2]

This intermarriage tactic was intended to be one of mutual protection as well as to facilitate trade with the indigenous population. This recommendation may have precluded applying the same condition to blacks, since they would have been less of a threat and had only their bodies for trade. Cadillac was a shrewd and shady operator, and this move proved effective. Soon there were four large Native American villages built within a short distance of the French village. "During the winter of 1701–02, six thousand Indians lived there," wrote historian Clarence M. Burton.[3]

Although sometimes through alcohol or bribery Cadillac did a good job of keeping the Indians from hostile acts against the

French, he was less successful managing the often disruptive bloodletting among the tribes, particularly the rivalry and jealously between the Ottawa and Miami groups, each believing the other was receiving the best trading bargains from the French. In 1706, while he was traveling, the worst outbreak occurred between Native Americans, an action that necessitated the involvement of the French to quell the conflict and the subsequent killing of thirty Ottawa warriors.[4]

Black slaves in Detroit were first mentioned in 1736, six years after Cadillac's death. The ethnicity of slaves is significant because there is confusion on the subject among the early historians of the city. Burton, however, seems to be clear on this matter. He identifies and distinguishes the blacks from the Native Americans, whom he identifies as Panis or Pawnees. After citing the "two negroes" belonging to Joseph Campau, he lists several Panis or Panisse, including one called Escabia, belonging to Joseph Parent, a local blacksmith, who is rumored to have lived among the Indians long before Cadillac's arrival.[5]

Were the "two negroes" the same as those mentioned by Dr. Norman McRae in his dissertation on the history of blacks in Detroit who he said were the property of Louis Campeau? The eminent professor notes that the majority of slaves in *Ville de troit*, or Detroit, "were panis and a few were black. It is difficult to know how many slaves were transported from New France to Detroit through regular business transactions and how many panis and blacks were brought to Detroit through the fortunes of war."[6] Moreover, McRae added, in 1736 an "unknown negresse" was buried by Father Daniel, which would record her as one of the first black women in the region.[7]

Listed among the spoils of war that went to the victor in the Indian battles were black slaves who were brought to Detroit. Others were captured during the Native American raids against plantations in the South. "Later some were brought to the city and the surrounding area by southerners who moved in with their chattels."[8] During an interview on National Public Radio, Native American authority Professor Tiya Miles of the University of Michigan verified such transactions:

> African-Americans who were enslaved in Detroit in the Great Lakes area were people who were sometimes themselves captives of Native Americans. So native people were moving . . . all around, north and south, east and west, interacting with other nations of native people, and were sometimes capturing black slaves from the South. And then black slaves who were captured by Indians would perhaps be passed along, just like the Native slaves.[9]

When the French conducted the first census in 1750, the total population in the city was 483 inhabitants, 33 of whom were slaves, both blacks and Panis. No distinction was made between black and native slaves. On September 10, 1760, the French surrendered the city to the British without a fight.

In 1761, a year after the change of rulers, James Sterling arrived in Detroit and Brian Leigh Dunningan wrote that by 1764, "he owned two big Negroes." He had difficulty selling them because they were without wives, "and likely to run away." Sterling's solution to the problem was to have his partner, John Duncan, buy two African women and send them to Detroit.[10]

There is no indication that blacks were involved in the Indian conspiracy led by Chief Pontiac, a leader of the Ottawa nation, in the spring of 1763. Under his leadership, a confederation of tribes was assembled with the purpose of attacking nearby British forts. While Professor McRae discusses a black slave woman named Catherine in 1752, she is not Catherine, the Ojibway maiden or "Chippewa squaw,"[11] who betrayed Pontiac's

attack on the city by divulging his plans to the British comman-
dant. "Every Englishman will be killed, but not the scalp of a
single Frenchman will be touched," she told Major Gladwyn (or
Gladwin), who had pressed her to end her lingering silence after
entering his room.[12] Pontiac, perhaps suspecting a trap, altered
his plan of attack, and the Battle of Bloody Run raged for three
months before the reinforced British soldiers were able to subdue the uprising.[13]

Near the end of the eighteenth century, a black slave woman
belonging to James Abbott, a partner in one of the largest trading firms in the city, was at the center of an episode that has been
given conflicting interpretations by historians.

Among the oldest accounts collected by historian Clarence
Burton, considered the dean of Detroit's history, is the story
of Jean Baptiste Contencineau, a Frenchman, and a black slave
woman, Ann (or Nancy) Wyley. The two concocted "a plan to
rob the storehouse and firm" of the man's employer, Abbott &
Finchly, and "then set fire in order to avoid detection." Their
purpose, according to Burton, was to gain possession of the contents of a box kept in the storehouse. On June 24, 1774, Contencineau, "at the request of the woman, set fire to the building and
carried away from it . . . the plunder he wanted in a small box
containing six dollars (piasters) of which four dollars were silver
and two dollars paper."[14]

The prisoners confessed, but each attempted to blame the
other. They were tried before Justice of the Peace Philip De-
jean of Fort Detroit, himself a slaveholder, possibly with a jury
and certainly with the approval of Henry Hamilton, the region's
lieutenant governor. Both were found guilty and sentenced to be
hanged, but there was such a public outcry against the sentence
that it became impossible to find an executioner. "Hamilton
agreed to free the woman from the penalty about to be inflicted
upon her, if she would act as executioner of the Frenchman. Of

course, she agreed and the Frenchman was accordingly swung off."[15] The execution unsettled the local population and they protested the act as unjust and illegal.

Professor McRae cited the case in his dissertation but concluded that both Contencineau and Wyley were "apprehended, tried and hung." Errin T. Stegich, in his essay on the incident in the anthology *Revolutionary Detroit*, spells the woman's name as Wiley and one of the employers as Finchley, but his narrative is very similar to Burton's and McRae's, citing both of them. A wildly divergent account occurs in Stephen Middleton's *The Black Laws in the Old Northwest*, in which he concludes that the pair conspired to flee from bondage posing as master and slave, a ruse reminiscent of the one used by William and Ellen Craft in their 1848 flight to freedom. Light-skinned Mrs. Craft dressed in male clothing and passed as a Southern planter traveling openly with her husband, who pretended to be her personal slave. However, lacking the money for travel, Contencineau and Wiley plotted to rob the master. "They agreed to break into their owner's home to steal the cash and clothing they needed before embarking on their journey." Middleton doesn't mention any apprehension or trial, stating that the conspiracy delayed them long enough for the owner to make them examples by reclaiming them and then hanging them in front of the other slaves.

A noted chronicler of Detroit's early days, Friend Palmer, supplies a coda to this incident. In his version, Ann Wyley, despite the strong plea for her manumission, was sentenced to death by a justice of the peace, and was buried on Larned Street. "When in 1817 the foundations of the church [Sainte Anne de Détroit Roman Catholic Church, the city's oldest church] were being excavated, the body of this unfortunate woman was found face downward," Palmer wrote. "It was supposed she was in a trance at the time of her burial."[16]

During the Revolutionary War, the settlements in Detroit were repeatedly attacked by the British with the help of allied Native Americans. A number of black Americans often found themselves between the combatants, a rock and a hard place that offered them little comfort and safety. Such was the situation of Jean Baptiste Pointe Du Sable, a fur trader who had been born in Haiti and later founded Chicago. Du Sable was arrested by the British, who charged him with being sympathetic to the Americans. In a letter, a British officer on September 1, 1779, observed that Du Sable was brought in custody to Detroit but apparently was a model prisoner. "The Negro, since his imprisonment, has in every respect behaved in a manner becoming a man in his situation, and has many friends who give him a good character." This "good character" may have allowed him permission to travel to various parts of the state under British supervision, and possibly spy for them.[17]

By the end of the war in 1783, Du Sable regularly traveled back and forth between Michigan and Illinois and was clearly a man of substance, according to historians. "Undoubtedly he owned one of the most complete establishments in the Middle West outside of Detroit and St. Louis."[18]

The 1782 census showed there were 179 slaves in Detroit, 101 of them females; thus over a nine-year period, the number of blacks in bondage had nearly doubled.[19] At this rate of increase, the next census counted more than 300 slaves in the city, representing about 5 percent of the total population. One of the city's largest slaveholders was John Askin. An inventory of his property in 1787 lists 6 slaves—3 black males, including Jupiter, whose estimated value was $450, much higher than the others; 2 "wenches," and 1 Panis. One of those women was Monette or Manette, with whom he fathered three children. On average, a good male slave could be purchased for £50, or $150, the price

Askin received for the sale of his slave Pompey. According to the Northwest Ordinance of 1787, slavery was not permitted, and so Askin and many others were in violation of the law, including William Macomb and Jean Cecot, each of whom owned 4 men and 4 women. (By the dawn of the nineteenth century, Macomb would own 26 slaves.) Simon Compau, William Forsith, and Thomas Cox owned 5 each. Even a woman, Alexis Maisonville, owned 4 slaves.[20] All told, seventy-eight families were slaveholders, about one in every four families in the city. Given that the majority of the slaves were women, it is obvious that domestic and household workers were more in demand than field hands or manual laborers.[21]

In 1795, Detroit was still under British jurisdiction, and the city was a de facto part of Upper Canada. Despite being illegal, slavery was in practice, and some black freedom seekers were not about to succumb to the order of the day. One such man was William Kenny, who formerly belonged to Alexander McKee, the deputy superintendent of Indian affairs. At some point, Kenny, a mulatto, had escaped from Detroit. David Tait was hired to find him and return him to his owner. Tait's search was frustrated at every turn, so much so that he resorted to expressing his exasperation in letters. Kenny was also adept with the pen and wrote a response to his former owner:

Dear Master—I embrace this opportunity to let you know that I am well and where I am. Likewise the reasons of my coming away (which I am very sorry I came away I did) it was occasioned by Capt. Elliots taking the liberties he did and abusing me in your absence the things which was left in my charge he took from me. I am in the North Western Territory living with a gentleman by name of Turner one of the judges of this Territory and he uses me extraordinary well.

Kenny goes on to relate with obvious sarcasm that he has encountered another man who was acquainted with his former master and who sends his regards. He closes by saying, "No more at Present. But still remains your obedient servant, William Kenny."[22]

In contrast, there were a number of enslaved blacks who were incredibly attached to their masters and found it extremely difficult to depart from them. The Jay Treaty forbade any more slaves to be brought into the territory, but total emancipation was way over the horizon.

There was no centennial celebration in Detroit in 1801, but if there had been one for its more than three thousand citizens, it would have hardly been a festive occasion for the city's uncounted black residents. Most of them were still caught in the throes of a legal system that left them languishing in limbo, a no-man's-land between freedom and slavery. Though Article VI of the Northwest Ordinance prohibited slavery, it was ineffective when it came to liberating those blacks already in captivity. Given their small population, any thought of a revolt would have been unrealistically naive and futile, though there were certainly a few who felt as Gabriel Prosser, Denmark Vesey, and Nat Turner did when they plotted their uprisings in the South. Only those slaves bold enough to paddle to the center of the Detroit River and drop anchor were safe from the ambiguous laws that made it precarious to be on either side of the river. Whether in Detroit or Canada, slaveholders had the upper hand, and in 1802 they sent a delegation to William Henry Harrison, the territorial governor, to insist that slavery was a necessity to fill the shortage of laborers, even though the shortage was diminishing.[23] An indecisive Harrison, an advocate for slavery and later the ninth president of the United States, did little to remedy the situation, thereby leaving any sort of repeal of Article VI to the electorate.

The first five years of the new century brought little change for black Detroiters. They were as chained to servitude as they were in the past, hammering at the anvil in the blacksmith shop, laboring on the construction of Sainte Anne's, weaving baskets, and preparing furs for their owners—endeavors for which they were not compensated. They could be sold for cash, traded for goods, and "even used as collateral for large purchases and debt resolution. In this way, they provided financial security to their owners and to the settlement at large."[24]

During the summer of 1805, a fire virtually leveled Old Town, the core of the city, leaving only one stone building standing. There were no fatalities, though one young boy was crippled. A careless pipe smoker was the source of the fire. He was tending his horses when a spark from his pipe ignited a nearby stack of hay. The stable was quickly engulfed in flames. Attempts to douse the fire with water from a furrier's vat proved futile after bits of fur clogged the firemen's hoses. A bucket brigade was summoned, including a number of blacks in the city, and they hurried to the scene but could not halt the spread of the fire. To salvage some of their goods, particularly the more expensive furs and other valuable items, storeowners loaded them in canoes and paddled out on the river away from the fire.[25]

A destructive four-hour fire was only a temporary setback for the resilient Detroiters, and the slaves were assigned the task of helping to rebuild the city under the guidance of Pierre Charles L'Enfant, who had designed Washington, DC, and who perhaps was assisted by his friend, black inventor and innovator Benjamin Banneker.

Not long after the building began, Peter Denison in 1807, was seeking freedom for his children. Held in captivity by William Tucker, Denison was allowed a lot of latitude by his owner, who resided in what is today Michigan's Macomb County, named after the wealthy slaveholder. When Tucker died, his will specified that Peter and his wife, Hannah, would be free upon the death of his widow, Catherine. Tucker bequeathed Denison's four children to his sons, but Denison sued to annul this provision. The case for his children's freedom was based on the federal law that established the Michigan Territory and outlawed slavery in it. The petitioners lost the suit, but Judge Augustus Woodward, for whom the city's major street would be named, ruled that three of the children must be consigned to slavery for life but the other one would be emancipated upon reaching his twenty-fifth birthday. Judge Woodward stipulated in a later ruling that if black Americans were to acquire freedom in Canada, they could not be returned to slavery in the United States. "Two of Denison's children, Scipio and Elizabeth, took advantage of this ruling by escaping to Canada for a few years and then returning to Detroit as free citizens."[26] Theirs was a landmark case and would be cited as a precedent in a number of appeals for emancipation by enslaved African Americans.

This was just the beginning of Peter Denison's celebrity. In 1808, the same year in which Thomas Jefferson signed a bill ending the US involvement in the international slave trade, Governor William Hull formed a militia to protect citizens and property against the local Native Americans, and Denison's role as a leader in it earned him further acclaim. Equally celebrated was African American slave James Robinson, among the most decorated soldiers in both the War of 1812 and the Revolutionary War.

Hundreds of African Americans served in the US Navy or were aboard privateers that plied the Great Lakes during the War of 1812. Commodore Oliver Hazard Perry extended a warm welcome to blacks who were desirous of being a part of the fleet that he was building. When his fleet defeated the British warships at Put-in-Bay on Lake Erie, he was effusive in his comments about the performance of black sailors. This battle marked a turning point in the war, and "the victory forced the British to pull out of Detroit, and much of what is now Michigan came under U.S. control, allowing Major General William Henry Harrison to cross Lake Michigan and defeat the retreating British at Canada's Battle of the Thames."[27] At this time there were approximately 144 blacks living in Michigan Territory and 24 of them were listed as slaves, 10 of them held in Detroit. After the war, a large influx of fugitive slaves entered the territory.[28]

Five years after the war, Lake Erie was again in the news with the building of the Erie Canal. By 1825, when the more than 350-mile canal was completed, it opened an international portal that facilitated the flow of white Easterners into the territory. As a result, that event was followed by the passing of a territorial law in April 1827 that restricted the entry of black migrants. It required all "Negroes in the territory to have a valid court-attested certificate of freedom and to register with the clerk of the county court." More grievous, a $500 bond guaranteeing good behavior was required to be filed by all black immigrants.[29] These onerous regulations had much to do with keeping the black population in check and limiting its growth in the city. The census of 1820 recorded 1,355 whites and 67 blacks in Detroit; by 1830 both groups had practically doubled to 2,096 whites and 126 blacks, of whom 32 were slaves.[30] During these early years, the black population in Detroit fluctuated between 2 and 5 percent, but it was always a vigorous and resourceful community.

2

THE BLACKBURN AFFAIR

Detroit in 1830 was a city in flux, where whites were primarily troubled by a wave of recent arrivals from the South, "blues people" seeking freedom from bondage. It was a warm summer night on July 6, 1831, when a young mulatto couple—Thornton, nineteen, and Ruthie or Lucie, as she was later called, who was a few years older—arrived, refusing to be relegated to lifelong bondage. They escaped from slavery in Louisville, Kentucky, without the help of the Underground Railroad and briefly resided in Detroit before moving to Canada. At the time of their escape, Lucie had already been sold for $300 and was to be sent down the river for resale in New Orleans or Natchez, where her fair skin made her much more valuable than in Louisville. Thornton knew time was not on their side, and with the nation in the midst of July Fourth celebrations perhaps among the celebrants they could move less conspicuously toward freedom. Traveling as a couple presented an additional challenge.

There were hordes of bounty hunters, who were ever watchful; they lurked in the shadows of docks, around train stations, and at other points of entry and departure, ready to grab an unsuspecting fugitive slave in order to earn the reward. A $25 bounty was set for the capture and return of Thornton to his master; it was a price far less than the $400 he could command on the auction block. Exhausted from a harrowing four-day trip by boat and stagecoach, the couple was invited to stay at the home of James Slaughter, a local black businessman.

Many Southern families were settling into Detroit's black community. It was an easy transition for the Blackburns. At the time, in Detroit, there were some discussions here and there about antislavery activities. It seemed familiar to them, especially the waterfront setting, which was much like the one they knew in Louisville. The black population was smaller but no less energetic, hardworking, and enterprising. It was only a matter of days before Thornton found a job as a stonemason.

"The Blackburns had settled in Detroit in hope that their troubles were behind them, but two disturbing events had occurred within their first two months in the city," Karolyn Smardz Frost wrote in *I've Got a Home in Glory Land*. "First came the news that a bloody slave uprising had been launched in Southampton County, Virginia. Originally planned for the same weekend as Thornton and Lucie's flight from Louisville . . . it had been delayed until August 22 because of the illness on the part of the riot's organizer. This was an educated and deeply religious slave named Nat Turner, a visionary with a gift for oratory."[1]

People received the news of Turner's revolt much as they had received *David Walker's Appeal*, a Christian manifesto to end slavery that was widely circulated in 1829. From city to city, even in the North, the racial tension was palpable. When he and his "army" were finished, the massacre of fifty-nine whites sent a chilling effect across the nation. Prophet Nat, as Turner was called, was pursued relentlessly by the law and outlaws. When they finally caught him, he was hanged and decapitated, and his head was posted near the uprising as a warning to others who considered violent means of liberation.

"The second incident had very serious personal implications for the Blackburns, although they would not realize it for some time."[2] Practically one year after their arrival in the city, as Thornton was walking through town, he bumped into a white man he knew from Louisville. They exchanged a few words, and Thornton left the acquaintance with the impression that he was now a free man.

On June 14, 1833, Sheriff John Wilson appeared at the Blackburns' home with an order to arrest them as fugitive slaves. He and his deputy, Lemuel Goodell, were to receive fifty dollars each after the trial, which was a legal requirement under the Fugitive Slave Act of 1793. The Blackburns were to be delivered to the dock at the foot of Randolph Street, then the primary business point in the city.[3] It took some legal maneuvering to bring them both before the judge. They were shocked to learn that James Slaughter, the black man who befriended them and with whom they lived upon arriving in Detroit, testified against them in court, recounting what they told him about their means of escape. Despite being a man of dubious reputation—it was said that he ran a bordello—his testimony was damning. Word of the trial spread fast among the city's fugitive slaves. The trial would be a test case on how free African Americans actually were in the territory.[4]

A supportive black community filled the courtroom.[5] Key to the case was the extent to which the Fugitive Slave Act of 1793 would be applied. If the defendants could present their papers of manumission, then they were beyond the reach of the law. But no such papers were offered in evidence by the Blackburns; certainly they knew that forgeries, if discovered, would doom them to even graver sentences.[6]

A group of outraged black citizens was no longer content to sit passively by and allow the wheels of justice to creak along. There were whispers of torching the city. "They met at the home of Benjamin Willoughby, a real estate speculator, financier and owner of a lumber business, who came to Detroit from Kentucky sometime between 1817 and 1830," journalist and author Betty DeRamus wrote. "He had worked as a laborer and acquired some money, often lending it to others. At his home, participants hatched a plot to free the Blackburns; the plan put Willoughby's own property and even his life at risk."[7]

The plan was part charade and deception. Once Sheriff Wilson allowed Mrs. Blackburn to receive visitors, Mrs. Caroline French and Mrs. Tabitha Lightfoot were chosen to enter her jail cell. While they chatted, Mrs. French changed clothes with Lucie. As Mrs. Lightfoot and Lucie left the jail under cover of night, they faked convulsive weeping, covering their faces. By the time the sheriff caught wind of the ruse, Lucie was across the river in Canada.[8] Changing places, however, left Mrs. French in the clutches of the law, and she faced the prospect of taking Lucie's place permanently. Fortunately, her father, Cornelius Leonard Lenox, a man of considerable wealth and clout, interceded and was able to get her released on a writ of habeas corpus. While out on bail, she fled to Canada, where she spent several months.[9] She would ultimately return to the city and resume living with her family. Meanwhile, with Lucie safe, her husband became the center of attention and retribution.

While Sheriff Wilson and the jailer transported Thornton from jail to a waiting steamer, they were attacked and their prisoner escaped. Apparently, the sheriff was intimidated by the crowd of angry black citizens who had gathered outside the jail when they discovered Thornton was being returned to Louisville.[10] To placate the enraged citizenry, "Blackburn requested that he speak to the crowd in order to allay their fears and to appease their anger. As the people crowded in to hear Blackburn, someone slipped him a pistol which he brandished and ran into a coach where he locked himself in, and promised to kill whoever attempted to recapture him."[11]

In the melee, with the assistance of several black Detroiters, Blackburn slipped from the coach and fled to a boat that took him to Canada. During the altercation, Sheriff Wilson was hit in the head with a blunt object, knocking his teeth out and fracturing his skull. He died a year later. There was one other fatality. Lewis Austin was shot in the lung and died two years later from the wound. Reunited with his wife, Thornton decided that living across the river from Detroit was not far enough from the greedy slave catchers. The couple continued their flight farther from Detroit.

In the wake of their capture, festering anger grew to a full-scale riot. On July 11, 1833, the jail was set on fire, and a few days later, the stables abutting the jail went up in flames killing a number of horses.[12] Blacks were accused of setting this fire, but there was no evidence they were involved. The situation had escalated to the point that two weeks later Mayor Marshall Chapin sent an urgent letter to Secretary of War Lewis Cass, requesting troops to stabilize the city. "The recent excesses committed in this city by the black population within its limits, and particularly the repeated attempts to fire the town," Chapin wrote, "have so far excited the apprehensions of our citizens for their property and lives. That I am instructed by the common council . . . to ask that a detachment of the United States troops may be stationed at this place, to act under the directions of the municipal authority until the excitement has subsided and tranquility is restored."[13]

Cass, a former governor of the Michigan Territory and a former slaveholder, acceded to the mayor's wishes, and martial law was declared. The heavy deployment of US troops and a complement of local militia suppressed the riot, and a sizable contingent of blacks bolted to Canada, leaving only about fifty or so to withstand the harsh indictments. Most burdensome was the posting of a $500 bond in order to remain in the city. Not since the British replaced the French as a dominant force in the city had there been such a dramatic change in the black population.[14]

According to historian David S. Reynolds, "Canada had abolished slavery but it did not have a firm policy on fugitive slaves. Imprisoned again, the Blackburns faced the bleak prospect of a forced return to the United States. In a landmark trial, however, a Canadian court ruled that they had committed no capital crime and could not be extradited to America. Canada was thereafter regarded as a protective home for fugitive blacks who wanted to live without fear of being recaptured and sent south."

The effects of the riot of 1833 lingered for nearly four years. It had created an immutable chasm between black and white Detroiters. This tension was in part responsible for the flight of many African Americans to Canada and other parts of the country. When Michigan gained statehood in 1837, there were only eleven blacks listed in the city's directory, the same number that arrived in New Amsterdam in 1626.[15] But as with most enumerations of blacks, this one was by no means accurate, because it included only the most prosperous citizens, not the majority who worked the docks, cleaned the streets, or were otherwise menially employed. In fact, the census of 1840 counted nearly two hundred African American residents. Whatever the number, they were resourceful and resilient in withstanding the blatant hostility of the white community.

Among these stalwarts were Madison Lightfoot and his wife, both of whom were pivotally involved in the Blackburns' escape;

Benjamin Willoughby; Robert Banks, who owned a haberdashery that sold used clothes; Peter Copper, a teamster who operated his own cab service; and one woman proprietor, Ann Butler, a laundress and possibly the widow of William Butler, a barber and activist.[16] The Butlers' freeborn son, who accompanied the Blackburns to Canada, was threatened with extradition along with the others.[17] By 1846, they were joined by such notables as Henry Bibb, the publisher whose slave narrative is among the most anthologized in the African American literary canon; the Rev. William C. Monroe, an abolitionist; William Lambert; and George DeBaptiste. These citizens were charter members of the burgeoning antislavery society that in 1837 had been forged by Shubael Conant, a white silversmith and watchmaker.[18] This organization had continued the antislavery activity begun in 1832 by a group of Quakers led by Elizabeth Margaret Chandler in the Raisin River Valley in Adrian, Michigan. At the top of their agenda was the boycott of any product produced by slave labor, particularly cotton. Historian Silas Farmer claimed that by 1836 "all the slaves were either dead or manumitted," so any movement against slavery was forged to protect those recently in flight from bondage.[19]

On October 24, 1839, a fugitive slave was abducted and claimed by bounty hunters from Missouri. Upon hearing about the capture, black and white abolitionists quickly assembled outside City Hall to prevent the US marshal from delivering the man from the courthouse to the jail. Fearing an attack from the abolitionists, the marshal called on the troops stationed nearby, and they were able to halt the demonstration. They apprehended one white and three blacks, placing them in a cell with the slave. After some pressure from the black community, the protesters and the slave were released, and the runaway's freedom "was purchased from his owner by citizens of Detroit who contributed the amount placed upon him by his owner."[20]

Although slavery was outlawed in the state, there were many instances in which slave catchers and bounty hunters ignored the law. There were also too many cases in which the government had to be pressured to enforce measures in protecting blacks that had been in place, more or less, since the enactment of the Northwest Ordinance in 1787. In addition, the *Detroit Free Press*, the city's first daily, along with headlines about the cholera epidemic and the financial panic of 1837, ran a rash of ads offering rewards for fugitive slaves. These factors were instrumental in the forging of a great abolitionist movement.

3

BLACK ABOLITIONISTS

Born in Trenton, New Jersey, William Lambert was twenty-one when he arrived in Detroit in 1838. He had visited the city on two previous occasions while working on boats that plied the lakes. With an activist background inculcated by Quakers, he wasted no time getting acquainted with like-minded abolitionists. When he wasn't working as a tailor, he could be found among the leaders of the city's antislavery organizations.[1]

His main preoccupation was working as a conductor on the Underground Railroad, assuring the safety of runaway slaves during their stay in Detroit and then escorting them to freedom across the river. He was a phenomenal conductor, and while he may have exaggerated the number of fugitives he guided to Canada, the general consensus among historians is that some forty thousand men, women, and children in flight from bond-age passed through his gentle and caring hands.[2] His prominence as a conductor was soon superseded by his skills as an orator when in 1840 he addressed the Michigan legislature demanding a constitutional franchise for an increasing black population that had grown to 707 in the state and 193 in the city.[3] These migrants often arrived with only the clothes on their backs. The churches were the most accommodating sanctuary for them.

Nowhere were the doors more open and the sanctuary more protective than the historic Second Baptist Church, the oldest black congregation in Michigan, founded in 1836 by thirteen former slaves. It was Detroit's seventh major church. Though not an ex-slave, Lambert was among the leaders of the congregation and worked closely with the church's first pastor, the Rev. William C. Monroe. Monroe had led a contingent of black members from First Baptist Church. Their departure was reminiscent of the action taken by Richard Allen and Absalom Jones in Philadelphia when they were dissatisfied with being consigned to "nigger pews."[4] In 1843, the Rev. Monroe presided over the first State Convention of Colored Citizens, held at his church. Lambert stirred the assembly with his eloquence.

By the time George DeBaptiste arrived in Detroit from Indiana in 1846, he had served as a conductor on the Underground Railroad for more than five years. The successful businessman was also a civic leader and a trusted friend of Monroe, Lambert, and a host of other antislavery advocates. A native of Virginia, where he was born free in 1815, DeBaptiste had traveled widely and was the steward and valet for President William Henry Harrison.

Given DeBaptiste's close association with Lambert, it's likely that they conspired in the usage of renegades, known as the McKensyites, who took slaves from their owners in order to resell them. "Sometimes they sold slaves three and four times before bringing them north." Lambert said he used these scoundrels, concluding that the ends justified the means.[5] DeBaptiste and Lambert created an elaborate system of communication that combined secret handshakes and passwords that they defined as the African American Mysteries: the Order of the Men of Oppression. This system made it possible to convey information from passengers to conductors on the Railroad, thereby facilitating safe passage. DeBaptiste, during his tenure as a conductor in Indiana, also devised a complicated way of switching horses and wagons to throw slave catchers off the trail of his horses, all of whom knew how to get from station to station in pitch darkness.[6]

Henry Bibb was born in 1815 in Kentucky. In his slave narrative, published in 1849, he mentions Michigan only in passing to indicate that he had spent the summer in the state in 1845. Although he didn't spend a great amount time in the city, his popular newspaper, *The Voice of the Fugitive*, was widely circulated after the Fugitive Slave Act became the law of the land on September 18, 1850.

The newspaper mainly focused on black folklore, slave superstitions, marriage, and escape episodes. It also revealed Bibb's literary skills. He was a consummate storyteller with a keen eye on politics and on the legal ramifications of slavery and the issue of property:

A slave from the State of Virginia, for cruel treatment left the State between daylight and dark, being borne off by one of his master's finest horses, and finally landed in Canada, where the British laws recognize no such thing as property in a human being. He was pursued by his owners, who expected to take advantage of the British law by claiming him as a fugitive from justice, and as such he was arrested and brought before the court of Queen's Bench. They swore that he was, at a certain time, the slave of Mr. A . . . and that he ran away at such a time and stole and brought off a horse. They enquired who the horse belonged to and it was ascertained that the slave and horse both belonged to the same person. The court therefore decided that the horse and the man were both recognized, in the State of Virginia, alike, as articles of property, belonging to the same person—therefore, if there was theft committed on either side, the former must have stolen off the latter—the horse brought away the man, and not the man the horse. So the man was discharged and pronounced free according to the laws of Canada.[7]

From his base in Canada, just across the river from Detroit, Bibb continued to agitate for freedom, often in concert with such luminaries and fellow authors as Frederick Douglass and William Wells Brown. Abolitionists, black or white, found it extremely perilous on the antislavery circuit in 1850.

When the Fugitive Slave Act was passed by Congress, it was essentially a compromise, allowing California to enter the Union as a free state. The balance between slave and non-slave states, which had been maintained since the Missouri Compromise of 1820, was tilted by the entry of California in favor of non-slave states, but in return the act empowered slaveholders by giving bounty hunters unlimited leeway in the capture of runaways. An affidavit from a slave owner to a federal marshal was all that was required for the return of their escaped "property." Suspected slaves had no legal standing whatsoever and no right to a trial. They were stripped of any means to defend themselves. The kidnapping of Solomon Northup nine years earlier was now government sanctioned. This was just the measure Bibb needed to push him more decisively to the emigrationist movement that was gradually galvanizing.

Bibb was soon one of a host of leaders who believed that being north of the "Cotton Curtain" was not enough to protect one from the "soul stealers." That group included Mary Ann Shadd, who was based in Chatham, Ontario.

There was no consensus about assimilation among the eminent emancipationists. Bibb and Martin Delany agreed on the need for a separate black identity and culture, but Shadd believed, as her father had taught her, that full equality could be achieved only by integrating with the larger white society. Their differing views on integration set them apart and created a heated rivalry, a schism over who would be the leader of the black community in western Canada.[8]

The integrationist/separatist dichotomy between Shadd and Bibb soon spilled over into their educational pursuits. Shadd, an unrepentant integrationist, vehemently rejected any form of caste system, whether based on race or any other characteristic, while Bibb's separatist philosophy anticipated a political vector that would later gain traction. More important, they disagreed on how funds should be raised to assist former slaves. The rivalry ceased, however, when Bibb's office was torched and burned to the ground in 1853. One year later he was dead.

After Bibb's death, a number of his associates in Detroit continued this struggle against caste, including the ever resourceful clothier Robert Banks, who had come to the city from the West Indies via New York City.[9] When Bibb and other members of the antislavery society were able to travel to various conventions, much of the financial burden was defrayed by Banks. In 1844 he was the only African American businessman listed among the economic elite. It was reported that he had twenty-five employees, including at one time or another Lambert and DeBaptiste.[10] Banks, along with the Rev. Monroe, was a vital conduit in the distribution of information from the East Coast; Banks was an agent handling subscriptions of *The Mystery*, a publication founded by Martin Delany, which later merged with Frederick Douglass's *North Star*.

The arrival of Wilbur Fisk Storey as the editor and publisher of the *Detroit Free Press* was not good news for black Detroiters. He wasn't behind the desk very long before he was hit with two libel suits. "His attacks on abolitionists, his denunciation of Negroes, and his eventual excoriation of Abraham Lincoln—particularly . . . after the Emancipation Proclamation—were so bitter that his legacy is a cruel caricature of editorial responsibility."[11] From his pen flowed a relentless surge of vitriol. He found a perfect whipping boy in black Republicans; the party in his estimation was a "monster of frightful mien . . . made up of white abolitionists, black abolitionists, and fugitives from slavery—this rabble of discord and destruction."[12] He was obsessed with race, and he wrote with the singular intention of ridiculing black Detroiters and those like John Brown, devoted to their emancipation.

Storey had no love for President Lincoln, either, or for the members of the Colored Vigilant Committee of Detroit, notably Lambert, DeBaptiste, and Monroe, who in 1858 gathered at William Webb's home when Brown passed through the city in transit to a convention in Chatham where he would present his Provisional Constitution, a document he had composed while living with Frederick Douglass for three weeks in Rochester, New York. During this meeting, Lambert agreed to be treasurer of what Brown envisioned as an antislavery government.[13]

A year later, on March 12, 1859, Brown returned again, this time with twelve or fourteen slaves he had liberated from Missouri. Many of the same men who had met with him at the previous meeting were on hand, but this gathering was distinguished by the presence of Frederick Douglass, who was in Detroit to deliver a lecture at City Hall.[14]

From the very inception of the slave revolt and Brown's plan to storm the arsenal, Douglass began to step back, cautioning his friend that he was headed for "a trap of steel" from which escape would be impossible.[15] Brown's loyal followers in Detroit were less forthcoming in their critique of his plan, and they extended their prayers and best wishes to him as he stood by the dockside watching the slaves he had emancipated board ships for Canada.

Brown's raiders were vanquished, the small contingent easily overcome after the initial success of their surprise attack on the federal arsenal at Harper's Ferry. Brown was captured and hanged, but his audacious act served as a catalyst to a nation that had to be stained with blood, Brown had said, in order to bring about the end of slavery.

"On April 12, 1861, a Detroit telegraph operator received the news that Fort Sumter had been fired upon." About a month later the First Michigan Infantry was on its way to Washington, DC. It was the first Western regiment to reach the capital and was soon the first Northern force to advance to South Carolina.[16]

It would be two years before black Detroiters could present arms and become agents of their own liberation. When they had an opportunity, after the Union Army had defeated the Confederates at Antietam, and once President Lincoln signed the Emancipation Proclamation and realized he could not win the war without his "sable soldiers," black Detroiters were ready to fight, ready to heed Douglass's clarion call—"Men of Color, to Arms!"

Men who had served without fear in ferrying fugitives to Canada were prepared for the rigors of war. They knew the danger of engagement, and their mettle had been annealed in their encounters with bounty hunters. Detroit is often overlooked as an important terminus of the Underground Railroad, but this legacy is part and parcel of the city's great history, a legacy that in its beginning was forged by such stalwarts as Lambert, De-Baptiste, Webb, Willoughby, and Banks.

These gallant warriors for freedom and justice put their indelible stamp on the quest for self-determination, a hallmark of courage and sacrifice.

4

FAULKNER AND FLAMES

Humanity wept, she lamented the sight,
The groans, blood and tears of that terrible night;
Yet, oh, may the town of Detroit never see
Such a day as the sixth of March, sixty-three.

—B. CLARK

Before black Detroiters could be fully engaged in the Civil War, there were some civic issues to overcome. For years the city teetered on the brink of racial turmoil fueled by the competition for jobs, the Enrollment Act of Conscription (the draft law), draft exemptions, and the issue of slavery. It took only a spark of misinformation to ignite the racial hostility, that tinderbox of bad feelings festering in Detroit's ethnic neighborhoods, particularly among the poor Irish and German working class.

By 1850, there were more than three thousand Irish Americans in Detroit, twice as many as the black population and representing a little over 15 percent of the residents of the city. In the 1880s, the number of Germans overtook that of the Irish and African Americans. With the advent of the Civil War and the Conscription Act, young German and Irish men were the majority of those drafted. Many of them complained about having to leave their jobs to fight whites for the benefit of blacks. They were even more incensed when black workers were hired to take their places. Lincoln's Emancipation Proclamation seemed to confirm their fears that the war was no longer to preserve the Union but to end slavery. On January 6, 1863, a celebration was held at Second Baptist Church to mark the proclamation, and exactly a century later President Lyndon B. Johnson dedicated a commemorative plaque memorializing the event.

These were some of the simmering issues that finally erupted when a black man was accused of raping a white girl. It was a chilly February day in 1863 when Mary Brown, a nine-year-old white girl, on her way to the post office encountered Ellen Hoover, a black girl she knew. Somehow they were enticed into a tavern owned by Thomas Faulkner and, once inside, lured to a back room where he raped Brown and possibly Hoover. "By late February," wrote Tobin T. Buhk in his book *True Crime in the Civil War*, "the alleged crime was front-page news in the city's two primary newspapers. Faulkner's racial identity was indefinite, though the *Free Press* and its rival the *Advertiser and Tribune*, jumped to conclusions and labeled him a 'negro.'"[1]

An examination of Mary Brown was ordered by a judge and conducted behind closed doors. Both the child's mother and the family doctor corroborated her story that the newspapers said was too fiendish to report. Meanwhile, Faulkner's lawyer bided his time, saving his defense for the trial. He had revealed that Hoover would be his star witness.[2]

Perhaps intimidated by Faulkner, Hoover's version of the event differed from Brown's. Later, with further coaxing and threatening her with jail time, she changed her story and said Faulkner had taken them both in the back room and closed the door.

Once more the newspapers aroused the public with inflammatory stories, lamenting the fact that if Faulkner was found guilty he could not be hanged since the death penalty had been abolished.

Unfortunately, the opening day of Faulkner's trial came almost simultaneously with the government's announcement of the new conscription law. Irish and German residents, already disturbed by a law that allowed those with $300 to avoid the draft, found the trial a perfect place to vent their discontent.

The trial lasted only two days. Faulkner was found guilty and sentenced to life in prison. This judgment was not enough for a mob that gathered outside the courthouse. As Faulkner was being escorted from the courthouse to the jail, the angry mob surrounded him, refusing to obey the commands of the provost soldiers guarding their prisoner. When they became unruly and began chanting "Kill the nigger," one of the guards fired several shots into the crowd. One man was killed and two were wounded, but this only enraged the mob. "If we got to be killed for niggers, then we will kill every nigger in town," someone in the mob screamed.[3]

There was no way to contain the fury, because there was no police force in Detroit at that time. No black person in the area was safe as the mob assembled and rushed downtown. There was no mercy for the first two black men they encountered and were relentlessly beaten to the ground. It's a miracle that Richard Evans, seventy-nine, survived the savage attack. He and his aged wife were together when the rioters fired on his home and battered down his door. One of them drew a pistol and shot Evans in the face, tearing the flesh to the bone. The old man fell to the floor and exclaimed, "You are now satisfied—you have done your deed, and shot me!" They left him there on the floor, thinking he was dead. Then they plundered the house, taking more than a thousand dollars from members of the distressed family.[4]

Another attack was on young Joshua Boyd, a mechanic who was hit in the head with an axe. After knocking him unconscious, the attackers dragged him from one location to another, repeatedly beating him with clubs and metal pipes. Boyd lingered in a comatose state for thirty hours before his mangled body expired.[5]

The mob knew better than to attack M. Dale, who stood in his doorway with a shotgun daring them to approach his house. One of his friends stood by, armed with an axe, and when the thugs saw their weapons, they quickly withdrew. Each time they neared his house, Dale lowered his gun and they retreated.[6]

By early March, on the fourth day of violence, more guns had arrived in the hands of federal troops, who were finally able to subdue the discord, but the city had been terribly damaged, leaving race relations in tatters.

In the wake of the turmoil, it was later learned that Faulkner wasn't black but of mixed Indian and Hispanic ancestry. Moreover, he wasn't guilty of raping the girls. They later confessed that they had lied, and after serving a few years in prison, Faulkner was released. The city had lost thirty-five buildings in the rioting, an untold number injured, and two people had been killed. No one was ever arrested, tried, or convicted for their deaths.[7]

During this period, the Confederate Army was wreaking havoc across the South and threatening to advance beyond the Mason-Dixon Line. It was time to put aside racial differences and to answer Frederick Douglass's call for unity. "There is no time to delay," he declared in a broadside from his home in Rochester on March 21, 1863. "The tide is at its flood that leads on to fortune. From East to West, from North to South, the sky is written all over 'Now or never.' Liberty won by white men would lose half its luster. 'Who would be free themselves must strike a blow. Better even die free, than to live slaves.'"

White soldiers from Michigan and Detroit had already tasted battle in the South as members of the First Michigan Infantry. Now was the time for black enlistees to test their mettle. In July, with the lingering aftereffects of the riot still an open sore on the city, Governor Austin Blair was authorized by the War Department to raise a regiment of black men to fight for the North. Many of the 1,500 African Americans living in Wayne County had already joined regiments, though they were still viewed as second-class citizens and denied the vote.[8] In October the black leaders in Detroit and around the state, including Sojourner Truth, held a meeting at Second Baptist Church, and hundreds of potential soldiers were in the audience, ready and able to become part of the newly formed First Michigan Colored Regiment. Of the 1,500 or so volunteers, one thousand of them had been born in slave states.[9] The colored troops from Michigan comprised one of nearly 150 such regiments in the Union Army. Their barracks were located on the city's lower east side. "The barracks were poorly constructed and during the following winter the men suffered from the cold, lack of good equipment, and sickness from which several died. Negro troops at that time were paid only $7 a month while the white troops received $10. In January 1864, the pay for all troops was changed to the same pay as the white troops received."[10] This action was similar to one taken by the black soldiers of Fifty-Fourth and Fifty-Fifth Regiments of Massachusetts, who stacked their rifles in a protest that ultimately brought about the change in pay. There was some resentment about the settlement, which to some seemed to suggest that black soldiers were concerned only about equal pay; on the contrary, one soldier wrote, they were protesting the principle of unequal treatment.[11]

By the winter of 1864, nearly 900 black men had enlisted in the regiment that was called Corps d'Afrique by the *Detroit Free Press*, and they were mustered into military service as the 102nd United States Colored Infantry. They left Detroit in March and saw battle almost immediately in South Carolina, Georgia, and Florida. In South Carolina, the troops, including two of Sojourner Truth's sons, were consistently brave under fire. On November 30, 1864, a detachment of the regiment consisting of 12 officers and 300 men left Beaufort and joined General Foster's column at Boyd's Landing, where they were engaged by Confederate forces. They distinguished themselves most gallantly in battle in the face of a vastly superior army; however, they lost 65 troops with many wounded during the three engagements. During its nineteen months in the field, the regiment lost 10 percent of its troops—about 140 soldiers and 3 officers, none of whom was black.[12] The historic Elmwood Cemetery on the city's east side is the final resting place for many of the casualties of the war. They had served nobly in the great war, whose victory and celebration was muted on April 14 with the assassination of President Lincoln. A river of tears flowed from Detroit's black community, and the soldiers in the field were no less mournful and distraught by the loss of the president.

At the war's conclusion, with the Union triumphant, the regiment mustered out and arrived in Detroit on October 17, 1865, to be paid and disbanded. Its soldiers had fought the good fight, and although they had removed their uniforms, many of them prepared for their next battle for dignity and human rights.

5

EARLY YEARS OF THE BLACK CHURCH

The social, political, and economic bedrock for black Detroiters was the church. It was in the sanctuary, the "loving arms" of the church that they sought refuge from the ravages of the day. Here they could find succor and salvation from the slights of poverty, the insults, and the racism that were so much a part of their daily travails. Two desires are significant to the emergence of the black church in Detroit—the need for spiritual nourishment and for a place to worship free of the white churches' discrimination.

On July 7, 1837, Madison Lightfoot, who was among the community leaders in the Blackburn affair, along with Cornelius Mitchell and William Scott, no longer willing to tolerate segregated seating at First Baptist Church, rose from the pews and walked out. Almost a year before in Detroit, Lightfoot and his wife—along with such enlightened communicants as Robert Allen, William Brown, Mr. and Mrs. George French (of Blackburn affair fame), Benjamin Read, the Rev. William C. Monroe, Samuel Robinson, and Richard Evans (who had been shot in the face during the riot in 1833)—had petitioned the state legislature to organize the Society of Second Baptist Church.[1]

Seven years after the riot, Detroit, like other northern enclaves, was experiencing a substantial growth in population as more and more blacks fled slavery. The census of 1840 listed two hundred African Americans in the city, and 15 percent of them belonged to Second Baptist Church.[2]

At the group's first meeting, in the home of one of the petitioners, the Rev. William C. Monroe was elected pastor, Lightfoot was chosen as the clerk, and French was elected deacon. By the time they held their third meeting, the state legislature had approved their request, and they decided to begin thinking about building a church. In the meantime, they used a building located on Fort Street, between Beaubien and Saint Antoine streets.[3]

The church leaders focused on outreach programs at Second Baptist, particularly an education curriculum for the children and an antislavery committee. By 1842, the day school was open for classes. William Lambert, Robert Banks, Lightfoot, and Benjamin Willoughby, a businessman of impeccable integrity, founded the Colored Vigilant Committee.

The next two to three years were productive for Second Baptist, especially for such tireless activists as Lightfoot, Lambert, Banks, and Monroe. One or more of them participated in practically every major state convention pertaining to abolition, temperance, or significant church affairs. Within a two-year period, the Rev. Monroe performed more than twenty marriages and officiated at funerals and baptisms. In 1846, he and Lambert left Second Baptist to establish Saint Matthew's Protestant Episcopal Mission. They moved farther downtown on Saint Antoine and Congress streets, leaving William Newman to lead the Second Baptist flock.[4]

The church continued to prosper under the Rev. Samuel H. Davis, who continued many of the programs launched by his predecessors. At the top of his agenda was the antislavery mission, which was complemented by several community programs in social services, education, and cultural activities. In addition, the church joined the Baptist Association for Colored People and later became affiliated with the Canadian Anti-Slavery Baptist Association and the Michigan Baptist Association.[5] These alliances were designed to broaden the church's reach beyond provincial groups and solidify its relations with Canadian activists. Moreover, the connection to Canadian Baptists also gave them ties to white ministers and churches of the same faith, something that was inconceivable in Detroit.

In 1854, a fire of undisclosed origin burned Second Baptist to the ground. Church services moved to an old schoolhouse that needed major repairs. It took three years before a new church was built, with the Rev. William Troy as the church's fifth pastor.[6]

With Monroe and Lambert at the helm, the newly formed Saint Matthew's congregation quickly surpassed Second Baptist and the Bethel African Methodist Episcopal Church, becoming the most influential black church in Detroit.[7] This influence, however, was short-lived, and with the passing of the Fugitive Slave Act in 1850, Saint Matthew's lost most of its congregation, the majority seeking refuge in Canada. Not until the 1880s would Saint Matthew's regain its former prestige.

The Bethel Church was established in 1841, having begun under the leadership of the Rev. Edward Heart two years earlier as

the Colored Methodist Church. From its inception and throughout the century, Bethel AME had the largest black congregation
in the city.[8] Bethel, whose congregation had been meeting at
various locations, including the city's Common Council office,
was able to construct its first church at a cost of $2,000, and was
officially dedicated on September 19, 1847.

The churches often competed to host major abolitionists. In
1858, the presence of radical abolitionist the Rev. Henry Highland Garnet guaranteed a standing-room-only audience at Second Baptist.

Garnet, with his usual oratorical brilliance, regaled the crowd
with a story about an incident in which a man, John Broady, had
enticed two brothers into the hands of slave catchers. Broady
convinced the brothers, John and James Williams, both escaped
slaves, to return to Kentucky with him to liberate other members
of their family. The brothers were trapped, and for the betrayal
Broady pocketed $300 in gold. When a group of black men in
Cincinnati heard about the incident, they pursued Broady, captured him, tried him in their "kangaroo court," and save for the
intervention of Garnet, would have killed him. Instead, he was
punished with three hundred blows with a paddle for his repre-
hensible act. Broady went to the police with his complaint and
pressed charges against his assailants; they fled from town. In
addition, he promised to tell everything he knew about the Underground Railroad.

Meanwhile, within a few months, the former vicar, the Rev.
Monroe, had parted company with Saint Matthew's. By 1859,
given his friendship with Mr. and Mrs. Henry Bibb and the further inducement promulgated in the speeches and sermons of
the Rev. Garnet, he was ready to consider a new faith. He found
the appeal of emigrationism irresistible, particularly after the
draconian enforcement of the Fugitive Slave Act of 1850. He
was soon off to Liberia, the US colony in Africa, as a missionary.[9]

Most black Americans were not interested in leaving the United States, believing that eventually the nation would live up to its hallowed creed. Though it brought unintended consequences, such as the riot of 1863, the Civil War was an indicator that change was on the horizon. Once again, amid the troubling and violent encounters, for the city's black residents the church became an important refuge from the hostile environment. However, even the church was reeling from the impact of injustice and, worse, from an economic climate that necessitated the sale of Saint Matthew's for $4,500 to Shaarey Zedek, a group of orthodox Jews who had withdrawn from Temple Beth-El.[10] The leaders of Shaarey Zedek and Beth-El were often sympathetic to the plight of black slaves. Several of them, such as Rabbi Liebman Adler of Beth-El and fur dealer Mark Sloman, were abolitionists who assisted fugitives' escape to Canada.[11] Adler never equivocated on his antislavery sentiments. Throughout his stay in Detroit, he was openly supportive of the Republican Party because of its stance on slavery. The members of Shaarey Zedek were steadfast in their fight against slavery, and they had even greater civic clout after laying the cornerstone for a new synagogue, the first to be built by Detroit Jews and the first building in the state specifically built as a synagogue.[12]

After the sale of the church, Saint Matthew's began its precipitous decline. That downward spiral would continue for a score of years before stability returned. Meanwhile, the smaller congregation met at various sites. The services often consisted of only Sunday school. The regular schooling begun in 1839 by the Rev. Monroe, also one of the teachers at Second Baptist, had vanished with him. At Bethel and Second Baptist, classes for children continued.

By the early 1880s, the gains made during the previous decade were fading fast. The influx of European immigrants in sections of downtown Detroit that were traditionally black quarters compounded the problems. The Jewish presence was particularly pronounced on Hastings Street, the main thoroughfare of what was gradually becoming a Jewish community. From 1880 to 1890, Detroit's Jewish population swelled from about a thousand to ten thousand. Gradually, Jewish merchants dominated the area. The most that blacks could expect from this emergence was the possibility of employment, primarily as custodial staff, stock handlers, shippers and receivers, or warehouse workers. They had little choice but to accept menial jobs as immigrants slowly replaced black workers as longshoremen, coopers (barrel makers), barbers, cooks, teamsters, and doormen. It made little difference if the newcomers were not fluent in English.

As in the future, the black churches were facilitators, providing the businesses with a steady flow of laborers who, church elders hoped, would benefit the coffers with their tithes. The churches resorted to a number of attractions to build their congregations. A powerful, charismatic preacher was an absolute requirement; his presence was complemented by a choir that could, depending on the denomination, either rock a church or hold listeners rapt with comforting spirituals.

At the dawn of the twentieth century, Second Baptist hosted several civic events. It was there that the Phillis Wheatley Home for Aged Colored Ladies, with the indomitable educator Fannie Richards as its leader, held its meetings. By 1898, the church had its first mortgage-burning ceremony after making its final payment of $700.[13] Richards, a native of Virginia, had arrived in Detroit with her family in 1851. Considered the city's first black teacher, she was the first to be hired on a permanent basis and was relentless in her determination to desegregate the city's public schools.

In 1890, an anonymous scholar composed a fanciful sketch of what he believed to be a composite of the typical black family in Detroit. James Wilson was the name given to the composite head of the family:

> He is 34, has a 32-year-old wife, an 8-year-old daughter, named Mary, and a 6-year-old son named Robert. A third child is due in five months. Wilson was born in Detroit, and his wife was born in Windsor, Ontario. His father was born free in Kentucky but moved to Ohio and then to Detroit in the 1850s to escape harassment. His mother was born a slave in Virginia, was emancipated and settled in Cass County, Michigan, by her former owners in the 1840s, and came to Detroit with her parents in the 1850s. The Wilsons are renting (and hope in a few years to buy) a small frame house on Hastings Street between Elizabeth and Columbia. There is a Negro neighbor on one side, a German on the other, and a Jewish family directly across the street. He lives one-half mile from work and usually walks there.[14]

The family was also probably a member of Bethel AME, Second Baptist, or Saint Matthew's.

The Lamberts and the Pelhams could never in any way be considered average families like the fictional Wilsons. One patriarch, Robert Pelham, was energetic, with a sunny disposition; the other, William Lambert, was slipping into the darkness of despair. In April 1890, Lambert was found hanging from a rafter in the woodshed at the rear of his house. A week before, Lambert, seventy-two, had been found unconscious, apparently stricken with a brain disorder, from which he nearly died. After attending church one evening, he took a length of doubled clothesline, climbed on a sawhorse, passed the loop through a ring in the rafter, placed the loop around his neck, and then kicked the sawhorse from under his feet.[15]

Lambert's death was a front-page story in the *Detroit Plaindealer*, a paper owned by the Pelham brothers. His funeral services were held at Christ Church, with the Rev. Dr. C. H. Thompson officiating. Among the pallbearers was attorney D. A. Straker, affectionately known as the black Irish lawyer, as well as Theodore Finney and Robert Pelham Jr. He is interred at Elmwood Cemetery.

Throughout his remarkable life, Lambert was a pillar of the community, an implacable foe of slavery armed with a steely resolve to uplift his people. In many ways, he stands as an unwavering beacon, a freedom fighter whose life and legacy is the template for self-determination.

6

BLACK ARTS IN THE GILDED AGE

The Gilded Age for Detroit occurred after the Civil War, from 1870 to the turn of the century. This was a bountiful era for a Midwestern city with an active port, and Detroit was an ideal location as a gateway to the West. Being on the winning side of the war and a staunchly Republican town also brought economic advantages. There was a gradual shift from wealth accumulated through land ownership to the development of a merchant class. Industrial growth, particularly in the manufacture of machine parts, teamster equipment, and stoves, was the mother of this emerging wealthy upper class. "In general, landownership re-mained important but became an auxiliary, rather than a main source, to major wealth until the real estate expansion of the 1920s."[1]

During this period, there was a proliferation of gentlemen's clubs, lodges, beer gardens, and various entertainment venues. These businesses, in their need for waiters, valets, busboys, coachmen, cooks, maids, and musicians, gave black Detroiters opportunities for employment. Particularly in demand were professional musicians. During the war, African Americans had acquired extensive experience in the regimental bands.

One of the most prominent bands was formed and led by Theodore Finney, who in 1857 had come to Detroit from Columbus, Ohio. When he joined forces with John Bailey, their thirty-three-piece orchestra was extremely successful and was among the first groups to feature syncopated music.[2]

According to several musicologists, Detroit was a proving ground for syncopated music, and Finney's arrangements were exemplary of the sound and rhythm. Finney's music, a reformation of the marching-band style soon to be popularized by John Philip Sousa, was a direct antecedent to the jazz-related brass bands that were to become so popular in the next decade. After Bailey's death in 1870, Finney reorganized the orchestra, and for several years it performed on the old steamer *Frank Kirby*, which plied the river between Detroit and Sandusky, Ohio.

When the bands weren't performing for white audiences, there were engagements at black concerts, formals, weddings, and other celebrations. By 1870, the black population had expanded to more than two thousand, still less than 3 percent of the city's population.[3] An increase in the population meant more performances for the musicians among the city's slowly emerging black elite.

Finney was not only a gifted and versatile musician, but also a savvy entrepreneur with interests in civic affairs. For the next twenty years, his orchestra would be an important institution and a training ground for some of the city's finest musicians. Fred Stone and Ben Shook, who later led their own bands, were two members of Finney's orchestra who gained considerable recognition.

Ensembles like Finney's were basically concert bands that played a repertoire that included parade marches and political rally songs, as well as concert arrangements for picnics and social functions. By the 1880s, however, these public performances were few, and musicians were employed mainly in "disorderly houses."[4]

When John W. Johnson settled in Detroit, his arrival marked the beginning of the brass bands. Born in 1865 in Ontario, Canada, Johnson had been trained as a cabinetmaker, but his interest in proficiency on the cornet gradually became a full-time endeavor. In 1884 he joined Dr. Carver's Wild West Show and toured the whole of Canada. After several years on tour, he settled in Detroit in 1890.[5]

For a brief period, after his Canadian experiences, Johnson was a member of Finney's orchestra. It was from this association that he learned more about music and how to develop his own organization. With the assistance of his wife, Katie, the Johnson household was a center of musical activity. After assembling his own band, he began performing throughout the city. His performances at Belle Isle and in Sunday-afternoon concerts at the old Germania Turner Hall were the talk of the town. It was through these performances that many aspiring musicians in Detroit improved both their musicianship and their job opportunities.

As it was with the brass bands in New Orleans led by John Robichaux, Johnson's brass band was a small but powerful aggregation of twelve to fifteen players. Like the previous decade's concert bands, his was in great demand. "The usual instrumentation of the brass bands was three cornets, one e-flat, two valve trombones, alto horn, baritone horn, tuba, one or two clarinets . . . snare drum and bass drum."[6]

The popularity of the brass bands, with their emphasis on the

Dixieland beat and the interplay among the horns, was slowly being overtaken by ragtime. This music associated with the renowned composer Scott Joplin was primarily performed by pianists. Joplin's name is inseparable from ragtime, especially his "Treemonisha," but Harry P. Guy, who migrated from Ohio to the city, claims the music originated in Detroit.

A musical genius, Guy as an organist and pianist provided an important bridge to classical music and the music of the black church. On Sundays he was the organist at Saint Matthew's Episcopal Church, and on secular occasions he accompanied the internationally known Fisk Jubilee Singers. Not one to take a social indignity without protest, he must have been incensed in 1882 when the Singers were denied hotel accommodations in Detroit—a blatant example of the city's continuing discrimination; by the late 1890s, only the theaters were free of discrimination.[7]

When his busy schedule permitted, Guy directed a boys' choir. He founded the first African American music academy in the city. He was also a fine composer, and his music bounced with syncopation. His stylish arrangements were used by top entertainers, such as Eddie Cantor, Bert Williams, and Sophie Tucker.[8]

A consensus of historians believes it was Guy, Fred Stone, and Ben Shook who were responsible for giving the Finney Orchestra and later derivative groups their unique drive and energy. By the 1890s, this propulsive beat and the blues tonality attracted a coterie of composers to Detroit, including W. C. Handy. It was after attending a rehearsal of Stone's Orchestra that Handy, who had toured the country as a cornetist with a circus band, first heard the moving syncopation of a Detroit band. In his autobiography, *Father of the Blues*, Handy recalled this visitation and his musical intentions: ". . . I had a secret plan to include a stirring ragtime number, 'My Ragtime Baby,' which our minstrel band had featured. It was written by a Detroit Negro, Fred Stone. I re-wrote the high-stepper and programmed it 'Greetings to Toussaint L'Ouverture' so that the manuscript sheets would create the impression of classical music without changing a note of the original."[9] Stone and Finney, according to some music experts, may have been the inspiration for Handy's "St. Louis Blues."

When Finney died, in 1899, the blues was just beginning to sweep the country. His band of musicians were crestfallen by his death, but they were not about to let his precious institution crumble. Ben Shook, who had come to Detroit from Ohio—like so many other musicians of the day—stepped in and guided Finney's orchestra quite capably for several years. The band prospered for a while, but it was hard to hold it together without a consistent flow of engagements. Gradually members began to drift away, joining other more productive units. But Shook was not dismayed. Like Fred Stone, his longtime Finney bandmate, he began assembling his own orchestra.

Shook not only handled the responsibility of fronting and booking his own band, but he was also a booking agent for other groups that played almost exclusively to white audiences. "He was a very fine musician and a pretty good agent," recalled Charles Victor Moore, who was in Shook's trumpet section, and saxophonist Johnny Trafton, also a member of the band, agreed.[10] He could make his violin sing, and Shook often showcased his rich baritone singing voice. Through Shook and Stone, the Finney tradition survived.[11]

With the arrival of the Gay Nineties, an era fueled by the musical genius of black composer James Bland, the Gilded Age was slowly coming to a close. Bland, of course, can't be credited entirely with that decade's reputation for alluring entertainment, though it was his songs "Oh, Dem Golden Slippers," and "Carry Me Back to Old Virginny," that brought him lasting fame, a bit of fortune, and unfortunate calumny from black

Americans. The latter song became the state song of Virginia until the 1960s, when African Americans could no longer stand to hear the song's demeaning lyrics, none more detestable than the line "There's where this darkey's heart am longed to go." Bland died of tuberculosis in Philadelphia in 1911, just about the time Charles "Doc" Cook launched his popular bands in Detroit and Chicago, principally on Saint Antoine Street, then the hottest thoroughfare in Paradise Valley—not that the entire valley was a paradise, according to the memory and poetry of Robert Hayden, who came of age there.[12]

Cook's music had a way of turning the most depressing moments into a fanfare of gaiety and jubilation. It is not clear when and where his music career began, although by the time he was eighteen, he was living in Detroit. Also, according to Albert McCarthy in his book *Big Band Jazz*, as early as 1909, Cook (or Cooke) was already active as a composer and arranger in Detroit.[13] One fact that backs up the testimonies of Moore and Trafton about Cook's musical acumen is that he was one of a few black Americans to earn a doctorate from the American Conservatory of Music.[14]

Before leaving for Chicago, Cook led several bands in Detroit; Cookie and his Ginger Snaps was one of the more memorable. Though Chicago became his home, he still ventured to Detroit for many of his concert dates, which carried him all over the Midwest. Cook firmly links the music of the brass bands with the first identifiable jazz in Detroit. He was a solid extension of Finney's music, having played with Fred Stone's Orchestra and later in Ben Shook's band.[15]

Almost matching Cook's popularity was Leroy Smith's band. Born in 1888 in Romeo, Michigan, located at the base of the thumb on the state outline, about a thirty-minute drive northeast of Detroit, Smith and his band was clearly within the society orchestra tradition—slow danceable waltzes and foxtrots with just a pinch of pep. His father was a trumpeter in Finney's Orchestra, and in later years, he praised his father for the lessons from one of the best private violin teachers in Detroit. It was Smith's opinion that the musicians twenty years earlier were better than those of the 1930s; he considered the earlier bands more versatile, not married just to swing.[16]

By 1914, Smith was leading a sixteen-piece ensemble at the Pier Ballroom, which was billed as a "ballroom of refinement," indicating that it catered to white audiences of relatively high social standing. After this gig, he departed for New York, and by 1921 he was a headliner at Connie's Inn, one of Harlem's most celebrated venues.[17]

The Finney, Stone, Shook, Guy, and Cook tradition was the lifeblood of Detroit's music scene for several decades. While their arrangements were imbued with elements of ragtime and early blues, they were also quite adept at performing spirituals or "sorrow songs," as W.E.B. Du Bois characterized the music in his book *The Souls of Black Folk*. Classically trained musicians, such as pianist Bertha Allena Hansbury and organist Frances Preston of Second Baptist Church were even more exemplary exponents of sorrow songs. Hansbury was a graduate of the Detroit Conservatory of Music and did postgraduate work in Germany. Upon her return from Europe in 1909, she began giving private lessons from her studio on East Forest Avenue. Within a decade, she taught more than three hundred students.[18]

Preston, an accomplished virtuoso pianist, was more a performer than a teacher, and she occasionally traveled and performed in recitals with a company of singers. She had moved to Detroit from Richmond, Virginia, with her parents and quickly immersed herself in school and church activities. "She took a course in Detroit Training School of Elocution and English Literature and graduated in 1882 at the head of her class."[19] Despite her busy schedule and commitment to the church, she took graduate courses that prepared her as a lecturer and organizer for the Women's Christian Temperance Union. She was personally responsible for generating more than seven thousand pledges against the sale and consumption of alcohol.[20]

Emma Azalia Smith graduated from Washington Normal School four years after Preston completed her studies. Her grandfather, Wilson Beard, arrived in Detroit in the 1840s, making her family among the first black residents in the city. A child prodigy, Smith learned to play the piano at three and later took private voice, violin, and French lessons. From 1887 to 1894, she taught at Clinton Elementary School. She became a member of the Detroit Musical Society, played in a black orchestra, and performed voice recitals throughout the city.[21]

By 1900, Smith was living and teaching in Denver, and there she met and married Edwin Henry Hackley, an attorney and editor of the city's black newspaper, the *Denver Statesman*. In 1905, Emma Hackley separated from her husband and moved to Philadelphia, where she became director of music at the Episcopal Church of the Crucifixion. Always seeking to spread her love for music, she helped organize the People's Chorus, which later became the Hackley Choral Society. The group proved popular in the Philadelphia area and gave her the opportunity to study voice in Paris in 1905–6. Among the notables who studied at the Choral Society were vocalists Roland Hayes, R. Nathaniel Dett, and Marian Anderson.[22] Hackley was especially concerned with Anderson's development, personally tutoring and guiding the young singer's early development. After Anderson's triumphs at Union Baptist Church, Hackley accepted her among the younger members of the People's Chorus.

"Before long, she gave her a solo to sing—'to inspire the other members to higher things,' [Hackley] liked to say. . . . Hackley had her stand on a chair as she sang. 'I want her to feel elevated, and, too, I want no one in the back of the hall to have the slightest difficulty in seeing her.'"[23]

Although a gifted singer, Hackley chose not to pursue a professional career. Instead, she devoted her life to instructing others. There were, however, occasional recitals, mainly to raise funds for various students and her choral society. Along with her teaching, Hackley was a journalist and an author. She published her own collection of music entitled *Colored Girl Beautiful*. In 1916, when her Vocal Normal Institute failed, she devoted more time to her research on African American folk music. Like her concerts and musicales, her folk festivals were very popular and were staged in cities throughout the country.

Despite failing health, she accepted an invitation to travel to Japan to participate in the World Sunday School Convention. A year later, in 1921, while performing in San Diego, Hackley collapsed onstage. Assisted by her blind sister, Marietta, Hackley was rushed back to Detroit and in 1922 died from a cerebral hemorrhage.[24]

Hackley's legacy lives on in Detroit, where her collection of memorabilia and artifacts is archived at the main branch of the Detroit Public Library. While she is remembered as a maven of classical music, she was also a committed activist and a highly respected literary critic. When her biographer asked her to name the twenty-five greatest people she had ever known, her list included Frederick Douglass, W.E.B. Du Bois, Booker T. Washington, the painter Henry O. Tanner, author Charles Chesnutt, activist Mary Church Terrell, feminist journalist Ida B. Wells, poet and novelist Paul Laurence Dunbar, and writer M. E. Lambert.

Mrs. Molly E. Lambert was the daughter of William Lambert, the legendary abolitionist. What her father represented in politics and religion, she did as an editor and author. Her articles appeared regularly in the *Plaindealer*, where she covered social, cultural, and political events. As an active correspondent for the paper, she often gave special attention to church affairs. In an article in 1891, she wrote very warmly about a divinity student, John A. Williams, who was feted with a sendoff party by the ladies of Saint Matthew's church. "A small but excellent company with repartee, and mirth laughter was most intensely enjoyed," she wrote. "The Rev. John Henderson and Miss M. Henderson, the Messrs. Anderson, Stowers, T. Lambert, and the 'Pelham brothers' with the Misses Meta Pelham, Julia Owen, Mrs. Ollie Wells, and Mrs. Will Ferguson assisted 'our Fred' [Pelham] in the honors [at] his beautiful home." This name-dropping of the town's black elite was part of Lambert's appeal to readers.[25] Her fans eagerly awaited each week for her roundup of the activities of the crème de la crème, which always included more than a dollop of juicy gossip.

Lambert was more than a name-dropping gossip columnist; she was a serious writer with more than a passing interest in high literature. She had a particular interest in the lives and work of black women writers. She published occasional poetry and articles in the *New National Era* (apparently while still a teenager, since Frederick Douglass discontinued the paper in 1874) and in the *AME Church Review*, as well as news about Saint Matthew's in its *Lyceum Journal*. Lambert also had a growing reputation as an essayist in several national publications.[26] She gained national attention while editing the Literary Department for Julia Ringwood Coston's *Afro-American Journal of Fashion*, which Coston launched in 1891. Mary Church Terrell, a women's-rights and civil-rights activist based in Washington, DC, added prestige to the publication as editor of the biographical section.[27]

In one of her final articles in the *Plaindealer*, Lambert was among a number of Detroiters who raved about a reading by Paul Laurence Dunbar.[28] In April 1893, three years after her father took his own life, she was even more eloquent and emotional when writing about her mother, Julia, and the illness that afflicted her as she approached death. "How happy the dearly loved one seemed," Lambert wrote after her mother had called her loved ones together, "as she smilingly passed from one to another in her gentle, motherly way. At the close of the day, she said to one of them: 'I'm glad we had such a happy time. I felt that I wanted to have you all here with me once more, if we never get together again.' Loving and beloved—there seems that someone has gone out of our lives whose place can nevermore be filled." Lambert concluded the obituary with the poignant poem "Mother," which had the ring of Wordsworth or Longfellow about it.[29]

During the Gilded Age, there was a close alliance among theater, dance, and the musical arts. "Two uncles of the late Fred Hart Williams, back in the 1880s, regularly held amateur and professional shows at the old Merrill Hall," Alma Forrest Parks wrote. "Fred Hart Ball, one of these enterprising gentlemen, was also the grandfather of Herb Jeffries, the Detroit-born balladeer."[30] Jeffries was a popular crooner who would go on to star as the Bronze Buckaroo in several Hollywood black Westerns.

When Merrill Hall was not available, Ball and his brother, Henry, would convert their barbershop, located on Gratiot and Beaubien, into a performance center. This was also a forum for lectures and presentations by Fred Hart Williams, Detroit's most productive author and historian. Williams was a tireless researcher and promoter of Detroit's black culture. He compiled a treasure trove of books, manuscripts, and articles, which is now in the Burton Collection at the Detroit Public Library.

Williams was interested not only in preserving Detroit's black history and culture, but also he played an active role in providing forums and theatrical events for a coterie of vaudeville artists and entertainers. Vocalist Sisseretta Jones, famously known as Black Patti, and Williams's aunt, Zoe Ball, often enlivened the theatrical scene with their performances in the Creole Belles. Azalia Smith Hackley was another performer and associate whom Williams occasionally sponsored.

Two of Fred Hart Williams's associates—Dr. Broadus N. Butler, later an assistant dean at the College of Liberal Arts at Wayne State University and chairman of the Association for the Study of Negro Life and History, and Nellie Watts, whose name adorned an annual concert series—continued his work after his retirement.

Alongside these developments in theater, the visual arts were also expanding. From the time that painter Robert S. Duncanson rose to prominence in the mid-nineteenth century, black artists in Detroit were inspired by his achievement and recognition. Though Duncanson is best known for his pastoral landscapes, his *Uncle Tom and Little Eva*, depicting a scene from Harriet Beecher Stowe's novel, hangs in the Detroit Institute of Arts. After traveling abroad and living in Ohio, he spent his last days in Detroit, where he died in 1872, just as the Gilded Age was getting under way.

Among the city's artists touched by Duncanson was Rose Poole Wise. A graduate of the Detroit School of Art, Wise expressed her artistic vision through watercolor. Her work was lauded by the Michigan Commission for the Chicago Exposition in 1915. A fellow Detroit painter at the exposition, John Spencer Jackson, also received considerable attention for his portraits. His painting of Sojourner Truth interviewing President Lincoln was highly praised. Jackson was equally skilled as a carver, using jackknives to sculpt images in wood.[31]

As the curtain descended on the city's Gilded Age, another, far more prosperous era was on the horizon—the heyday of the automobile industry. In a rented workshop on Mack Avenue, Henry Ford began tinkering with a vehicle to replace the thriving trade in carriages. In 1904, the Ford Motor Company was founded, and the auto age began. Whether R. E. Olds had a car on the road before Ford is academic. Ford set the pace, and behind came other automotive pioneers—William C. Durant, the Dodge brothers, and Walter Chrysler. When Ford began mass-producing his Model T from an assembly line in Highland Park, his company's production was unrivaled. Ford symbolized the automobile industry.

The Gilded Age had provided black workers with countless employment opportunities, but Ford and car manufacturing were an incomparable boon for black Detroiters. A ceaseless wave of European immigrants pushed black workers out of the service jobs as cooks and maids in hotels, restaurants, and homes, but the automobile factories needed janitors and laborers in the foundry. By 1915 black workers began to fill this void. This was the beginning of Ford's enduring relationship with black workers, a story that is vital to the city's history.

For the most part, that relationship between the man who said "History is bunk!" and black Detroiters was a troubled one, a classic black-and-white battle and clearly an unequal one. James Baldwin, during an appearance in Detroit in 1980 as a participant on a panel on black English at Wayne State University, put that relationship in stark terms, so typical of his ability to speak truth to power. "I'm talking about the auction block," he said at the beginning of his speech. "We are also talking about the automobile assembly line. I want to make this clear, sitting in your town, talking in your town.

"One of the architects of this peculiar town is a man named Henry Ford, who is probably responsible for building it," Baldwin continued, "paying workers black and white, clubbing down workers black and white—who was a friend of Hitler's; who was no friend of the Jews. (He hadn't yet heard about us.) I challenge anyone alive to challenge me on that."[32]

Some black artists with the right connections in the union, particularly those skilled in the mechanical arts and in illustrating, lettering, and design, were occasionally employed by the automobile manufacturers. Each of them, in Baldwin's terms, was beholden to Henry Ford and the other architects of Detroit.

7

THE PELHAMS AND
THE BLACK ELITE

Robert Pelham Jr. was a Detroit delegate to the National Afro-American League meeting on May 18, 1890. On the agenda was Michigan's affiliation to the national organization, whose express purpose was to achieve full citizenship and equality for black Americans.[1] He was thirty-one and in the prime of his extraordinarily productive life. There was still much work to be done in preparation for the meeting. On the political front, there were election issues to handle; there were cultural and social events to oversee. Pelham was a perpetual networker, an inveterate traveler, and he needed more than a day to deal with sundry other activities, particularly his work on the inventions that would later give him a special status in Detroit and elsewhere.

Some of the energy and creativity he possessed was inherited from his father, Robert Sr., a robust mason and plasterer, who with his wife, Frances, arrived in Detroit from Petersburg, Virginia, in 1861, two years after Robert was born. He was born free, and at a very early age his mathematical skills and intuition were evident. The education system his parents sought out was perfectly suited for young Pelham, and he sped through what was generally a twelve-year process in nine years.[2] Obviously, he was double-promoted, a practice that would exist for years in Detroit's public school system as a reward for smart students.

Pelham was a high-school student when he began working at the *Daily Post*, which advocated Republican principles and was where he would remain in various capacities for twenty years, working under the *Post*'s editor and owner, Zachariah Chandler, who would later hold several political offices, including mayor, senator, and secretary of the interior under President Grant. These positions gave Pelham an opportunity to be mentored in his work as a journalist. Empowered by this mentoring and tutelage, he approached his brother, Benjamin, who also worked at the *Post*, with the idea of starting their own paper, and in 1883 the *Detroit Plaindealer* rolled off the presses. It seemed a good idea in a city with a black population of nearly three thousand—practically a paper per person given its average circulation—a burgeoning middle class, and a sizable contingent of potential subscribers in the region. When it appeared, Frederick Douglass forwarded a letter to the Pelhams declaring that the paper "meets my warm approbation."

Joining the Pelham brothers in the creation of the city's first successful black newspaper were Byron G. Redmond and two community stalwarts, William H. Anderson and Walter A. Stowers. In its earliest iteration, the paper consisted of six columns and eight pages. It carried many ads, both business and classified. The *Detroit Plaindealer* got off to a good start and created quite a buzz in the industry, eventually pulling in subscribers from throughout the nation. In fact, it was a model for other black-owned publications, such as the *Chicago Defender*, especially after it grew from a small folio to more than twenty pages. Not only was the paper distinguished by its hard-hitting editorials, especially its persistent rebuke of the *Free Press*, but also it was one of the first newspapers in the West to utilize typesetting machines, and by 1890 it was alone among the papers to have in its office a Rogers typographical composing machine. To appeal to its national readership, the paper relied on stories sent from throughout the country, as it did not have reporters in other cities. Its downtown offices were a beehive of activity, all of it overseen by managing editor Robert Pelham. All the fancy graphics and a wide range of coverage were not enough to keep the paper afloat, however. More subscriptions and broader advertising were needed in order to sustain it.

After it folded in 1893, the Pelhams shifted their focus to the Afro-American League. While Robert and Benjamin assumed leadership roles in the burgeoning organization, their brother, Fred Pelham, was busy earning his degree in engineering at the University of Michigan. At thirty, he was younger than Robert, Benjamin, and Joseph (who lived in Missouri and was a delegate to the league's convention in Chicago in 1890) but no less accomplished and perhaps even better educated. Among the highlights on his impressive résumé was his stint at the Michigan Central Railroad Company, where he worked as an assistant civil engineer. His ingenuity was lavishly praised, and he earned a plethora of accolades for the uniquely designed and constructed skew arch bridge, a masonry vault over the Dexter River a few miles northwest of Ann Arbor.[3]

His work was also praised in Detroit and, according to the

manager of Citizens Street Railway Company, Fred was a resourceful and creative engineer in redesigning the curves in the city's rail system. Among his many affiliations were his memberships in various engineering societies; he was also a Sunday school teacher at Bethel AME Church.[4]

Meanwhile, Benjamin was busy on the political front and was instrumental in electing the Wayne County treasurer. For this endeavor, he was rewarded with an appointment as the treasurer's junior clerk. His bookkeeping and clerical skills modernized the record-keeping system for the county. He married Laura Montgomery of Sandwich, Ontario. They had two children, a daughter, Frances, and a son, Alfred, who was born in 1900, the same year Benjamin transferred to the office of the register of deeds. In this capacity, he continued his modernization and organizing wizardry, thereby speeding up the processing of information.[5]

Notwithstanding the commitment of the Pelhams, the Afro-American League or the National Afro-American League, as it was renamed two years after its founding, never really gained traction. The league was the brainchild of T. Thomas Fortune, the editor of the esteemed *New York Age* newspaper, and Bishop Alexander Walters of the African Methodist Episcopal Zion Church in Washington, DC. They envisioned and the Pelhams endorsed equal opportunities for black Americans, especially voting rights and desegregation of public accommodations, along with a cessation of lynching.[6] At the dawn of the twentieth century, the organization anticipated in many ways the mission of the Niagara Movement and the NAACP, with their commitment to challenge Jim Crow laws from a legal standpoint. The league had a promising start, winning two lawsuits in which Fortune was personally involved. He also was instrumental in challenging the Supreme Court decision upholding the Civil Rights Act of 1883, which ruled the Civil Rights Act of 1875 unconstitutional, thereby allowing unequal treatment in all public spaces and accommodations. But without support and donations from members and advocates, there was no way the league could continue in its fight against racism and discrimination. It disbanded in 1893 but resurfaced five years later under the rubric of the Afro-American Council.[7]

With the demise of the League, Robert Pelham, like his brother, shifted gears, dedicated himself to being a clerk and a good public servant. This was accomplished with his eye for detail as a special agent of the General Land Office and as an inspector for the Detroit Water Department.[8] He and his wife, Gabrielle Lewis of Adrian, Michigan, whom he had married in 1893, left Detroit in 1900 for Washington, DC, where she was a prominent figure in musical circles. She had earned a bachelor's degree in music from Adrian College in Adrian, Michigan, the first woman to do so, and she would be the first person of color to have an official position with the Michigan State Music Teachers' Association.

Before the couple departed for the nation's capital, they were honored by the governor and showered with praise and affection by the noted journalist and activist Ida Wells Barnett, who once wrote for the *Plaindealer*. She effused: "Mr. Pelham is the busiest man I know of anywhere."

At the city's bicentennial celebration in 1901, there were few black Detroiters among the spectators. Confined to the lower east side and paying exorbitant rent, most had very little to celebrate.[9] If there was one benefit for the poorer denizens in the community— the majority of them, when they were lucky enough to be employed, sweeping the streets, shining shoes, or doing laundry—it was living cheek by jowl with the striving black middle class, or the black elite. The economic depression that hobbled the nation in 1893 was still a lingering problem in black America, and black

Detroiters were not exempt. Possible employment in the emerging automobile industry had yet to reach the black community. Black-owned businesses provided some jobs, and their successes gave the less fortunate something to which they could aspire. Even black entrepreneurs of means had their own challenges to overcome. Many of them were what W.E.B. Du Bois defined as the "talented tenth"; they were well-educated and prepared to fight for a larger piece of the American dream. Others in the black community adhered to the ideas of Booker T. Washington as members of his National Negro Business League. It was a momentous occasion when, in October 1900, Washington was invited to dine with President Theodore Roosevelt.[10]

In August 1900, when the National Negro Business League held its first meeting in Boston, Mrs. Susie Smith, a chiropodist and manicurist, was the only delegate from Detroit.[11] Nor was any person from Detroit or Michigan mentioned in the records of any future proceedings of the League, which is perhaps why in 1903 Washington found it necessary to travel to Detroit to speak at the Light Guard Armory, not about the absence of black Detroiters from his annual meetings but about racial harmony. Washington may have had another reason to be there. He was under furious attack, particularly by the radical Democrat Du Bois, and more aggressively by the militant Boston publisher, William Monroe Trotter. Detroit's growing black community and its seeming neutrality on the heated differences between the major leaders may have been the comfort zone in which he sought to make his appeal. The attempt to broaden his base in the Midwest was certainly important to him toward the end of his life, and Detroit—and particularly Henry Ford—was high on his agenda. He had secured a letter of introduction to Ford in 1915.[12] The Wizard of Tuskegee may have used that moment to generate sympathy in the North and tamp down the furor caused by Du Bois's attacks on his accommodationist and assimilationist beliefs. It was not until 1926, eleven years after Washington's death, that the League established a branch in Detroit.[13]

Gradually a new black middle class emerged in the city, replacing the previous one that was inclined to push for integration, as opposed to desegregation. "Integration had never worked as a viable survival strategy for the majority of black Detroiters in the late nineteenth century," historian Richard Thomas concluded. "Having one's sons and daughters attend white universities, white churches, and fashionable parties could not build and sustain the community to which they belonged by race and history. In hard truth, however, such achievements were mere tokens masquerading as universal race progress. In the end, the harsh hand of time demanded a reckoning. New leadership was needed if blacks were to survive and progress."[14]

A relentless wave of white immigrants had a devastating impact on black-owned businesses, especially those related to the service industry, in which black butlers and maids once cornered the market. An increasing scarcity of businesses may have diminished the prospect of Detroit's black citizens taking advantage of Washington's network of black entrepreneurs. The network served as an umbrella for black owners to support each other beyond their often isolated precincts. By the 1900s, the extent to which the small black elite was involved in such enterprises was marginal; many of them opted to earn their living as civil servants, or as Thomas observed, to find a way to get on the "government payroll."[15] The downward spiral into unemployment or underemployment of many Detroiters, their purchasing power diminished, meant that the small black businesses no longer could depend on consumers of any color to patronize their stores. Many of these businesses—printing companies, accounting firms, funeral parlors, barbershops and beauty salons, doctors, dentists, and lawyers—belonged to the black elite, and the most prosperous of them traced their lineage back at least two generations in the city, state, or Canada.

Many of Detroit's black elite were close associates of the Pelhams. There was William W. Ferguson, a native Detroiter whose father, Joseph, was among the city's first black physicians and who was married to Evalina Richards, Fannie Richards's sister. After attending the city's public schools, William completed courses at the Detroit College of Law. It was his press, one of the largest in the city that printed the *Plaindealer*. He was married to Emma Pelham, Robert and Benjamin's sister. In 1890 he sold the company and, like so many of his colleagues and associates, went into the real estate and investment business, neither of which were labor intensive or provided a significant number of jobs. Three years later, in 1893, he served a term in the lower house of the Michigan legislature, successfully demonstrating that blacks could aspire to political office in the state.[16]

Ferguson had ties with another member of the black elite: attorney D. Augustus Straker. For years they had been friends, and in November 1892, they shared a news story in the *Cleveland Gazette* when Ferguson was elected to the state legislature and Straker to the circuit court as a commissioner. They came even closer together when Straker represented Ferguson in a discrimination lawsuit. Although most of Straker's clients were white, he still had room on his docket for a black client with enough money, particularly one of Ferguson's prominence. Straker's civil rights activism and his intense opposition to discrimination gave him an additional incentive to represent Ferguson in his lawsuit. When Ferguson retained him, Straker had been awaiting trial for a case that involved a doctor who had been refused service at a restaurant. Ferguson and Moses "Fleet" (short for Fleetwood, but also indicative of his speed) Walker, a baseball star in Syracuse in the International League, had been told by the restaurant's owner, Edward Gies, that he could serve them in the saloon but not in the dining room. At the trial, this was his testimony. The judge ruled in favor of the defendant on the grounds that the requirement of "separate but equal" had been satisfied in accordance with the Michigan Civil Rights Act of 1885.[17]

Straker took his appeal to the Michigan Supreme Court. In *Ferguson v. Gies*, the justices ruled that the judge in the lower court was in error, thereby vindicating Ferguson, Straker, and another client who had a similar complaint. "The supreme court reversed the jury's decision and ordered that only the question regarding the amount of damages to be awarded should be resubmitted to a jury," wrote David Katzman, citing the court records. "Straker returned to Detroit and reargued the case before a jury, but the panel disregarded the spirit of the Supreme Court's mandate and awarded Ferguson damages of only six cents."[18] In another encounter with a bigot nine years later, in 1900, Ferguson, rather than taking his case to court, took the law into own hands. A white racist objected to Ferguson's eating with white patrons and confronted him, calling him a "nigger." That was the last thing he said before Ferguson decked him with two punches.[19]

Ferguson's friend, Moses Walker, was also involved in a fracas, in 1891, when he was attacked by a white gang while visiting friends in a tough section of Syracuse. He pulled out his pocketknife to defend himself and in the melee killed one of his assailants. Walker received no sympathy from the press, which reported that he was drunk at the time, but given his popularity and the unfairness of the charge, the public sided with him. At his trial, the jury acquitted him in less than an hour. The verdict was greeted with a resounding ovation from the spectators.[20]

The cheers were like the ones he heard while performing on the baseball diamond in the Negro Leagues, where he was considered one of the immortals. Tall, slender, and handsome, Walker was the first black to play in the major leagues; in 1884 he joined the Toledo Blue Stockings of the American Association. After playing at the University of Michigan, his brother, Welday, joined him on the team. Walker was the son of a doctor and was born at a way station on the Underground Railroad. He grew up in Steubenville, Ohio, where he attended integrated schools and played on integrated baseball teams. At the age of twenty, he enrolled in Oberlin College. He was as gifted in the classroom as he was on the ball field. In his final year at Oberlin, he was the star catcher. He left the school before graduating but later attended the University of Michigan for two years, again excelling as a player. "Later in life, after leaving baseball, he became a businessman, inventor, newspaper reporter, and author," wrote baseball authority and historian James A. Riley. "Embittered, he became an advocate of racial separation, supporting a 'back to Africa' policy for American blacks."[21] Walker's forty-seven-page pamphlet *Our Home Colony: A Treatise on the Past, Present, and Future of the Negro*, published in 1908, is a searing attack on colonialism and racism. The only solution to America's race problem, he wrote, "is the entire separation by emigration of the Negro from America."

There must have been occasions when D. Augustus Straker thought he was back in South Carolina, so rabid was the racism and discrimination in Detroit. Straker was born poor in Barbados, and after his father died, things got worse. Determined and steadfast, he was able to acquire some formal education. For a while he worked in a tailoring establishment. A plea to his mother rescued him from the realm of needle and thread and placed him back on the academic path.[22] At Codrington College, on the island, he was embraced by the principal and placed under the guidance and instruction of the Rev. Joseph Durant, a well-known educator, astronomer, and linguist. By the time the brilliant Straker was seventeen, he was sought out to teach at public schools in Bridgetown, the capital. His reputation as a teacher and scholar soon attracted the attention of a Protestant Episcopal bishop in Kentucky, who invited him to America.[23]

In 1868, Straker was asked to deliver a speech in Kentucky on international law and the necessity to create a tribunal to help arbitrate and settle disputes. From this auspicious debut in America, he was offered an opportunity to study for the ministry, which he later rejected when he learned that it would not be a refuge from racism. After a brief stint teaching at a freedmen's school, he left Kentucky and enrolled at Howard University, where he obtained his law degree. He was subsequently employed as a secretary for O. O. Howard, the president of the university and chief of the Freedmen's Bureau.

It wasn't all nose-to-the-grindstone for the bachelor. He found time to marry the niece of Fannie Richards, Detroit's doyenne of education.

In 1875, after being appointed a customs inspector in Charleston, South Carolina, he stepped down from his position at Howard. Thereafter he practiced law and took a similar customs position with the government until the death of President James Garfield. He served three terms as a representative to the South Carolina legislature and then became dean of Allen College. His wife convinced him that Detroit would welcome his vast experience, and ever restless, he followed her advice. After the monumental victory in the Gies case, Straker was elected the first African American judge in Michigan.[24] In 1892, when he and Ferguson were saluted in the press for their electoral victories, he learned that the white members of the Detroit Longshoremen's Union No. 1 had drawn the color line, forming their own union under the International Longshoremen's Union of the United States. This separatist move infuriated the black community, and it left some seventy African American members in No. 1 without a cent in the treasury. They rallied, elected new officers, and paid back expenses. "The fight will be carried to the docks," the members promised.

Meanwhile, the black elite chose to deal with issues that most immediately jeopardized their upper-class status. Those were matters of property, civil rights, and integration—not desegregation—and opportunities to acquire wealth without the traditional encumbrances. Other than those in flight from servitude, most of the free blacks who arrived in Detroit in the 1840s and 1850s came from Virginia, Kentucky, or the Northeast, plus a few from Canada. Given what they had been told of the opportunities there, migrants often came from the Southern border states. The Pelhams, Richardses, DeBaptistes, Lamberts, and Fergusons, and Straker from Barbados via South Carolina, formed the foundation of what later would somewhat derisively be called the "cultured 40," referring to the black elite.[25] To some extent, they were representative of Du Bois's "talented tenth," endowed with a gift of leadership and the troubling "double consciousness"—a feeling as though one's identity is split into warring factions.

A story in one of the local newspapers summarized this situation when it reported that "There is a colored elite more exclusive than any other society in Detroit, which has its old families, its professional classes, its nouveau riches clamoring for recognition, its afternoon teas, its dances, its club studies, and most of the other duties and diversions which make up the life of white society in its most exalted strata."[26]

It is inaccurate and irresponsible to suggest that the black elite bore anything but a passing resemblance to white Detroiters; though they were similar in some ways, racism enforced vast differences. The black elite certainly found ways to take advantage of the adverse effects of discrimination by establishing businesses to service the black community. Even those advantages seldom amounted to more than a momentary benefit, however. Only in the businesses with steady perennial demand, such as burying the dead, was there enough money for owners to present any resemblance to the white upper class. Many in the black working class were only one paycheck from poverty. Even so, *they* were better off than their brothers and sisters who had no work but the scavenging of utter destitution. In such a society, how can the black elite be blamed for expropriating a bit of well-being and solace from their bourgeois pretensions and from fruitful associations with those white Detroiters who would accept them.

In no way can Mrs. Molly E. Lambert be considered an uppity black elitist with little concern for the less fortunate. Any community would be blessed to have her in its precincts or have her literature on its bookshelves. The fruit, they say, never falls far from the tree, and Lambert amply embodied the spirit and moxie of her antecedents. She was truly exemplary of her father, William, in her "race woman" attitude. As a journalist, she covered the appearance in town of Paul Laurence Dunbar, the esteemed poet, who was there mainly to bolster the campaign drive for Mayor Hazen Pingree, the choice of the black elite. Apparently Pingree's team and a Dunbar poem, "Vote for Pingree and Vote for Bread," made a difference.[27]

To honor the poet, black civic leaders established the Dunbar Memorial Hospital. Founded by Dr. James Ames and a dozen or so other black doctors in 1918, the hospital was housed in a building erected in 1892. A photo of the founding doctors graces the cover of Ken Coleman's book *Million Dollars Worth of Nerve*, mainly a history of Black Bottom and Paradise Valley. There, in 1922, Dr. Ames poses in front of the hospital at 580 Frederick Street. With him are several venerable members of Detroit's elite, including Drs. Henry Cleage, Robert Greenidge, and Lloyd Bailer.

A year before Dunbar Hospital was opened, Dr. David North-cross and his wife, Daisy, founded Mercy Hospital in Black Bottom. The structure wasn't as impressive as Dunbar's Queen Anne style with a dash of Romanesque highlighted by a bay-windowed gabled dormer cascading across the front façade, but the service it provided was on par. Dunbar was once surrounded by similar structures, but now it stands alone, a landmarked solitary structure and the home of the Detroit Medical Society (DMS), which had a number of distinguished black doctors as members, including Dr. Ames, Dr. Joseph Dancy, Dr. A. L. Turner, and Drs. David and Daisy Northcross, who were among the creators of the DMS's predecessor, the Allied Medical Society.

Among the most civic-minded of the black elite was educator Fannie Richards, who devoted time and attention to both elderly black women and deprived youth. In 1898, she and Mrs. Mary McCoy, the wife of the great inventor Elijah McCoy, established the Phillis Wheatley Home for Aged Colored Ladies. Naming it after a black female poet balanced it nicely with the name of the city's first black hospital. According to a story in the *Detroit News*, there were only seven women in the home in 1900.[28]

The decade from 1900 to 1910 was not good for black Detroiters, no matter their class. When immigrants from Europe began arriving in the city at the turn of the century, they gradually began to replace black workers in the good-paying positions as domestic servants and in the hotels. This decline in occupational status had a deleterious effect on the black elite and the "Negro continued to retrogress down to the year 1915."[29] If the black elite was experiencing an economic downturn, the city's black working poor were reeling from an even more devastating blow.

As historian David Katzman noted, the majority of Detroit's factory workers from 1890 to 1910 were foreign born, and for some companies, like the Dodge brothers, they were the preferred choice. "In 1890 there were no blacks in the brass and ship industries, and only twenty-one blacks were found among the 5,839 male employees in tobacco, stove, iron, machine and shoe industries." The overall picture for African Americans interested in the manufacturing and mechanical pursuits was no better. According to the 1900 census, only 139 blacks were listed, and 47 were in the building industry.[30] Nor were blacks visibly employed in brewing, furniture making, woodworking, and printing. If their employment percentage approached their population ratio, it was in dressmaking for women and house painting for men.[31] Most black women worked as domestics or laundresses, while the majority of black men were unskilled laborers, except for those able to hold on to their jobs as barbers. They mainly serviced black patrons, since the European immigrants, who were given freedom to leave their departure and destination points, had replaced them behind the barber chairs.

Some African Americans decided to open their own businesses. Wilson Beard, the grandfather of vocalist Azalia Smith Hackley, had been in Detroit since the 1840s. He established a laundry to take care of his family and hired eight to ten employees. Later Azalia's father, Henry Smith, opened a curio shop, which contained a collection of rare ancient coins that later became a valuable addition to the city's library, an added attraction for visitors.[32] Even more prosperous was James Cole, who before his death in 1907, was considered the richest black man in the city. He began to accumulate his wealth during the Civil War, when his grain store and livery stable brought him a lucrative contract with the Union Army. As his wealth increased, he began to invest in real estate and other small businesses.[33] Cole's wealth—estimated at $200,000—and his business savvy often combined with his general interest in the welfare of the black community. In 1919, Cole opened what would become the oldest black-owned funeral parlor in the city. It grew to become a vital and cherished institution, and emulating its impressive wakes, other funeral homes, including Swanson's, Diggs' (now Stinson-Diggs), McFall's, and Mason's, followed.

In contrast to the relative prosperity of the black elite, there was the salt of the earth, the city's toiling class, those fortunately employed just above the economic fault line of society. These African Americans were the street cleaners, haulers, bootblacks, steamer refuelers, and longshoremen, workers at all the menial jobs less desired by the Europeans. For black men trying to raise a family, these jobs were nothing to sneer at. They would have to do until the factories began offering them opportunities, albeit only the grimiest and lowest-paid positions in warehouses and foundries. This was a very intense period of racism in America. The Spanish-American War only exacerbated white racism, because the enemies, whether Spanish, creole, mestizo, or native, were all of a darker shade and were considered people of color. In the years between 1889 and 1903, on the average, every week, "two Negroes were lynched by mobs—hanged, burned, mutilated."[34] The arrival of millions of immigrants to America radically shifted the composition of the nation's working class, and nowhere was their presence more keenly felt than in Detroit, where they represented a preponderant percentage of the workforce. They brought with them their own prejudice against blacks, and too many of them hardened this animosity to assure themselves of their place in the American hierarchy.

Like many other Americans, the new arrivals often believed the mean-spirited stereotypes about black Americans. They picked up these elements of white oppression from various aspects of American culture—from newspapers such as the *Free Press* and later from films like *Birth of a Nation*, from their native-born coworkers, and even from ex-President Grover Cleveland who, during a speech at a Madison Square Garden fund-raising event for Booker T. Washington in 1903, asserted that blacks were ignorant, lazy, and shiftless.[35]

There were a few black workers hired as iron molders in the foundries of the stove companies. By 1900, Detroit was among the nation's leaders in the production of cast-iron stoves. Making a stove involved nearly two dozen departments, all dependent on the foundry. To produce the metal castings, molten iron was poured into the mold cavity. After cooling, the wood-framed flask that held the sand mold was dismantled and the casting shaken out from the sand. Each casting then had to be further cleaned and polished; then the parts were assembled and voilà!—the stove.[36] Back in the fifties, travelers up and down Jefferson Avenue or on their way to Belle Isle used to marvel at the giant stove—said to be the largest in the world—with WEL-BILT inscribed on the side, which hovered near the entrance to the bridge. Visitors driving on I-94 to Detroit from the airport are often stunned to see a huge roadside Uniroyal tire as part of an advertisement and were jokingly told back then, "You ain't seen nothing yet. Wait till you see the stove." At one time the Iron Molders Union was one of the city's largest and most effective. Black workers were in the union, according to the report of the Seventh Annual Conference on the Study of the Negro Problems, held in Atlanta in 1902. Nearly two hundred pages of the study are devoted to tallies of black artisans in state-by-state listings. In Michigan in 1900, there were 15,816 black artisans, including 731 barbers and hairdressers, which constituted the largest category. There were 235 lumbermen and rafts men, 122 carpenters and joiners, and more to the point, 28 iron and steel workers in the local plants. Most of the black women artisans fell into three categories—dressmakers, milliners, and seamstresses, of whom there was a total of 194.[37] The study underscored the presence of longshoremen, carpenters, and engineers. According to the Longshoremen's Union, Detroit had 60 members. The union also noted that Detroit was one of the few cities where blacks were employed as motormen and conductors on the street railways.

No indication was given for the number of black members in the Iron Molders Union, other than stating that there were very few. In Toronto at the union's annual convention in 1902, the race question was raised by a delegate from the South who said that blacks should be excluded from the union, but delegates from the North and Canada advocated for black membership. Later, when the secretary of the union was asked about a resolution on the issue, he asked to be left alone because he had more important matters on his agenda.[38]

Indecision, ambivalence, and rejection were the prevailing options exercised by trade unions when it came to enlisting black members. From the Brotherhood of Boilermakers and Iron Shipbuilders to the Stonecutters Association, blacks were not wanted, hadn't applied, or were barred by the group's bylaws.[39]

Things were a lot different at the Knights of Labor, which by 1886 had approximately seven hundred thousand members, of whom sixty thousand were African Americans. Obviously, depending on the region, some of the union's locals had both black and white members, while others had separate (but "equal") organizations.[40] During the early 1900s, Booker T. Washington and W.E.B. Du Bois had their own ideas about the unions. Uppermost in Washington's mind was the dichotomy between black workers in the South and those in the North. His focus was mainly on black agricultural workers, 34 percent of the black workforce in 1900. In the Southern states, he wrote, the trade unions had not hindered the progress of black skilled laborers or of black workers in special industries, such as coal mining and iron mining, etc. But in border-state cities like Saint Louis, Baltimore, and Washington, black bricklayers and carpenters were a rarity. He was saddened by what he observed on the campus of Howard University as a building was being erected. "Every man laying brick on this building was white; every man carrying a hod was a Negro. The white man, in this instance, was willing to erect a building in which Negroes could study Latin, but was not willing to give Negroes a chance to lay the bricks in its walls."[41] Those knowledgeable about Washington's use of examples will note how similar it is to others, and this one could have easily come to mind, for at Tuskegee the students made the bricks and constructed the school's buildings.

Du Bois attacked union favoritism as a symptom of capitalism as well as racism, decrying, ". . . the practice among employers of importing ignorant Negro American laborers in emergencies, and then affording them neither protection nor permanent employment, and the practice of labor unions in proscribing and boycotting and oppressing thousands of their fellow toilers, simply because they are black. These methods have accentuated and will accentuate the war of labor and capital, and they are disgraceful on both sides."[42]

8

DETROIT AND WORLD WAR I

I'm goin' to Detroit, get myself a good job
Said I'm goin' to Detroit, get myself a good job
Tried to stay around here with the starvation mob.
Yeah, I'm goin' get me a job up there in Mr. Ford's place
Uh huh, goin' get me a job up there in Mr. Ford's place
Stop these eatless days from starin' me in the face.
When I start makin' money, she don't need to come around
I said when I start makin' money, she don't need to come around
'Cause I don't want her now, Lord, I'm Detroit bound.[1]

—BLIND BLAKE

Two things commanded the nation's attention between 1915 and
1920—the Great Migration and World War I. One was a domestic,

demographic shift of population, and the other, an international conflict. Both had a dramatic effect on American social and political life. And both had meaning and effect on black Detroiters. As it was during the days of slavery, Detroit was a primary destination during the Great Migration. Many of these migrants traveled along the same byways as the fugitives on the Underground Railroad, perhaps with less fear but with a similar apprehension about what awaited them on the other side of the Cotton Curtain, and how real was the so-called promised land.

By the middle of the decade, this movement had reached critical mass. Henry Ford's announcement of paying workers at his automotive plants five dollars a day was an additional stimulus for black Americans eager for a fresh start in life. Carole Marks, in her book *Farewell—We're Good and Gone*, adds another factor to the push-and-pull tug of this historic demographic shift. "First, a majority of the migrants of the Great Migration were urban, nonagricultural laborers, not the rural peasant usually assumed. Secondly, black migrants left the South not simply to raise their wages but because they were the displaced mudsills of southern industrial development. Thirdly, much of the mobilization of the migration was orchestrated in the board rooms of northern industrial enterprises."[2]

Five dollars a day instead of five dollars a month seemed too good to be true, and in too many instances, it was. Of course, this was by no means the first illusion the newcomers would struggle to transcend. A year or two after Ford's announcement, an African American newspaper, the *Chicago Defender*, picked up the beat and became the drum major for the march of black migrants to the North. These future workers were not aware that one of Ford's motives for five-dollar-a-day pay was to impede the growth and effectiveness of the Industrial Workers of the World and the Communist Party. Offering workers what he viewed as a decent salary would, he hoped, be incentive enough to keep them from the pull of an alternative economic system. Nor did these workers know or care about Ford's racial ambivalence. Emblazoned in the headlines was the call to the lowly to abandon the land of lynch law. Blacks getting their hands on one of the papers was akin to their ancestors having a copy of David Walker's *Appeal* in the 1830s. It was as if they possessed a subversive weapon with intentions of overthrowing the government. The *Defender* posted job opportunities, train schedules, and other pertinent information for those wishing to venture north, particularly to Chicago, though Detroit and other industrial centers were also listed. From the responses the paper received, it was clear that the migrants were fully alerted; even if they had no idea where Detroit was on the map, they knew it had to be a better place than where they were. This letter, addressed on May 29, 1917, from a hopeful in Greenville, Mississippi, is an example of this yearning:

> Dear Sir: this letter is from one of the defenders greatest frends. You will find stamp envelope for reply. Will you put me in tuch with some good firm so I can get a good job in your city or in Cleveland, Ohio or in Philadelphia, Pa. or in Detroyet, Michian in any of the above name states I would be glad to live in. I want to get my famely out of this cursed south land down here a negro man is not good as a white man's dog. I can learn anything any other man can. Not only I want to get out of the south but there are numbers of good hard working men here and do not know where they are going and what they are going to.[3]

Between 1910 and 1920, New York State experienced a 66 percent rise in its black population; in Chicago there was a 148 percent increase, and Detroit, with a 611 percent surge, was by far the fastest-growing African American urban center.[4]

John Dancy, the Detroit Urban League stalwart, was both a witness and a member of this black population explosion in Detroit. As he noted in his memoir, there were 5,741 blacks in the city in 1910, according to official census figures, although the enumeration of blacks, no matter what year, is always questionable. "At the time I came here," Dancy recalled, "the Negro population was estimated at about 17,000. By 1920, when there was another official census, the figure had risen to 40,838; and in the next 40 years this increased a dozen-fold."[5] The swelling black population meant one thing to local businesses and another to Dancy and his colleagues at the Urban League, whose immediate responsibility was to make sure the new arrivals were not left out in the cold, literally and figuratively.

Prior to Dancy's arrival in Detroit, Forrester B. Washington was the secretary of the league. He had done a lot of groundwork, welcoming the newcomers with provisions and teaching them survival skills for the North. Suddenly, almost overnight, Detroit's dramatic increase in population put the city in the national spotlight; it became a symbol of full employment, high wages, and a better life for African Americans.[6] By 1917 a representative number of black workmen were employed throughout the industrial sector, including 1,100 at Packard Motor Car Company, 200 each at Ford and the Continental Motor Car Company, and 100 at Michigan Central Railroad.[7] At the beginning of the automobile industry, black workers were vital, and Packard took the lead in hiring them, though mostly as unskilled workers, as at Ford, which quickly surpassed all other companies in the number of African American employees.

Detroit was soon overflowing with new arrivals from the South. The city became an ideal test case for the National Urban League on how to deal with a dense population in need of social, political, and economic assistance. The National Urban League, the brainchild of sociologist Dr. George Edmund Haynes, had been in existence eight years when Dancy came aboard in 1918. Haynes, a professor at Fisk University in Nashville, had conducted a survey of African American conditions in the city and presented a summary of the report in 1918 in New York City at the annual meeting of the Home Missions Council. He selected Detroit because it was a typical industrial center receiving a large influx of new migrants. It was a good choice. After a series of faltering steps, the Detroit branch of the Urban League finally gained traction, due to the correspondence between the league's national director, Eugene Kinckle Jones, and the administrators at the Associated Charities in Detroit. This exchange of letters mirrored in intensity and concern others shared with the *Chicago Defender.*

The letters from both parties expressed a bit of uncertainty on how to proceed and how to overcome the cumulative problems. With Washington and Dancy at the wheel, policies gradually fell into place. Washington, who had earned a master's degree in social work from Columbia University, settled in Detroit in 1916. In only a few months, he had created a model comprehensive plan that would later be emulated by other branches. "You cannot do much for a man spiritually until you have given him a healthy and wholesome physical environment," Washington opined. "In other words, 'you cannot grow lilies in ash-barrels.'"[8] But Detroit proved to be potent compost, especially given the metaphorically rich soil of densely populated Black Bottom.

Moral uplift, very similar to the teachings of Booker T. Washington, was a primary strategy in Forrester Washington's plan to assure that his charges were prepared for jobs and shielded from the lure of less wholesome activities such as gambling, prostitution, and frequenting bars and nightclubs. If the social agency was not doing its job, unsavory attractions would take control, and the newcomers would eventually become undesirables. To prevent migrants from being seduced by "demoralizing elements," Washington resorted to a tactic used by women in the reform movement's Dress Well Club and warned the newcomers not to wear audacious, flamboyant outfits that would mark them as country bumpkins, not ready for urban complexities. He was also aided and abetted by the Young Negroes' Progressive Association (YNPA), which helped steer migrants toward redeeming social affairs, dances, baseball games, and even into organizations like the Boy Scouts and the Camp Fire Girls. A decade or so later, the League, under Dancy, inaugurated the summer sojourns to Green Pastures, a highly regarded recreational camp.

Washington's tenure as director of the branch lasted only two years. Before turning the reins over to Dancy, he had been highly successful in developing community-building strategies to help the migrants get their footing, wrote historian Richard Thomas, but it was left to Dancy to devise and perfect those long-term programs that could—and did—sustain the black community through tough times.[9] "One of the first things I had attempted to do when I took up my duties in Detroit," Dancy related, "was to work in close cooperation with other social agencies such as the Children's Aid Society, the various settlement houses and similar organizations."[10] Dancy's mission was to provide a warm and friendly greeting for the migrants, decent housing, and preparation for a job. He often carried out the first of these obligations personally. Once during a two-day period, he took a break from the office then located at 1911 Saint Antoine, and counted 270 people as part of the steady stream of migrants entering the city. Getting a job wasn't that difficult during the early years of the migration; in fact, in those days recruiters roamed the South looking for laborers. In one year, he reported, they supplied 19,000 black workers in response to job requests. The biggest challenge for Dancy and his cohorts was housing. "There was much doubling up of families, in houses that, in many instances, were unfit for human habitation. Conditions grew worse. Rents were high. The average rent for white families was $30 a month; for Negro families, it was closer to $50, and the Negro got worse housing for his money."[11]

This was the period when Marjorie Ramsey Lewis's parents arrived in Detroit from a small town outside of Chattanooga, Tennessee. They arrived in 1915 still haunted by memories of life in the South.

"My grandfather purchased property, a house, and moved his family to Chattanooga," she recalled. "The KKK did not want them there so they burned a cross in the yard. All six of my family members were sharp shooters. One by one they would target practice in the yard. The police next door let the Klan know he was on our side. I guess the Klan felt the risk was too great. So, my family won the battle and lived there without another burning." Civil rights activist Charlie Cobb in his book *This Nonviolent Stuff'll Get You Killed* wrote: "Few if any white terrorists were prepared to die for the cause of white supremacy; bullets, after all, do not fall into any racial category and are indiscriminately lethal. . . . In place after place, a few rounds fired into the air were enough to cause terrorists to flee."[12]

Lewis's uncle and father were among those black Detroiters who volunteered for the army and marched off "to make the world safe for democracy."

"In 1915," Lewis continued, "they migrated to Detroit. In 1917 my dad and uncle, Raymond Ramsey, were drafted into the army. They were in the 372nd Infantry which was loaned to the French. My uncle received the top honor, the Croix de Guerre from the French."[13]

Along with the highly decorated 372nd Infantry was the 371st Infantry (mainly composed of black recruits from South Carolina), three all-black National Guard regiments, the 369th Infantry (the legendary Harlem Hellfighters), and the 370th Infantry; all were part of the 93rd Provisional Division, provisional in the sense that it never attained full strength. The three National Guard units were turned over to the French.[14] The 372nd Infantry, formed in 1918, was composed of six National Guard units from Ohio, Maryland, Tennessee, Massachusetts, Connecticut, and Washington, DC. Two hundred fifty draftees from Illinois, Ohio, and Michigan were transferred to fill out the regiment. Two white officers headed the unit, in which there was a lot of racial tension.[15]

Colonel Charles Young knew firsthand about racism and discrimination in the armed forces, both in and out of uniform. He earned his colonel or "full-bird" status in the Spanish-American War, as a leader in the Philippines, and under General Pershing in Mexico. The son of former slaves, Young was born in a log cabin. He believed that although he was more than fifty years of age he still had "strength for the fight" and the readiness to serve his country. The top military brass thought otherwise, rejecting him due to age. To prove he was physically fit, Young rode a horse from Wilberforce University in Ohio to Washington, DC. When the army turned him down a second time, he began to accept the rumors that he wasn't wanted because if they had allowed him to reenlist as a colonel, he would have been in command of troops, and that could not be tolerated.[16] This action against Colonel Young occurred in 1917. Although he was officially retired, he continued to campaign on behalf of young blacks in the army. His tour brought him to Detroit, where Dancy was given the task of handling his accommodations. Dancy wrote that there was no hotel room available. The city's only black-owned hotel, the Biltmore, was filled to capacity. Each attempt Dancy made to provide a place for him was turned down by Young. "Don't worry about me," he told Dancy, "the [Urban] center is warm and I can make a bed here with my overcoat and be completely comfortable."[17] The next day he gave a rousing speech at the

Light Guard Armory, located at Brush and Fort streets. He held the huge audience spellbound and clearly inspired a number of young black men to join the army. Five days before the war ended, Young was granted permission to serve.

Young's speech was similar to the one delivered by Frederick Douglass during his recruitment drive for young black men to join the Union Army to fight the Confederate forces. Of the nearly 368,000 black draftees who served in World War I, about 90 percent were assigned to labor, supply, and service units. Only 11 percent of all black military forces saw combat—the National Guard units and a few Southern draftee units.[18] As for other fighting men and women, only the navy had a substantial number—11,000 blacks, most of them working in the galleys as cooks and mess stewards. There were no blacks in the marines, the air corps, the army field artillery units, or the Army Corps of Engineers.

A number of black Detroiters distinguished themselves in the war, including Second Lieutenant Coit Ford, who served overseas. After their military service, other soldiers spent valuable time in the city. Both Harry Haywood and Robert Poston were active politically, though in different ideological camps. Haywood is remembered mainly in political circles for his book *Black Bolshevik*, which chronicles his beginnings in Omaha, Nebraska, then on to Moscow and membership in the Communist Party. During the war, Haywood (his birth name was Hall) was a member of the 8th Regiment, an Illinois National Guard unit. When he was deployed overseas, his unit, like the other all-black National Guard units, was attached to the 93rd Division. This placed him in the same division as Michigan's 372nd Infantry.

"Bullets whizzed over our heads," Haywood wrote, recounting conflict in the last major battle in Europe, in the Argonne Forest, located in a long strip of rocky mountain and dense woodland in northeastern France. "All of us scrambled to get into the communication trench which opened on the valley. Second Lieutenant Binga Desmond, our platoon commander (and the University of Chicago's great sprinting star) fell from the embankment on top of me. Fortunately, he was not hit. But even with his 180 pounds on my back, I am sure I made that ten or fifteen yards to the communication trench, crawling on my hands and knees, as fast as he could have sprinted the distance."[19] Haywood went on to become a major leader in the party and often returned to Detroit to speak, but none of his appearances was more publicized than his powerful speech in defense of James Victory, a World War I veteran, who in 1934 had been accused of slashing and raping a white woman. Attorney Maurice Sugar, representing Victory, was able to get an acquittal for his client by exposing the weakness of the prosecution's case in contrast to Victory's alibi. This wasn't Sugar's first involvement in a high profile case. Two years before, he represented survivors of the Ford Hunger March. Six men died during a massive protest march of laid-off workers at the Ford Motor Company's Rouge Plant in Dearborn. The march was to present a list of demands to the company, but it was met with tear gas from a phalanx of police. Five of the slain marchers were white. The lone black man among the fatalities was Curtis Williams, who died three months after the altercation. He was denied burial beside the five white men in Woodmere Cemetery. According to some accounts his ashes were scattered by plane over the Ford plant.[20]

Haywood's political counterpart Robert Poston had traveled widely since the early 1900s after leaving his hometown of Hopkinsville, Kentucky. Before enlisting in the army in 1918, there were brief stops in Nashville, Boston, and at Howard University in Washington, DC. Within three days, probably because of his college background, he was promoted to sergeant and then recommended for a commission. An altercation with a racist sergeant put an end to his rapid ascent, and soon he was snared in a legal fight for his life that led to an honorable discharge within a year. He never made it overseas.[21] Back in civilian life, Poston launched a publishing company in Hopkinsville but ran afoul of printers who refused to print his paper after he reported that returning black veterans were placed at the back of parades. He tried to publish a newspaper in Nashville, but it proved to be too expensive. Ultimately, he and his brother, Ulysses, landed in Detroit and began publishing the *Detroit Contender*. "Within eight months the new paper had surpassed all its local rivals in circulation."[22] Their paper was perfectly poised to cover Marcus Garvey's celebrity. Enthralled by the charismatic leader, they joined his Universal Negro Improvement Association (UNIA).

Garvey made Poston an assistant secretary general of the UNIA. The industrious Poston brothers—Ulysses rose in rank to become an editor at the organization's paper, the *Negro World*—provided the movement with a solid Detroit base. The presence of Detroiters J. A. Craigen, F. Levi Lord, and John Charles Zampty, who often traveled with Garvey as his adjutant general, greatly enhanced the organization.[23]

Zampty had migrated from the West Indies to Detroit to work for the Ford Motor Company. He was employed there until he opened his African export and import shop uptown on Woodward Avenue in the mid-1950s.

When the Poston's paper lasted less than a year, the brothers shifted their journalistic efforts to Garvey's paper, and two years later, Robert married the gifted sculptor Augusta Savage. He died in 1924 on a ship returning from a business trip to Liberia. By this time Haywood was a member of the Communist Party and to some extent connected to the African Blood Brotherhood, a militant coterie of activists with ties to the Communist Party who sought to infiltrate the Garvey movement for recruitment purposes. Except for an occasional visit to attend a rally and to confer with party comrades in Detroit, Haywood's base was in either Chicago or New York City.

Though they were never around very long, when they were in town, Poston and Haywood were prominent political figures, even if philosophically they were at opposite ends of the spectrum. The Great Migration brought thousands of people with diverse beliefs to the city—Garveyites, communists, socialists, and, as we will see, various significant religious leaders, both Christian and Islamic. During this time, many immigrants from the Caribbean became permanent residents of Detroit.

Elijah Poole, who later became Elijah Muhammad, was also a follower of Garvey before meeting the seductive W. Fard Muhammad, or W. D. Fard. Poole and his wife, Clara, and their children left Georgia and arrived in Detroit in the early twenties. They settled first in Hamtramck, a Polish enclave, before moving to Black Bottom. For Elijah, war was not the answer (and with the advent of World War II, he would spend time in prison as a conscientious objector). Despite the lure of the bustling automobile industry, his preference was Fard and his religious ideas. For black soldiers returning home from a war, the amalgam of cultlike religion, restrictive covenants, the rise of industry, and a budding black middle class made Detroit a unique urban matrix. Many veterans went directly to the newly opened Dunbar Memorial Hospital, where a cadre of competent doctors—Dr. J. W. Ames, medical director, Dr. A. L. Turner, and Dr. Joseph Dancy, John's brother and the hospital's first intern—awaited them. Ossian Sweet was another young doctor on the hospital's staff.[24]

The first two decades of the twentieth century were relatively promising for black Detroiters, who in the previous decades had witnessed nothing but lynch law and raw indifference to their humanity and quest for equal rights. Detroit was blossoming industrially. Black and white residents had come a long way from the Underground Railroad and the riots of the past. Even so, they were not naive about the challenges ahead, the need to build coalitions to make the city more governable and more accommodating to all of its citizens. Though factories were mass-producing an array of useful products, for many black workers they resembled the plantations—owners like the slaveholders, the supervisors like the overseers, the foremen like the drivers, and security guards like the pattyrollers (slave patrols). For them the working conditions were a form of neoslavery. There was still a lingering despair, an unrelenting disparity between black and white income, housing, education, and decent employment.

DR. SWEET AND MR. FORD

By 1925, the budding Garvey movement was grinding to a halt after its leader was convicted and sentenced to the Atlanta Penitentiary for mail fraud. His flock of followers believed the charges were trumped up to stifle his movement. The chanteuse Josephine Baker and soprano saxophonist Sidney Bechet could no longer endure the country's racism and took their flagging careers to Paris. Much closer to home, Dr. Ossian Sweet was on his way to a major confrontation with bigots as he moved into an all-white neighborhood on Detroit's east side.

The job market, which had been robust during the previous five years, was beginning to slide into recession. A hopeful sign, however, was found in the work of the labor leader A. Philip Randolph, who organized black workers into the Brotherhood of

Sleeping Car Porters. Similar recruitment was occurring in Chicago, where the nascent American Negro Labor Congress was convening for the first time. The two organizations shared many members and the purpose of improving working conditions and civil rights for black Americans.

During this era, Dr. Sweet's case was the centerpiece. An editorial in New York's *Amsterdam News* declared unequivocally that the court case could possibly be the most important "ever figured in all the history of the United States." What if the situation was reversed? the paper's editors asked. "Imagine that a mob of Negroes has resented a white family's moving into a colored neighborhood; and, in defending themselves, the besieged white family had shot and killed a colored man. What grand jury in the United States would indict the white family for murder in the first degree? What police officer would take the stand and testify that they were not acting within their rights protecting themselves? Why, then, should Negroes be charged with murder? Who dare to defend themselves and their property?"[1]

This *Amsterdam News* editorial was reprinted by the *Cleveland Gazette*, an indication of the extent to which the case resonated nationally. In all the African American papers and some major white dailies, Dr. Sweet's case was front-page news for several weeks. Even the *Detroit Free Press* covered the incident and the subsequent trial, albeit discreetly. "We Must Fight If We Would Survive," the *Gazette* editorial blasted in a twenty-four-point headline, and none did so more unswervingly than Dr. Sweet and his wife, Gladys. The Sweets did not walk blindly into this fray. Both were aware of the possible repercussions of their audacity, the likes of which had been brutally forecast on the city's west side months before, where, in three separate incidents, black families had sought to integrate an all-white neighborhood.

If Dr. Sweet was a bit naive about the situation, Gladys certainly could not have been, because she was born and raised in Detroit. Dr. Sweet's introduction to racism occurred during his youth in Bartow, Florida, when he witnessed the lynching of a black man. In 1911, he came to Detroit to work during a semester break from his studies at Wilberforce University. Choosing to work in Detroit between semesters for the next three years was not an arbitrary decision. Like thousands of black Americans— and eventually millions—he was among the first to heed the siren call to workers that was emanating from Detroit. However, he was not employed by the Ford Motor Company, but as a bellhop at various hotels and a vendor at Bob-Lo Island Amusement Park.

Sweet was a young man in Detroit at a most propitious time in America's history. From Europe the drumbeat of war was getting stronger. In America, another major migration was taking shape; the Ku Klux Klan, covered in white sheets, was marching boldly in the streets; and Detroit felt the impact of several social, political, and economic shocks. Ford's offer of five dollars a day must have had special resonance for Sweet, who grew up in Florida, where the daily rental of a horse and wagon for cartage cost the same. Even so, he would have welcomed a chance to earn that much, and it would have put him on a faster track to purchase that Model T, which was much less expensive than the nearly nineteen thousand dollars he paid to purchase the house on Garland during that fateful year of 1925. By then, more than a decade since Ford's offer of a job in exchange for loyalty to the company, autos were rolling off his assembly line in Highland Park and the River Rouge plant in record numbers. Unrivaled, the Tin Lizzie soon became the epitome of the motor vehicle, the veritable sine qua non of transportation and, as Beth Tompkins Bates wrote in her thorough study of Ford and black workers, the Ford was "synonymous with the word 'car.'"[2]

Although 1914 is the year cemented in the memories of migrants setting off in search of River Rouge or Highland Park, an industrial Valhalla, it wasn't until 1919 that Henry Ford stepped up the process of hiring black workers. This occurred eleven years after the company was incorporated, which was the same year the Wright Brothers took to the sky. "After World War I, Ford hired thousands of African American men to work for the FMC [Ford Motor Company], a policy decision that launched black workers on the road to modernity so they, too, could take part in Ford's 'new world.'"[3]

Getting a job at Ford, no matter what year, had to be a boon to the black unemployed, and in 1919, with the nation rocked by racial disturbances and the spilling of so much black blood that it was called the Red Summer, such a job was a balm for the miserable circumstances that seemed to relentlessly batter black Americans. Ford wasn't the only automobile company searching for black workers. At the beginning of the 1920s, Dodge and Packard were eagerly recruiting, but even their combined total didn't equal the thousands who were employed.

John Dancy, head of the Detroit Urban League (DUL) and the Rev. George Bundy of Saint Matthew's Church may have had close and cordial ties to Henry Ford, but when it came to counseling on African American affairs, the Rev. Robert Bradby of Second Baptist Church was at the top of Ford's list. "It all started one day in 1918," wrote historian Richard Thomas, "when Charles E. Sorenson [Sorensen], the plant manager of Ford Motor Company, invited Mr. Bradby to his office. Since 1910 the Canadian born Bradby had been the pastor at Second Baptist. During his 18-years of leadership at the church, he had demonstrated a tenacity and was known not to cower before the city's elite. Sorenson showed Bradby a number of knives and other weapons that had been confiscated from black and white workers, and asked him to help manage the racial conflicts in the plant and to recommend 'good Negro workers' to the Ford employment office."[4] Thus, the portals to heavenly wages at Ford opened with the Rev. Bradby as the gatekeeper, a position he would hold for nearly a quarter of a century.[5] And of course, the Rev. Bradby wasn't the only minister at Ford's beck and call.

Near the end of the decade, the percentage of black workers at Ford was greater than the percentage of blacks in the city's population. Blacks numbered some fifty thousand out of a total population of a little over 1.5 million, or 3.3 percent, while blacks at Ford represented at least 10 percent of the overall workforce. The Ford Motor Company was the largest employer of African Americans in the city.[6]

There weren't as many job opportunities for black women, women like Shahida Mausi's great grandmother, who arrived in the city in 1918 from South Carolina and went directly to the Rev. Bradby's church, seeking comfort and assistance for herself and her three children. "When the church was unable to help her, she played the numbers and hit 420 for enough money to get her started," said Mausi, the city's current culture maven. Some years later, the family purchased a home on East Ferry, and, incidentally, the address was 420. "That house has been in the family since the 1930s," she said, adding that today it is ideally located near the M1 rail line under construction on Woodward Avenue.[7]

Business was bustling again at Ford after a terrible recession in the early 1920s, but there was growing dissatisfaction from the salesmen, executives, and even some consumers, who insisted that it was time to dump the Model T and move on to a more efficient car. It is not known if any of these complaints reached Dr. Sweet and his wife as they drove around town in their Model T, gathering the essentials for their new home. Among these essentials was an arsenal of rifles and ammunition. Dr. Sweet's intent to be ready for racist attacks would soon be construed by the prosecution as grounds for its conspiracy charge against Dr. Sweet.

The Sweets, a young black married couple seeking the American dream, desired a comfortable home in a quiet neighborhood where they could raise their children. Instead of settling in to enjoy domestic bliss, they faced an angry mob of white neighbors, all determined to stop what they viewed as a violation of their restrictive covenant.

When Dr. Sweet and his wife, Gladys, moved to 2905 Garland, they had been living in cramped quarters with his wife's relatives. They wanted a home beyond the teeming Black Bottom. Word of their purchase spread, and a mob of neighbors assembled outside their home, cursing and threatening. The second day, September 9, was noisier. The Sweets were joined by two relatives—Otis and Henry Sweet, Dr. Sweet's brothers—and seven other friends and associates. Terrified by the hostile crowd and by a subsequent barrage of stones and other objects, Henry later admitted that he fired two shots, one of them a warning shot over the heads of the mob, the other into the crowd. Two white men were shot. Eric Hogsburg was wounded in the leg, and Leon Breiner died from a bullet to the back. Shortly after the shooting, all who were in the Sweets' home were arrested and a trial date was set. Deciding who would defend the eleven—the Sweets: Ossian, Otis, Gladys, and Henry; John Latting, Norris Murray, Joe Mack, Charles Washington, Hewitt Watson, William Davis, and Leonard Morse—was a source of contention that was finally settled when the NAACP insisted that they retain the best lawyer in the land, Clarence Darrow.

The racial animus and the restrictive covenants faced by the Sweets were becoming increasingly common in Northern neighborhoods.[8] Equally repugnant was the rise of the KKK; by the time the Sweets settled on the east side of Detroit, there were more than twenty thousand Klan members in the city. Phyllis Vine, in her book *One Man's Castle: Clarence Darrow in Defense of the American Dream*, provides a perspective on Dr. Sweet's

Southern background, which taught him to *expect* an attack by a white mob. His education began at Wilberforce Academy in Ohio, where he experienced the teachings of Booker T. Washington and W.E.B. Du Bois. Vine recounts an incident that Sweet witnessed in Florida when he was seven years old. It needs no novelistic touches to embellish the grisly reality of the lynching of a black man, Fred Rochelle, accused of killing a white woman. "When the entire posse had assembled, Rochelle was dragged to the spot and tied securely. The mob poured drinks for spectators while he cried for mercy. They ignored him and instead behaved as if they were guests at one of the popular outdoor parties. Eventually Mr. Taggart [the leader of the mob] was ready, and they took their places so he could strike a match. For the next eight minutes, Rochelle shrieked. Flames climbed up his legs, formed a curtain around his torso, and draped his face. After the flames died back, souvenir hunters pocketed pieces of his charred remains—a digit, part of the femur, a piece of his foot."[9]

Vine graphically depicts the Great Migration, with "140 trains arriving daily," before moving on to assess how dynamic Detroit was becoming, a fitting environment for Sweet's achievements in medicine and his association with a number of the city's black movers and shakers, including attorney Julian Perry and Dr. Alexander L. Turner, Sweet's colleague, who had encountered a similar mob attack on the city's west side. While Detroit was rapidly expressing appealing elements of modernity, there were still remnants of the vicious, racist past. "Detroit is Eldorado," one magazine gushed, but, at the same time, there was the other Detroit, where pestilence, violence, and squalor festered to make life almost unbearable for most black Detroiters bottled up in Black Bottom. The Garland neighborhood, comprised of working-class whites, stood in stark contrast to the ghetto.

When the trial began on November 9, the opening statement was delivered by defense attorney Arthur Garfield Hays, not Darrow. After stating his theory of law and the right of self-defense, Hays told the court and the jury that "to shoot to protect oneself is a right arising from the necessities of a particular situation as the facts appear to the person involved." The persons involved, the state of mind of the defendants, he said, was a "trapped state of mind induced by what has happened to others of their race, not only in the South where their ancestors were once slaves, but even in the North in the states which once fought for their freedom."[10] By contrasting the Northern and Southern experiences of black Americans, Hays invoked the lynching Dr. Sweet witnessed as a child. He could have gone further with his analogy, by noting, for example, that twenty-five blacks had been killed in Detroit while in police custody in 1925, eight times the number killed under police supervision that year in New York City, whose black population was at least twice as large.[11]

At one point during the deliberations, one of the prosecutors defined the mob outside the Sweets' house as merely a "neighborly" gathering. He went on to say that Darrow "'. . . is going to make his own witnesses liars when he tells of that crowd. I don't know how long he is going to talk—two hours, maybe; maybe two days. He is going to tell you about that howling, bloodthirsty crowd—' With masterful timing, Darrow interjected, 'just neighborly.' Laughter erupted in the packed courtroom, the judge's reprimand followed."[12]

Darrow didn't mention the howling, bloodthirsty crowd when he cross-examined Ray Dove, who lived directly across the street from the Sweet home. "You didn't want him there?" Darrow asked Dove. "I am not prejudiced against them, but I don't believe in mixing whites and blacks," Dove answered. "So, you didn't want him there?" Darrow repeated. "No, I guess not . . ." Dove said.[13]

When Dr. Sweet took the stand, a collective sound of exhalation filled the courtroom. With his usual debonair demeanor, he took the oath and stared intently at the jury. He was questioned by attorney Hays, and at some points in his testimony, it was as if he were recounting the lynching he had witnessed many years ago.

Q: *What did you do when you got home on the evening of September 9th?*
A: First thing I remember is my wife telling me about a phone conversation she had with Mrs. Butler, in which the latter told her of overhearing a conversation between the motorman of a street car and a woman passenger, to the effect that Negro family had moved into the neighborhood and they would be out before the next night.
Q: *When did you first observe anything outside?*
A: We were playing cards; it was about eight o'clock when something hit the roof of the house.
Q: *What happened after that?*
A: Somebody went to the window and then I heard the remark, "The people, the people."
Q: *And then?*
A: I ran out to the kitchen where my wife was. There were several lights burning. I turned them out and opened the door.

I heard someone yell, "Go and raise hell in front, I'm going back." I was frightened, and after getting a gun, ran upstairs. Stones kept hitting our house intermittently. I threw myself on the bed and lay there a short while. Perhaps fifteen minutes, when a stone came through the window. Part of the glass hit me.
Q: *What happened then?*
A: Pandemonium—I guess that's the best way of describing it—broke loose. Everyone was running from room to room. There was a general uproar. Somebody yelled, "There's

someone coming!" They said, "That's your brother." A car had pulled up to the curb. My brother and Mr. Davis got out. The mob yelled, "Here's niggers! Get them, get them!" As they rushed in, the mob surged forward fifteen or twenty feet. It looked like a human sea. Stones kept coming faster. I ran downstairs. Another window was smashed. Then one shot. Then eight or ten from upstairs; then it was all over. . . .

Q: *State your mind at the time of the shooting.*

A: When I opened the door and saw the mob, I realized I was facing the same mob that had hounded my people throughout its entire history. In my mind, I was pretty confident of what I was up against, with my back against the wall. I was filled with a peculiar fear, the kind no one could feel unless they had the history of our race. I knew what mobs had done to my people before.

Chief Prosecutor Robert Toms [objecting]: Is everything this man saw as a child justification for a crime 25 years later?[14]

At the beginning of his closing argument, Darrow slowly reviewed some of the critical moments of the trial and the various testimonies with the jury, never losing eye contact with them. "If I thought any of you had any opinion about the guilt of my clients, I wouldn't worry, because that might be changed," he said, pausing to make sure they were with him. "What I'm worried about is prejudice. They are harder to change. They come with your mother's milk and stick like the color of the skin. I know that if these defendants had been a white group defending themselves from a colored mob, they never would have been arrested or tried. My clients are charged with murder, but they are really charged with being black. . . . You are facing a problem of two races, a problem that will take centuries to solve. If I felt none of you were prejudiced, I'd have no fear. I want you to be as unprejudiced as you can be."

He told the jury that every policeman at the scene knew the crowd was after Dr. Sweet, his family, and friends. But no one batted an eye, he said. "Draw upon your imagination and think how you would feel if you fired at some black man in a black community and then had to be tried by them. . . ." Mob psychology, he explained, is the most dreadful thing with which man has to contend. The mob was waiting to see the sacrifice of some helpless blacks, he continued. "They came with malice in their hearts."

Darrow paced between the judge and the jury, always directing his statements to the jury. "The Sweets spent their first night in their home afraid to go to bed," he intoned, turning for a moment to face the Sweet family seated in the front rows. "The next night they spent in jail. Now the State wants them to spend the rest of their lives in the penitentiary. The State claims there was no mob there that night. Gentlemen, the State has put on enough witnesses who said they were there, to make a mob."[15]

Darrow's closing argument was among the best the famous lawyer had ever uttered, said Kevin Boyle, author of *Arc of Justice*. "I ask you gentlemen in behalf of my clients," Darrow implored the jurors. "I ask you more than anything else, I ask you in behalf of justice, often maligned and downtrodden, hard to protect and hard to maintain, I ask you in behalf of yourselves, in behalf of our race, to see that no harm comes to them. I ask you gentlemen in the name of the future, the future which will one day solve these sore problems, and the future which is theirs as well as ours, I ask you in the name of the future to do justice in this case."[16] But four weeks of give and take, and Darrow's powerful phrases, earned them only a mistrial. Nothing had been solved, and rather than a brighter future, Darrow was reacquainted with the same old nasty, dismal past.

Leaders of the NAACP viewed the result as a "partial victory," which to a certain degree was right for them, for the exposure the organization received surely added to its growth. During the year, 380 new affiliates were organized with more than 200 weekly newsletters. Meanwhile, the city's 80,000 African Americans wondered, would the outcome be any brighter for the Sweets in the second trial?[17]

The second trial, which began in April, was much like the first, except for John Dancy's testimony. He deftly explained that a black family moving into a white neighborhood doesn't bring down the property values but rather enhances them, because blacks usually were charged double the price paid by whites. Once again the prosecution and the defense—and Darrow was now joined by a new attorney, Thomas Chawke, whose reputation as a mouthpiece for the underworld was legend—had to renew the legal tactics of before. The prosecution pushed its conspiracy charge and the defense insisted that a man's home was his castle and he had every right to defend it.

"Henry Sweet, Negro, was acquitted of a charge of murder by a jury," an editorial in the *Boston Herald* declared on May 13, adding that the "trial was an echo of Detroit's race disturbance."[18] Prosecutor Robert Toms had focused the entire case on the conviction of Henry Sweet; he kept his promise and dropped the charges against the others. Judge Frank Murphy, who used the trial as a springboard to a career as the city's mayor, the state's governor, US attorney general, and a Supreme Court justice, warned the spectators not to allow their emotions to interfere with acceptance of the verdict. "Accept it courageously and with good will," he said.[19]

The celebration for the defendants, particularly for Dr. Sweet and his wife, was short-lived, because within a few months they lost their daughter, Iva, to tuberculosis, which she probably contracted from her mother, who was exposed to it during her time in jail. Two years later, in 1928, the illness felled Gladys, leaving the good doctor without comfort or rudder. By 1960 the mob violence, the trials, and the trauma it brought to his family, was an accumulation of heartbreak that overwhelmed him one evening when Dr. Sweet could take no more.

The Ford Motor Company's replacement of the Model T with the Model A was a shift to recover from the financial crisis of 1927. To switch, the company had to shut down the Rouge plant and pink-slip thousands of workers, including more than 1,500 black employees. Other automotive plants were experiencing similar signs of the incipient economic depression, an ominous harbinger of collapse. At the General Motors' Pontiac plant in 1929, there were 29,000 employed in the spring. By the fall the number had dwindled to 14,000.[20] The bad news hit the black community first. There were other telltale signs that the Great Depression was on its way, though it had long ago taken up permanent residence in Black Bottom and the other devastated zones of the nation. "Hey, the depression came we didn't know the difference" was a common sentiment among many black Detroiters.

The Sweet trials were not only a referendum on race, but also a political platform, with the outcome of the city's mayoral race contingent on the results. During the Sweet trials, Judge Murphy was fully aware of the political implications of his presence on the bench. He knew what was at stake and how beholden he was to the city's black electorate, which had helped him secure his position at Recorder's Court. Of greater concern was his handling of the trials, knowing how pivotal that would be in the mayoral quest that most Detroiters assumed he was on. In 1923, black Detroiters, some of them defying their loyalty to Henry Ford, sided with Murphy in an election "that pitted the traditional Protestant industrial elite—Ford interests—against the larger population of Catholic immigrants and blacks. Murphy, a lawyer and activist in the Democratic Party, had big ambitions, especially for an Irish Catholic politician in a city controlled by

Anglo-Saxons," observed author Beth Bates.[21] In effect, the black vote—but one wonders how many of the fourteen thousand newly arrived migrants from the South were eligible to vote— was Murphy's for the asking. With a Klan candidate lurking on the horizon, the upcoming election was becoming increasingly significant for black Detroiters.

Few of them were caught in such a political quandary as the Rev. Robert Bradby of Second Baptist Church. "While Bradby used his church effectively as a hiring hall for jobs at the FMC, his close affiliation and support for Frank Murphy's reform agenda revealed that Bradby's expectations for black Detroiters included much more than inclusion in the mainstream industrial job market. Indeed, Bradby's close working relationships with both Henry Ford and Frank Murphy exposed his deep ambivalence toward Ford."[22] In 1930, with the election months away, Bradby had time to weigh the consequences of taking a political position.

Charles Denby wasn't plagued with this dilemma. As a recent migrant from Dixie in the late 1920s, he had no vow of loyalty to Ford or anyone else. In the city since 1924, he found work in the factories, mainly at Graham Paige, where it was his job in the foundry to shake out the oil pan under the motor. "I never wanted to work for Ford, and I never did work there," Denby wrote in his autobiography. "Everyone talked about it; they said it was the house of murder." Perhaps not exactly murder, to defuse Denby's exaggeration, but working at Ford was the source of jokes depicting the exhausted, overworked worker. "Every worker could identify Ford workers on the streetcars going home at night," Denby continued. "Every worker who was asleep was working for Ford. You'd see twenty asleep on the cars and everyone would say, 'Ford workers.' Many times the conductors looked over the car and shook a man to tell him it was his stop. On Sunday, Ford workers would sleep on the way to church."[23]

Notwithstanding Denby's aversion to Ford and its found-ries, the impending Depression caused him to change his mind about the company. When he heard that they were hiring, he was among the five hundred in line for fifty to one hundred jobs. When a representative informed them that they had hired the men that they needed, Denby thought it was just a ploy to get people to leave in order to hire those who stayed. Along with hundreds of others, he stayed. The pushing and shoving forced the company to call the fire department, which doused the men with water. Because it was the dead of winter, soon their clothes were frozen as hard as bricks. Denby said, "That's the first and last time I went to Ford to look for work."[24]

Nor was Beulah Alexander Young conflicted about allegiance to Henry Ford. In the early years, there were no black women working at Ford. In fact, it was not until 1946 that gender was added to the UAW-Ford nondiscrimination clause. Young, like many others who were involved in the women's club movement, had a clear choice in the upcoming elections, giving her support to Murphy. From her bully pulpit at the *Detroit People's News*, the paper she owned, Young could state her case like few others. She must have done a good job, because her husband, Dr. James Percy Young, was later appointed city physician by the victorious Mayor Murphy.[25]

At that time, one of the main purposes of the clubwomen was to counter stereotyped negative news about the black commu-nity. Young was a tireless advocate for a more positive reportage. Among her colleagues in this endeavor were Mamie Bledsoe and the indefatigable Nellie Watts. Even the black publications were taken to task for their penchant to report only on the sensational stories, many of them justifying the practice on the grounds that it sold papers. As the Depression loomed, the women began to focus less on negative media coverage and more on the diminish-ing prospects of employment, particularly for black Detroiters.

The clubwomen, black and white, were concerned about the decline in employment, the lagging new car sales, and the decrease in construction. Major building projects—such as Albert Kahn's Art Deco Fisher Building and two connections to Canada via the Ambassador Bridge, a project in which a black engineer, Cornelius Henderson, helped to develop structural steel—were a boon to the city's growth and employment. During Herbert Hoover's administration, the clubwomen reported that Detroit was the city hardest hit by the Depression.

10

WHITE BALL AND
THE BROWN BOMBER

In the late 1920s, before the Great Depression, when black Detroiters weren't preoccupied with making a living, they found a measure of relief in following the Detroit Stars baseball team and their rivals in the Negro National League. Only a boxing match featuring Joe Louis, the Brown Bomber, could compete with the feats of Turkey Stearnes on the diamond. Having Turkey slugging the ball and running the bases, however remarkably, were not enough to tilt a contest between the Stars and the team from Saint Louis in the spring of 1926. The Stars lost the game,17–16.[1]

Richard Bak, in his book on the Detroit Stars, found an interesting connection between the Sweet trials, the second of which ended in 1926, and the Stars. At the time of the trials, Moses Walker was an officer of the baseball club and at the same time vice president of the Detroit Chapter of the NAACP. Bak suggests that, as an arbiter between these entities, Walker may have solicited funds from the well-paid baseball players to help in defraying the legal expenses of the trials.[2]

Whenever the Stars were in town and appearing at Mack Park or Hamtramck Stadium, it was always a festive occasion, particularly when they were playing against one of the stellar teams in the Negro National League. For baseball fans, this was a great opportunity to get away from their mundane, depressing routines. The excitement at the game always intensified when Norman "Turkey" Stearnes flew around the bases, his arms flapping. Equally entertaining were his teammates: Clarence "Spoony" Palm, Christopher Columbus "Crush" Holloway, and Leon "Pepper" Daniels. Even when they weren't scoring many runs and winning ball games, the fans could count on the amusing antics of the team's manager, Elwood "Bingo" DeMoss.[3]

By the summer of 1926, Stearnes had been with the Stars for three years. If there were a collector's baseball card for the lefthander, it would highlight his lifetime batting average of .352 in the black leagues and .313 against barnstorming white major leaguers. He led the league seven times in home runs and hit an astonishing .474 in playoff games. Stearnes, a native of Alabama, hit more home runs in the Negro Leagues than the incomparable Josh Gibson and Buck Leonard.[4] His statistics in 1927 were typical of his all-star performances: He played in more games (82), had more at-bats (301), more hits (113), the highest average (.375) and hit more home runs (20) than any of his teammates. He led the team in doubles, triples, and stolen bases.[5] These statistics compared favorably with those amassed by Ty Cobb, the racist Georgia Peach, who in 1926 was both a player and manager of the all-white Detroit Tigers.[6] He vowed never to play against black players. Cobb's salary was $50,000 a year, and Stearnes was lucky if he earned more than $1,000 for a six-month season, playing about half the number of games afforded by white leagues. Then for the other six months of the year, the players had to find other employment. Despite their celebrity status, many of them accepted jobs at the auto plants. Like other black workers, they were relegated to the wet deck or the paint department.

If the Detroit Stars had one fan who was always in attendance at their games no matter how well the team was doing, it was Henderson "Ben" Turpin. He was hired as a police officer on August 1, 1927, and assigned to the Third Precinct on Gratiot Avenue. Many of his off-duty hours were spent keeping up with Stearnes and the Stars. There may have been other black police officers in the city, but few could match Turpin in stature. "From all accounts," wrote Cheryl Wells, "Turpin's off duty time was spent pursuing his love of baseball and supporting the Turpin's Athletic Club and still he found time to volunteer his supervision at the neighborhood theater." Though he earned enough money to live in some of the better neighborhoods, he chose to live in Black Bottom, where his club was located.[7]

His record as an officer of the law was unrivaled. In twenty-five years of service, he received only two demerits. "One of these was for shooting a Purple Gang hit man while off-duty on October 14, 1929 at 11:30pm." After the hit man pulled a gun and aimed it at him, Turpin shot Louie Bryant, a member of the notorious gang, which sold booze during Prohibition. Turpin was charged with first degree murder, but a Recorder's Court jury acquitted him, and he later received a Meritorious Citation for "Exceptional Bravery."[8]

Turpin, Stearnes, and John Roesink, the owner of the Detroit Stars, must have endured unrelieved grief when the news reached them that Mack Park had gone up in flames on July 7,

1929. The fire blazed for hours and was officially ruled an accident. Hundreds of fans, trapped behind a chicken-wire screen, were rescued by members of the Stars. The disaster was a terrible setback for Roesink and the team. They played the remainder of their home games in Dequindre Park. Despite the tragedy, Stearnes appeared unperturbed as he continued to compile impressive box-score numbers.

Among the black Detroiters saddened by the fire was fifteen-year-old Joe Barrow. When he wasn't working out at the gym, he rarely missed a game at the park.

Joe Barrow was his birth name, but he would achieve international acclaim as Joe Louis. Black Detroiters watched Louis's meteoric rise from a stumbling amateur at the Brewster Center gym to become heavyweight champion of the world. Before he was anointed the Brown Bomber because of his ability to knock an opponent out with one punch, he put in hours and hours of hard work and training. After obtaining a job at Briggs auto-body plant, earning $25 a week, he quit school. The work was backbreaking, leaving him with little desire or energy to work out in a gym. "I pushed truck bodies to the sprayer on the assembly line. The tape would come off the body covers and land on the floor sticky side up. The tape would gum into the dolly wheels, and you'd get a real workout pushing those truck bodies. I would leave the factory around five o'clock, go home for dinner. Working that hard kind of made me forget about boxing."[9]

Louis did not forget about the Purple Gang. According to him, the gang, composed of Jewish members, operated on the Detroit River, held close ties to Al Capone in Chicago and mobsters as far away as Louisiana. It was Turpin who intervened when Louis was being recruited to be a member of another gang on the east side. His intervention rescued Louis from the clutches of a crew of hoodlums, all of whom ended up in prison.[10]

Turpin wasn't the only person looking out for Louis. John

Roxborough and Julian Black, despite Louis's unpolished skills, recognized that he was a diamond in the rough and took him under their wing. The Roxborough family came to Detroit in 1899. Now with ties to a number of unsavory businesses, none more lucrative than the numbers racket, John had been a star athlete at Eastern High School, along with his brother, Charles. In order to complete the makeover, Roxborough moved Louis into his home and helped him refine his table manners and eating habits. Roxborough had some of his suits altered to fit his young fighter and made sure he had the best boxing equipment. All he needed now was a good business manager, a task Black assumed, and a top trainer—enter Jack "Chappie" Blackburn, who was a stern trainer, and as Barney Nagler wrote, "he looked the part. A bony face, marked by a scar on the left cheek and set off by beady eyes that peered out of angular slits, he appeared as an instrument of discipline. Usually taciturn, he was informative and kindly where Louis was involved. He knew boxing as a serious business and instilled in his pupil an early devotion to the course."[11] The work overalls worn at Briggs were replaced by Everlast boxing gear, and rather than punching a clock, Joe began tearing into a punching bag. He left his stepfather, Pat Brooks, and his brother, Deleon Barrow, at Ford while he set out on a journey to fame and fortune.

It took Louis about three years to establish himself as a top-ranked amateur. He often told reporters he couldn't remember his first bout, which must have been in the early 1930s. Prior to pulling on the gloves to face an opponent, Louis devoted many hours to learning how to move in the ring, mostly from Holman Williams. He put his prodigy through hours of rigorous training and footwork at the Brewster Center. After a grueling session with Williams, Louis would go to work at one of the jobs he held, even sometimes delivering ice. Invariably, young black boys waited outside the gym wanting to help him carry his boxing gear.

Louis was accustomed to the attention and allowed them to tote his gloves and other gear. One of the skinny kids stood out from the rest; he could walk a block on his hands and was very nimble on his feet. "When he moved to New York, I missed him," Louis said. "He was a real nice kid. His name was Walker Smith. Later they changed his name to 'Sugar Ray Robinson.'"[12]

By 1934, when Louis was launching his professional career in the ring, the Negro Leagues were barely making payroll, and the devastating fire at Mack Park in 1929 hadn't helped matters. During the bleak summer of 1931, with unemployment spiraling off the charts, few Detroiters, black or white, had the money to attend a ball game, whether it was to watch the Tigers at Navin Field or the Stars at Dequindre Park.[13] Instead of lining up to see Stearnes play or even to see Louis fight, people spent their time in the many bread lines throughout the city.

The collapse of the Negro National League in 1931 was a blow to the Detroit Stars. A few of the players became teammates on the Detroit Wolves of the East-West League. "The league was founded by Cumberland Posey . . . he combined the Wolves with his other team, the famed Homestead Grays."[14]

Black baseball fans in Detroit in 1935 had no choice but to enjoy the Detroit Cubs, a barnstorming semipro team. They had no league affiliation and very few players of the caliber the Wolves possessed. After Joe Louis knocked out former heavyweight champion Primo Carnera and then Max Baer in 1935, he gave serious thought to owning a baseball team—he often said that if he hadn't become a successful boxer he would have tried to play ball. That dream never became a reality, though he did sponsor a softball team called the Brown Bombers. This was about as close as boxing would come to baseball, and as Louis ascended to become a champion, the Negro Leagues became a fading memory.

11

THE TURBULENT THIRTIES

My heart is aching
for them Poles and Greeks
on relief way across the sea
because I was on relief
once in 1933.
I know what relief can be—
it took me two years to get on WPA.
If the war hadn't come along
I wouldn't be out of the barrel yet.
Now, I'm almost back in the barrel again.
To tell the truth,
if these white folks want to go ahead
and fight another war,
or even two,
the one to stop them won't be me.
Would you?

—LANGSTON HUGHES, "RELIEF"

Depression. The word captured both the economic and psychological condition in America, and black Detroit was doubly encumbered. It was a time when "white people had less money to spend on themselves, and practically none to spend on Negroes, for the depression brought everybody down a peg or two," wrote Langston Hughes. "And the Negroes had but few pegs to fall."[1]

There was wide confirmation that black Detroiters suffered the most during the Depression, which arrived officially on Black Monday and Black Tuesday, October 28 and 29, 1929. "Of all the sufferers," wrote Paul Kellogg, "perhaps the Negroes, as the newest comers to Detroit, were hardest hit. A social worker in a Negro district told me of their predicament, but it was set down in cold figures at the City Department. Of the 4,029 families given relief that November, 1,118 were colored, or 28 percent. These included 5,137 persons out of the 86,000 colored population in the city. More than one out of twenty, in the old hard phrase, 'were on the town.' . . ."[2] In too many instances, being on relief failed to halt the marshals with orders to evict. Thanks to Joe Billups, one of the first and most notable black leaders of UAW Local 600, many evicted families had their furniture returned to their homes soon after the marshals placed it on the sidewalk. To guard against the marshals or deputy sheriffs returning, Billups left someone behind to alert the office of the local, a tactic that he had perhaps acquired while a member of the Communist Party or the Auto Workers Union. It was a game of cat and mouse, and the Unemployment Councils often came out on top because the landlords had to pay the marshals or deputy sheriffs to return for a repeat performance. In an interview, Billups said, "So few landlords would pay it again because the same thing would happen all over again."[3]

Evictions were a nationwide concern. They surfaced in literature, nowhere more gripping than in Ralph Ellison's *Invisible*

Man, in which activists come to the rescue of the evicted, much as Billups did in Detroit.[4]

The dozen or so Unemployment Councils in the city were not the only extension of the Communist Party. There was a sizable contingent of militants in the League of Struggle for Negro Rights (LSNR). Among the more prominent members was the poet Langston Hughes, later to be president of the organization. In 1930, the league was forged out of the remaining members of the American Negro Labor Congress with the purpose of further galvanizing and radicalizing the black community. Central to this effort were the theoretical ideas put forth by Harry Haywood, who a generation later would settle in Detroit. His manifesto called for full black liberation and was forcefully backed by the Southern delegates to the founding conference in Saint Louis, where no voice was more fervent than that of Mary Dalton, one of the Atlanta Six, a group of communist organizers charged under Georgia's Insurrection Act and facing capital punishment.[5] By 1935, the league had run its course and morphed into the National Negro Congress. This radical progression eventually set the stage for the emergence of a number of black labor leaders, of whom few were as charismatic and bellicose as Coleman Young.

Young, like many of Detroit's luminaries, was born in Alabama and followed that straight line of migration to the city in 1923, close to the time that Judge Murphy was adjusting to his position in Recorder's Court. Young was five years old, the son of a tailor who set up his shop in the heart of Black Bottom. On Saturday's he had a part-time job cleaning Dr. Ossian Sweet's clinic, which at that time was located above Ike Portlock's cleaners. Young recalled in his autobiography that an additional responsibility was to answer the phone when Sweet was off "to lunch with his lovely nurse, Miss Smith." While minding the office, he remembered, "It occurred to me that a dollar was an exceptional amount for a man to pay a kid for an hour or so of secretarial work, but it also occurred to me that Miss Smith was an exceptional lunch companion."[6]

In 1936, Young was eighteen and working as an electrical apprentice in the Ford Motor Company electrical program. Although he excelled in all the tests, a white man with lower scores, whose father was a foreman at the plant, got the only job available. Young was dispatched to the assembly line. Motivated by the unfair results of the electrical program, he was eager to join the year-old UAW. It didn't take long for Young's maverick nature to get him in trouble. Suspected of being a union sympathizer, he was accosted by one of Ford security chief Harry Bennett's goons. Young decked him with a steel rod, ending his days at Ford. Following his dismissal, he had several menial jobs and hustled in the pool halls while maintaining a radical outlook and militant attitude that was quite compatible with that of the Rev. Charles Hill, pastor of Hartford Avenue Baptist Church. "Reverend Hill was an old-time hellfire and brimstone preacher whose moral convictions carried him to the presidency of the Michigan branch of the National Negro Congress (NNC)," Young wrote. "The NNC provided a progressive forum for black working people, and it naturally acquired a political accent, but it was Reverend Hill's simple passion and courage that drove the organization and inspired young ideological upstarts like me."[7] Much of Young's affection for the union movement came from the influence of the Rev. Hill, whose church hosted the founding of Local 600, which eventually became the largest union local in the world. He admired the minister's defiance of Henry Ford as well as Ford's minion, Donald Marshall, whose job it was to see that Ford workers toed the line and voted Republican. Ford once wrote Reverend Hill to inform him that he would fire all the members of his church who worked at Ford if the church continued to be used for union meetings. "Reverend Hill told Ford to go to hell," Young wrote.

Young was one of many Detroiters who joined with the established civic leaders supportive of the Rev. Hill's audacity and fearlessness. John Dancy of the Urban League, soon-to-be-Congressman Charles Diggs, militant labor activist Snow Grisby, and attorney Harold Bledsoe all looked forward to sharing a foxhole with Hill as they began to develop workers' councils and formulate a strategy to involve blacks in the union movement, which for the most part excluded them from membership. Dancy did not readily adopt a pro-union position; thus he stood in opposition to the Urban League's national leaders, most notably Lester Granger and Eugene Kinckle Jones. Under pressure from the national office, he eventually supported the UAW-CIO, though he chose not to dwell on his reluctance to change his anti-union stance in his memoir.[8]

When Detroit's Civic Rights Committee (CRC) was formed in 1933–34, though perhaps not at the very start, the Rev. Hill was among the key organizers. The organization was allied dutifully with Franklin Delano Roosevelt's administration and his New Deal policies. The president was determined to make his vision a reality on the local level. The CRC was one of several important political groups taking shape in a city that was ablaze with union activity, civil protests, and the legal defense of constitutional rights. Members of the Booker T. Washington Trade Association (BTWTA), led by the Rev. William Peck of Bethel AME Church, who came to Detroit in 1930 from Oberlin, Ohio, were among those who aided the defense of Angelo Herndon, the young Communist agitator in Georgia facing charges of insurrection for organizing workers, as well as that of the Scottsboro Boys, the nine youths who in 1931 were falsely accused of raping two white women on an Alabama train.

As Young related, there was very little middle ground in the city at that time. The atmosphere was polluted by proponents of virulent, toxic racism and bigotry. None were more fascistic than Father Charles Coughlin and Gerald L. K. Smith, who were widely known for spewing their Klan-like anti-Semitic hatred on radio and at various forums. To ensure his place in the fight against these right-wing zealots, Young became the secretary of the Detroit chapter of the NNC.[9]

Black women were not absent from the front lines of battle. Led by Fannie Peck, Reverend Peck's wife, the Housewives' League of Detroit often stood shoulder to shoulder with their male counterparts, equally concerned about the discriminatory practices of white businesses and about poor housing, and simultaneously advocating for self-determination, particularly for black small businesspeople. They were a critical support team for the BTWTA, Beth Bates wrote, and "Peck's strategy encouraged alliances between working-class and middle-class clubwomen who no longer valued 'respectability' so highly."[10] She was also deeply committed to Bethel and rarely missed a Sunday school session with her young charges, unless of course duty called at Parkside Hospital or the Women's Missionary Society, where she was a board member. In 1936, she organized the Fannie B. Peck Bethel AME Church Credit Union, which for years remained a stable institution.[11]

When the Rev. Horace White arrived in Detroit in 1936, he was welcomed by the Rev. Peck, both graduates of Oberlin's College of Divinity. Although he arrived in the city six years after Peck, he was soon carving out a leadership position as the pastor of Plymouth Congregational Church. The Rev. White "was as well-spoken as he was outspoken," wrote historian Angela Dillard. It was also the same year that Charles Diggs Sr. was elected the nation's only black state senator. "White, Hill, and [Canon Malcolm] Dade formed the core of a pro-Union Black religious movement, but they were also part of a much larger network of progressive activists," Dillard noted. "The same year that White arrived in Detroit, Louis Martin, a recent graduate of the University of Michigan, became the editor of the *Michigan Chronicle*, a subsidiary of the *Chicago Defender*." Martin, a skillful writer and an astute politician with national connections, gradually turned the paper around, and it became a vocal opponent to the Republican, anti-union *Detroit Tribune*.[12]

Louis Martin was a formidable operative for Ford, particularly as the company sought to keep its black employees in check; he was firmly against the campaign to establish the UAW in its plants. The headlines in the late 1930s in Detroit reported the conflict brewing in the automobile industry; the Ford Motor Company, with its sizable number of black employees, was at the center of the struggle. For the most part, the faith and trust that black workers expressed toward their employer is understandable—paychecks from the automobile companies put food on their tables, kept a roof over their heads, and were the path to greater prosperity. Black workers were reluctant to participate in the strikes against the companies and felt uncertain about the promises made by the emergent union. After all, there was a four-century history of white betrayal to counsel hesitancy and prudent neutrality. A few blacks even went so far as to stand shoulder to shoulder with Ford's security forces as they brutally attacked union members, and some joined the legions of strikebreakers who dared to cross the picket lines surrounding the plants.

The complexity of the fight for collective bargaining in the automobile industry is thoughtfully analyzed by labor historians August Meier and Elliott Rudwick, who wrote that progress came gradually on the job front given the "tangled web of interaction among Negro advancement groups [the National Urban League and the NAACP], black workers, officers in union locals, International UAW leaders, corporate managements and the various concerned federal agencies."[13] Out of this matrix of turmoil was forged an unbreakable alliance between the black workers at Ford and those at Chrysler, General Motors, and the other plants where the UAW-CIO had been chosen to represent them. On both sides of the shifting encounter emerged a cadre of men and women, black and white, who would play decisive roles in the city's overall development—Shelton Tappes, Horace Sheffield Sr., John Conyers Sr., Emil Mazey, Geraldine Bledsoe, R. J. Thomas, Reverend Robert Bradby, John Dancy, Reverend Everard Daniel, and Gloster Current—were among a number of unsung heroes and heroines that also included Walter Hardin, Christopher Alston, Joe Billups, Leon Bates, Oscar Noble, Veal Clough, and the Reverend William Bowman.

With the advent of World War II and the urban riots in the early forties, this alliance between black workers and the unions would again be tested. During the extremely troubling moments the existing camaraderie was stretched to the point of breaking; however, the end result brought greater understanding among the participants and broadened opportunities in the industrial complexes for black workers.

Whether from the pulpit, the foundry, or the political arena, Detroit's black community has always been active and highly volatile. There has been a dependable minority who refused, under any circumstances, to abide insult or neglect. This unyielding impulse was certainly the case during the Depression, no matter how dispiriting it was for most residents. Action from the black community's cultural and black nationalist realm seemed irrepressible, and out of Black Bottom in the thirties would come a musical pulse that renewed what had always been there and a religious development that was relatively new—Islam.

There was only a trace of Islam in Detroit before Elijah Poole (Elijah Muhammad) arrived. He was the avatar of an unorthodox form of Islam passed on to him by W. D. Fard. "I was born in Georgia, went to public school in Georgia and was never out of the state of Georgia until I was 25 years of age," Muhammad declared in his book *Message to the Blackman in America*. "I married and had two children and moved to Detroit in April, 1923, from Macon, Georgia where I worked for the Southern Railroad Company and the Cherokee Brick Company, the latter as a tram road foreman and builder. I never was arrested and served no jail terms on any charge or charges until 1934."[14] He told a reporter that he moved to Detroit "because I thought the life might be better, but even there the first year I saw my people shot down right in the street without any justice whatsoever."[15]

Muhammad was the son of sharecroppers, and both his father and grandfather were circuit preachers who, during his childhood, inculcated in him a strong sense of religious belief. Also during his childhood, much like Dr. Ossian Sweet, he witnessed the lynching of a black man for no other reason than he had supposedly insulted a white woman. That impression lived with him for years, and it made him ripe for the messianic appeal of W. D. Fard. During their first encounters, Poole quizzed Fard about his name and who he was. "I asked him, 'Who are you, and what is your real name?' He said, 'I am the one that the world has been expecting for the past 2,000 years.' I said to him again, 'What is your name?' He said, 'My name is Mahdi; I am God, I came to guide you into the right path that you may be successful and see the hereafter.'"[16] Depending on the source, Fard was the reincarnation of Noble Drew Ali, the founder of the Moorish Science Temple, who died in 1930 or, as Poole later as Elijah Muhammad put it, "had come to us [reincarnated in Fard] from the Holy City of Mecca, Arabia in 1930." It has been estimated that between 1930 and 1934 he recruited eight thousand followers among black Detroiters. "The rapid growth of the first Temple [located in Black Bottom] was accompanied by the establishment of various subsidiary organizations, among which was the University of Islam for the training of 'Moslem' youth and families in the 'knowledge of their own' as distinct from that of the 'civilization of the Caucasian Devils.'"[17]

The FBI records about Fard revealed that he spent time in prison and committed some less than prophetic actions. When he began assembling his following, he formulated a number of theories and concepts, several of which were brought to fruition by Burnsteen Sharrieff Muhammad (or Mohammed), the wife of John Muhammad, one of Elijah's brothers. According to attorney Gregory Reed of the Keeper of the Word Foundation in Detroit, a cache of rare documents was found in the attic of the home where Burnsteen Muhammad lived. As the result of her courses at Commerce High School, she possessed the clerical skills that enabled her to translate Fard's dictations into curricula, proposals, and various programs. Reed discovered among more than one thousand documents a copy of "The Secret Ritual of the Nation of Islam," which converts never actually saw but memorized in order to certify their membership and grades from the University of Islam, founded by Fard. A sample exam problem gives an idea of intellectual fare at the university:

The uncle of Mr. W. D. Fard lives in the wilderness of North America, and he is living other than himself; therefore, he weighs more than his height and his blood pressure registers more than thirty-one. This killed him at the age of forty-four years. The average person breathes three cubic feet of air per hour, but the uncle of Mr. W. D. Fard breathes three and seven-tenths of cubic feet of air per hour. How many cubic feet of air did Mr. W. D. Fard's uncle breathe in forty-four years? How many atoms does he breathe in all of his forty-four years when one one-hundredth of a cubic inch contains two hundred million atoms?[18]

With the same air of mystery that brought him into contact with Elijah and his followers, Fard disappeared. According to Malcolm X, he was seen in Harlem in the sixties. Muhammad, no longer buttressed by the Mahdi and besieged by the Detroit police department, vanished like his mentor, gathered his flock, and relocated to Chicago.

Even so, Temple No. 1 remained in Detroit and would later prosper under the leadership of Malcolm's brother, Wilfred. Muhammad was gone, but a large number of his flock continued his teachings, and they were among the activists who inspired a new generation of political organizers that emerged in Detroit. Minister Muhammad and the Nation of Islam solidified the foundation of black nationalism, providing a wellspring of social and political thought that would be manifested in several organizations throughout the country. These political formations were not confined to the tenets of Islam but also found formidable expression in the Christian theology promoted by the Rev. Albert Cleage. By the late sixties, some of Muhammad's "do for self" philosophy was evident in Cleage's vision: "Through the concept of self-determination," Cleage said in a speech in 1968, "black militants have been able to give unity to a people fragmented by oppression and have begun the laborious process of transforming the black ghetto into a black community."[19]

Elijah Muhammad, influenced by Marcus Garvey and possibly the Moorish Science Temple movement of Noble Drew Ali, extended their notions of black nationalism. Cleage and a coterie of others would apply a more militant tone to nationalist demands as the fight for self-determination flowered in the sixties.

12

BOOM TOWN

In the summer of 1941, months before the bombing of Pearl Harbor, an influx of newcomers overburdened the city's housing stock. These arrivals were Detroit's second major wave of migrants. The Detroit Housing Commission, expecting federal grants, approved two sites for the development of housing projects for defense workers. Its members envisioned units similar to the Brewster Projects, which had been constructed in Black Bottom several years before.[1] As Beth Smith Jenkins observed in her master's thesis, a site on the northwest corner of the intersection of Dequindre and Modern streets was set aside for African Americans. The original site designated for whites was located several blocks away, on the northwest corner of Mound Road and Outer Drive.

The problem began when the federal government stepped in and overruled the proposal for the African American site. Only one site, at Nevada and Fenelon streets in a white neighborhood, was approved and designated for white occupancy. Given the urgency of the housing situation, the City Commission, with the Rev. Horace White as the sole black member, did not oppose the federal government's decision.[2]

A bitter tug-of-war ensued. The pressure from blacks and white liberals forced Washington to reverse its decision, and the plan for projects for black occupants was restored. On September 29, 1941, the public housing project was named Sojourner Truth, in tribute to the abolitionist and women's rights advocate whose gravesite is in Battle Creek, Michigan. "On the night of February 27, 1942, a fiery cross was burned in a field close to Sojourner Truth Homes," Jenkins wrote. "That same night one hundred and fifty white pickets patrolled the project with the avowed purpose of preventing occupancy by Negro tenants assigned to the first twenty-eight units. By dawn the crowd of picketers had grown to twelve hundred, many of whom were armed."[3] What would be called the Sojourner Truth riot erupted the next morning when two cars driven by blacks crashed through a line of white picketers. The bold action sparked a bombardment of bricks from whites. Blacks retaliated from the opposite side of Ryan Road. Only after the police placed the blacks under protective custody was the riot halted. Even so, the skirmish broke out again in smaller encounters and a great number of blacks and whites suffered injuries. To keep the peace, Mayor Edward Jeffries dispatched a large contingent of police officers to the scene. More than a hundred people were arrested for disturbing the peace and carrying concealed weapons. It was also decided to delay any further attempts to move blacks into the units, in the hope that time would mollify the protesters on both sides. Meanwhile, the occupants who had been promised the units were given temporary quarters in the Brewster Public Housing Projects. Workers from UAW Local 600, led by Horace Sheffield and Shelton Tappes, manned the picket lines and raised funds at weekly mass meetings to continue the protest.[4]

It's no surprise that coverage by the white, mainstream dailies—the *Detroit News*, the *Detroit Free Press*, and the *Detroit Times*—was flush with "unconscious racism," an assessment offered by Matthew W. Kapell. A counternarrative emerged from the pages of the *Michigan Chronicle*, the city's black weekly. It implied that the endemic racism of the period, from the KKK and other fascist influences, caused the outbreak. Kapell is careful to note the differences among the three white dailies. The *News* and *Times* tended to "emphasize collusion with America's World War II fascist enemies and a need to return to order quickly for the war effort. The *Detroit Free Press* offered less organized reporting by both noting detail on violence against Detroit's African-Americans and suggesting that those same African-Americans were somehow responsible for the terror perpetrated against them."[5] The Rev. Charles Hill, noted for his activism in the community, defined the situation as "a crisis of all America. Our enemies are the same. . . ."[6]

Not until April 17, after a long, drawn-out investigation, did the National Housing Agency render a decision and establish a program for black occupancy. Eleven days later, Mayor Jeffries deployed more than 1,000 police officers and 1,600 National Guard troops to protect the families who moved in.

One lesson learned from the Sojourner Truth debacle was the need for the city and federal governments to stand firm with unwavering decisions. Vacillation was disconcerting for both blacks and whites, only intensifying the anxiety of newcomers, whose primary concerns were getting jobs and decent housing. Early in 1941, Navy Secretary Frank Knox, to short-circuit racial tension in the defense industry, issued an ultimatum to the naval ordnance stations condemning the refusal of white employees to work with African Americans. Any such refusal, he decreed, would be viewed as disloyalty to the government; by his order, those involved "are not only subject to immediate dismissal but may be prevented from obtaining employment in other establishments engaged in war production."[7] But an official sanction from on high sometimes loses its clout by the time it reaches the plant floor, having very little impact on the animosity among workers.

At the Ford, Packard, Dodge, Murray Body, and many other firms, in too many instances the company and the union were on the same page with regard to the treatment of black workers. Management and the unions, faced with the problems of converting production from cars to tanks, as well as the attendant issues of seniority and transfer of workers, sought to avoid dealing with bigotry, tossing that responsibility to the government, which had no day-to-day oversight. Twice in August 1941, a group of Negroes in the Dodge foundry stopped work for a short while to protest management's arranging for the transfer of only white foundry workers, no Negroes, to production jobs at the Chrysler tank arsenal.[8] Movement from the hot, dangerous foundry to the production line was a big step up, and of course, whenever black workers were upgraded, the whites were outraged. In September 1941, when the Packard Motor Company transferred 2 black polishers to defense work, approximately 250 white workers staged a forty-minute sit-down strike, which halted the unit's operations. A few months later, in January 1942, white workers repeated the action at the Hudson Motor Company.

The crux of this issue originated with the founding of the UAW-CIO and job security. Most black workers were content just to have a job, and they knew that upgrading and admittance into apprentice programs were out of the question. Black workers were restricted to unskilled labor and foundry work, and neither they nor the union seemed to care. "Not only did colored union members generally accept this situation," wrote Robert Weaver, who would become secretary of housing and urban development, "but in certain instances they encouraged its development. At one of the large automobile factories in Flint, Negroes were employed as laborers, machine cleaners, and truck drivers and the local union classified all Negro employees as janitors."[9]

Classification as janitors gave black workers seniority, and no matter what other actual work they did, their status as janitors was secure. These circumstances were altered considerably with the shift to defense work. A new transfer agreement among management, the government, and labor limited the number of janitorial jobs in war production. Black workers had to struggle, either for upgrading or for a new interpretation of the union contract. By the summer of 1941, President Roosevelt, under the threat of a mass march on Washington, had already begun to take action on discrimination in the workplace. He issued Executive Order 8802, creating the President's Committee on Fair Employment Practice, a name soon slightly rearranged for a better acronym as the Fair Employment Practice Committee, or FEPC.

The new committee stepped in to forcefully push the policy of nondiscrimination. This action was greatly strengthened and enhanced by contracting agencies, especially the War and Navy departments. Gradually, from plant to plant, Detroit began to modify its color-caste occupational patterns. "The UAW-CIO had become convinced that it had to face honestly and aggressively the problem of opening new and better jobs for its Negro members, [and] . . . the most difficult problem in this area was to be that of achieving employment opportunities for Negro women."[10] Later in 1942, President Roosevelt, under continuing pressure from A. Philip Randolph and his union cohorts, issued an executive order, a stronger directive. As a result, more than seventy-five thousand Black Detroiters were employed in the war plants.[11]

As the war intensified, more troops were needed, which meant fewer male workers in the plants. This was the opening women needed to enter the workforce via temporary employment in the rapidly growing war machine. Soon Rosie the Riveter, various colors and ethnicities, became indispensable to the war effort. Becoming a black Rosie certainly was Louise Thomas's aim when she enrolled in a defense training course at Commerce High School. In 1942, after passing the course with relative ease, Thomas, one of the twenty-eight thousand able-bodied black women in Detroit available for work, hurried to Ford's Willow Run bomber plant, which was in need of female riveters. Frustrated after two failed attempts to gain employment, she returned to the school to confer with her instructor and overheard him telling another black woman that Detroit factories would never hire them. She voiced her complaint in a letter, the gist of which was: "If I were a white woman, instead of a Negro, my school credentials and my O.K. slip for work at the Ford Willow Run plant would mean something and I would now be working on a defense job . . . riveting war weapons to help our nation win the war. It is time for those in authority to get behind these issues and help get a square deal for Negro women in [the] defense industry. We, too, are Americans."[12]

Black women like Thomas registered their complaints with a number of institutions, including the NAACP (whose Detroit branch since the early thirties had been among the nation's largest), the UAW, and the federal government, demanding that they enforce the FEPC policy of nondiscrimination. The response was inadequate, so it wasn't unusual to find women rallying outside the plant gates or passing out leaflets assailing Ford minions like Willis Ward, accusing him of being an Uncle Tom and a sellout.

"Mr. Ford," one flyer argued, "Negro women and men will and must play their rightful part in helping win this war."[13] These actions were successful. The number of black women employed in the war industries made an astronomical leap from very few in 1942 to fourteen thousand by November 1943. Of course, in many instances the jobs they held were classified as nonessential; still, they were earning more money than they would have doing domestic work.

For many black women in the 1940s with little education, especially young women recently arrived from the South, domestic work was the only available employment. Such was the lot of Katherine Brown, who was twenty-two and a new migrant from Alabama. She was on a bus from Louisville, Kentucky, traveling to Alabama, when she met a woman who told her about someone in Detroit who was looking for women for housecleaning jobs. She followed up and was asked for references. From a friend, she got a letter of reference and mailed it to the woman in Detroit, who immediately responded and sent her a ticket to travel from Alabama to Ypsilanti. She later recalled this story while traveling to her great granddaughter's high school graduation ceremony at Eastern Michigan University. "This is the very city where I arrived in 1941," she said. "I rode the bus all the way from Alabama to Ypsilanti and the woman picked me up and drove me to her home in Detroit and that began my connection to the city."

After two years of domestic work, her reliable girlfriend Hazel told her they were hiring at Ex-Cell-O, a small company on Oakman Boulevard that made aircraft engine parts and electronic parts for the defense industry. "When I got there at seven o'clock in the morning, there was already a long line of people but since Hazel knew the foreman I was hired. Plus, I had some experience working at the Briggs factory."[14]

The work at Ex-Cell-O was much easier and the pay was better, she said. "All I had to do was to attach a wire to a bulb and push it on down the line." Katherine was one of one hundred black women employed at Ex-Cell-O, one among a veritable army of black women in the workforce at the plants. Like her, many of them had been cleaning houses in the suburbs of Detroit and elsewhere before the men were called off to military service. "Well, it was good while it lasted," she sighed. "But like all good things, it came to an end when the war was over and I went back to cleaning houses." Even during her employment in the plants, Katherine maintained her relationship with the housewives, working for them on the weekends and during special occasions such as Bar Mitzvahs and Jewish holidays.

Katherine's relative success was an exception, for even during the war, black women were on the bottom rung of the employment ladder. Even when they were lucky enough to be hired, they were often shunned by the white workers—male and female— who often would refuse to work with them. "At Packard," wrote Thomas Sugrue, "whites walked out on a hate strike in 1943 when three black women were placed as drill operators. . . . In January 1943, fifty leading war production plants in Detroit had women workers, but only nineteen hired black women."[15]

In 1940, James Boggs, like Katherine, had migrated to Detroit from Alabama. He was hired at the Chrysler assembly plant on Jefferson Avenue, where he would remain for nearly thirty years. His path to the factory from the farm did not come via trade school but as a result of the war. "Hitler and Tojo put me to work in the plant," he often remarked, referring to the Nazi and Japanese leaders with no intention of allegiance to their fascism or any possible alignment with the remnants of Satokata Takahashi's pro-Japan movement.[16] Takahashi's presence in Detroit began during the Great Depression; his objective was ostensibly to arouse sympathy for Japan by pretending that it was the champion of oppressed nonwhites, which he did through an organization called The Development of Our Own. "If there is a political lesson to be learned from pro-Japan movements among blacks during the Great Depression," wrote Ernie Allen, "it is perhaps that the waters of self-determination continue to run deep within the African American national community even during times of significant class conflict. . . ."[17]

As a member of Local 7 of the UAW, Boggs became active in union politics, accepting a position on the local's organizing committee, more popularly known as the "flying squadron," which provided support and protection for striking workers. Boggs was part of "a generation of black workers who found in the UAW a platform for various forms of working-class black activism. They developed organizing skills, gained exposure to many currents of radical thought, and used the union as a political base from which to mount efforts to address racial discrimination both inside and outside the plant. Boggs thus joined black UAW members who, as they moved in and out of black institutions, constructed significant networks of black political activity."[18]

Coleman Young put his political and union activity on hold, or, more accurately, he shifted much of it to his affairs in the military. "In our neighborhood, only fools went off to war," Young wrote. "And the only fools were me and my brother George."[19] Young's behavior and achievements in the army mirrored his success in civilian life. He rapidly advanced from a buck private to OCS (Officer Candidate School); upon graduation he attained the rank of second lieutenant. Ever restless and with a military file increasingly full of reports about his words and deeds in opposition to the flagrant racism and discrimination he was encountering, he decided to transfer to the US Army Air Corps. Trained as a bombardier/navigator, even as a member of the legendary Tuskegee Airmen, Young refused to go along with the protocol, to be a dedicated serviceman with nothing on his mind but dropping bombs on the enemy. The closest and most threatening enemies for him were the white officers he encountered as he was bounced from one outpost to another in the South, including his native Alabama, where hostile interactions were almost a daily routine. His militant attitude followed him from the barracks to the company headquarters. His defiance spread, and while it earned him enduring respect from his fellow black soldiers, many of them from Detroit, it was a thorn in the side of his commanding officers.

Young was not ordered into combat, but he had plenty of confrontations with white military police and first sergeants. On more than one occasion, he was arrested for protesting against the restrictions that kept him from exercising his rights as an officer to enter facilities set aside for them; the black officers were not allowed to congregate with the white ones, a prohibition that was untenable for the defiant Young. Hardly a week passed that didn't find him in hot water for violating the Uniform Code of Military Justice, being insubordinate to a superior officer, or acting like an inveterate troublemaker. Thanks to fellow Detroiters Gene Savage, Robert Millender, John Simmons, and Hayes Porter, he had companionship as well as the secretarial support he needed when facing court-martials. After his discharge from the service on December 23, 1945, despite his provocative behavior, Young began receiving mail from the army urging him to extend his military obligation by joining the reserves. "But I preferred not to set foot on a military base again, and because I never served in the reserve—or maybe because I never filled out the papers correctly—I wasn't officially discharged in the eyes of the Army until 1950, which I didn't realize until I read it in my FBI file a few years ago."[20]

Young was reluctant to re-enlist; Elijah Muhammad avoided service altogether. On May 8, 1942, for the second time, Muhammad was arrested in Washington, DC, by the FBI for not registering for the draft. "When the call was made for all males between 18 and 44, I refused (not evading) on the grounds that, first, I was a Muslim and would not take part in war and especially not on the side with the infidels. Second, I was 45 years of age and was NOT according to the law required to register."[21] According to noted historian and activist Ernest Allen, Muhammad was arrested again in Chicago in September 1942, in a series of highly publicized raids conducted by federal agents. Muhammad and eighty-four other African Americans were detained; nine women and three men, including Muhammad, were charged with sedition, the remainder with draft evasion.[22] The sedition charge was dropped, but Muhammad was convicted of encouraging draft resistance. His arrest in the nation's capital was a strong indication that he had been on the move and was no longer based in Detroit, though the main Temple was in Chicago. Eventually Muhammad was sentenced to the federal correction institution at Milan, Michigan, thirty miles southwest of Detroit. From July 1943 to August 1946, he served three years and one month of his five-year sentence. Upon entering the prison, he was given a standard psychiatric evaluation, wrote Louis De Caro. He was diagnosed as schizophrenic because he claimed to have had visual and auditory communications with Allah.[23]

While he was in prison, Muhammad's wife, Clara, struggled to keep his flock together, even after the Chicago police closed down Temple No. 2 under the pretext that it was affiliated with the Japanese. That allegation stemmed from Muhammad's association with Takahashi, the Japanese radical fascist. Muhammad's imprisonment turned out to be a blessing in disguise, wrote E. U. Essien-Udom. It helped to establish his claim to leadership. The fact that he had been incarcerated was an integral part of the "Messenger's charisma, enabling him to liken himself to the persecuted prophets of the past. For his followers, his persecution is not only an important qualification for his leadership, but also evidence of his sincerity and the divinity of his mission."[24]

In 1946, when Muhammad was released from prison, Malcolm Little was going in. Not only were they geographically miles apart, Elijah in Michigan and Malcolm in Massachusetts, but they also served time for different reasons. As fate would have it, however, they were on a similar path of engagement, and thanks to his siblings, Malcolm by 1948 would be a member of the Nation of Islam. He was still four years from release from prison and residence in Detroit. During the Depression years, membership at Temple No. 1 in Detroit had reached eight thousand but had begun to decline significantly by 1945.[25] One of the basic tenets for members of the Nation of Islam was the Yakub theory, which posited that white people were created as a race of devils by selective breeding conducted by an evil black scientist named Yakub (the biblical Jacob) about 4,600 BC. Despite their outspoken hatred for white people, the black Muslims cannot be blamed for the Detroit race riot of 1943. In fact, if their behavior then was like it was in 1967, they probably stood on the sidelines, imploring black Detroiters not to participate in the looting because they were breaking the law.

This advice was ignored by thousands of Detroiters—black and white—after a minor incident ignited the volatile animus when the disturbance reached its peak. "The riot began like those in 1919, with direct clashes between groups of Negroes and whites," wrote Harvard Sitkoff. "Over 100,000 Detroiters crowded onto Belle Isle on Sunday, June 20, 1943, to seek relief from hot, humid city streets."[26] Suddenly, after some jostling among visitors, the ninety-degree weather seemed to get even hotter. Charles "Little Willie" Lyon, a young black man, assembled a bunch of friends seeking revenge on the "hunkies," after having been attacked a few days earlier by whites as he tried to enter Eastwood Amusement Park at Eight Mile Road and Gratiot. Willie and friends broke up family picnics, beat up some boys, and started a melee on the bridge connecting the island to the city. Fights broke out all over the island. From the playground to the bus stops, blacks and whites were ripping into each other ferociously. Several white sailors from a nearby armory, who were angry about a previous incident in which blacks had attacked one of them, went to the bridge and fueled the furor. Like a wildfire, the riot and rumor spread beyond the island into the city, coiling dangerously around Black Bottom and Paradise Valley, where from the stage of Sunnie Wilson's Forest Club, a patron named Leo Tipton screamed, "There's a riot at Belle Isle! The whites have killed a colored lady and her baby. Thrown them over a bridge. Everybody come on. There's free transportation outside!"[27]

Inflamed by the story, blacks began to assail any white person they saw, precipitating a brutal response from white policemen. With their revolvers drawn, they used their nightsticks to beat blacks indiscriminately. In retaliation, blacks broke store windows along Hastings Street and vandalized white-owned businesses in other parts of the city. Katherine Brown and her girlfriend, just home from their jobs at Ex-Cell-O, changed clothes and rushed to the streets to join a crowd of black residents on their way to Russell Street. Someone had thrown a brick through Isaac's Market window; there, unlike on Hastings Street, the looting was intense, with folks grabbing anything they could carry. Katherine had a Virginia ham and a can of Swift's chitterlings when she returned to her apartment on Cardoni Street. "One of the reasons I didn't stay out there very long is that the police and the National Guard were patrolling the street and I saw a man get shot in half," she recalled. "He was running from the pawn shop on Holbrook with an armful of clothes when they shot him down. That was enough for me."[28]

Practically every store on Russell Street on the North End was vandalized except Barthwell's Drug Store on the corner of Russell and Alger. "My father had eleven drug stores and three ice cream parlors with thirteen flavors, all of them delicious," Magistrate Judge Sidney Barthwell Jr. said. "My grandfather, Jack, came to Detroit from Cordele, Georgia in 1919 and worked at Ford's River Rouge plant for 33 years. People obviously knew my father and respected him and his business. That's why they didn't break the windows like the others. That store on Russell Street was his first store, opened in 1933, even before the one in Black Bottom."[29] William Hines arrived in Detroit from Albany, Georgia, the same year as Jack Barthwell, and they became very close friends. Hines remembers buying ice cream from his soda fountain. "Then I went back to him as one of the first black liquor salesmen in the state of Michigan. Mr. Barthwell had five liquor licenses, so they hired me to crash the market. He did accept me, but he let me know that I had to make my own way. It wasn't easy because my competition was Jewish and they were heavy in the wine business."[30]

Some of the black businesses were rapidly expanding, and within a few years they would top the nation in their independence—in competition with the Jewish merchants, who actually were not that disturbed by the rioting that destroyed many of their stores. They felt they could do more business with the competition gone, but that wasn't necessarily the case, for with the others gone, the predators could now focus on the Jews. Nowhere were the Jewish merchants more devastated by the riot than on Hastings Street. This street was densely populated by blacks and was, in the opinion of the Urban League's John Dancy, a veritable cesspool of filth and squalor, but it also "contained a number of small businesses operated by whites, mainly Jewish merchants. The mob began to stone and destroy these shops; the destruction spread until practically all the white-owned businesses in the Negro section had been attacked."[31] By daybreak, Hastings was littered with debris and broken glass, and unwanted merchandise was strewn along the entire street from one end to the other.

According to a report by Thurgood Marshall, the two days of mayhem produced thirty-four corpses, twenty-five of them African American, seventeen killed by the police. These deaths, the police claimed, were justifiable homicides because the victims were looting the stores on Hastings Street.[32] In addition, nearly two thousand people were arrested, the majority of them black, and an unknown number were severely wounded, most of them black. Not one white person was convicted of any crime committed during the riot.[33]

The expected reports, none of them favorable for black Detroiters, came a week later. Mayor Jeffries established an interracial committee to assess what had happened, but it did not consider issues of racism, housing, or employment, nor did it call for a grand jury investigation. It determined that whites were culpable only for retaliating against black attacks and that the police had been exemplary in carrying out their duties. Mayor Jeffries's staff also produced an appropriately named white paper, which reached the same conclusions, commending the police and taking the black leaders to task if they continued to criticize police behavior. Both reports were accepted and approved by the Common Council.[34]

"I have always said that the 1943 riot could have been avoided," wrote John Dancy. "The problems that led to it were apparent long before the riot occurred. A year earlier, the National Urban League had conducted a study of specific areas of racial friction in Detroit and presented its findings to an interracial study committee established by the mayor."[35] The riot also reverberated beyond the destruction in Detroit. The riot renewed A. Philip Randolph's March on Washington Movement, which two years previously had threatened to bring the nation to a halt. "Riots are the result of the government policy of segregation of and discrimination against Negroes," Randolph said as his group gathered for a meeting in Chicago. Not only was his movement refueled, but the tremors from the riot in Detroit also had an impact on elections throughout the nation.[36]

The wave of destruction in Detroit couldn't compare with the obliteration of Hiroshima and Nagasaki that brought World War II to a cataclysmic close in August 1945. Americans were still recovering from the death of President Franklin Delano Roosevelt, and the sorrow lingered longer among black Detroiters, for he had been sympathetic to their plight. Also, there was their deep admiration of Eleanor Roosevelt. Residents of Black Bottom forever cherished her visit to their neighborhood on September 7, 1935, when she attended the groundbreaking ceremony for the Brewster Projects.[37] To see her seated in the back of a plane with a Tuskegee Airman at the controls was an unforgettable image for many black Americans.

But it was her husband's pen that signed those executive orders that made the lives of blacks a bit more tolerable, although on at least one occasion he had been forced to acquiesce to the "fierce urgency of now" expressed by A. Philip Randolph and his unwelcomed march on Washington.

With the war abroad over and at least a scintilla of domestic tranquility in the city, black citizens in the Bottom and Paradise Valley were no longer willing to tolerate Southern hostility up south, as they termed their disturbingly familiar new locale. This new non-subservience was increasingly evident from those who had served in the US military and were now returning to earn their piece of the American pie in the factories of Detroit, which were slowly making the conversion from war production back to manufacturing Oldsmobiles, Chevrolets, Fords, Buicks, Dodges, and Cadillacs. This change also meant that Katherine Brown and many other black women were no longer needed; if they were among the fortunate few, they could return to domestic service.

By the late 1940s, "more and more blacks were eager to join the union movement," Coleman Young noted. "The labor challenge was no longer organizing the emboldened black workers but enlisting the whites who had fought them on Woodward Avenue and the Belle Isle Bridge."[38] The often irreverent and obstreperous Young led this unionizing struggle as politics and civil rights began to coalesce. He became the first African American to serve on the executive board of the Wayne County CIO (Congress of Industrial Organizations) Council in 1947.

The convergence of organized labor and the burgeoning civil rights movement created opportunities for Young and a number of other aspiring leaders. One such aspirant was Cora Mae Brown, a native of Alabama, who was eight years old when she arrived in Detroit in 1922. Her journey toward political and social prominence was managed well by her family. They made sure she had the best early educational training, followed by enrollment and graduation from the prestigious Cass Technical High School, before sending her off to Fisk University in Nashville. At Fisk, one of her professors was the renowned sociologist E. Franklin Frazier, author of *Black Bourgeoisie*. When she returned to the city, she acquired a job as a social worker in the Women's Division of the Detroit Police Department. With the experience she gained there, she was perfectly poised to assist young black women during the Great Depression and into the war years. Always eager to improve herself, Brown entered Wayne State University Law School and earned her doctorate of jurisprudence in 1948. She was entering the legal arena at a most propitious time, just as the US Supreme Court was sounding the death knell of racially restrictive covenants. The cases in this decision—*Shelley v. Kraemer, Uricolo v. Hodge,* and

McGhee v. Sipes—would have special significance for the budding young lawyer, especially the last, because the McGhees lived in Detroit, on Seebaldt Street on the city's west side.

After receiving her law degree, Brown's next goal was to enter the electoral arena. Although she failed in her first two attempts at winning a seat in the Michigan State Senate, she succeeded in 1952, becoming the first African American female state senator in Michigan—and in the nation. At the top of her legislative agenda were fair housing and equal employment. With finesse and determination, she made great progress toward these objectives and other civil rights objectives. In 1956 she ran for Congress but was defeated. However, there was a payoff for someone of her immense talent—she was appointed special associate general counsel of the US Post Office in 1957, a position she held until her death at the age of fifty-eight in 1972. She is buried in the historic Elmwood Cemetery.

When Cora Brown finally arrived in the state senate, Charles Diggs Jr. had been there a year. For several years, they served simultaneously. Diggs was born in Detroit in 1922, the same year Brown came to the city with her family. Both attended Fisk University, but Diggs had also been a student at the University of Michigan for two years, 1940–42, before heading to Nashville. In 1943, he was drafted into the US Army Air Corps and stationed at Tuskegee Army Airfield. After he was discharged from service, Diggs returned home and began working at the family funeral home on Saint Aubin Street, which was located directly across the street from Young's tailor shop. "We lived upstairs, and the funeral parlor was downstairs," Diggs said of the family's new location at 1939 Saint Aubin. "We were renting the place."[39] The family also ran an insurance company employing about a hundred agents, and along with selling burial insurance policies, the only ones in the state, they were selling the Democratic Party, which was just beginning to make some headway among blacks who traditionally voted Republican. Diggs Sr. parlayed his lucrative business into politics and was elected to the Michigan Senate. The younger Diggs followed in his father's footsteps successfully in both business and politics, but his most fruitful endeavor began in 1954, when he was elected to Congress and acquired the political influence needed to usher important bills through the legislative process. In 1955 he shed light on such national issues as the Emmett Till case. Along with several black reporters, he was among the daily observers who attended the trial of the men charged with Till's murder in Mississippi. They were seated in the courtroom's section for black spectators.

Gradually black Detroiters began to move beyond Black Bottom and Paradise Valley. Many of them had accumulated enough savings to move to the city's west side, mainly to the neighborhood bounded by Tireman, Grand River, Buchanan, Bright, and Central streets. But the shadow of segregation still lingered and curtailed their entry to the YMCA located at West Grand Boulevard and Grand River.[40] It has been documented that whenever black aspirations are denied and when social and political prohibitions block them from enjoying their full civil and human rights, in the words of Booker T. Washington, Marcus Garvey, and Elijah Muhammad, they begin to "do for self." Barred from white social clubs, black Detroiters in 1949 created the Cotillion Club, a place for young professionals to associate, mingle, and refine their skills. It was also a place where future leaders—such as Charles Diggs, Judge Damon Keith, representative and attorney George Crockett, and the city's first black councilman, Bill Patrick, could strategize while they were entertained by music played by the city's finest orchestras.

13

BREAKTHROUGHS

Mr. George Jackson once lived in the Bottom but now had a home on the west side and was the owner of a brand-new Cadillac. He worked at the Ford Motor Company, but owning a Cadillac, with its flashy fins, a powerful V-8 engine, and trade-in value of $700, was a manifestation of status.[1] His was a noticeable breakthrough—an ordinary worker who showcased his upward mobility by parking a Cadillac in front of his home. Such a luxury, however, wasn't obtainable in the early 1950s for the Binion family, who moved to Detroit's Eight Mile Road district fresh from the Mississippi Delta. Even so, theirs was a significant breakthrough: they had broken away from the Jim Crow shackles that tied them to sharecropping and hopelessness.

"My family moved to Detroit from Mississippi with hundreds

and thousands of other families making their way to northern cities from the South," recalled artist McArthur Binion. "My father and my uncle (they'd married two sisters) came to Detroit, got work in the Cadillac plant then sent for their families. There were eighteen of us in a two-bedroom house at Eight Mile and Monte Vista." John Binion, McArthur's first cousin, amplified the memory. "When my father, and McArthur's father, Uncle Earl, showed up at the plant they didn't have to take a test. They were asked to make a muscle and because they were fresh from doing farm work, their muscles were well-developed. They were singled out, along with other southern young men and hired immediately." Eventually, there were six Binions employed in several automobile factories, many of them working more than forty years before retiring.

"We broke the color line in our neighborhood in 1952,"[2] McArthur added, "and were the first African Americans on our block"—but not the first in the neighborhood. Katherine Brown and her children had been living on Pinehurst, a block away, for two years, and there was one other family, the Foremans, who must have been the first blacks in the neighborhood to move beyond the six-foot wall that separated blacks and whites. The white wall ran for several blocks between Mendota and Birwood, beginning at Eight Mile Road. Some of the kids in the neighborhood would play ball against the wall or challenge each other by walking on it. "I had never seen my boys so excited," Katherine said of the Binions' moving in. "They came home yelling about how many boys and girls got out of a truck."[3]

Working at Cadillac, like the Binion men, was one thing; owning one of the cars they made was another. Most of the former sharecroppers were content just to see the other side of the Cotton Curtain, whether or not they could afford a luxury car. The powerful-looking Cadillac symbolized another notable breakthrough—General Motors had surged ahead of Ford and become the largest, richest corporation in the world, the first corporation in the history of humankind to gross a billion dollars a year. This rise to fiscal dominance was, in part, facilitated by Walter Reuther and the UAW in 1948, with the historic agreement that guaranteed wage increases tied to a cost-of-living index.[4] The bitter hundred-day strike of 1945–46 was clearly in the past. The union, in effect, became a junior partner.

The racial situation at the Chevrolet plant and throughout GM reflected strong support for discrimination and continued resistance to upgrading black workers or even hiring them. There was little help from the UAW, whose record on race relations continued to be mixed.[5]

Discrimination was also evident in the city's neighborhoods, particularly on the lower east side. What the government and city agencies defined as urban renewal meant "Negro removal" for many of the residents in Black Bottom and Paradise Valley. "My father's tailor shop was plowed under in 1950," Coleman Young lamented. "Mabern's barbershop bit the dust a little later. Ours was the first neighborhood to be eliminated, with long stretches of stores and houses being demolished seemingly at random."[6] It took merely three years for the black community on the lower east side to be leveled; in the end more than seven hundred buildings were razed and some two thousand black families forced to relocate.[7]

When the Dies Committee, aka the House Un-American Activities Committee (HUAC), set up shop in Detroit in 1951, many black activists scurried for cover, but not Coleman Young. His courage was never more evident than in his refusal to hand over the membership lists of the local chapter of the National Negro Congress, an organization HUAC had defined as subversive. "I refuse to answer that question," Young told the committee when he was asked if he was a member of the Communist Party. He invoked his First Amendment rights and declared, "I have no purpose of being here as a stool pigeon, I am not prepared to give any information on any of my associates or political thoughts."[8] Young's defiance and tart-tongued responses were broadcast on local radio. His attorney, George W. Crockett Jr., had represented Paul Robeson, Claudia Jones, and much closer to home, Carl Winter in similar bouts with HUAC.

Jones had been arrested and tried for un-American activities under the Smith Act, which was written so that labor organizing and agitation for equal rights could be construed as sedition and treason, the same as actually fighting to overthrow the government by force. Defending political activists in New York City, Crockett was operating outside of his familiar base in Detroit. But in Detroit, he was part of a breakthrough when he and his law partners Dean Robb, Morton Eden, and the inestimable Ernest Goodman formed the first integrated law firm in the nation. Furthermore, they secured an office in the Cadillac Tower Building, which had a policy of not leasing space to African American law firms.[9]

Crockett, a native of Jacksonville, Florida, and a graduate of Morehouse College and the University of Michigan Law School, was a no-nonsense attorney. When defending Robeson, Jones, and eight others accused under the Smith Act, he was charged with contempt of court and served four months in jail himself. Despite the conviction, he was not disbarred and later served as legal counsel for the Mississippi voter-registration project of Freedom Summer 1964. It was in this capacity that he asked Michael Schwerner, Andrew Goodman, and James Chaney to investigate a church burning, the assignment that led to their murder.

While her husband was busy on the legal front, Ethelene Crockett, having raised three children, earned a medical degree from Howard University in 1942. She completed her internship at Detroit Receiving Hospital, and because no Detroit hospital would accept an African American woman physician, she did her residency in New York City. Finally in 1952, she was accepted at a hospital in Detroit, becoming the first black woman in her field of obstetrics and gynecology to practice in the state. By now Detroit's African American population had increased to more than three hundred thousand, and Dr. Crockett brought her share of new babies into the world.[10]

It was often said that between them Dr. Ethelene Crockett and Dr. Charles H. Wright delivered more than ten thousand black babies—and a few white ones. Both doctors had experienced a similar path. Faced with the same obstacles that prevented Dr. Crockett from having a residency in Detroit, Dr. Wright, a native of Alabama with a medical degree from Meharry Medical College in Nashville, Tennessee, went to Cleveland and New York City to fulfill the requirements to practice obstetrics and gynecology in Detroit; he began practice there in 1953. After establishing an enviable record in private practice, he was admitted to practice at Hutzel Hospital and certified as a general surgeon in obstetrics and gynecology in 1955.

A year before Dr. Crockett began her tenure at Hutzel Hospital, John Conyers Jr. was returning home from the Korean War; Malcolm X had risen to become the national spokesperson for the Nation of Islam; and the country would soon be embroiled in three of the most important milestones in its history—*Brown v. Board of Education*, the murder of young Emmett Till in Mississippi, and the Montgomery Bus Boycott, marked by the emergence of Dr. Martin Luther King Jr. and Rosa Parks. Conyers, like his future colleagues in Congress Charles Diggs and Charles Rangel, was an army veteran, a member of the 127th Combat Engineers, an all-black unit. He was a lieutenant when his unit was activated in 1950, but they had been well back from the front lines of battle. "I didn't have a bad experience," he told the *Detroit Free Press*. "In a way, it gave me travel I might not have otherwise experienced. I like to think that my worldview was broadened by my military experience."[11]

Traveling abroad was to prove beneficial for Malcolm X, though it happened after his years in prison. His confinement in prison harnessed Malcolm's restless, intrepid spirit. He had time to reflect and redirect that energy in more positive directions. He was fortunate to have a loving family who were members and active participants in the Nation of Islam. Malcolm Little gradually evolved into Malcolm X, and later El-Hajj Malik El-Shabazz. "My going to Detroit instead of back to Harlem or Boston was influenced by my family's feeling expressed in their letters," Malcolm recorded in his autobiography. "Especially my sister Hilda had stressed to me that although I felt I understood Elijah Muhammad's teachings, I had much to learn, and I ought to come to Detroit and become a member of a temple of practicing Muslims."[12]

Malcolm's odyssey is one of the best-known stories in the American canon, but much less known is Charles Diggs's pilgrimage to Mississippi to witness the trial of the men accused of killing Emmett Till. In the summer of 1955, Diggs was in his first year as Michigan's first African American congressman, having been elected in November 1954. He arrived at the trial accompanied by attorney Basil Brown and businessman James Del Rio. A rather reserved personality, unperturbed by the chaos around him, Diggs, without swagger or defiance, moved through the racist hostility that permeated the town of Sumner, where the trial was held. Simeon Wright, Till's first cousin, who was sleeping next to him in the bed when he was abducted, said he remembered seeing Diggs enduring the "hot and humid courtroom with the rest of us. He was the only elected official from the North and he stood up to the courtroom officials who at first tried to block his entry."[13]

A counterpart to the black nationalism expressed by Malcolm X and the Nation of Islam was emerging: black Christian nationalism. The Rev. Albert B. Cleage Jr., the son of an outstanding physician in Kalamazoo, Michigan, would be among the leading proponents of black theology and self-determination. Cleage Senior was one of the founders of the black-owned Dunbar Hospital and was appointed the City Physician in 1930 by Mayor Bowles. Cleage Junior graduated from Northwestern High School and earned his bachelor of arts degree in sociology from Wayne State University in 1932. Before taking a job as a social worker in the city's Department of Health, he studied briefly at Fisk University under the eminent sociologist Charles S. Johnson. From the Oberlin Graduate School of Theology he earned his bachelor of divinity degree in 1943, the same year that he married Doris Graham and was ordained in the Congregational Christian Church. His first pastorate was at the Chandler Memorial Congregational Church in Lexington, Kentucky. Before returning to Detroit in 1951, he pastored several churches in other cities. Two years later, there was an amicable parting from Saint Mark's Community Church, when he led a group of followers to form the Central Congregational Church. It was around this time that his concept of black Christian nationalism and the Shrine of the Black Madonna began to emerge. His Black Christian Nationalist Covenant stated:

Declaring ourselves to be God's Chosen People, created in His image, the living remnant of the lost Black Nation, Israel, we come together as brothers and sisters in the Black Christian Nationalist movement. We are disciples of the Black Messiah, Jesus of Nazareth, who by His life and by His death upon the cross, teaches us that nothing is more sacred than the liberation of Black people. We covenant together, and pledge our total commitment to the task of rebuilding a Black Nation with power, here on earth. We will do whatever is necessary to achieve self-determination for Black people. We will fight the injustice, oppression and exploitation of all Black people. As members of the Black Nation, we are bound together in an inseparable sacred brotherhood. To the service of His sacred brotherhood, we pledge our lives.[14]

At the same time that the Rev. Cleage was heeding the call of black Christian nationalism, another minister, the Rev. C. L. Franklin, who had assumed the pulpit at New Bethel in 1946, was increasing his congregation. There was no nationalistic inclination in his church, but rather meetings that brimmed with the old-time Baptist religious fervor and rousing gospel music that he had absorbed in Memphis. With each one of his fiery sermons, Franklin's flock seemed to increase, and none of his sermons was more popular than his version of "The Eagle Stirreth Her Nest."

In this famous sermon, the eagle symbolizes God and his care and concern for his people. "The eagle has extraordinary sight," Franklin preached. "Somewhere it is said that he can rise to a lofty height in the air and look in the distance and see a storm hours away. . . . I want to tell you God has extraordinary sight. He can look behind that smile on your face and see the frown in your heart. God has extraordinary sight."

This sermon was recorded by Franklin in 1953. Author Nick Salvatore describes how, after a few more metaphors, Franklin, more than warmed to his topic, spoke of how the eagle built its nest and prepared the eaglet for the world. "It was at this juncture that C.L. shifted gears," Salvatore wrote. "In place of that conversational tone, a musical expressiveness emerged to carry the message forward as [he] whooped, or chanted the remainder of the sermon. He sang in key modulating his voice from near-falsetto to guttural rasp, creating a dynamic cadence both with his words and the interplay created by his voice, the audience's response, and the occasional percussive beat of his hand hitting the pulpit."[15] This powerful and popular recording is one of the reasons black Detroiters lined up outside his church to attend his services.

Whenever she could, Katherine Brown would visit the church. During the mid-fifties her days were consumed with keeping a roof over her head and making sure her four children ate a balanced meal each day and had decent clothes to wear to school. By 1956, she was among the lucky few to get an apartment in the newly built Jeffries Projects, named after the father of the mayor who had been ineffective during the Sojourner Truth Housing debacle that sparked the riot of 1943. From her sixth-floor apartment in building 601, she could see Poe School (now Edmonson), partially concealed by several other fourteen-story buildings in the complex. In many respects, the Jeffries, with its thirteen towers and 415 low-rise units capable of housing more than 2,100 families, resembled the Brewster Projects, and the younger inhabitants of each saw the others as mortal enemies. There was basically a turf war between the two gangs based in the two projects. They contested each other in sports and entertainment, but much of their animosity would soon be mollified with the advent of cultural programs and development of the music industry, which would thrive as a result of their mutual cooperation. The merger of their aspirations was personified by the working relationship between Diana Ross from Brewster and songwriting geniuses Lamont and Reginald Dozier from the Jeffries projects. Later Lamont combined his talent with Brian and Eddie Holland, and they wrote a trove of top hits, a soundtrack for their generation. In fact, many young performers from both projects trekked over to Third Avenue, to Fortune Records, owned by Jack and Devora Brown, to make inexpensive demos in hopes of matching the popularity of Nolan Strong and the Diablos or Andre Williams, whose recording "Bacon Fat" was a hit in 1956. At that time, another big hit record was Little Willie John's "Fever," which may have provided John with the money to leave Jeffries for greener pastures, the newer projects on Six Mile Road. Little Willie starred in football and could run with the best in the games between Jeffries and Brewster teams, many of which occurred in the trench where the John C. Lodge Freeway was under construction. Mack Avenue was the street connecting "the bricks," along which the boys from Brewster probably loosened up during the stroll to the Lodge.

The Chrysler (I-75), John C. Lodge (M-10), and Edsel Ford (I-94) freeways all came with the force of destructive tornadoes to black neighborhoods. By 1958, the building of the Lodge alone had taken out more than two thousand homes and other buildings. Even more were demolished to make way for the Ford Freeway.[16] Out of the destruction of longstanding neighborhoods emerged the vertical communities, high-rise buildings with relatively affordable rents. For a moment, the change seemed to forecast a bright future. Black Bottom became a veritable Camelot.

From the mid- to late fifties, the city of Detroit was in a state of transition; the black community was watching large portions of it being dramatically transformed. The altering of neighborhood grids was something most black Detroiters had grown accustomed to, like poverty, discrimination, and being often deprived of federal and municipal assistance. Being shortchanged was nothing new for them, though cultural ingenuity was always in abundance. Three notable black artists were seemingly undaunted by the expected uncertainties in their communities. Playwright Ron Milner, when not excelling at baseball or basketball at Northeastern High School, was at his old typewriter working on the great American novel or one of the plays that one day would make it to Broadway. As a teenager he had already received some recognition in the *Michigan Chronicle* for his creativity and writing ability, which came as a stunning surprise to his teammates.

Painter Al Loving, three years older than Milner, graduated from Cass Technical High School in 1951 when he was sixteen years old. In 1955, he traveled to India with his father, a professor of education administration at Wayne State University, who had received Fulbright and Ford Foundation grants. The images Loving saw there, especially the array of brilliant colors, profoundly affected his artistic outlook. Bassist Ron Carter, like Loving a graduate of Cass Tech, was just beginning to learn the fundamentals of his instrument but already acquiring the recognition that one day would place him in that great ensemble formed by Miles Davis. They were exemplary of the talented young men on their way to ensuring that the city's rich cultural tradition in music and the arts extended into future generations.

Three young women were also on the verge of wider recognition. Carlene Hatcher Polite, the daughter of UAW officials, began her artistic career as a dancer at the Martha Graham School of Contemporary Dance with professional performances in New York and Detroit from 1955 to 1963. Always an aspiring writer, she put her creative impulses on hold and worked in the civil rights field with the Detroit Council for Human Rights and the NAACP. Then it was time to follow her heart to Paris and into the world of literature. In 1966, when she was thirty-four, she published in French *The Flagellants*, her first book. It was later translated into English. By that time, she was back in the States, teaching at the University of Buffalo. The title of the book worried a few Detroiters, who feared that it would be unflattering to the city or its denizens. But only the first chapter had any reference to the city other than calling it the Bottom. New York City got far more attention. Her female protagonist, Ideal, abandoned the Bottom because it was too provincial. Her hope was that New York City would satisfy her craving for a broader spectrum of opportunities.

While Polite was touring with Martha Graham and writing, Shirley Woodson Reid, a graduate of Chadsey High School, was blending colors on an easel and earning the first of her degrees in fine arts, which she received in 1958 from Wayne State University. As an education specialist in the Highland Park school system, she blended her artistic talents with her love of teaching young people. Art history also commanded her time and attention. She was invited as a member of the National Conference of Artists to lecture or participate as a panelist at countless exhibitions and seminars.[17] Her artistic gifts were not limited to oils and canvases, and her predilection for jazz and literature was nurtured by her husband, Edsel, who maintained an intimate connection to Detroit's jazz community.

Detroit's jazz scene in the early 1950s was a hothouse of bebop. One of the style's progenitors, Charlie "Yardbird" Parker, was a regular performer in the city and a magnet attracting a retinue of hopefuls, particularly alto saxophone players intent on capturing his searing lyricism. There were singers, too, such as Betty Carter, who sought to emulate Bird's swift arpeggios and intervallic leaps. Lionel Hampton was so impressed with her ability to swing and scat that in 1950, when she was twenty-one, he contracted her to tour with his band. Their appearance at the Paradise Theater with Illinois Jacquet's powerful tenor sax up front rocking the balcony was particularly memorable for the Northwestern High School grad, who had honed her natural gifts at the Detroit Conservatory of Music. Hampton's wife, Gladys, also deeply admired Carter's rhythmic finesse and unique harmonic acumen, and dubbed her Betty Bebop, an apt sobriquet for her intuitive feel for the complexity of the new music. It was a brief and bountiful stint that Carter had with the temperamental Hampton, who fired her numerous times before she decided to embark on her own solo career. By the 1960s in duets with Ray Charles, she received greater recognition.[18]

When she wasn't on the road, Carter was a dynamic member of a coterie of jazz notables who honed their skills at a bevy of nightspots from Black Bottom to the North End, from Baker's Keyboard Lounge on Livernois near Eight Mile Road to the El Sino on Saint Antoine Street, the once-fabled thoroughfare of Paradise Valley. The regulars, the city's numerous jazz aficionados, were up front at the Blue Bird Inn on the west side, or at Klein's Show Bar on Twelfth Street, or at the World Stage on Woodward near Davidson, particularly on Tuesday nights, when many of the performers were associated with the New Music Society, under the direction of guitarist Kenny Burrell. The society's members, which at times numbered more than five thousand, were among some of the finest musicians in the city, from the young to the veterans. It was there that Pepper Adams, Roy Brooks, Donald Byrd, Lonnie Hillyer, Charles McPherson, Bernard McKinney (Kiane Zawadi), and Lucky Thompson first enthralled standing-room-only crowds.[19]

On the weekends, jazz lovers, most of them young beboppers, filled the Blue Bird Inn, eager to get as close as possible to the bandstand to hear tenor saxophonist Billy Mitchell, featuring either Barry Harris or Tommy Flanagan on piano with Elvin Jones on drums. Ernie Farrow, Will Austin, Paul Chambers, Doug Watkins, or Ray McKinney were among the fabulous bassists on the stand on any given evening. No matter the ensemble, it was always quite able to provide an invigorating vehicle for such guests as Bird, Curtis Fuller, Thad Jones, Wardell Gray, or Miles Davis, who was a frequent guest during that period, when he struggled to overcome his heroin addiction. "There were some good musicians in Detroit and I was starting to play with some of them," Davis recalled in his autobiography. "That helped me and a lot of them were clean . . . and they looked up to me because of all the things I had done . . . and since they were clean it made me want to stay that way."[20] Davis said that people were packing into the Blue Bird to hear them play, and it wasn't unusual for Betty Carter or Yusef Lateef to drop by and sit in.

By the mid-fifties, Lateef could do that only occasionally, because he was fronting his own group at Klein's Show Bar. Taking the gig at Klein's meant that Lateef could no longer keep his part-time job at Chrysler. Playing almost nightly at the bar gave the band—Lateef on saxophones, oboe, and flute; Hugh Lawson on piano; Austin or Farrow on bass; Louis Hayes on drums; and Curtis Fuller on trombone—a lot of experience in a short time. In the spring of 1957, Lateef got a call from Ozzie Cadena of Savoy Records, who expressed an interest in signing the group based on the recommendation of a friend. Thus began Lateef's long and productive career as a recording artist.[21]

In 1959, while Lateef was adding more recordings at Savoy and later at Prestige Records to his discography, bassist Ron Carter was finishing his classical studies at the Eastman School of Music in Rochester, New York. A graduate of the renowned Cass Tech High School that had produced such musical stalwarts as Roland Hanna, Donald Byrd, Kenny Burrell, Paul Chambers, and a host of others, Carter was well aware of the awesome responsibility of carrying on that tradition, though it took him a while and a few unexpected setbacks to settle into the jazz sphere. There was also a solid family legacy to uphold, particularly from a father who had come to Detroit in the early fifties, when he was one of a very few blacks employed as a bus driver by the Detroit Street and Railways Company. Carter's father had spearheaded a breakthrough in employment for black workers in the DSR, but his son was unable to make similar inroads into Detroit's classical music world. This later proved to be a boon for his many jazz fans. At the dawn of the 1960s, as jazz was experiencing a variety of styles, from Charlie Mingus and Ornette Coleman to Duke Ellington and Dave Brubeck, an innovative leap by Miles Davis ended one era and set the stage for the next. He chose Carter as his bassist as they took the music to a new and exciting plateau. "I arrived at the right time," Carter told his biographer, Dan Ouellette. "After all, it's all about timing."[22]

Timing is essential for all musicians, and in the mid-fifties, Detroit was overflowing with them. Other than the Blue Bird Inn, owned by Clarence Eddins, there were no black-owned clubs. Eddins became sole owner of the Blue Bird Inn, located on the city's west side, when Buddy Dubois was shot and killed in 1956. Within a year, Eddins began to transform the Inn, which had been operating since the early thirties. The renovation was geared to the development of jazz, in which bebop was gradually supplanting swing. The club was expanded with redesigned seating to increase its capacity. The stellar house bands were always a draw for local and nationally acclaimed musicians, and the club's reputation increased with occasional performances by Miles Davis, then living in Detroit. Davis recalled playing at the Blue Bird for "several months as a guest soloist in Billy Mitchell's house band."[23]

Whether he was actually performing at the Inn or not, a rumor of his being there was enough to draw a flock of acolytes. As the club flourished, Eddins was able to bring in name acts, and soon the Inn was a crucible of modern jazz. For a score of years, into the seventies, it continued to be one of the city's most significant night spots.

Eddins, who died in 1993, left a legacy and template that Bert Dearing continues in the twenty-first century through a network of successful business enterprises, including a nightclub, a restaurant, and a theater. Entrepreneurship has been essential to the black community and its drive for self-determination.

14

FROM MOTOWN TO SHOWDOWN

While the blues and jazz continued to occupy a large swath of Detroit's cultural front, rhythm and blues with a tinge of pop was gradually gaining a foothold, thanks to Berry Gordy Jr. and the Motown experience. Meanwhile, there was a developing disharmony between the unions and the city's black workers. "The merger of the CIO with the AFL in the middle of the decade indicated to many blacks a declining commitment to the battle for job equality . . . this came at the very time that the NAACP legal victories and the dramatic rise of Martin Luther King to public prominence signified a revolution of expectations that was spawning a new [militancy] among black Americans. In this context the old, still unsolved issues of job discrimination in the factories and the lack of representation in the highest councils of the auto union assumed a new urgency."[1]

A leading voice in this new surge, one willing to address the union's recurrent ambiguity, was Horace Sheffield, a union organizer and a man well informed about the inner and outer workings of the labor movement. He spoke before the US Civil Rights Commission in 1960, three years after he had helped to found the Trade Union Leadership Council (TULC). His main complaint at that time was the general ineffectiveness of the UAW's Fair Practices Department, which he contended was missing in action when it came to getting skilled jobs for black workers. Their presence in the plants had dramatically increased, but black workers still constituted a fraction of 1 percent in such trades as carpentry and tool-and-die making. "Even at Rouge where there were 12,500 black workers, fewer than 250 of them were among the 7,000 in the skilled trades. With blacks now 25 percent of the workforce at major Detroit companies like Chrysler and GM, the situation was becoming increasingly volatile, and their grievances about exclusion from the skilled trades represented one of the principal issues raised by TULC."[2]

While Sheffield and his comrades were shaking up things on the labor front, in 1957 attorney William Patrick Jr. integrated the city's municipal chambers as the first African American member of the City Council. This was a harbinger of militant agitation on the horizon. Patrick's victory was aided by support from the UAW-CIO as well as an impressive campaign team, led by attorney Damon Keith. The union had apparently been put on notice by Sheffield's activism. That Keith had time to help Patrick is quite remarkable, since his main responsibility was to bring in business for his newly formed law firm, which included attorneys Herman Anderson, Myron Wahls, Joseph Brown, and Nathan Conyers, John's brother. "I was doing a lot of community work with the NAACP, United Negro College Fund, with the churches, and so my name was being bandied around," Keith told his biographers. "People were coming in to see me, and after I'd interview them, I would introduce them to Nate or Herman as clients."[3] Or to Wahls, who was not only a quite competent attorney but also a highly respected pianist. When he wasn't in the courtroom, Wahls was refining his chops on the keyboard, brushing up on the latest compositions from the world of jazz, particularly bebop.

With Patrick in the city council and Keith and his cohorts ready to take up the legal fight to level the playing field in the unions, Sheffield was further emboldened and was given additional support from stalwart labor activists such as Nelson Jack Edwards, Robert "Buddy" Battle, and Marc Stepp. With them on board, he could focus on strategy and tactics as they pushed the TULC into ever more militant demands for an end to the practice of relegating blacks to the lowest-paying and most onerous jobs. Since the end of World War II, the relationship between the union and black workers had been fairly cordial and respectful, but these warm feelings resulted from wartime necessities. Now the radical aggressiveness of Sheffield and his allies exacerbated the unraveling of unity between the workers and the union. Inevitably, the simmering resentment of white union members and leaders came to the surface, and the discord mushroomed into larger social and political issues as the decade came to a close.

The essential problem had been summed up in "Big Boss Man," a blues evergreen recorded by John Lee Hooker who sang, "Can't you hear me when I call?"

Whether the big boss man was a straw boss on a farm or a foreman in a factory, Hooker's call generally went unanswered, much like the demands by Sheffield and his cohorts. Hooker's blues plea was ignored at the point of production, and his music meant very little to the new generation of black Detroiters, their youthful impetuosity eager for a brand-new beat.

The Gateway to Freedom International Memorial to the Underground Railroad, commemorating Detroit's role in the Underground Railroad, is located at Hart Plaza on the riverfront. It was sculpted by Edward Dwight, after winning a competition. It was dedicated on October 20, 2001. *(Photo by Dale Rich)*

William Lambert (1817–1890) was among the leading abolitionists in Detroit. As a conductor on the Underground Railroad, he helped thousands of runaway slaves continue their flight to freedom in Canada. *(Photo courtesy of the Detroit Historical Society)*

Fannie Richards, a native of Virginia, became the first African American teacher in the city's school system by the 1860s. She was a teacher for more than fifty years, and she was inducted into the Michigan Women's Hall of Fame for her contribution to education. *(Courtesy Archives of Michigan)*

Emma Azalia Hackley (1867–1892) excelled as a singer in several genres, but her lasting legacy was in the realm of music education. An extensive musical archive at the Detroit Public Library is named in her honor. *(Courtesy of the E. Azalia Hackley Collection of African Americans in the Performing Arts, Detroit Public Library)*

Elijah McCoy, the great inventor, was born in Canada, but beginning in the 1870s he resided in and around Detroit, where he continued his innovations in lubricating systems. So vast was the number of patents and his authority, he was deemed "the real McCoy" to distinguish him from imitators. *(Courtesy of the Burton Historical Collection, Detroit Public Library)*

This scenic shot is along a creek that runs through Elwood Cemetery, where a coterie of black and white notables rest in eternal peace, including Lewis Cass, Coleman Young, and William Lambert *(Photo by Herb Boyd)*

A black man battered and bloodied during the race riot of 1943. *(Photographer unknown)*

The 606 Horseshoe Lounge was built in 1936. Before it was demolished in 2000, it was the last bar in Detroit's Paradise Valley, an entertainment and business district. *(Photo by Dale Ric)*

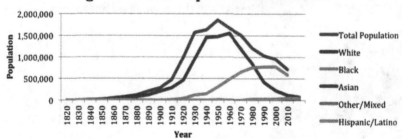

Fig. 2 Detroit's Population over Time

Legend:
- Total Population
- White
- Black
- Asian
- Other/Mixed
- Hispanic/Latino

This chart shows that from 1920 to 1930 there was an increase of 80,000 in Detroit's black residents; another population explosion occurred from 1940 through 1950, when the black population doubled. *(Photo courtesy of Mask Magazine)*

The great boxing champion Sugar Ray Robinson shares a magazine with Joyce Finley (Garrett). *(Photo courtesy of Shahida Mausi)*

Milton Henry (Brother Gaidi); Jaramogi Abebe Agyeman (Albert Cleage); Thomas "Beans" Bowles; Kwame Ture (Stokely Carmichael), and an unidentified man.

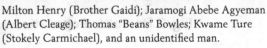

Congressman Charles Diggs addresses a crowd in Washington, D.C., in 1972 at the first African Liberation Day celebration.
(Photo by Dale Rich)

This is Hitsville, U.S.A., the original Motown headquarters, on West Grand Boulevard. *(Photo by Dale Rich)*

Berry Gordy's mansion at 918 West Boston. *(Photo by Dale Rich)*

The wall near Eight Mile Road, once a line of demarcation separating the black and white communities. *(Photo by Dale Rich)*

Rosa Parks with Mayor Coleman Young at his inaugural prayer breakfast in January 1975 at Cobo Hall.
(Photo by Dale Rich)

Shahida Mausi holds a picture of her great-grandmother.
(Photo courtesy of Shahida Mausi)

On the left, partially obscured, is *Michigan Chronicle* reporter Jim Ingram. Councilwoman Erma Henderson and attorney Ken Cockrel join him at a press conference in the early 1970s. *(Photo by Don Van Freeman)*

Ribbon-cutting ceremony on Friday, August 31, for the opening of the new Detroit Jazz Center, 2110 Park Avenue. *Front Row:* Herb Boyd, executive director of the Detroit Jazz Center; Representative John Conyers (first congressional district); State Senator John Faxon. *Back Row:* John Sinclair, chair of the Detroit Jazz Center; State Representative George Cushingberry Jr., and State Senator David Holmes. *(Photo by Leni Sinclair)*

Concert on Washington Boulevard. *Front row (l to r):* Miller Brisker, Wendell Harrison, Vincent York, Ernie Rodgers, Teddy Harris *(standing),* Malvin McCray, Sam Sanders, Arnold Clarington, and Beans Bowles. *Second row:* Vaughn Klugh, Marcus Belgrave, Ron Jackson, Herbie Williams, Steve Hunter, Donald Towns, Jimmy Wilkins, Ed Gooch, Brad Felt. *In the rear:* Rod Hicks, two unidentified members, bassist Melvin "Skull" Jackson, and Roy Brooks. *(Photo by Leni Sinclair)*

Nadine Brown, *Michigan Chronicle* reporter; Rosa Parks; Elza Dinwiddie; Katherine Brown; a Wayne State University student; a faculty member at Wayne State; Herb Boyd; and Alex Haley. All are listening to Almitra Dye, Boyd's daughter, read from Boyd's first publication of student essays in response to Haley's *Roots* in 1977. *(Photographer unknown)*

Yusef Lateef signs his autobiography for Katherine Brown at the Jazz Festival in 2007. *(Photo by Herb Boyd)*

Shrine of the Black Madonna. *(Photo by Dale Rich)*

Artist Bennie White Ethiopia studying his mural of Malice Green, who was killed by the police on November 5, 1992. In 2013, the mural was demolished along with the building located at Warren and Twenty-Third Street. *(Photo by Dale Rich)*

Ron Scott, with the megaphone, leading a demonstration in the summer of 2010 in downtown Detroit following the police shooting death of Aiyana Jones. The woman to the left of Scott is Jewell Allison, who organized the protest. In back of Scott is activist Carl Dix of the Revolutionary Communist Party. *(Photo by Herb Boyd)*

Summer of 2014 advisory council and history collective, including George Gaines, with the purse; Gene Cunningham, kneeling; and Elza Boyd, center. The others are Marsha Music, Greg Hicks, Ron Lockett, and Charles Simmons. The photo was taken by Herb Boyd at Reggie Carter's house.

David Rambeau, actor, director, and pioneer in black television, in the rotunda at the Dr. Charles Wright Museum of African American History in 2014. *(Photo by Herb Boyd)*

Artist McArthur Binion and his daughter, Stella, in New York, at the Lelong Gallery, in 2016. *(Photo by Herb Boyd)*

Civic leader Ron Lockett and former mayor Dave Bing at Northwest Activities Center, in 2016. *(Photo by Herb Boyd)*

Power of Togetherness is Charles McGee's twenty-five-foot sculpture outside the Charles H. Wright Museum of African American History. *(Photo by Herb Boyd)*

Roy Brooks, famed percussionist and bandleader. *(© 2017 Barbara Weinberg Barefield)*

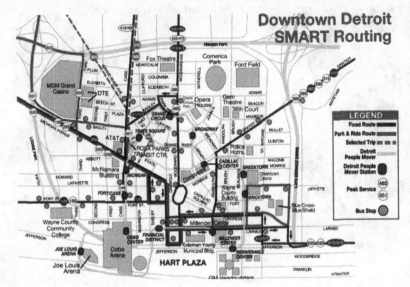

(Photo courtesy of smartbus.org)

Rosa Parks's home. *(Photo by Dale Rich)*

15

A BRAND-NEW BEAT

Berry Gordy Jr.'s dream of starting his own record company wasn't farfetched but rather a logical extension of his success as a songwriter. Several of rhythm-and-blues singer Jackie Wilson's hits from 1957 to 1959, including "Reet Petite," "To Be Loved," and "Lonely Teardrops," were co-written by Gordy. An intuitive businessman, Gordy began thinking about owning and controlling his creative products.

Remarkably, when Gordy borrowed the $800 from his family to start his Tamla label, it wasn't Wilson who recorded the first song but Marvin Johnson with "Come to Me," one of several tunes he composed with Gordy. What began as a fruitful partnership splintered bitterly, however, over who was the composer and rightful owner of the songs they had written together. Johnson felt he had been shortchanged and ripped off.

It's hard to identify where Gordy got his musical genius, but his entrepreneurial drive was clearly in the family's DNA; his father was an enterprising businessman. In 1936, when his family moved to Black Bottom, Gordy was six and a half years old. "It was an important turning point for the family. Pop had finally seen his struggles pay off. During those Depression years—he had not only survived—hustling his way from being an apprentice plasterer to getting his contractor's license and hiring men to work for him—but had saved enough money to make a down payment on our very own two-story commercial building on the corner of Farnsworth and St. Antoine Streets, not far from that first little grocery store he had been running."[1]

Working with his father was grueling, backbreaking labor that toughened his muscles and at the same time made him think that there had to be a better way to make a living. Even so, he put his body to another test in the boxing ring, and as a reasonably good featherweight, he shared the card at least once with heavyweight champion Joe Louis. But the smell of liniment and the sitting in the corner waiting for the bell soon gave way to his first love: music. In 1956 he met Jackie Wilson, another former boxer, and their collaboration was almost as magical and productive as Gordy's was to become with Smokey Robinson a few years later.

Gordy first met Smokey when he and his group, the Matadors, were auditioning for a contract with a local recording company. Though unsuccessful, they caught Gordy's attention, who praised them and offered Smokey some songwriting advice. After listening to nearly one hundred of Smokey's songs, Gordy suggested that he work on telling a story in his music. "That's how it all started between Smokey and me," Gordy related. "Our relationship was simple. I wanted to teach, he wanted to learn.

He started bringing me songs on a regular basis. I continued to turn them down just as regularly, but I knew it was a matter of time before he'd come to me with something I'd really like."[2]

Gordy recalled that in January 1958 or a year earlier, according to Smokey, that day arrived. "It happened while I was watching *American Bandstand* on TV. The Silhouettes were singing 'Get a Job,' number one song in the world, when it hit like a bolt of lightning. Get a Job? *Got a Job!*" Within minutes Smokey composed his response and hurried to Gordy. "This is it! I got it!" he exclaimed bursting in on Gordy's meeting. "'Got what?' Gordy asked. "Got a Job," Smokey responded, "our first hit. . . . Berry helped me whip it into form, the group started some serious rehearsing, and we cut it over at United Sound in the early part of November 1957. Flip side was 'Mama Done Tole me.'"[3]

"Got a Job" gave Gordy and Robinson what they needed to seal their partnership, the hit and financial boost Gordy sought to form his own company. At the time, the majority of Detroit's working class was struggling to hold on to their jobs or hoping to receive one more unemployment check. The downward spiral of the economy and the disappearance of jobs were indices directly connected to the ever shrinking manufacturing base, especially the reduced output of the automotive industry and the closing of plants. When Packard suspended operation in 1956, it was an ominous indictor that the industrial decline was fully under way. "I felt like someone had hit me with a sledge hammer," one Packard worker said.[4]

None of the gloomy workplace impact came as a surprise to James Boggs. Since his arrival from Alabama, and while working at Chrysler, he had been warning workers of the impending downturn, with a special concern about overtime and automation. "In every plant the company is demanding more productions from the workforce," he wrote in 1958. "Dodge and Chrysler workers have been sent home twenty-three days before completing an eight-hour day. The company says they are not producing up to their work standards. Over a hundred men have been fired or given days off for not meeting these standards."[5] Of course, black workers were disproportionately harmed by these layoffs or firings, especially those who by the late fifties were unfortunate enough to be employed at Ford, where the Edsel was running out of gas and gaining little traction with car buyers.

The only black workers immune to the vagaries of the plant were the entrepreneurs, owners of their businesses. It was advice similar to this that Smokey Robinson urged on Berry Gordy. Rather than being at the mercy of other producers and labels, why not start your own? "Why work for the man, when you can *be* the man?" Robinson told his mentor.[6] With Robinson by his side, Gordy took that advice all the way to the bank, particularly after counting the cash flow from the team's first million seller in 1960, "Shop Around," on the Tamla label. In Gordy's world, a label or two does not constitute a company. He always had a bigger plan. "Because of its thriving car industry, Detroit had long been known as the 'Motor City,'" Gordy wrote. "In tribute to what I had always felt was the down-home quality of warm, soulful country-hearted people I grew up around, I used 'town' in place of 'city.' A contraction of 'Motor City' gave me the perfect name—Motown."[7]

Robinson recalled that beginning: "West Grand Boulevard was the name of the street. Berry had bought a routine, B-Flat two-story house on the same strip as a funeral home and a beauty shop. We were wedged in between. . . . Downstairs became headquarters. Kitchen became the control room. Garage became the studio where we'd cut 'Way Over There' and 'Shop Around.' The living room was bookkeeping, the dining room, sales. Berry stuck a funky sign in the front window—'Hitsville, USA'—and we were in business."[8]

Ironically, it was the factories and their assembly lines after which Gordy patterned his production procedure. After a writer composed a tune, Gordy matched it to a particular group; they rehearsed and refined it, and then it was reviewed and finalized by Gordy and his team of producers. When the song rolled off this assembly line of musicians and arrangers, the finished product was like a new Cadillac. This was the beginning of the brand-new beat that Gordy envisioned. The compilation of hits would be the soundtrack of a generation.

16

BING AND BANG

On the political front, Congressman Charles Diggs's influence had grown exponentially. Following the national census, he successfully pushed for the creation of a second black-majority congressional district. Equally prosperous at that time was the House of Diggs, the family-owned funeral home, which, like so many black-owned funeral parlors—Stinson's, Swanson's, McFall's, and Cole's (the oldest dating back to 1919)—faced little competition in burying African Americans. No doubt the black-owned parlors benefited from the passage in 1961 by the state legislature of a bill prohibiting racial discrimination by private cemeteries.

Inseparably linked to the black-owned funeral homes were the black churches, and in the 1960s, few pastors could rival the pulpit power of the Rev. Clarence LaVaughn Franklin. He arrived in Detroit in 1946 for his installation at New Bethel Baptist Church, and by the late fifties he had risen to a leadership position in both the sacred and secular realms of the city. During this process, he had transformed himself from anything resembling a Mississippi-born, country circuit preacher from Memphis. His hair was "conked," that is, straightened with lye; his suits were purchased from Kosins, one of Detroit's top haberdasheries, and he cruised around town in a brand-new Cadillac. These accouterments added luster to his charisma and magnetic voice. It was easy to understand how he could move a church to ecstasy. His ability to mesmerize a congregation did not extend to calming the rancor at the National Baptist Convention, however, particularly the dispute between two leaders he admired. Even so, he was determined to resolve the conflict.

The Rev. J. H. Jackson, who had led the convention for nearly thirty years, riled many members, including Dr. Martin Luther King Jr., for his opposition to church involvement in the civil rights struggle. Although Jackson had backed the movement during the Montgomery bus boycott, he decided that the organization should no longer be involved. Mediating this split, which Franklin did without leaving the convention, was not easy. Franklin was facing two other challenges—how to keep his Metropolitan Civic League for Legal Action afloat and how to help his daughter Aretha navigate her crossover from gospel to popular music. Meanwhile, his Civic League had lost what little clout it had had.

Aretha's situation proved more complicated. "Eighteen in 1960, she already had two children and had left high school before graduating. She also possessed a considerable reputation from her gospel recordings and tour appearances. Her musical abilities were exceptional, and when she told her father of her desire to record popular music, the preacher father and this talented gospel-performing daughter became the talk of the church world."[1] It would have been hypocritical on Franklin's part to block his daughter's desires, because he had introduced her to all types of music. If Aretha wanted to follow the likes of Sam Cooke and Ray Charles in leaving the sacred for the secular without sacrificing any of their soulfulness, then Franklin fully supported her.

In the fall of 1960, her recording of "Today I Sing the Blues," was among the top R&B tunes in the country. "Just when my career was getting started . . . Detroit was undergoing major changes. For one thing, an urban renewal program meant the end of the New Bethel of my childhood. The Chrysler Freeway was being built right through Hastings. The church—in fact, the entire neighborhood—was being torn down for the highway. (Daddy spoke of how the Catholic Church, only one block away, was saved from demolition while ours was not. He couldn't explain why)."[2]

By 1962, little explanation was needed when the Gotham Hotel, which had stood as a lodestone since 1943, was closed. When business partners John White and Irving Roane bought the nine-story building, located at the corner of John R Street and Orchestra Place, it had become a choice alternative for notable blacks who weren't welcome in the downtown hotels.[3] It was equivalent to Harlem's Hotel Theresa, with similar architecture, accommodations, and in particular, a similarly spacious dining room and bar. In 1958, when the great bluesman B. B. King remarried, the ceremony was performed at the Gotham with the Rev. Franklin officiating. In 1964 an era came to a shattering close when the wrecking ball began demolishing the building. Paradise Valley had lost its centerpiece. The leveling moved inexorably up and down the route of the Chrysler Freeway, ripping the heart out of Black Bottom so folks in the exurbs had another, faster way to get in and out of the city.

The early sixties in Detroit was a time of political optimism among black residents. Among the brightest prospects was Wade Mc-Cree Jr., whom President Kennedy appointed to the federal district court. There was more jubilation when Governor John Swainson appointed Otis M. Smith to the Michigan Supreme Court, a position a black man hadn't held since Reconstruction. McCree and Smith joined Damon Keith, who in 1960 was the commissioner of the State Bar of Michigan. Such flexing of legal and political muscle was a prelude to the 1961 mayoral election, in which black voters were a key factor in attorney Jerome P. Cavanagh's upset victory over the incumbent Louis Miriani.

With a liberal mayor holding the reins, blacks expected a dramatic change in the often brutally racist behavior of the police, which was sanctioned by Miriani. They even hoped that Cavanagh would live up to his promise to do something about the white "homeowners' rights" movement ceaselessly instigated by Mayor Albert Cobo during his years in office (1950–57) and continued by Miriani. Blocking the open-housing law was of central importance to the white homeowners who were determined to keep their neighborhoods segregated. Inevitably, the tide of black residents won out. They were tired of being forced to live in inferior and inadequate housing, but rather than live together, white homeowners began to move out of the city. Thus began white flight from the "black invasion" and the city's population shrinkage. The 1960 census revealed a precipitous dip in Detroit's population, from nearly 2 million to about 1.6 million. This 9 percent loss was a harbinger of population shift.

To Cavanagh's campaign in 1961, attorney Keith devoted a considerable amount of time and energy. When he returned to the firm, Willie Horton was one of his important clients. "After leading Northwestern to a city championship in 1959, he piqued the interest of numerous major league teams, including the Detroit Tigers—even though he was just a teenager." Horton, a native of Mississippi, arrived in Detroit when he was about fourteen, and after being taught the rudiments of baseball in the neighborhood where he lived near the Jeffries Projects, he was a star at Northwestern High School, Keith's alma mater. At the request of Horton's parents, Keith became the star's legal guardian. "I was flabbergasted," Keith would recall. "Legal guardian meant I would be responsible for him in every way. I couldn't believe they were asking me that. But they said, 'Mr. Keith, we believe you can take care of our son. We trust you to watch out for his best interest.'"[4] Horton was still in high school when he signed with the Tigers for a $50,000 bonus, three times the salary Keith was earning. The money was followed by glory. It should be noted that one of Horton's high school teammates was Katherine Brown's son, the captain of the team. Another was Alex Johnson, who became a major league star, winning a batting title in 1970.

One of Mayor Cavanagh's first acts upon taking up residence at Manoogian Mansion—the first mayor to do so—was to issue an executive order prohibiting racial discrimination in hiring and promotion practices in the city. Next he appointed George Edwards, who previously had served as a justice on the Michigan Supreme Court, as the new police chief, a move that was enthusiastically supported by the black community, given Edwards's liberal credentials. Another bold stroke from Cavanagh was the implementation of an affirmative action program throughout the city agencies. Even Coleman Young applauded the new mayor. "Detroit politics in general took a new sensitivity under Cavanagh," he wrote. "He was an active player in the War on Poverty, at the same time working to reverse the decline of the central business district by brisk office construction."[5] Cavanagh's progressive policies, as Young viewed them, provided a wedge of opportunity for all Detroiters. Opportunities, too, for a platoon of black activists who in many respects were far more militant than Young.

Much of the incipient militancy sprung from activists who had been influenced by Malcolm X. In speech after speech, and even more vociferously after the provocative 1959 documentary *The Hate That Hate Produced*, Malcolm gained wider exposure. To him the documentary demonized the Nation of Islam, but it provided him with a useful platform to further his attack on Christian preachers and the "so-called black leaders." Among Detroit's radical leaders were James Boggs, the Rev. Albert Cleage, Milton and Richard Henry, Coleman Young, and John Watson. Perhaps the least known of these men was Watson, whose long political history began in the early sixties when he was dismissed from the Congress of Racial Equality for being too radical. "A few years later," observed Dan Georgakas and Marvin Surkin, "he was expelled from SNCC, along with the entire Detroit chapter, because the group had advocated direct action in the North as well as in the South. During the next few years, he worked with NAC (Negro Action Committee), the Freedom Now Party, and UHURU."[6]

Other than a few minor demonstrations, Uhuru (*uhuru* is the Swahili word for "freedom") had very little presence beyond the campus of Wayne State University, where it was composed of a small group of militant activists who spouted revolutionary rhetoric, read Karl Marx, Frantz Fanon, Mao Tse-tung, Che Guevara, V. I. Lenin, Fidel Castro, C.L.R. James, and of course, Malcolm X. "Our mission as expressed in our speeches and writings during that period was a combination of civil rights desegregation, labor rights for Black workers, socialism; Pan Africanism and what some of us called a Black revolutionary internationalism," said Charles Simmons, a member of the group and later an international correspondent for *Muhammad Speaks*.[7] In the fall of 1963, Watson and other members of Uhuru, most notably Luke

Tripp and General Baker, protested a ceremony staged by the city's civic leaders announcing their bid to host the 1968 Olympics. Among the prominent guests at the event was track and field star Hayes Jones from Pontiac who approached the podium bearing a replica of the Olympic torch. "As the national anthem played, Jones . . . didn't receive a hero's welcome. Protestors from an array of local civil rights organizations carrying picket signs used the occasion to point out the hypocrisy of Detroit's bid to host an event symbolizing international brotherhood while housing discrimination remained rampant and legally sanctioned due to the city's unwillingness to pass an open-housing ordinance."[8] The protestors were quickly arrested, only fueling Watson and Baker's militancy.

Uhuru may have been the most rebellious of the groups demonstrating for open housing, but it wasn't the only one. The local branch of the NAACP and various church leaders also took to the streets, one group encircling the Detroit Civic Center. The various demonstrations had some impact, but it was the black real estate brokers who supplied the telling blow. Whether the Realtors were true believers in open housing and racial integration or merely "blockbusting opportunists," as many were called, the results were the same: white residents fled at the first sign of a black family moving into the neighborhood. "The tactics of blockbusting brokers and speculators were simple. They began by selling a house in an all-white block or neighborhood to a black family or using devious techniques like paying a black woman to walk her baby through a white neighborhood to fuel suspicion of black residential 'takeover.'"[9]

The die had been cast. The fight for open housing loosed the torrent, leaving white residents only one recourse, or so they felt—move to the other side of Eight Mile Road.

17

MARCH TO MILITANCY

In the summer of 1963, black residents were less concerned about what was happening on the blockbusting front than the news that Dr. Martin Luther King Jr. was coming to town for a civil rights march down Woodward Avenue. On June 23, on the Walk to Freedom, more than 125,000 people gathered behind King, who was joined on the front line by UAW leader Walter Reuther, funeral home owner Benjamin McFall, real estate speculator James Del Rio, and the Rev. C. L. Franklin. For the leaders of the march, this was a dress rehearsal for King's more momentous gathering two months later in the nation's capital. The "I Have a Dream" speech he delivered in Detroit was not as elaborate as the one in DC, but there were some special remarks for Detroiters: "I have a dream this afternoon that one day right here in Detroit, Negroes will be able to buy a house or rent a house anywhere that their money will carry them, they will be able to get a job."[1] King had touched on two burning issues in the city that were particularly well-received by the open-housing advocates.

Two weeks later, the hope and inspiration of King's speech in Detroit was washed away by the death of Cynthia Scott. She was shot and killed by the police during a confrontation in downtown Detroit. Scott grew up on the North End and lived in an apartment one floor above Katherine Brown, who, like others on Cardoni Street, knew her as Bay-Bay. She was always big for her age and stood about six feet tall as an adult. According to the police, Scott, twenty-four, had a long arrest record for prostitution, and on this occasion, a day after the July Fourth holiday, she was accosted by two police officers, who claimed they saw her with money in her hands and therefore assumed she had just finished rolling a client. The police claimed that when Theodore Spicher, a white officer, attempted to arrest her, she slashed at him with a knife and then walked across the street as though the affair were over. Spicher drew his gun and shot her twice in the back. But that wasn't enough to stop her. She turned to face Spicher, who fired once more, hitting her in the stomach. She fell dead.

"City prosecutor Samuel H. Olsen quickly exonerated Spicher solely on the testimony of the two policemen," wrote Nick Salvatore. "Olsen, whose reputation was already dismal among black residents, refused to credit the statements of other eyewitnesses, all of whom were African Americans, because he considered their accounts 'too biased.'"[2] When Katherine Brown heard about it, she couldn't believe it was Bay-Bay, and remembered her as a little girl who was tough enough to stand her ground against some of the neighborhood bullies. Whites as usual shrugged off the killing of a black sex-care provider as unimportant, while blacks, based on common experience, assumed that she was merely resisting a police shakedown to keep the cash she'd earned on her back. Rallies were called by Uhuru and the Rev. Cleage at 1300 Beaubien, police headquarters, after Scott's death had been ruled a justifiable homicide. Attorney Milton Henry was retained by the Scott family to represent them in a lawsuit filed against the city and its police force. In any event, Scott's death—or murder, as some activists charged—was a catalyst for new political formations and a renewed impetus for those already in the streets protesting police brutality. No one was surprised—and certainly not the police—that GOAL (Group on Advanced Leadership) was among the organizations protesting the exoneration. According to FBI files, GOAL had been in existence since October 1961, and in April 1962 was officially registered as a nonprofit educational corporation. "GOAL," the FBI reported, "was organized to hasten the Negro's achievement of full human rights and full human responsibilities."[3] The FBI also had under surveillance the Freedom Now Party, formed in August 1963, and agents reported on Malcolm X's famous "Message to the Grass Roots" speech on November 10, 1963. This event, sponsored by GOAL in collaboration with the Northern Negro Grass Roots Leadership Conference, was held simultaneously with a more conservative conference convened by the Rev. C. L. Franklin. At one point, the two entities had been one, but when Franklin heard that black nationalists and members of GOAL were involved, he excluded them, thus prompting the Rev. Albert Cleage to form an alternative rally at King Solomon Baptist Church. Malcolm X, the Rev. Cleage, and radical journalist William Worthy were the main speakers. During his speech, Malcolm X mentioned that Congressman Adam Clayton Powell Jr. was in town, ostensibly to address those assembled by the Rev. Franklin at Cobo Hall. The Rev. Cleage, the only Detroiter Malcolm X cited, had emerged as one of the most outspoken and fearless black leaders in the city.

Peniel Joseph, in his book *Waiting 'Til the Midnight Hour: A Narrative History of Black Power in America*, summarizes this period of politics in Detroit with keen insight, noting, "Collectively, their political struggles placed them at the forefront of an informal coalition of militants whose intellectual thought, political manifestoes, and community organizing were early examples of Black Power."

In 1964, the Rev. Cleage was the gubernatorial candidate on the Freedom Now slate, which included his brother, Henry Cleage, who sought to unseat prosecutor Samuel Olsen, and Milton Henry, who ran against John Conyers Jr. Michigan wasn't the only promising base for the party, but, as in the other elections, the candidates were unsuccessful then, although remnants of the party and its outlook flowered several years later with the creation of the Black Slate, which would become significant in the election of future candidates, including Coleman Young, who was endorsed by the slate.

From the time in 1957 that Rosa Parks and her husband arrived in Detroit, the civil rights icon worked tirelessly for Conyers. Parks's commitment to fight Jim Crow—North or South—was unrelenting. There was less cohesiveness and commitment, however, in the Freedom Now Party. "Within two weeks of the election, the Rev. Cleage and Grace Boggs resigned from the party, having experienced a power shift to the Henry brothers [Milton, Richard, and Laurence] and their supporters."[4]

A more notable political development occurred when Coleman Young announced his bid for the Fourth District seat of the state senate. Young easily defeated community activist Nelis Saunders and joined Basil Brown, the only black legislator in the state senate. When the unrepentant Young ventured back to his neighborhood after the victory, he was greeted in the customary manner: "'Hey, motherfucker!'" Young recalled. "I turned to my offender, eyed him gravely, and set the record straight. 'From now on,' I said, 'it's *Senator* Motherfucker.'"[5]

Detroit activists were shocked when they heard that Malcolm X's house, in East Elmhurst, New York, had been firebombed on February 14, 1965. They were relieved that no one was injured, but they knew their plans to present him at a forum that evening had to be canceled. They were wrong. Stunning many of his followers, who were certain that he would be too traumatized to travel, Malcolm fulfilled his promise to speak. In his speech that evening at Ford Auditorium, he thanked Milton Henry and his Afro-American Broadcasting Company for inviting him and then addressed a broad range of subjects, from his recent trip to Africa and the Middle East to the Ku Klux Klan, excoriating the civil rights leaders for their ineffectiveness. He touched the audience when he mentioned Detroit. "I know Dearborn; you know I'm from Detroit. I used to live here in Inkster. And you had to go through Dearborn to get to Inkster. Just like driving through Mississippi when you got to Dearborn. Is it still that way? Well, you should straighten it out."[6] A week later, Malcolm (now El-Hajj Malik El-Shabazz), was gunned down at the Audubon Ballroom in Washington Heights, a neighborhood in uptown Manhattan.

Herman Ferguson, a member of Malcolm's Organization of Afro-American Unity, witnessed the assassination and recalled flashing yellow lights, possibly indicating that the entire incident was being filmed. "It does not seem that we only had Malcolm with us for about thirteen months after he left the Nation of Islam," Ferguson lamented. "Yet in that short period of time, Brother Malcolm cast his shadow over our Movement in so many ways. He changed our focus from civil rights to human rights. He influenced the birth of many Black Nationalist organizations (the Black Panther Party, the Republic of New Afrika, the Black Liberation Army, to name just a few). People who fight for their freedom from oppression and for national liberation know his name worldwide."[7]

About a month later in Alabama, another fighter for justice from Detroit was the target of racist assassins. Viola Liuzzo, thirty-nine, was brutally killed by men who hated her. Liuzzo, the only white female martyr of the civil rights movement, was emotionally troubled after watching clips of *Bloody Sunday* on television March 7, 1965, in which marchers were beaten fiercely by state troopers near the Edmund Pettus Bridge in Selma, Alabama. A mother of five children, married to a Teamsters union member, and a student at Wayne State University, Liuzzo, who owned a 1963 Oldsmobile, may have seemed an unlikely person to drive all the way to Selma to participate in the march. She was a member of the NAACP, and at Wayne State on March 12, she joined 250 other students at the federal building singing "We Shall Overcome."

This was her first real civil rights demonstration in the South. In Selma, she took on a number of duties, including welcoming people to the march and chauffeuring residents back to Selma after they had completed the fifty-four-mile march to Montgomery. She and Leroy Moton, a young black man, had just dropped off passengers in Selma and were on a return trip to Montgomery on Highway 80 when a car with Klan members and an FBI informant that had been following them pulled alongside. They opened fire. Liuzzo was shot twice in the head and the car careened into a ditch after Moton grabbed the wheel. The Klansmen inspected the damage and seeing blood all over the place concluded that both were dead and drove off. After they departed, Moton, covered with the dead Liuzzo's blood, climbed onto the highway and hailed a ride. Two weeks after her death, burnt crosses were found on the lawns of four Detroit homes, including the Liuzzo residence.

Among those attending Liuzzo's funeral on March 30 at Immaculate Heart of Mary Catholic church on the city's west side was Dr. Martin Luther King Jr. He was there for the high requiem mass on the second day of mourning proclaimed by Governor George Romney. Also present were civil rights leaders Roy Wilkins of the NAACP, James Farmer of CORE, the Rev. James Wadsworth, Congressman Charles Diggs, attorney Milton Henry, and "rival union presidents Walter Reuther of the United Auto Workers and James R. Hoffa of the Teamsters."[8]

Rather than attending the funeral services, students at Northern High School staged a walkout in protest of what they felt was an inferior education. The walkout began on April 6, 1966, after an editorial by honor student Chuck Colding in the student publication was censored. He had strongly criticized the school's subpar curriculum and the leadership of Principal Arthur Carty. The students demanded that Carty be removed, or they would not return after Easter recess. In response to the students' demand, School Superintendent Samuel Brownell "temporarily reassigned the principal to the central office, ostensibly to study the situation at Northern, and he placed the school under the authority of two high-level administrators."[9] On April 19 a school board meeting failed to resolve the crisis; in fact, it made things even worse by refusing to remove Carty. The next day, out of more than 2,307 enrolled at the school, only 183 students showed up. Students, including Colding, and members of the Wayne State University faculty set up a Freedom School under the direction of economist Karl Gregory. What began as a small disturbance at Northern soon spread throughout the city and commanded daily media coverage. Meanwhile, Dr. Gregory and his volunteers continued to hold sessions at the makeshift school and were soon joined by a few Northern teachers. Near the end of April, the students at Northern voted to return to class one day before a scheduled citywide boycott. This protest was just a first alarm; the dissent would simmer for months before it erupted again two years later.

Related to the issues raised by disgruntled students were salary complaints from teachers. Tension had grown considerably around the millage by which school districts were allocated funds. The demands presented by the Detroit Federation of Teachers were finally met, and the teachers rejoiced in a pay hike of $700, giving them an annual salary of $9,300. A strike was averted, wrote education authority Jeffrey Mirel, but the $7.5 million per year for salaries left the "school board in serious financial straits."[10] The school board took another blow when the millage proposal failed to get the votes it needed for a 2.5 mill tax increase. This was a measure favored by black voters but soundly rejected by white voters, which came as no surprise in the longstanding debate about the allocation of funds to the school districts. Mirel recalled: "Beginning in 1965, even though the state had channeled more resources to schools in the Motor City, the city's schools were still considerably underfunded. In 1967–68, despite serving 14.23 percent of students in the state, Detroit received only 11.37 percent of the state school aid."[11] Things would get worse, and the only alternative was a demand for another millage vote and, if that failed, a lawsuit.

18

THE MOTOR CITY IS BURNING

Ooh, the Motor City is burning, babe, there ain't a thing in the world that I can do
Don't you know, don't you know, the big D is burning, ain't a thing in the world lil' Johnny can do
My hometown burning down to the ground, worser than Vietnam
It started on 12th and Clairmount that morning, I just don't know what it's all about
It started on 12th and Clairmount that morning, I don't know what it's all about
The fire wagons kept comin', the snipers just wouldn't let them put it out . . .

—JOHN LEE HOOKER

In 1966, a small riot on Kercheval Street on the east side was a precursor to the major urban rebellion that rocked the city. To some degree, the discontent and volatility of the student eruptions were transferred to various militant groups and to people generally fed up with the systemic maladies that even the liberal promises and policies of Mayor Cavanagh could not cure. The spring offensive launched by the high school students evolved into a more heated showdown by the summer of 1966. The intersection of Kercheval and Pennsylvania streets was ground zero for the disturbance precipitated by the police, mainly by the notorious "Big Four" (a patrol car with four policemen inside) who accosted a group of black males on the corner, a gathering that to them, as in slavery times, constituted unlawful assembly. They were able to scatter some of the youths, but three of them were obstinate and determined to stand their ground. A commotion followed; it drew a crowd, forcing the police to call for backup. The presence of a hundred cops, many of them members of the TMU (Tactical Mobile Unit), a kind of SWAT team, was sufficient to momentarily halting an outbreak of violence. But soon Molotov cocktails and other objects began to rain on the police, allegedly thrown by members of the Afro-American Youth Movement. On the next evening, August 10, there was a tense standoff between the residents and the police, each side waiting for the other to make the next move. However, not a shot was fired, and rather than victims drenched in blood, both sides were soaked by a heavy rain that dampened the potential confrontation. These militants were not Black Panthers, who would emerge in the fall in California, but they expressed similar concerns. General Baker, Rufus Griffin, and Glanton Dowdell, participants in the Kercheval disturbance, were arrested, charged with carrying concealed weapons, and placed on five-year probation.[1]

There is a standard narrative of the rebellion that exploded in the early hours of July 23, 1967: A squad of vice police raided an after-hours club, a "blind pig," located on Twelfth Street and Clairmount. A celebration was under way for two Vietnam veterans who had recently returned home. More than eighty people were arrested. As the celebrants were being led into paddy wagons, an angry mob gathered and, spurred on by an agitator, began to hurl things at the police.

"It was so chaotic in the streets that I was unable to get my morning papers to deliver," recalled Conrad Mallett Jr.[2] He said his usual routine was to arrive early in order to have the *Detroit Free Press* to his customers by six in the morning. Ironically, three days before the rebellion erupted, his father, Conrad Mallett Sr., Mayor Cavanagh's executive secretary, had led a roomful of mayoral aides through a mock riot scenario. It was a profile complete with not only the conditions that might fulminate the disturbance, but also a plan of action. In many respects, Mallett was prescient.[3]

During the melee, somebody smashed the window of a nearby clothing store. The vandalism spread like wildfire as looters broke into store after store, except those marked SOUL by African American proprietors. The fires came next. "On Monday alone," remembered Arthur Johnson, then executive secretary of the local NAACP, "almost 500 fires were burning. Firefighters from as far away as eighty miles were called to the city."[4] Marcena Taylor, the city's first black firefighter and soon to be first battalion chief, took part in extinguishing the flames. Motown singer Martha Reeves said she was onstage at the Fox Theatre in the middle of "Dancing in the Street" when someone rushed in and told her the city was on fire. She went calmly to the stage, made her announcement, and she and the Vandellas quickly packed their bags and headed for the next gig, in New Jersey.[5]

In an attempt to halt the uprising, Johnson, along with good friend Damon Keith and Representative John Conyers, took to the streets. When they arrived at the epicenter of the disturbance, they were met with jeers and epithets from the crowd; the most stinging insults called them Uncle Toms. Conyers tried to placate the crowd with calming words blasting from a bullhorn, but that only incited them more, and eventually he and his cohorts were forced to run for cover. Unable to stem the tide of revolt, the men conferred and decided that the best thing to do was to head to police headquarters, where they were notified that the mayor, the governor, and Police Commissioner Ray Girardin had assembled to discuss what measures to take to stop the spread of chaos and destruction. "They were vacillating on whether or not federal troops should be brought in," Keith recalled. "At one point, President Johnson called in from Washington. They put him on speakerphone, and he talked about sending a force in to deal with the violence. That's how bad the situation had gotten."[6] It was so bad that even a civil rights icon like Rosa Parks, and her husband, Raymond, were not spared in the plunder and pillage. Parks, employed by Conyers, lived near the heart of the upheaval on a street that one day would bear her name. Not only was Raymond's barbershop looted and their car vandalized, "One of the troopers threatened to hit him on the head with a rifle," Parks said in an interview in 1980.[7] The Parkses had traveled a thousand miles from night riders in white sheets only to be confronted by their counterparts in blue uniforms.

Another associate of Keith, Johnson, and Conyers was Recorders Court judge George W. Crockett Jr., whose radical bona fides were incontrovertible. When hundreds of people arrested in the rebellion arrived in his courtroom, he once more demonstrated his unique way of administering justice. Lines of Detroit City buses, jammed with mostly black people charged with misdemeanors, encircled Recorders Court. With no more room at this location, the arrested were dispatched to Belle Isle, which after a while resembled a concentration camp. "I came into the limelight because I refused to set high bail to keep these people locked up," he told a writer. "I let them go on their personal promise to come back when I got ready for them. The other judges were fixing bail at $10,000. To show you how brash I was, I sent a letter to each of the judges telling them what the Eighth Amendment of the Constitution required and what the Michigan Constitution required on reasonable bail. I was mad as hell."[8] Bail, in Crockett's glossary, was a "security guarantee, not a tool of punishment and discrimination."

Jim Ingram, a columnist at the *Michigan Chronicle*, was not among those who stood in Crockett's court. He had been released from custody after being arrested along with his brother and two other companions for allegedly being at a gas station where a ban had been placed on the selling of gasoline. "We were taken to the 7th Precinct, I knew that because the ride was very short and the doors were flung open and somebody started yelling, 'Run niggers, run,'" Ingram said, recalling the incident for *Eyes on the Prize*, the documentary series on the civil rights movement.

An officer started slinging us out of the van. I couldn't see that clearly what was going on in front of me but I was the last one out of the van and I saw my brother in front of me being swung at. There were National Guardsmen on the right and police on the left and they were swinging rifles . . . and red pick ax handles and I was trying to dodge some of the swings. I don't know how I got through there with only being hit hard one time with a rifle barrel and that's what broke my right arm. We sort of ran I guess as fast as we could and tried to dodge those, some of them were really swinging quite wildly. . . . It was like I was going to myself, 'What have we done?' I mean they, we were guilty of Lord knows what in these guys' minds, you know. I mean they were treating us like we were hardened criminals or something. And all we were doing was attempting to buy some gas in a gas station. We were in the wrong place at the wrong time.[9]

Eleanor Josaitis was in the wrong place at the wrong time, too, according to her husband. He was pretty angry but mainly because his wife had dared to venture out into the chaos. At the time, she was an associate director of Focus: Hope, an organization that she had cofounded with Father William Cunningham to help the needy. "My husband and I had been down to the seminary where we had mass. We looked out the windows at all the smoke. The following day I came back and walked the streets with Father Cunningham. When I got home that night, that's the only time my husband ever said a harsh word to me in thirty-six years. He grabbed me by the shoulders: 'Do you know what you're doing?'"[10] During the five days of turmoil, forty-three people were killed, two white women among them, including Helen Hall. She was visiting Detroit on business from Illinois when she was allegedly killed by a sniper. Sniper fire, or the rumor of it, also took the life of the only black female who died in the riot, Tanya Blanding, who was four years old when she was killed by gunfire from a National Guard unit stationed in front of her house at 1756 West Euclid near Twelfth Street. Blanding was the rebellion's youngest victim, and her death intensified the anger and resentment in the black community. A bullet from a .50 caliber machine gun ripped through her tiny body from a guardsman who mistook the flash of a match from the apartment where she lived for sniper fire. More than two hundred mourners attended her funeral, and no criminal charges were brought against the guardsman.

Many whites, such as Joann Castle and her family, packed a few items and moved to safer turf outside the city limits. "An article appeared in . . . [the] newspaper saying that blacks were going to attack homes on Boston Boulevard," Castle recalled in an unpublished manuscript. "Don [her husband] and Patrick Mason set down an edict: women and children must leave. Our neighbors from Taylor were on vacation. They called to offer us the use of their home. Rosemarie and I drove to Taylor with all the young children and spent one night. There was no time for preparations: grab your pajamas and go. There were two of us and nine children. We were upset that we were sent from our homes and drove back the next morning. There were rumors of cars of blacks on the freeways moving toward the suburbs. In reality, the freeways were deserted."[11]

Aubrey Pollard, Carl Cooper, and Fred Temple were the only three victims to get any semblance of justice as victims of the rebellion, and theirs came as a result of community activists organizing a people's tribunal. A group of committed activists—Dan Aldridge, Ken Cockrel, Lonnie Peek, Glanton Dowdell, and others came together after the three men were killed by the police at the Algiers Motel on Virginia Park. They didn't need H. Rap Brown's fiery pronouncements; they were incensed enough by the "murders" and sought some form of retribution. When the word spread that Brown, the former chairman of the Student Non-violent Coordinating Committee was coming to town—mainly invited by Aldridge and his wife, Dorothy Dewberry—thousands assembled at the Dexter Avenue Theater to hear him. They were not disappointed. "There was a town called Motown, now it ain't no town," Brown began. "They used to call it Detroit, now they call it Destroyed. I hear ain't nothing left, but Motown sound. And if they don't come around, you gon' burn them down." He had the crowd cheering with approval. And then he touched on the three dead men: "What happened at the Algiers Motel must not be allowed to be repeated. The tribunal to be held must be made legal by the people. If the murderers are found guilty, and they should be, the brothers should carry out the execution."[12]

The tribunal was originally scheduled to be held at the Dexter Avenue Theater, but Brown's incendiary speech perhaps put a damper on that possibility, and a new venue was chosen: the Rev. Cleage's Central United Church of Christ on Linwood Avenue. On trial were a black security guard and police officers Ronald August, Robert Paille, and David Senak. They were charged with killing the three young men in cold blood. A roster of notables from the activist community was selected to fill the roles of the various courtroom officers: Milton Henry was assigned to be lead prosecutor; attorneys Sol Plafkin and Russell Brown were chosen to defend the accused; and with a freshly minted law degree, the judge and moderator was Ken Cockrel. In the jury box was author John Oliver Killens, who had worked with Malcolm X in writing the principles for the Organization of Afro-American Unity; bookstore owner Ed Vaughn; and the esteemed Rosa Parks. As expected, to a great cheer from the more than two thousand people in the church, the officers were found guilty. It was the most satisfaction the victims and their families would ever get from the tragedy, because the officers were later acquitted in the official trial.[13]

In the wake of the devastation, there were 43 dead citizens and 473 injured. More than 7,200 were arrested, a few for having mismatched shoes and naked mannequins. Some 2,500 stores were vandalized or torched. There were nearly 400 homeless families, and 412 buildings had to be demolished. The overall damages totaled between $40 and $80 billion. Among the losses were a popular nightspot, an irreplaceable bookstore, and nearly a block of homes after a gas station exploded. The police fingered one man, Michael Lewis, known as "Greensleeves" because of the apparel he wore that morning, as the culprit who started the civil disorder. A series of rallies and pressure from protesters was successful in getting his bail reduced, and eventually the charges were dropped, so the city fathers had to find somebody else to blame. For a while, bookstore owner Ed Vaughn was viewed as a suspect, even though he was out of town. They certainly couldn't blame Julius L. Dorsey, a fifty-five-year-old private guard who was posted in front of a market when he was accosted by two black men and a woman. "They demanded he permit them to loot the market. He ignored their demands. They began to berate him. He asked a neighbor to call the police. As an argument grew more heated, Dorsey fired three shots from his pistol into the air. The police radio reported: 'Looters, they have rifles.' A patrol car driven by a police officer and carrying three National Guardsmen arrived. As the looters fled, the law enforcement personnel opened fire. When the firing ceased, one person lay dead. He was Julius L. Dorsey."[14]

Months before the Kerner Commission released its report summarizing a summer of discontent primarily in Detroit and Newark, the city leaders had already embarked on some of the remedies proposed by the commission and, to some degree, anticipated the concern voiced by psychologist Kenneth Clark, who viewed riot-commission reports with a jaundiced eye. During his testimony before the Kerner Commission, he said they were like "Alice in Wonderland—with the same moving picture reshown over and over again, the same analysis, the same recommendations, and the same inaction."[15]

Mayor Cavanagh had placed too much stock in media reports about the city's tranquility. In the midst of the rebellion, still stunned, he called civic leaders together to form the New Detroit Committee. The following accounts were underscored by a gaggle of business leaders and corporate heads, none more prominent than J. L. Hudson Jr., president of Hudson's, the city's largest department store at that time and the third largest in the country behind Macy's in New York City and Marshall Field in Chicago. With Hudson at the helm, Cavanagh and his committee members were mindful of the criticism emanating from black community activists, who, as they expected, would not be invited to this blue-ribbon affair, which in the end could only apply Band-Aids and symbolic gestures to the systemic problem. "One well-known militant, Milton Henry, told the committee members that black nationalists should be involved in the reconstruction of the city. Reverend Cleage outlined areas in which cooperation between blacks and the committee was possible. Lorenzo Freeman, a WCO [West Central Organization], however, disagreed with the idea of an interracial committee, saying it was 'passé.'"16

To mollify the complaints from black militants, three were added to the nine so-called black moderates on the thirty-nine-member committee, with former councilman Bill Patrick as president. To some extent, the inclusion of Frank Ditto also helped to assuage some of the criticism about the lack of community activists on the committee. "Frank Ditto and his work on the volatile east side of Detroit gained national attention and was featured in *Time Magazine* (June 13, 1969) as an example of 'a black militant who can work in the upper echelons of white society while retaining their independence and the respect of the blacks on the street,'" observed Joann Castle, who was among those involved Catholics concerned about the city's welfare. "It may be that Detroit was unique in the way blacks and whites worked together in the late 1960s and early 1970s. There are many possible reasons for this, one being the city's working class history and its strong union base."17

A rebuke came from the traditional African American organizations, such as labor leaders, various ministers, the Cotillion Club, and the Booker T. Washington Business Association. Even the *Michigan Chronicle* was neglected in the call. New Detroit was barely off the ground before it was met with a headwind of disgruntled citizens, each organization screaming about exclusion. Out of this rumbling resentment evolved the City-wide

Citizens Action Committee (CCAC). Another organization that stood in opposition to CCAC was the Detroit Council of Organizations (DCO), headed by the Rev. Roy Allen, president of the Council of Baptist Ministers. "The DCO became the 'voice of the ins,'" wrote urbanologist Sidney Fine, "just as the CCAC was the 'voice of the outs.'"[18]

A bifurcated city experienced another chasm, this one between the black militants and the moderates, who were ascendant, in such organizations as the Wolverine Bar Association, the NAACP, and eventually the DCO, which claimed to represent some thirty organizations and an impressive number of black Detroiters. The DCO quickly commanded the top political leadership in the city. For the most part, this was a familiar division, with the militants expressing separatist tendencies and the other side supporting the integrationist solutions.

New Detroit struggled to find some middle ground, though it leaned toward the CCAC, which soon was uplifted by a check for $85,000 from the Interreligious Foundation for Community Development. Despite this financial support, which allowed the Rev. Cleage to invest in the Black Star Co-op, where African dresses, dashikis, and other garments were produced and sold primarily to African American nationalists, the CCAC failed to gain the traction necessary to overcome attacks "from traditional civil rights groups . . . and to elicit the support of the masses of black Detroiters."[19]

Neither the DCO nor the CCAC had the answer to the city's pressing social and economic problems. None of these makeshift organizations, even when cobbled together as a coalition, could solve the dismal condition of the 24 percent of young black men between the ages of sixteen and twenty-four who at the time of the rebellion were unemployed. Their resentment was especially sharp because while the bottom economic rung had fallen off the economic ladder, those on the rungs above them were making headway. When Damon Keith was nominated by President Johnson as a federal judge for the Eastern District of Michigan, they were pleased. He was greeted with cheers like those that Geraldine Bledsoe Ford had received one year before, when she was elected to Detroit Recorder's Court, the first African American woman judge in Michigan. With Judge Wade McCree on the bench in the US Court of Appeals for the Sixth District, it seemed that Michigan blacks might finally see some justice. However, there wasn't much of that for the 678 African Americans arrested during the rebellion; 64 percent of them were charged with looting and faced time in jail or a fine, though most of them had no criminal record. If they were lucky, they ended up in George Crockett's courtroom where leniency abounded.

Two years after the rebellion, Judge Crockett extended his unique sense of justice once more when he was summoned in the middle of the night and immediately convened a session of his court at police headquarters. A police officer had been shot and killed outside the Rev. Franklin's New Bethel Baptist Church, where black nationalists, principally members of the Republic of New Afrika (RNA), were holding a convention. The police stormed the church and arrested more than 140 activists, holding them incommunicado for hours. Crockett ordered the release of 130 of those arrested, ruling that their detention was in violation of Michigan law. Even William Calahan, the Wayne County prosecutor, had to accede to this ruling. Like Judge Bruce M. Wright in New York City, who earned the nickname Turn-'em-loose Bruce for a similar attitude toward mass arrests and high bail as a tool of suppression, Crockett was hated by the police, so much so that they organized a campaign to impeach him. A bumper sticker said it all—SOCK IT TO CROCKETT! He was denounced by the governor and reprimanded by both houses of the Michigan legislature. But the push for impeachment, which began with the step of bringing Crockett before a Judicial Tenure Commission, backfired when the commission upheld the judge's position that the blanket arrests were illegal.

If Crockett had opened a fissure in the criminal-justice system, attorney Ken Cockrel drove a wedge into it after he was retained to defend Al Hibbit, who was one of the men accused in the shooting death of Police Officer Ronald Czapski near New Bethel Baptist. Two other RNA members, Chaka Fuller and Rafael Viera, were also arrested and charged. In his defense of Hibbit, Cockrel established himself as one of the brilliant legal minds in the country. He also demonstrated that his courtroom demeanor wasn't limited to mellifluous colloquy. When his client's bail was doubled, he called the judge a racist monkey, a honkie dog fool, and a thieving pirate. Cited for contempt of court, he replied that his language was consistent with that spoken about similar subjects in his community. During his own trial, Cockrel was defended by his law partners, and among the witnesses called was Professor Geneva Smitherman, a linguist, whose testimony provided context for Cockrel's expressive language. Eventually all the charges were dropped, and Cockrel rose to another legal level with his successful defense of Hibbit, mainly by attacking the jury-selection process, asserting that it denied his client a jury of his peers, that is, working-class African Americans. Another jury was impaneled, with a black majority, and Hibbit and the other defendants were exonerated.

Cockrel and his law partner Justin Ravitz, used a similar call for a jury of peers in defense of James Johnson, a factory worker, who was accused of killing three fellow workers. Again, Cockrel got the jury he wanted, jurors with work experience in factories. Johnson was presented as a man with deep psychological problems stemming from the time in his childhood when he witnessed the dismembered body of his cousin after he was lynched by a white mob. Later, during the trial, Cockrel took the jurors on a tour of the plant so they could see for themselves how dangerous Johnson's job was. This was the coup de grace that freed Johnson. Cockrel argued that the oppressive work conditions led to Johnson's mental breakdown. Not long afterward, Cockrel's legal finesse would once again command media attention.

The crack in the criminal-justice system applied by Crockett and widened by Cockrel had been long in the making. Both men were important in the evolution of Detroit's radical period that came in the wake of several key developments in 1968, a memorable year for the world and the city. On a global scale, the war in Vietnam occupied most of the headlines, and even more so the often violent confrontations with those who opposed it. The Tet Offensive by the Viet Cong at the start of the year ignited a wave of protests throughout Europe, most dramatically in Paris. There were the assassinations of Dr. King in April and Robert Kennedy two months later. King's death triggered riots throughout the nation. On April 4, 1968, everything changed, said Ron Lockett, executive director of the Northwest Activities Center, who at that time was a student at Eastern High School and a Black Power advocate. "We took over the school," he remembered. "Two students climbed the flagpole and took down the Stars and Stripes. Our protest was so strong that when we came to school after the break the name of the school had been changed to Martin Luther King, Jr. High School."[20] Adding to the yearlong turbulence was the police violence at the Democratic National Convention that August in Chicago. It was against this grim backdrop that a convergence of student activism, wildcat strikes by black workers, and the founding of grassroots organizations gave Detroit the leading role on the nation's black political stage. At the forefront of this energized base of reinvigorated activism were the students at Wayne State University, including Ron Lockett, Ron Hunt, Victor Stewart, Glenn Shelton, Lonnie Peek, Gene Cunningham, Sylvia Williams, Geoffrey Jacques,

Homer Fox, Alice Tait, Arthur Bowman, Reggie Carter, Kathy Gamble, and Ozell Bonds.

"In the autumn of 1968," wrote Dan Georgakas and Marvin Surkin in their thorough discussion of the era, "Wayne State University had almost 35,000 students. Most of them lived at home and most of them worked."[21] The university, composed of eleven colleges, including the highly nonconformist, politicized cadre of students at Monteith College, was basically a commuter school with few students living in the few dormitories. Most of the students were white. Although the black students, numbering between 2,500 and 3,500, at this urban university, located in the middle of an African American community, represented 10 percent of the student population on campus—a percentage much higher than at the University of Michigan and Michigan State—it was still minuscule compared to the percentage of blacks in the surrounding population, and while these students were admitted, too many of them did not graduate.

The Daily Collegian, the student newspaper, was a lily-white operation with little social or political relevance for the black students. Nor were conditions any better in the classroom, where a narrow Eurocentric curriculum was being taught. "We were a tiny minority in the classrooms and virtually forgotten when it came to seeing our history and culture represented in the syllabus," said Gene Cunningham, who would succeed John Watson as the editor of the *South End*, the renamed *Daily Collegian*.[22] The long, hot summer of '67 had to some degree emboldened the black students that fall when they returned to classes. By the fall of '68, their outlook and determination gained more traction—and more students. With this new sense of power and President William Keast and his administration on the ropes, fearful of having disorders on Wayne's campus like those that had been developing elsewhere since the spring, they organized themselves and began to issue a number of demands, including an increase in black student enrollment, a black students' union, and the creation of a Black Studies department. These demands were eagerly promoted in the newly revamped, radicalized *South End* under the direction of Watson, who was ably assisted by his white managing editor, the intrepid Nick Medvecky, an ex-paratrooper and veteran political activist.[23] With Watson, his hair uncombed for months and his glasses held together by a wad of white tape, and the skinny Medvecky at the wheel, the *South End* maintained a vital link to grassroots organizations, such as the local branch of the Black Panther Party, and to the growing army of young blacks in the city's plants, especially at Dodge Main in Hamtramck. Main was a bubbling cauldron of protest about work conditions and dissatisfaction with the UAW, which, during the most heated exchanges with black workers, was said to stand for "U Ain't White." In effect, the struggle taking place on campus mirrored the uprising in the plants, and there would soon come a time when the students and workers would be one and the same, despite the *South End* banner that declared ONE CLASS CONSCIOUS WORKER IS WORTH 100 STUDENTS! An effective bridge between the students and the militant workers was the *Inner City Voice*, where Watson had sharpened his ideological perspective and journalistic skills before arriving at the *South End*. For a while they coexisted, sometimes sharing stories just as they shared a revolutionary objective.

As the students and several radical professors began their negotiations with President Keast, his shock of gray hair and tailored suits embellishing his New England demeanor, and Arthur Johnson, then a vice president of community affairs, it was agreed that an Association of Black Students would be formed with Lonnie Peek as the chair. Meanwhile, plans were under way to establish a black studies program, with the students to be given a considerable voice in its planning, staff, and faculty.

19

OUR THING IS DRUM!

Concomitant with the upsurge of radical developments on campus, workers in the plants had pushed ahead with the formation of the Dodge Revolutionary Union Movement or DRUM. The radical labor tradition imbued in the white union movement finally, on May 2, 1968, connected with black workers. It would have been perfectly apropos if blues singer Joe L. Carter had rendered lines from "Please Mr. Foreman" when some four thousand black and white workers at Dodge Main staged a wildcat strike together, protesting a speedup on the assembly line. "Please, Mr. Foreman, slow down this assembly line," Carter sang, "I don't mind workin' but I do mind dying." The refrain from the Chrysler bosses was not blue but pink as a disproportionate number of black workers were fired, including General Gordon Baker Jr. In a letter to

Chrysler Corporation three days after his dismissal, Baker refused to allow his discharge to go unanswered. "Even though you have falsely placed the banner of leadership of a wildcat strike upon my shoulders I shall wear it proudly," he wrote. "For what more noble banner could a black working man bear? In this day and age under the brutal oppression reaped from the backs of black workers, the leadership of a wildcat strike is a badge of honor and courage."[1] Rather than ridding itself of a nuisance and silencing Baker's powerful voice, the company inadvertently gave him a larger forum and a leadership position that would be a driving force in the various iterations of the Revolutionary Union Movement.

In the beginning was DRUM, and among its sixteen demands were an end to racism in the UAW, revision of the grievance procedure, elimination of all safety and health hazards in the auto industry, and a more vigorous fight by the union against production-line speedups and ever increasing output quotas. "The companies should double the size of their work force to meet the present workload."[2] In July, DRUM called for another strike at Dodge Main, and more than three thousand black workers stayed home for two days. The strike gave the organization the publicity it needed to spark the formation of other rallies and strikes. Suddenly, there was CADRUM (GM's Cadillac plant), FRUM (Ford), ELRUM (Chrysler Eldon Avenue plant), and even an UPRUM, a UPS contingent. There was such a rash of strikes and spinoffs from DRUM that an umbrella group was forged— the League of Revolutionary Black Workers (LRBW). "My role as one of the founders was to see that League policies were implemented and to hold it all together with all the personalities and egos," recalled Michael Hamlin.[3] The other founding members of the league, who composed the Executive Committee, were General Baker, Ken Cockrel, John Watson, Luke Tripp, John Williams, and Chuck Wooten. In June 1969, the league was incorporated, and four months later, it opened its headquarters at

179 Cortland in Highland Park. It was off to a promising start, accelerated by ancillary movements from students and white radicals, including Sheila Murphy, Jack Russell, Joann Castle, John and Leni Sinclair, Ron Glotta, and Frank Joyce. Hamlin had his hands full trying to harmonize the differing tendencies and ameliorate the frictions within the ever expanding League. As it is for any mass-based organization, it was impossible to control the flow of folks who congregated at headquarters or showed up at the various rallies and demonstrations. Each member of the Executive Committee, for example, was under extreme pressure— hounded by external problems from Chrysler with its subpoenas and the police with their harassment, and internally by the inability to detect or prevent infiltration by agents provocateurs from law enforcement agencies. Then there were the personal fights and bickering, the blatant male chauvinism, the abuse and attacks on women, and the antagonistic behavior of black members toward any whites, however well meaning, who dared step into headquarters. "We had instances of rape, the impregnation of a sixteen year old honor student who had joined our youth arm and so forth," Hamlin lamented. "So you could imagine the opportunities that gave official law enforcement to come down on us, on top of the internal demoralization this caused. And I couldn't be there all the time to keep order among these elements."[4]

For a while these internal contradictions were minimal and didn't hamper the league's growth, which extended all the way to Italy, where its strategies and tactics were admired and appropriated by Italian workers. "Outwardly," wrote Ernie Allen (Mkalimoto) who joined the league in 1970 and served as its director of political education, "the League operation was extremely impressive. Even those with prior political experience could not help but be moved by the seriousness, dedication, and camaraderie of League members who followed impossible schedules to get the job done."[5] Interestingly, in a city crowded with an amalgam of differing organizations, the league maintained a relatively harmonious relationship with them. "We existed side by side with the Black Panthers and other organizations in the black community like the RNA [Republic of New Afrika]," General Baker told Bob Mast. "We pretty much dominated the politics in Detroit."[6] That "domination" had more to do with the power of the personalities at the top of the league than with the size of the organization, which never exceeded more than a hundred active, ready-for-the-ramparts members.

In addition, as Allen notes in his thoroughgoing analysis of the strengths and weaknesses of the league, it was succumbing to a "false sense of organizational success in other areas: the creation of the League film 'Finally Got the News,' the proliferation of LRBW offices in the Detroit area, participation in a book project which had engaged hundreds of liberal whites, as well as growing media attention which the League was attracting nationwide."[7] Another illusion of success arrived with the money James Forman had collected from the Black Manifesto. No longer affiliated with the Black Panther Party and only marginally connected to SNCC, Forman was content to rest on the laurels he had earned as a leader in the civil and human rights struggle. What beckoned him to Detroit was a phone call from Mike Hamlin and the National Black Economic Development conference, led by the eminent minister Lucius Walker, to be held at Wayne State University under the auspices of the Interreligious Foundation for Community Organization (IFCO). Forman was invited to speak at the conference by Dorothy Dewberry, a colleague of his from SNCC. Simultaneously, an invitation was extended by Hamlin to him to observe the inner workings of the league. Meeting with Hamlin and league members was a priority for Forman, but after several sessions with them, it was decided that the conference, (later known as BEDC), could be a useful event to attend in order to seek funding to finance some of the league's objectives. "Since the conference was being staged by 'Christians,'" Forman wrote, "we felt it was the right occasion to demand reparations from the Christian churches for the centuries of exploitation and oppression which they had inflicted on black people around the world."[8]

On April 26, 1969, about the same time that the league was in the early stages of consolidation at the conference, Forman delivered his Manifesto. A week later in New York City at Riverside Church, he delivered the same address, which received far more notice and notoriety there. After a lengthy discourse on racism and exploitation, and how black workers helped to build the most industrialized nation in the world, Forman cut to the chase. "We are therefore demanding of the white Christian churches and Jewish synagogues, which are part and parcel of the system of capitalism, that they begin to pay reparations to black people in this country," Forman recited. "We are demanding $500,000,000 . . . this total comes to 15 dollars per nigger."[9]

According to the Manifesto, the money would be earmarked for television stations and publishing houses in four cities with only Detroit mentioned in both categories; a southern land bank; a National Black Labor Strike and Defense Fund; and an International Black Appeal, among other initiatives. The Interreligious Foundation for Community Organization (IFCO), headed by the Rev. Lucius Walker, was designated to distribute the funds in accordance with the mandate. The Manifesto was signed by a number of well-known Detroiters, who constituted a steering committee, including league members Luke Tripp, John Watson, John Williams, Ken Cockrel, Chuck Wooten, and Mike Hamlin. Other notables were Daniel Aldridge, Howard Fuller (Owusu Sadaukai), Julian Bond, Vincent Harding, Lucius Walker, Peter Bernard, Howard Moore, and Renny Freeman of New Detroit. Fannie Lou Hamer was the only woman listed.

Somewhere along the way, things fell apart. Forman announced, "Many forms of support that we thought would be forthcoming failed to materialize. Key to this was the retreat of IFCO from support of the Black Manifesto."[10] The actual amount of money funneled to the League by BEDC remains a mystery, though whatever funds were obtained were more than the organization had on hand, and the creation of Black Star Publishing was a major recipient of the funds. Some of the money was invested in the film, *Finally Got the News*, that was to promote the League, which it did with a modicum of success. A larger sum was piped into the publishing company overseen by a white printer, Fredy Perlman. A black woman, Helen Jones, was in charge of the day-to-day operation, and assisted by former SNCC member Monroe Sharp who had returned to the states from Tanzania to work with the League. Other than posters, placards, flyers, and pamphlets, the most costly endeavor was the printing of Forman's book *The Political Thought of James Forman* that was not enthusiastically received by the rank and file members. Many of those who criticized the book had not read it, basing their responses on others' opinions. Those critics reported that it was a waste of time and money, and that Forman's ideas at that time were imprecise with no clear direction nor analysis.

When assessing the positive and negative aspects of the League of Revolutionary Black Workers, the valiant efforts of the workers and students should not be minimized. It would be disingenuous to ignore the organization's faults—its structural problems, the tension created by its varied social and political composition, the recurring disconnect between the leadership and the rank and file, and the trouble that arose from the Black Manifesto and its bounty of funds—even though it provided the league with temporary funding that freed members from soliciting and helped generate longer-term financial support. These issues came to a head by 1971 with the "Easter Purges." The league's Executive Board voted unanimously to expel seven members, charging them with insubordination and alleging that their spouses were "security risks." "Principled criticisms of the organization, as well as measures designed to address its fundamental problems, had been offered; the only 'counter' which the EB [Executive Board] could find in its political repertoire was that of 'hardline policy,'" wrote Ernie Allen, one of the seven purged. "The effects of that policy on the rank-and-file as well as on the EB itself constituted the immediate causes leading to the break-up of LRBW."[11] Complicating matters was the presence of white women, the wives of Mike Hamlin and Ken Cockrel, which didn't please the black women in the organization. There may have been a special dispensation for Jane Fonda, who moved to Detroit in 1971 to participate in the Winter Soldier investigation, in which Vietnam veterans were asked to testify about the atrocities they experienced. Fonda was introduced to Cockrel, learned of the league and its mission, and expressed an interest in working to help them. Nick Medvecky, who was John Watson's managing editor during his tenure at the *South End*, recalled a trip that he, Watson, and Cockrel made to San Francisco in 1972, which must have occurred after the series of letters between Cockrel and Fonda. During that trip, Fonda and Donald Sutherland were shooting *Steelyard Blues*, Medvecky wrote. "Jane and others passed us onto a variety of left contacts in or associated to that industry."[12]

According to Patricia Bosworth, Cockrel told Fonda, "There is no one in the movement, no real activist, who's a movie star. Stay with it, we need you. Own your leadership."[13] They held each other in high regard as indicated in letters between them. Fonda had received a film treatment from Cockrel on the subject of drugs, but she told him that her friend actor Donald Sutherland had found it "unprofessional." Still, she was interested in knowing more about the Black Workers Congress (BWC). In his reply, Cockrel expressed his excitement in hearing from her, and though he was disappointed about the assessment of the treatment, he must have been thrilled to see Fonda's political references to Cheddi Jagan of Guyana. He explained to her the "many internal changes" that had occurred within the BWC and "as for the film project, your assessment is absolutely correct, but that situation is no longer of any import, at least not in the context of Black Star Productions. Moreover, I regret that I was in such situation with the shit being so 'untogether.'"[14]

The collapse of the league, in the eyes of General Baker, was mainly the result of trying to do too many things and losing focus on organizing in the plants. "We had Black Star Productions, Black Star Printing, two Black Star bookstores, Black Conscious Library, and all these other facilities we had gathered around us," he recalled. "In the split we lost our intellectual wing that we relied heavily on to be our spokesmen . . . we went on a kind of retreat. We had to."[15]

Call it a retreat, a strategic withdrawal, or just another path away from the "hard line" for some of the key players in the league. While Baker maintained his ties to the workers, Watson raised dogs, Cockrel geared up for a successful run for City Council, Hamlin and his closest comrades formed the Black Workers Congress, and Forman went back to school and did some union organizing in the nation's capital. In the wake of their departure, there were only the remnants of their Camelot-like moment when a generation was convinced that the revolution was just around a corner in Detroit and elsewhere, when there was hope that a Black United Front would be the answer to the stultifying retrenchment. There were a number of accomplishments the league could document as part of its legacy, including its impact on the UAW's racist policies and the promotion of African Americans to leadership posts. It instilled in the youth a more class-conscious outlook and a new appreciation of working-class culture. And by its endeavor and experience, it highlighted mistakes to be avoided in the future.

20

UNDER DURESS FROM STRESS

As the sun was setting in 1971 for the League of Revolutionary Black Workers, it was rising in several sections of Detroit's social, political, and economic firmament. Things were looking promising for Motown with the release of Marvin Gaye's breakthrough recording "What's Going On." And African Americans were making some headway in the upper echelons of the big three—GM, Ford, and Chrysler—as well as automobile dealers. If the league was in a political retreat, Gaye, his emotional state always an issue, was looking for a refuge from the public after the death of his singing partner, Tammi Terrell, which rocked his musical future. When he proposed his concept album *What's Going On* as the solution to societal problems and his own troubled condition, Gordy and his management team resisted. They said the songs were too long, too formless, and would find no appeal or traction with listeners, even his most devoted fans. Gaye told them that either they'd release the album, or he'd never record for them again. "The ploy worked," wrote his biographer David Ritz. "Marvin won, and the winnings were bigger than even he had imagined. His first self-produced, self-written album altered not only his career but his very life."[1] The album's narrative, Gaye's antiwar message, and his plea for peace both in the world and his troubled life were all the therapy he needed to recapture his musical genius, to reclaim his place among the best soul singers and composers of his generation. Curtis Mayfield, Isaac Hayes, David Porter, and others had provided the funky wedge, but Gaye supplied the passionate cry, the urgency that gives his music an eternal presence.

Whatever the revolutionary content of the Motown sound, it meant little to the machinations of the Detroit Police Department. There was a foreboding uptick in police violence with the creation of a secret unit in the city's police department, the dreaded death squad STRESS, an acronym for Stop the Robberies and Enjoy Safe Streets. This undercover decoy squad was fully mobilized and operating with alarming and frightening effect. Each evening extended the pattern of ever more disturbing assaults on the black community, particularly its young men. Mayor Roman Gribbs, an ex-sheriff of Wayne County, who had defeated black candidate Richard Austin in 1969, and Police Chief John Nichols were determined to reduce crime in the city by brute force, even if it meant reducing the black population. During STRESS's first year as a death squad–cum–SWAT team, the city's police force had the highest number of civilian killings per capita of any American police department.[2] During its three and a half years of existence, STRESS officers shot and killed 24 men, 22 of them African American. So Gaye's question was never more apt. In effect, one third of the homicides were committed by STRESS, which represented only 2 percent of the total department. To justify these numbers, which included the body counts of more than five hundred raids without search warrants, the unit's commander, James Barron, cited the dangers the *cops* encountered when invading people's homes. Among the STRESS officers, none was as seemingly problematic as crew chief Raymond Peterson. Before he was assigned to STRESS, he had amassed a record number of complaints. During his first two years on the squad, he took part in nine killings and three nonfatal shootings.[3] Bullets from Peterson's gun killed five of the victims. No charges were brought in any of these cases. Two years later, in 1973, criminal charges were brought against him after he shot and killed a man—in self-defense, he claimed. But the knife recovered at the scene belonged to Peterson. Peterson was acquitted of the charge, but he was dismissed from the police force after the trial. In 2012, the name Raymond Peterson appears in *Unity*, a quarterly published on behalf of retired police officers and firemen, praising the publication and submitting a donation.[4]

On at least one occasion, the STRESS unit wasn't content to be gunning down black citizens. STRESS officers were cruising down Rochester Street on the west side on March 9, 1972, when they observed a man carrying a gun enter an apartment building. They were not aware that the man was an off-duty Wayne County deputy sheriff on his way to a card game with fellow officers. Thinking they had stumbled upon an illegal gambling establishment, the officers barged through a door that was left partly ajar. The deputies thought the intruders were there to rob them and opened fire. According to tenants in the building, some thirty shots were fired. One of the bullets struck Deputy Henry Henderson, forty, who died an hour later at Detroit General Hospital. Four other deputies were wounded, but none of them seriously.

Detroit police commissioner John F. Nichols and Wayne County sheriff William Lucas, the first black to hold the post, took charge of the investigation. They told the press the shoot-out resulted from a tragic misunderstanding. "This could have happened to any police unit," Nichols said, "and it could have turned out the same way."[5]

Anti-STRESS feelings reached their peak on December 4, 1972, when four undercover cops engaged in a shoot-out with John Percy Boyd, Hayward Brown, and Mark Bethune. They were basically concerned with the eradication of heroin in the black community, an issue of serious concern that the law enforcement agencies were giving no serious attention. "Johnny, Hayward, and Ibo [Bethune] were at my house when they planned to take the drug dealers out," said poet/musician Sadiq Bey. "They were determined to rid the community of the heroin dealers."[6] If the officers were there on a stakeout, their attention was soon riveted on the three armed young men, and in the exchange of gunfire, four of the STRESS officers were wounded.

This prompted a strong reaction from the Detroit Police Department. Almost immediately, the police began conducting one of the largest manhunts in the city's history. Practically everyone associated with the three, especially their family members, were targeted, harassed, and had the doors to their homes kicked in. Most egregious were the police assaults on the families of John Boyd and his first cousin, Hayward Brown. One evening when John Clore, Boyd's stepbrother, returned to his home, it had been ransacked. He then went to the home of his parents, Dorothy and Siegel Clore on Charest on the city's east side. About two hours later, without warning or a search warrant, five uniformed police officers crashed through the front door, barging in with their rifles pointed at the family members. Behind them came ten more officers, and while some held the family at gunpoint, the others searched the house and seized two unloaded hunting rifles and shotguns owned by Siegel Clore. According to the lawsuit filed by Dorothy Clore, her son was forced to lie on the floor handcuffed while he was searched. Subsequently, he, his girlfriend, and his stepsister, Melba Boyd, were arrested and held for several hours without being charged. "The suit said that later the same night Siegel Clore received a telephone call from a man who identified himself as a Detroit police officer and threatened to blow up the Clore home."[7] Hayward Brown's family was also targeted and harassed when the home belonging to his mother, Odessa Brown, was raided and searched without a warrant.

The illegal procedures against the Clores and the Browns were among the fifty to one hundred complaints and documented cases brought against the police department. Durwood Furshee, a fifty-seven-year-old unemployed security guard, would also have been a complainant had he not died of police gunfire after they stormed his home on December 8. Believing they were a gang of robbers breaking into his house, he opened fire and was killed in a barrage of bullets from the STRESS officers.

Three weeks later, on December 27, another shoot-out with Boyd, Brown, and Bethune occurred, and this time one officer, Robert Bradford, was killed, and another, Robert Dooley, was wounded. Some accounts mistake who was killed and who was wounded, but as Patrolman Doug Heady later recalled the incident, upon receiving a radio run that day that announced that two persons in front of 9234 Schaffer, possibly police officers, had been shot, "My partner Bob Walden and myself were the first car there. Bob Dooley was lying in the street by their car . . . he had been shot several times. Bob Bradford was lying face down in the driveway, and had been shot several times . . . Bob Bradford died in my arms that night."[8] Officer Dooley informed the police who the assailants were, and a massive alert went out for their arrest. Later, that evening, Police Commissioner Nichols appeared on television and described the three as "mad-dog killers." After weeks of holding the black community hostage, the police announced in January 1973 that Brown had been captured and beaten severely when they brought him to the precinct. Meanwhile, it was widely reported that Boyd and Bethune had eluded the police and, disguised as a priest and nun, escaped to Atlanta.

While Brown was awaiting trial, Boyd was killed by a police officer on February 23, along with his half-brother, Owen Winfield. Four days later, on the rooftop of Morris Brown College, Bethune was shot and wounded by the police, and then reportedly took his own life.

Retained to defend Brown, Cockrel sprang into action. In typical fashion, he flipped the script. Instead of Brown on trial, it was STRESS. After a series of trials on more than a dozen charges, Brown was acquitted. When the verdict was announced, the courtroom was seized with bedlam as spectators cheered and raised their fists in triumph. Brown's acquittal meant that his dead partners were also technically freed, little consolation for the Boyd and Brown families. They could take pride in the fact that the three were instrumental in derailing STRESS and what may have been their overall plan to allow the drugs to flow thereby creating a multitude of craving addicts to prey on their neighbors and families.[9]

Cockrel's victorious court battles, from New Bethel to Brown, made him a highly regarded public figure, one who, if he played his cards right, could one day become mayor, although that option would have to be delayed a few years. The politically savvy Coleman Young was gathering his campaign forces to challenge Nichols and to make certain that STRESS, having left 22 fatalities in its murderous wake, all but one an African American, by any other name would never again run rampant, arresting and harassing innocent citizens. About the same time that Brown was celebrating his liberation, Young was ready for a serious mayoral bid, though Richard Austin was being touted as the odds-on favorite to be the city's first African American mayor, if he chose to relinquish his post as Michigan's first black secretary of state. He chose not to run. This left Young with the opening he needed, but there was still the formidable John Nichols. When the primaries were over, Young had come in second, so in Detroit's nonpartisan mayoral system, the two were set to go head-to-head, and the issue of the police and its poor relations with the black community was a point Young drove home during his campaign.

The election came down to race—a black man versus a white man; one labeled anti-cop for opposing police lawlessness, the other epitomizing the city's police. There was no gray area between Coleman Young and John Nichols, only black against blue. Councilman Mel Ravitz, no relationship to Cockrel's law partner, Justin Ravitz, was another candidate, who with UAW backing could not be taken lightly. But after a dismal showing in the primary, Ravitz stepped aside, and the union had no other choice but Young. "On election day, I became the goddamn mayor of Detroit," Young said in his typically colorful language. "There wasn't a single precinct in the city that was close—Nichols took the white ones and I took the black ones—but the final count fell within four percent, with 234,000 votes for me and 216,000 for the commissioner. To top it off, my victory was accompanied by that of my running mate, the new city charter."[10] Young wasn't naive about his victory, feeling that the city was his because the whites no longer wanted it. He relished the opportunity, even if he had been given an empty bag. Diana Ross, topping the charts with "Touch Me in the Morning," sang his praises at Cobo Hall, and the party was on—that is, until he delivered his acceptance speech. He told all the dope pushers, rip-off artists, and muggers that it was "time to leave Detroit. Hit Eight Mile Road. I don't give a damn if you're black or white, or they wear Superfly suits or blue uniforms with silver badges. Hit the road."[11]

This was the beginning of Young's mandate, which would be relentless for the next twenty years. His strong language about getting out of Dodge, that a new marshal was in town, was questionable, since white flight had been under way for more than a decade. It was noteworthy that Detroit had its first black mayor and the City Council had its first black female member, Erma Henderson. Winning a council seat, even an unprecedented one—and later becoming its first black president for twelve years—was almost routine for Henderson, since she had learned so much about the process as a campaign manager in William Patrick's successful race in 1957. Most useful for Patrick was Henderson's long and deep relationship to Detroit's black community, which began in 1918, when she arrived with her parents from Pensacola, Florida. She was a product of the city's public schools, a student leader at Eastern High School, and a graduate of Wayne State University, from which she later earned a master's degree in social work. As a social worker, she expanded her already impressive contacts, which would be crucial in her endeavors as a public servant. The new black mayor and councilwoman had been friends since childhood.[12]

As the political glass ceiling was cracking, blacks were also making their way into the city's corporate hierarchy. In January 1971, the bold and charismatic Philadelphian Leon Sullivan, having flexed his innovation muscles in the realm of employment and civil rights, was named the first African American on General Motors's board of directors. A year later, Jerome "Brud" Holland, who had distinguished himself in many endeavors, including serving as ambassador to Sweden during the Nixon administration, joined the board at Chrysler. In 1973 Clifton Wharton, the president of Michigan State University, was elected as Ford's first black board member. At this time, the small group of African American automobile dealers included Ed Davis, the nation's first black car dealer, with a Chrysler-Plymouth dealership on Dexter Avenue; Clarence Carter, GM's first black car dealer in Detroit; and Nathan Conyers, the brother of Rep. John Conyers, with his Ford dealership on Fourteenth Street and West Grand Boulevard. They were hoping those appointments would improve sales and provide the help that they needed to prevent more black dealerships from closing their doors. One plan to prevent the failures was the formation of the National Black Automobile Dealers Association. Robert Hill, owner of one of the first black dealerships in the West, in Compton, California, became executive director. Hill quickly sought funding from the Commerce Department to get the organization functioning, but it was too late to salvage Davis, the pioneer, who shuttered his operation in 1971. Davis, like the other dealers, began to realize that blacks don't necessarily buy from black dealers. The dealerships owned by whites were not doing that well either. Moreover, there were the challenges of black customers qualifying for credit and the limited number of "marginal risks" allowed a dealership. "The consumer had to have confidence in the merchant, which meant the merchant must establish credibility," said Hill. "My credibility is affected when I can't get the customer financing and another dealer can. It's affected when I can't service his car and the other guy can. The consumer responds to that, whether he's black or white."[13] There were sundry other bumps in the road for black dealerships—management deficiencies, financing, and location—but when Davis closed shop, Hill may have known that the handwriting was on the wall.

By the time Young celebrated his first year in office, STRESS was gone, and so was Motown, which in 1972 ceased operations in the city and moved to Los Angeles. With the city and the nation reeling from an economic downturn, Berry Gordy was among the city's entrepreneurs who began to consider other venues and ventures for his investments and aspirations. Such an option was not available for the city's leader. The Roman Gribbs administration had left Young with a financial crisis that could only be solved by trimming the staff and cutting spending, which he did surgically. Young took control of the city at the lowest ebb of automobile production since 1950. He was hardly sworn in when the oil embargo kicked in, and this only added salt to an economic wound created with the announcement that American Motors was packing it in and bound for Southfield.[14] For Young, an additional woe was a reluctant populace who refused to support his appeal to legalize gambling. (In 1996, two years after a casino opened in Canada, the mayor's dream of casinos in Detroit finally became a reality after the City Council approved the proposal.) However, Young was able to appropriate $35 million from the state by emphasizing the importance of the city's major institutions—the Detroit Zoo, the Detroit Public Library, and the Detroit Institute of Arts—that were visited and enjoyed by residents of the entire state.[15]

21

MUSES AND MUSIC

The city's major cultural institutions received a cash infusion, but the lesser known community-based organizations had to seek other means of financial support. Their directors and board members knew that it was futile to expect any trickle-down funding from Young's windfall from the state. Many of them survived by charging admission and soliciting donations, much as Boone House had done in the past. Boone House, which flourished in the early sixties, was the brainchild of the Rev. Theodore Sylvester Boone, for many years the pastor at the historic King Solomon Baptist Church on Fourteenth Street. Born in Texas, Boone attended college in Iowa and later earned his law degree in Chicago. Before he left Texas for Detroit in 1941, he was arguably the most prolific black writer in the state, having authored fifteen books, including one on the philosophy of Booker T. Washington. Over the next decade, he wrote twelve more. When he was approached by a coterie of Detroit writers to use his parish as a meeting place, they obviously knew of his devotion to the craft.

Boone House, despite the indefatigable efforts of poet Margaret Danner, existed for only a couple of years, from 1962 to 1964. Still, it was the inspiration for a number of writers, none more significant than Dudley Randall. A native of Washington, DC, Randall moved to Detroit in 1920. He was thirteen when he published his first poem in the *Detroit Free Press*.[1] After military service in World War II, Randall worked in the post office while earning a degree in library science. For the next five years, he was a college librarian at Morgan State and Lincoln University in Missouri. In 1956, he returned to Detroit and was employed at the Wayne County Federated Library System. To protect the rights to his poem "Ballad of Birmingham," about the four little black girls killed in a church bombing in 1963, Randall published it himself. Out of this necessity, Broadside Press was born.

Broadside Press was much more than a local phenomenon; it had international impact. Melba Joyce Boyd, an editor, noted that between 1966 and 1975, the press published "eighty-one books, seventy-four of which were poetry, including single collections by forty poets, and of those forty, fifteen authored two or even three titles."[2] Randall may not have been aware that J. Edgar Hoover's agents had alerted him about the press after the publication of *For Malcolm*, an anthology dedicated to the slain leader.[3] Broadside Press was a prodigious undertaking during this era when black studies and the arts were being revived.

In 1975, near the end of its productive run, Broadside published Sterling Brown's *The Last Ride of Wild Bill*. During a visit to Detroit, the esteemed scholar, poet, and raconteur shared the poem and a few of his tall tales with an audience at Your Heritage House, founded by Josephine Harreld Love in 1969. They were enthralled by his voice, its melodic cadence, the dramatic interpretation of his characters. A year later, the staff at the press were among those joyful readers to learn that one of their own, Robert Hayden, who once lived in Black Bottom, was named the first African American poet laureate of the United States. Hayden's poem "Those Winter Sundays" offers his memory of his father during those days in Paradise Valley, an extension of Black Bottom, in which he observed his father's early rising and hard work with "cracked hands that ached."

Although Hayden was respected by Randall, many of the poets and writers during the intense period of black nationalism in the late 1960s took exception to his work, dismissing it as irrelevant to the black arts movement. In 1966, at a Black Writers Conference at Fisk University, when Hayden announced that he was not a "Negro" or "black" poet, but simply a poet, he incurred the animus of many black artists, including Haki Madhubuti.[4] When Madhubuti—under his birth name, Don L. Lee, also a Broadside poet—wrote his critique of Hayden, he questioned Hayden's editorship of a Negro anthology, given his resistance to being labeled a Negro poet: "If one doesn't wish to be judged or recognized as a 'Negro' poet, why advertise as such?"[5]

Madhubuti may have denounced Hayden in the 1960s but he still studied his works, including him among other influences, such as Hoyt Fuller, Frantz Fanon, Paul Laurence Dunbar, Jean Toomer, et al. He said they confirmed that any "people who control and define their own cultural and political imperatives . . . should be about the healthy replication of themselves and the world they walk in."[6]

In 1967, when Madhubuti created Third World Press, he stated that it was a direct outgrowth of Broadside Press. Early on, he expressed in action what he later meant by a "healthy replication of ourselves" by following in the footsteps left by his mentor. "I am the man I am today in part because of Dudley

Randall," he told *Detroit News* reporter Betty DeRamus. "I . . . stayed in his house. He taught me what was possible."[7]

Five years after Madhubuti launched his press, Naomi Long Madgett, a Detroit poet, founded Lotus Press. Madgett arrived in Detroit from Virginia, a well-traveled path, eventually earning a master's degree in English from Wayne State University. She was a member of a group of writers, including Oliver La-Grone, James Thompson, Margaret Danner, and Randall, who met at Boone House. When she began Lotus Press, she claimed it was out frustration with both "white publishers" and rigid, even opportunistic, nationalist independent black presses.[8] Undoubtedly, Broadside Press was not included in this denunciation, because Madgett's admiration for Randall was expressed on many occasions. "He was my friend and colleague in the community of poets who flourished during the 1950s and 1960s in Detroit," she told a reporter.[9] By the twenty-first century, Broadside and Lotus were united under the same ownership.

Publishing black books in Detroit, other than Broadside and Lotus, was never a thriving business. Except for Vaughn's, the Shrine of the Black Madonna, and a few operated by churches, black-owned bookstores were nonexistent. In the turbulent 1960s, Vaughn's on the far west side and the Shrine on Linwood were where Broadside and Lotus Press publications could be found. The stores were bountiful with books chronicling the movement and African American history and culture, as well as other Afrocentric artifacts popular during the period.

"I bought my first copy of Malcolm X's autobiography from Vaughn's," said Ron Hunter. "It was also a place where you could get the latest pamphlets on the struggle against apartheid in South Africa or the anti-colonial wars in other parts of the continent." Besides offering books, magazines, journals, and African artifacts, Vaughn's, like the Shrine, was a meeting place that hosted authors and their signings and served as a center for organizations to conduct workshops and lectures.

Sometimes literary and musical events were joined at such locations as Club Ibo in the north of the city or at the Detroit Creative Musicians Association on East Ferry near Wayne State University, another place where artists could gather and express their creative ingenuity. Don Davis's United Sound Systems extended such occasions into recording sessions, none more provocative and controversial than those with a band called Death, a band that presaged the frantic punk music popularized by the Sex Pistols and others. The band followed a long line of greats who had recorded at the studio, which was located on Cass Avenue in the 1930s before moving to Second Avenue. In 1948, John Lee Hooker recorded "Boogie Chillen" there; ten years later, it was the site for Marv Johnson's "Come to Me," and by the time Davis purchased the studio in 1971, it was the prime studio for sessions by George Clinton and Parliament-Funkadelic. To some degree, Death—consisting of the Hackney brothers, David, Bobby, and Dannis—wasn't unanimously endorsed by Davis, whose Groovesville Productions studio was where they cut their demo in 1975. Davis was interested in signing the group if they would agree to change the name. A shrewd businessman and a fine guitarist, Davis felt that the band's name would have no commercial appeal. By this time, he was preoccupied with stabilizing the First National Bank, the state's first black-owned bank, where he was CEO.

Davis may not have had the wherewithal to help the city or struggling artists, but Rep. John Conyers was instrumental in facilitating funds, literally and figuratively blowing his horn on their behalf. Few possessed his insight when it came to securing funds through the National Endowment for the Arts. He knew firsthand the plight of the city's artists, particularly the

painters, sculptors, and dancers, and he later made a similar effort, though in vain, to secure reparations for African Americans
whose ancestors had toiled without pay through his House Resolution Bill 40 in 1989.[10] Conyers often credited his inspiration
for the bill to real estate agent Ray Jenkins, whom Detroiters
knew as Reparations Ray. Few people were as relentless and determined as Ray was in the demand for reparations. One of his
favorite stories as a real estate agent was the time he was showing
a home to Stevie Wonder, who toured the home by feeling the
walls. Much of Ray's spirit and legacy on reparations—he died
in 2009—can be found in the imaginative work of Ta-Nehisi
Coates, particularly the very informative series on the subject in
the *Atlantic*.

As a once promising saxophone player and chair of the Detroit
Jazz Center in 1977, Conyers was in a prime position to assure
that the city's musicians received some of the allocated funds.
Edna Ewell Watson, one of the few black women of prominence
in the League of Revolutionary Black Workers and the former
wife of John Watson, was on guard to make sure black artists
would not be shortchanged when the cash flow began. Watson
provided a vital link between the realms of arts and activism. In
1976, she supervised Communities United for Action (CUFA),
which sponsored a program and exhibit to showcase the works
of black artists. At the Jazz Center, she was the administrator of
the Pioneer Jazz Orchestra under the direction of Sam Sanders.
The Jazz Center was just one of the artistic coalitions flourishing
in the city at that time; it was largely an offspring of the Strata
Concert Gallery, which earlier in the decade, guided by Kenn
Cox and Charles Moore, had featured such jazz greats as Elvin
Jones, Charlie Mingus, Max Roach, Ornette Coleman, Archie
Shepp, and Herbie Hancock. Pianist and music educator James
Tatum; Tribe, the brainchild of Wendell Harrison and Phil Rane-
lin; the Jazz Development Workshop, led by Harold McKinney

and Marcus Belgrave; and RAPA House, with Ernie Rodgers at the helm, were a few of the organizations and institutions consciously involved in maintaining Detroit's cultural and artistic pulse. Not only were the cultural presentations of the highest order, but also they were successful in attracting and sustaining a sizable audience of fans and supporters.

Hundreds of Detroiters were in attendance at the Ford Auditorium on April 9, 1978, to pay tribute to Paul Robeson, who would have turned eighty on this date. Mayor Young and Paul Robeson Jr. were the honorary chairpersons, and the advisory council included Dr. Charles Wright, Judge George Crockett, librarian Clara Stanton Jones, Dr. Geneva Smitherman, historian Dr. Norman McRae, and Tommye Gail Myrick as artistic director.

Among the entertainers at the evening concert were Harold McKinney and the All-Star Jazz Band, the Detroit City Dance Company, with choreography by Carole Morriseau, and the Brazeal Dennard Choral Group. These local artists were complemented by appearances from vocalist Chet Washington and actor Robert Earl Jones. It was a weeklong tribute to Robeson, who had visited Detroit many times, most notably at the invitation of the Rev. Charles Hill of Hartford Memorial Church. "Paul Robeson had many close friends in our city," recalled Dr. Charles Wright, who wrote a biography of Robeson. "The first major appearance was in the late 1930s, when Paul appeared in concert at the Masonic Hall under the sponsorship of Miss Nellie Watts."[11] He filled the auditorium, and a similar audience paid tribute to his legacy during that birthday celebration in 1978.

In 1979, Charles McGee, along with artist Jean Heilbrunn and others, founded the Contemporary Art Institute of Detroit (CAID) in an attempt to invigorate the art scene. McGee was ten years old when he arrived in Detroit from rural South Carolina. The big city, with its noises and flashing neon lights, was all new to him, and so was school. When he entered elementary school, he couldn't write his name, but at an early age his artistic skills were already beginning to develop. After a formal education in art, he embarked on his own career, and now his paintings, assemblages, and sculptures are on permanent display at such local institutions as the Detroit Institute of Arts and the Charles H. Wright Museum of African American History.

McGee's works are in Troy Beaumont and Detroit Receiving hospitals, and on constant display for riders of the downtown Detroit People Mover who pass through the Broadway station. His versatility as an artist matches his energy, and he seems to be perpetually involved in one project or another. "As long as I'm on the face of the earth, I plan to keep step as best I can. I think that the body certainly is going to slow down, has slowed down, but the mind, if you cultivate it, can keep on ticking. But it needs oiling just like a machine. And it all comes out of the type of person that you are too. I'm just so hungry for it that I don't know what it means to have my cup full," he told a *Metro Times* reporter.[12]

Toward the end of the decade, in 1978 and 1979, Allied Artists Association was formed and launched a number of concerts to save the endangered Orchestra Hall/Paradise Theatre. Headlining the concerts were such notables as Dizzy Gillespie, Yusef Lateef, McCoy Tyner, and Donald Byrd, along with a corps of local musicians, including Sam Sanders, Teddy Harris, and the Hastings Street Jazz Experience, featuring Miller Brisker and Ed Nelson. These concerts were all reasonably successful, and they drew additional attention to the aims and goals of those who were interested in salvaging the historic building from the wrecker's ball.[13] Besides preserving a historic landmark, the artists had a self-interest in saving the venue, a stage where they often performed.

The Allied Artists Association (AAA) was able to get organizational footing after receiving a $7,500 grant from the National Endowment of the Arts. Two other local organizations were also recipients of grants—Your Heritage House ($20,750) and Concept East Theater ($20,000).[14] The AAA was comprised of a number of artists from various fields of endeavor—painters, poets, playwrights, graphic artists, journalists, musicians, and dancers. In order to survive, they believed it was necessary to merge their talents and skills and form an organization to oversee their individual and collective needs.

22

COLEMAN AND COCKREL

In the mid-1970s, Detroit's hopeful signs on the cultural front masked the problems in the economic realm. Searching for relief, Mayor Young believed he had an ally in Washington, DC, now that a former congressman from Michigan, Gerald Ford, had succeeded Richard Nixon as president. Having averted a riot in the Livernois-Fenkell section of the city in the summer of 1975, Young was among several mayors invited to the White House for the announcement of President Ford's plan for revenue sharing, a move no doubt facilitated by his resident guru, Emmett Moten.[1] According to Young, Ford pledged $600 million of federal money for a Detroit subway. That promise was never realized, unless you count the funds received that were used to build the People Mover.

Mayor Young veered clear of the school busing controversy, choosing instead to focus on President Jimmy Carter's administration, which had put a number of federal incentive programs in motion. In the fall of 1976, Young received $5 million from the government and wanted to use it to begin to finance his dream of building an indoor stadium next to Cobo Hall. He had to maneuver around a lot of pushback on the project, since both the Detroit Pistons, the basketball team, and the Red Wings, the hockey team, had expressed no intention of continuing to host their games in any downtown facility. Obviously they had witnessed the successful flight of the football Lions to the Silverdome in Pontiac, where there were sufficient parking lots and white patrons. After many court dates and fund-raising efforts, the deal was finalized for a hockey arena, not a stadium. Keeping the Red Wings in Detroit was key to Young's objective. Once he got the club's owner, Bruce Norris, to sit down with two other local movers and shakers—retailer Max Pincus and Joey Nederlander, owner of the Fisher Theater—a deal was cut. Now all Young needed was to generate about $40 million to complete construction. He was able to do this by borrowing against future block grants from the federal government. "When the arena was finished—before the approval of all of our federal loans actually came through—the naysayers whined that we had built it with smoke and mirrors," Young said. "What the hell else did we have?"[2] Young topped off this triumph by naming the building the Joe Louis Arena, a place where white men played and the only thing black was the puck. It wasn't until 1984 that the Red Wings franchise signed its first black player, Brian Johnson, a right winger from Montreal. He played in only three games before being sent back to the minors.

In November 1977, Mayor Young won reelection by a wide margin. To some extent, winning a second term was a testament to his popularity. "I have a long relationship with Mayor Young," said the Rev. Charles Butler. ". . . I know the mayor to be an extremely brilliant man. Some folk think that he is uninformed, blunt, and stupid because he doesn't mind using some choice words from time to time."[3]

Without question, the mayor had a large following, a particularly huge and effective black constituency. But there were detractors, political activists who were critical of his administration and its policies. "When Carter was president," said community activist Roger Robinson, "Young could have mobilized the entire city. He could have taken a quarter million people to Washington to demand justice for Detroit and urban America. He had that skill, and clearly had the roots and analysis to have done something like that. He could have, in fact, put together a class and urban coalition that went across many lines, and used Detroit as the example. But he didn't, and that's the failure."[4]

Robinson's disappointment was shared by many Detroiters, especially those on the left. Young's shortcomings were all the more glaring to those who cherished his leftist background and put their faith in his promises. Attorney Ken Cockrel, who was not a true believer, mounted the greatest opposition. His successful bid for a council seat in 1977 was the political springboard required to ensure him a run in the next mayoral race. Sheila Murphy, his future wife, was instrumental in his campaign, as she would be in the subsequent organizing of the Detroit Alliance for a Rational Economy (DARE), which would be a kind of research arm for the councilman.

At that time, irrational was clearly the best word for Detroit's economy; its wheels were spinning, but it was going nowhere fast. Nor was there any real concrete progress in race relations by the time of the mayoral election of 1977. It became less a black-versus-white contest than a black-versus-black when Councilman Ernest Browne sought to stop Young from winning a second term. Browne hoped to win the election by appealing to white voters, but more and more of them were fleeing. Browne's gambit was dead on arrival, and Young won decisively, unlike his narrow victory over Nichols in 1973.[5] As Young commenced his second term in office, Cockrel was beginning his first on the council. Many envisioned a political showdown.

The euphoria from Young's victory was gradually swept away like the confetti at Manoogian Mansion. With the city on the brink of economic collapse, the Young administration had to contend with a shrinking industrial base that was inextricably tied to the manufacturing of automobiles and related industries. In 1978, the unemployment index was becoming grimmer, fast approaching 20 percent. Again, with smoke and mirrors, Mayor Young was able to get the unions and financially beleaguered Chrysler—on the verge of experiencing its first billion-dollar annual loss—to the negotiating table and win a few concessions from each to stave off a crisis that in reality only the federal government could rescue them from. When the government stepped up and bailed out Chrysler, Detroit and the Young administration finally exhaled. Despite the infusion of cash, all was not well at the company. Nothing resonated as balefully as the plight of workers punching the time clock for the final time at Dodge Main, which closed in 1980.

As the saying goes, when one door closes, another one opens. Dodge Main was gone, but a new GM plant was on the way. By force of eminent domain, the Polish neighborhood was demolished. The protests mounted to stop construction of the plant were futile. The *Metro Times*, an alternative newspaper, had just begun its run, and the Poletown story got it off to a most auspicious start, thanks to the fearless reporting of the late Jeanie Wylie, who was among the protesters arrested. She believed that to get to the heart of the story she had to be a participant. That way she would understand the passion and loss felt by thousands of displaced homeowners. "Detroit was nearly bankrupt when it made the decision to level Poletown in order to accommodate GM's new Cadillac plant," Wylie wrote. "Times were extremely hard for city residents. Businesses had been fleeing Detroit for some time. Certainly something had to be done, but I question whether the solution was for General Motors and the City of Detroit (and the union, the church, and the media) to coalesce to displace 4,200 people."[6]

A large number of African Americans were displaced too, but they were grieving more when the layoffs hit the Detroit Police Department. This story was chronicled in the *Metro Times*'s first edition with a profile of Sergeant Willie Bell, president of the Guardians of Michigan, a five-hundred-member black police officers association. Bell, an eleven-year veteran, recalled that there were very few black police officers in the higher ranks before Young became the mayor. "Before Coleman," or BC, as he called it, "affirmative action was only a token activity." He was particularly perturbed by the recent layoff of seven hundred officers, of whom 75 percent were African American and 40 percent were women. The Detroit Police Officers Association (DPOA), representing 3,700 officers, mostly white, refused to discuss alternative layoff plans. "Can you imagine the hostility," he said, "if the police would have been laid off without using the seniority rule?" By this rule those last hired would have to be the first to go.[7]

In the summer of 1979, Detroit's economic woes were exacerbated by a deeply emotional one for the community when the venerable Rev. C. L. Franklin was shot by a burglar in his home on LaSalle Boulevard. Alerted that someone had pried open the screen and climbed through his upstairs bedroom window, Franklin retrieved his pistol and confronted the burglar. There was an exchange of gunfire. Franklin was hit twice. One bullet struck his right knee, and the other ruptured the femoral artery in his right groin. By the time the ambulance arrived, Franklin, sixty-two, had lost a lot of blood. As he was being removed from his home and taken to Ford Hospital, he went into cardiac arrest. It was later estimated that his brain was without oxygen for nearly a half hour. When his family arrived at the hospital, the esteemed pastor was unresponsive and comatose. The New Year arrived, and Franklin remained in a coma. The cost to maintain him at home, where he would be better treated and possibly recover, was extremely high, and to meet these expenses, Aretha summoned the faithful to plan a benefit concert at Cobo Hall.[8]

The Rev. Dr. Clarence LaVaughn Franklin died on Friday, July 27, 1984. It took two days of "homegoing" at New Bethel to accommodate the thousands of mourners. The services included words of praise from the Rev. James Holley, Robbie Smith, and noted *Michigan Chronicle* religion writer Robbie McCoy. Mayor Young, in consultation with the family and Fannie Tyler, Franklin's private secretary, trimmed the list of speakers, leaving it for the Rev. Jesse Jackson to begin the remarks from dignitaries. Jackson's sermonette recounted Franklin's magnificent odyssey with a particularly sonorous note about how his influence reached well beyond Black Bottom, "beyond New Bethel into the heart of Black America."[9]

Franklin's death left the city with a gaping spiritual hole that several ministers sought to fill, including the Revs. Holley, Charles Adams, Malcolm Dade, Charles Butler, Nicholas Hood, James Wadsworth, and Wendell Anthony, who succeeded the Rev. Wadsworth at Fellowship Chapel after his death in 1986. Anthony, a graduate of Wayne State University, where he was a student activist, would later head Detroit's branch of the NAACP. Detroit's nationally recognized pastor was stilled, black unemployment continued to hover around 25 percent, and the decennial census was about to show that, like the economy, the city's population was spinning downward. The Republicans were gearing up for their July convention in the city, and the hope was that they'd shell out a few bucks and give the local consumer index a jolt. Still, the cowboy—or Prune Face, as Mayor Young called Ronald Reagan—was on the horizon, and it was time for the Democrats to run for the hills, or the suburbs.

Cockrel wasn't running for the hills but contemplating a run to supplant Young. Cockrel objected vehemently to Young's development plans, particularly his promise to give General Motors tax breaks. "I don't see how we can justify giving a multi-billion dollar corporation tax relief, when we are asking our citizens to dig down into their own pockets," Cockrel said.[10] Young was outraged when he learned of Cockrel's stance on his plans, though it shouldn't have come as a surprise. "I think Ken is a bright young man, probably has a political future, although I'm amazed at some of his positions he has taken on tax incentives—the whole question of whether GM needs the money. They ain't running no . . . welfare program."[11]

Near the end of his fifth and final term in office, Young was on a plane flying back from Lakeland, Florida, where he had been invited to the spring training camp of the Detroit Tigers. He was traveling with Emmett Moten, head of the city's Community and Economic Development Department (CEDD). "Mr. Mayor, let me ask you something," Moten said. "Now that you are near the end of your political career, who would you like to see become the next mayor?" Moten said the mayor thought for a second or two, and then said there were two men he liked for the position. "Dave Bing and Kenny Cockrel," he replied. "Both are smart, hard working young men and I think they can do the job."[12]

By the fall of 1979, Cockrel seemed less concerned about keeping his membership in the Detroit Alliance for a Rational Economy (DARE) separate from his role as a councilman. In September, at the Sacred Heart Seminary, he was a speaker at the conference on city life sponsored by DARE. Cockrel questioned the priorities of a system that gave Max Fisher [chairman of Marathon Oil] $12 million but couldn't find funds for the Detroit General Hospital. He said the whole process of electoral politics was a facade. "It does very little to change structures that systematically screw the economically oppressed," he stated. "It's time the people of Detroit made its demands heard. It's time the city council and the mayor respond to the people who voted for them, or maybe we need some electoral upheaval."[13]

When Cockrel assumed his seat on the city council, a minor electoral upheaval had occurred. It's probably not so incredible, given Detroit's history of labor activism, that two of the city's most prominent elected officials were at one time affiliated with leftist organizations and avowed Marxists. Even so, in 1979 they were not ideologically compatible. Dan Georgakas and Marvin Surkin summed up Cockrel's influence thus: "When conventional politicians, historians, and unionists talk about seminal groups of that time, they don't acknowledge the League [of Revolutionary Black Workers, of which Cockrel was a founder and leader]. Coleman Young's autobiography doesn't mention them once. We think that's a testimony to how much they feared the League and the movement the League represented."[14]

23

POSTINDUSTRIAL BLUES

Detroit City
It was the finest city it was
Yes, Detroit City
It was the finest city it was
I'm crazy 'bout that city
And I love its pretty girls
When you leave that city
And you feel this kind of love
When you leave that city
And you feel this kind of love
Just one goes out easy
And you find a good place to go
You don't need a lot of money
To have a real good time
You don't need a lot of money
To have a real good time
Just be a real good boy
And everything will turn out fine.

—FATS DOMINO, "DETROIT CITY BLUES"[1]

According to the Census of 1980, there were 1.2 million people in Detroit. The non-Hispanic white population constituted a little over 34 percent; blacks represented more than 63 percent, and Latinos, about 2 percent. Along with this black numerical majority, of which there was a serious undercount, depriving the city of state and federal money, came the unwelcome prospect of deindustrialization, the disappearance of jobs that the city's working class had depended on for years. "Like my father," said one young black man, "when I graduated from high school I wanted to work at Ford, buy me a car, and get on with raising a family." His dream and plans belonged to thousands of Detroiters, but ahead of them loomed the nightmare of automation, cybernation, outsourcing, and the general relocation of the factories that had been so indispensable to the livelihood of their fathers and grandfathers.

A more ominous menace was taking shape as well—the spread of opiates, particularly heroin, and cocaine. With the traditional routes to middle-class success closed, young black Detroiters sought other means of survival, mainly via the underground economy. Too many black youngsters succumbed to the lure of the loudspeakers from cars operated by Young Boys Inc., advertising the income to be made from running drugs. The gang, widely known as YBI, had been around the city for several years, but with the economy in a downward spiral and job opportunities increasingly unavailable, they seized on the desperation of the poor youngsters who could peddle their drugs without facing prison terms if caught. Between 1978 and 1982, YBI, through three separate subgangs—Big Boy, Raymond, and WW, so named after the gang leaders—controlled most of the heroin trafficking in the city. They became so notorious that they are cited in an international encyclopedia of drugs.[2] According to police estimates, at its peak the gang had revenue of $7.5 million a week.

Young Boys Inc. was a plague on the Young administration, and something had to be done about it, especially the health crisis it was creating with the epidemic explosion of drug addiction. From the very beginning of the Young administration, George Gaines had been the actual director of the Health Department—whenever the appointed director left, Gaines, who had a master's degree in public health, was in charge. "They would get another director, and then he would leave," he said. "I would run the department again." The directors, Gaines confided, left for various reasons. Some were not prepared for the job and others couldn't handle the pressure. Compounding the heroin peril was the outbreak of HIV, which the medical community believed was related to the sharing of needles by addicts. Gaines said he discussed the problem with Mayor Young.

I told him there are forty thousand addicts in Detroit. If we don't do something this neighborhood is going to be devastated with HIV. He said, "How are they going to get it?" I said they share needles. He said, "You got to do something." What we did was until we got the needle exchange program, we gave out bottles of bleach so that the addicts could clean their needles. We showed them how to clean their needles. In a sense I am sure that that made some difference here. Because it got to be a pattern that you just don't clean the needle with water, you use bleach. We got the concept from San Francisco and we called it "teach and bleach." Later we learned that it was not very efficacious. Coleman said, "Give them the needles. They ought to have the needles." I said, you can't do it, it is against the law. We finally got the law changed, the Ordinance changed. He was a progressive person to work for; that is the kind of person he was.[3]

After the law enforcement agencies were able to arrest its leaders and break up YBI, some remnants remained. Later they would be responsible for the scourge of crack cocaine in the early and mid-1980s.

When playwright Ron Milner finished his comic operetta *Crack Steppin'* in 1981, it had nothing at all to do with drugs, which the writer absolutely abhorred. It was a fast-paced soulful musical produced by Barry Hankerson and had an extended run at the Music Hall, featuring choreography by Clifford Fears. The only thing with a bigger wallop at that time in the city was newly crowned WBA welterweight champion Tommy "Hit Man" Hearns, who had a date with WBC champion Sugar Ray Leonard to unify the weight division. Meanwhile, Mayor Young was trying his best to unify a city that was between extreme pain and agony, according to Felix Rohatyn, the noted finance wizard who had rescued New York City and was answering Young's call for help. Rohatyn concluded that one of Detroit's problems was the drain of revenue from suburbanites. He confirmed what Young had been saying all along, but of course with different words and in a different tone. A special election to impose an increase in the income tax was the only remedy for a city about to belly up.

In 1981, after much political horse trading and legislative finagling, the tax referendum was passed, and it was clear sailing for Young after another landslide victory. On the other hand, Councilman Cockrel, the presumed mayoral heir apparent, disillusioned by his inability to use his Council position to improve conditions in the city, decided not to run for reelection. This was a move, several pundits concluded, to prepare for his run for mayor in 1984.

To shore up his standing on the cultural front, Mayor Young tapped Dudley Randall of Broadside Press to be the first African American poet laureate of Detroit. One of Randall's first acts was to drive to Lansing and corral several legislators to discuss the proposed dissolution of the Michigan Council of the Arts and how that would harm the children of Detroit. A year before, in 1980, Randall had written a poem, "Detroit Renaissance," dedicated to the mayor. "Together we will build / A city that will yield / To all their hopes and dreams so long deferred," he wrote with lines that are vintage Randall and with intimations of Langston Hughes. There was also an echo of Aldous Huxley about the creation of a "brave new world."[4]

A towering symbol of this "brave new world" was Young's Renaissance Center, which by 1981 was four years old, preparing to host and celebrate the second annual Detroit International Jazz Festival, in partnership with the older Montreux Festival, whose personnel had arrived from Switzerland. There was often much discussion about Detroit linking its jazz tradition with New Orleans, because the cities shared the seminal backbeat to their music. But as Emmett Moten said—and as a native of New Orleans who was Mayor Young's economic development czar he knew exactly what he was talking about—"Detroit is older than New Orleans but has never taken advantage of its heritage."[5] At most major jazz jamborees, the main attractions are usually the internationally recognized musicians, and the plans here were no exception. With vocalists Sarah Vaughan and Detroit's own Betty Carter as headliners, local musicians were naturally concerned as to what extent the festival would improve their lot. "This year we plan to have a better balance between local and national acts," promised pianist Kenn Cox, a member of the program committee. Pianist/composer Harold McKinney, while praising the event, still had some reservations about the overall concept. "All the decisions are from the top down," he lamented. "They have the money but they don't know anything about the music."[6] McKinney, the vice chairman of MUSIC (Musicians United to Save Indigenous Culture), said that the festival placed far too much emphasis on entertainment and not enough on the economic and political conditions facing the musicians. "The music must be put into a larger cultural context. The festival could be an event that educated as well as entertained," he said, evoking MUSIC's founder, percussionist Roy Brooks, and his portmanteau word *edutainment*.[7] Griot Galaxy was one of the local groups slated to perform at the festival, one that would not only balance the lineup but would tilt it toward the avant-garde, a term detested by Faruq Z. Bey, the nominal leader and saxophonist, because of its militaristic origins. In the city's Cass Corridor near Wayne State University, not too far from Verne's Bar and the Vernor Ginger Ale billboard, was Cobb's Corner, where Griot Galaxy often alternated with organist Lyman Woodard and his band.

With no cover charge and featuring some of the finest jazz and blues musicians in the city, Cobb's Corner was jam-packed every night of the week. Most of the patrons were students at Wayne State or part of the veritable army of homeless and unemployed residents who lived nearby in an assortment of shelters, including the Salvation Army's Harbor Lights. When the downtrodden denizens, many of them on some form of public assistance, were not crowded in Cobb's for the music, they stood in the soup lines scattered from a church pantry on the east side to a rescue mission on the west side. Even those lucky few holding down a job at one of the automobile plants were struggling to make ends meet, on the average making less than twelve dollars an hour. The cost of living, rent, taxes, and the other bills left them with little money for an evening out, a movie, or a game of their favorite sports team. The laid-off workers at Chrysler knew it was futile to think they would be called back soon, and even if they were, they knew there was no way they could expect the high wages they once commanded.[8] Reaganomics was the law of the land, and Mayor Young's castigation of the president practically eliminated any chance of federal aid for the city. The "winter of crisis" the mayor had predicted in December 1982 arrived with little relief in sight.

As usual when bad times hit the city, black Detroiters bore the brunt of the storm. They were the majority in the long lines at the Soup Kitchen Saloon, but not for a handout. Located on the east side near the city's waterfront, the Saloon was Detroit's home of the blues, where such performers as Albert Collins and the duo of Sonny Terry & Brownie McGee kept the music tradition alive at this 140-year-old watering hole. When blues diva Sippie Wallace was booked at the joint, an overflow crowd was guaranteed, and she never failed to please with her way of wrapping her wonderful voice around the issues of the day. "She didn't make you cry in your beer," said the saloon's owner, Brian McDonald. Her songs were tales of woe, he said, "but they were the kinds of stories where everybody lived and saw the next day." She and Bonnie Raitt were close associates and often performed together.[9] The blues permeated the city. It was as if John Lee Hooker's voice was echoing from every nook and cranny, every shelter and back alley, every unemployment and welfare office. Aspects of the blues spilled from the paintings of Charles McGee, Allie McGhee, Al Loving, Harold Neal, Ibn Pori Pitts, Bennie White, and Gilda Snowden; from the sculpture of Oliver Lagrone; from the punches of boxer Alvin "Blue" Lewis; from the leaps and pirouettes of Carole Morriseau; and from the plays of Bill Harris. Soon its baleful moan began emanating from the churches, never more sorrowfully than from the choir at New Bethel Baptist Church when their songs and prayers were extended to their stricken leader. As ever, Mayor Young got it right. The winter crisis seemed long and unbearable.

On July 25, 1984, Judge Horace Gilmore relieved some of the depression for black Detroiters when he ordered the city to rehire eight hundred black police officers who had been laid off by Young during the budget cuts in 1979–80. This action gave fresh meaning to the blues. The mayor was also caught in the grip of a civil case in which the city was accused of violating federal racketeering and antitrust laws. At the crux of the lawsuit filed by officials of Oakland County was the charge that suburban constituents overpaid for water and sewer services because "of the city's sludge-hauling contract with Vista Disposal, Inc., which is operated by one of Mayor Young's protégées, Darrlyn Bowers." Bowers and Charles Beckham, the former city Water and Sewage director, were convicted in federal District Court of bribery and conspiracy in a related case. Young recalled that the government's special prosecutor attempted to involve him in the case as an "unindicted co-conspirator," but there was no basis for it, despite a taped conversation, which was deemed immaterial. Much of the case centered on an alleged bribe of $16,000 that the prosecution claimed Beckham received.[10] On the witness stand during the trial, Beckham told the court that the content of the envelopes supposedly containing the money was nothing more than details of a contract and a reading of Bowers's water meter. The feds were unable to snare Young, but both Beckham and Bowers were convicted and sentenced to four and a half years in jail. The taint of Vista stuck to Young throughout his succeeding years in office. John Feikens, the federal judge overseeing the case, had appointed the mayor as receiver of the Water and Sewage Department, making Young the shit czar, as he called the assignment. Judge Feikens had once co-chaired the Michigan Civil Rights Commission with Damon Keith and now believed that the Young administration was not prepared for the receivership. According to Young, Feikens had authorized the wiretaps of his friends and entrapped them in the sludge scheme.[11] Young believed the feds were out to take him down. In his autobiography he expressed feelings that he was under surveillance, the target of eavesdropping, and the victim of innuendoes.

All of these court proceedings meant very little to blue-collar Detroiters, black or white. Most of their attention was riveted on
the Tigers and a pennant race that would find them winning the
title in a wire-to-wire romp and defeating the San Diego Padres
4–1 in the World Series. For a moment in the city, the often
troubled race relations were perhaps benefiting from the smooth
fielding and timely hitting of Tigers shortstop Alan Trammell
(white) and second baseman Sweet Lou Whitaker (black). It's
hardly news that most of the fans at the game were white, but
whites were a minority in the cheap seats. The so-called Bleacher
Creatures were mostly black fans, cheering from seats that put
them closer to Chet Lemon, the fleet black centerfielder who
covered as much ground as the grass.

This was the Tigers' first World Series since they'd beaten
the Cardinals in 1968, a victory that was followed by a wild
celebration with a spree of vandalism. It was worse in 1984 as
thousands lined the streets to cheer the conquering heroes when
they assembled at Kennedy Square. Suddenly that evening celebration morphed into a citywide conflagration. To Mayor Young,
it was a civic disturbance akin to Devil's Night, the night before Halloween that had lit up the city a year before, in 1983.
This was a far cry from ringing doorbells, soaping windows, and
turning over garbage cans that was the mischief of the previous
generation of children. "For reasons no one understands," wrote
Ze'ev Chafets, "America's sixth largest city erupted into flames.
Houses, abandoned buildings, even unused factories burned to
the ground in an orgy of arson that lasted seventy-two hours.
When it was over the papers reported more than eight hundred
fires. Smoke hung over the city for days."[12] A few years later,
during another outbreak of flame and fury on Devil's Night,
Chafets was stunned to see elderly black men with long black
coats covering their bathrobes standing on their porches armed
with shotguns and garden hoses. They were just the opposite of

the large number of young black men who were arrested during the night of flame and mayhem, which perversely had become a kind of tourist attraction.

Tourists to Detroit, particularly those with an interest in the city's black nationalist tradition who wanted to visit the Shrine of the Black Madonna, were welcomed at the church by the esteemed Rev. Cleage (Jaramogi Abebe Agyeman). His church, later renamed the Pan-African Orthodox Christian Church, had a formidable political arm called the Black Slate. It played a decisive role in the city's politics, beginning in the early seventies when it helped elect Mayor Young. In 1981, it was the organization behind the election of Barbara Rose-Collins to the City Council. While the Black Slate continued to endorse candidates and orchestrate various social and political events, Pastor Agyeman managed the church and the Black Slate from Houston. Although Jaramogi was no longer a visible force in the city, his former comrade-in-arms, the tireless James Boggs, was still as voluble as ever, his pen no less capable of speaking for the powerless. From this radical perspective, black Detroit and its denizens, including Latinos, Native Americans, and Asians, were expendable to the powers that be. "Our communities have been turned into wastelands," Boggs wrote. "Public transportation is not only constantly breaking down but its cost has become prohibitive. Crime has become so normal that we fear one another more than we used to fear wild beasts."[13] Boggs made this comment in September 1984, and it contradicts Mayor Young's assertion a few months later when he proudly proclaimed—citing an award from the International Society of Crime Prevention Practitioners—that Detroit had the best crime-prevention program in the country. Boggs and Young were right about the hostility directed at the city from the suburbs, given that Detroit was fast becoming the blackest city in the nation. As more than one commentator noted, it was hard to distinguish whether the hatred was for Young or the city; for black (and white) Detroiters, the two were inseparable.

The suburban disconnect was a pressing reality for Detroit in 1985, but Boggs's point about the fear factor in the city should not be minimized. During an hour-long presentation of *American Black Journal*, a local cable-television show hosted by Ed Gordon, teen violence was the topic discussed by a panel consisting of Dr. Emeral Crosby, the principal of Pershing High School; James Younger, head of the Detroit Police Department's felony prevention division; and Professor Hartford Smith of Wayne State University's School of Social Work. It was a lively discussion that included a number of call-ins and one unidentified young man on the show who said that everyone he knew carried a gun, "not with the intent of hurting anyone, but simply to protect themselves from attack." He said he had been shot once in front of his home. Smith chimed in that America's cities were becoming populated with more sophisticated delinquents than ever before, a situation exacerbated by a deteriorating sense of community. "We've seen for the first time in American society the tip of a very ugly iceberg," Smith said. "We live essentially in a community of strangers, which leaves many youth to their own tactics of survival."[14]

Detroit's internal violence was given an even larger platform of exposure when the ABC News television show *Primetime* promised a balanced portrait of the city with Mayor Young at the center. But Young had been snookered; the purportedly objective story was basically a dreary account of a city gone down the tubes with little indication of hope or uplift. As if to accentuate what the panelists had discussed on *American Black Journal*, the *Primetime* segment closed with a "mourning mother sobbing over her son's grave, one of a series of poignant shots that were portrayed as extemporaneous but which many people felt were contrived," Young recounted.[15]

Contrived or not, the show left an indelible stamp on Detroit as a city overrun by violence, the "murder capital" of America, a designation first applied in 1974 but not accurate until 1987, when there were 62.8 homicides per 100,000 residents. There was clearly a steady escalation of murders in the city, so much so that in 1986 Pistons star Isaiah Thomas led a march against crime. Ironically, just as the marchers, led by Mayor Young, started the procession downtown, an announcement came that a police officer had been killed by a man who thought he was a prowler.[16]

Detroit got a spiritual and musical uplift when the Winans, the city's legendary gospel group, released their fifth album, *Decisions*, in 1987 on the Qwest label, particularly from "Ain't No Need to Worry," featuring Anita Baker. The single earned the group and Baker a Grammy. With lyrics like "Ain't no need to worrying / What the night is gonna bring / Because it will be all over in the morning," it was just the message a depressed community needed to shake off the negativity bombarding it from near and far.

A grave concern for many black residents in the mid-1980s was crack cocaine, use of which spread like wildfire across the country. In Detroit and elsewhere, especially among the poor, powdered cocaine gave way to crack, a stable, dampness-resistant form of the alkaloid more easily stored and sold in small quantities to the nonwealthy. Nearly every neighborhood had at least a "master chef or two" who could cook the rocks to perfection. "At first it was like a fad, almost recreational but it soon became something else, and suddenly all the fun was gone," users often confessed. He was talking about the rapid buildup of *tolerance*, the brain's weakening response to successive doses, which in susceptible persons leads to a strong psychological dependence unlike the physical addiction of heroin yet sometimes rendering a person unable to stop smoking it until either all of the money or all the rocks are gone. In 1986, according to one report, Detroit registered the nation's fastest acceleration of crack abuse. It was estimated that at least fifty thousand metro Detroiters were hooked on the little rocks, and, unsurprisingly, most of them were young black men and women. The distribution of crack was a $1 billion-a-year business in the city, and it left thousands of users doing almost anything for the next hit on the pipe.[17]

There's a scene in Nubia Kai's play *Parting* that captures the attitude of young black men in the late eighties reflecting on what their parents had to do to make a living, especially when employed at the Ford Motor Company. Sudan, one of Kai's main characters, laments to Sherrie, his girlfriend, that his father

> . . . didn't mind workin'. Nigger worked his ass off and acted like he loved it. Thought he was the John Henry of Ford Mo. Company. He be braggin' about how they use to come out to the factory the night before it opened and stand in line. . . . He did that every night for five months till he got re-hired in '36 and brag about it! See, workin' for Mr. Ford was a prestigious thing back then, but it ain't about shit to me 'cept slavery. I guess I didn't inherit that John Henry mentality from him. I say crush the muthafuckin' railroads and the monsters who own it.[18]

Kai dramatized what James Boggs had been preaching for years about the rapid deindustrialization, outsourcing, and the closing of factories that for generations were a reliable source of income. "There are no industries coming to our cities to employ them now that capitalism has reached the multinational stage," Boggs explained.[19] From his perspective, even if Sudan had wanted a job at Ford like his father, his chances in the late eighties were slim to none. Boggs recognized what thousands of young black Detroiters would soon discover—that the traditional jobs once waiting for them when they came of age were no longer available. This was a transitional phase of the auto industry. Plant after plant was shutting down; between 1987 and 1990 only one new plant opened in the country, a General Motors Saturn factory, a multibillion-dollar project designed to win back buyers of Japanese automobiles.[20] A new day had arrived, and it didn't include the young black hopefuls from the high schools of Detroit.

Sudan would have been a perfect role for actor/director Earl D. A. Smith, but by the time Kai had finished her play, Smith had joined the ancestors. Death cut short his promising career, which had begun in the early seventies with leading roles in *Rashomon* (1973) and *Devour the Snow* (1979) at the Marygrove Theater. His leadership role in the founding of the Black Theater Department at Wayne State University was well established by the time he was featured in the film *Freedom Road* (1979) or in Shakespeare's *Julius Caesar* at the college's Hilberry Theater. "He was a fantastic actor and very effective teacher," recalled Peggy Coley, one of his students. "I can still remember his directing me. Earl was a taskmaster and he was absolutely devoted to the development of Black Theater at Wayne State. It's too bad he died so soon."[21]

Although Smith was not a member of the Concept East Theater, founded in 1960 by Woodie King Jr., along with David Rambeau, Cliff Frazier, and others, his intention was to instill that same independence and creativity within the academies where he taught and performed. The mantle he and Concept East left behind was adopted in 1985 by Council Cargle and his wife, Maggie Porter, when they founded Harmonie Park Playhouse in the basement of the Madison-Lenox Hotel. Cargle was a versatile and busy actor who earned his bachelor's degree from Wayne State University and when not on the stage could be found at Michigan's Thirty-Sixth District Court, where he was a deputy clerk for District Judge Denise Page Hood. After the judge took a position at the city's Recorder's Court in 1989, Cargle retired and devoted his time to the theater, not only his own but practically everyone in the city, including the Detroit Repertory Theater, the Jewish Ensemble Theatre Company, the Attic, the Unstabled, and Plowshares Theater Company. After a performance or on weekends, he was part of the audience at the 101 Lounge, where he joined pianist and vocalist Kris Lynn waiting his turn to sing.

Detroit's lawyers were jubilant to learn that Judge Hood had been chosen to serve on Recorder's Court. That joy was stifled, however, when attorney Ken Cockrel died on April 25, 1989. Cockrel, fifty, died of a heart attack days before he planned to announce his mayoral bid. According to his wife, Sheila Murphy, he had completed the petition process for his candidacy.

Few possessed Cockrel's mastery of the language, "fine voluble colloquy" as one friend observed of his rapid-fire delivery with a complement of words that often flew over the heads of his listeners. "Not sure what he said, but it sure sounded good," was the reaction of many in earshot of his eloquence. Noted sociologist Michael Eric Dyson, who grew up in Detroit, said he was directly influenced by Cockrel's linguistic agility. "He talked so much, he was called TV," recalled his brother, Jesse Cockrel.[22] On April 29, his charisma and extraordinary odyssey were recalled at a memorial service at the Rackham Auditorium. Local activist and cultural leader John Sinclair was among those in attendance; he lamented that Cockrel was "cut down from within at perhaps the height of his considerable powers as a champion of the people and spokesman for human and economic rights."[23] The tributes for him came from a disparate coterie of friends and associates, including Justin Ravitz, Mike Hamlin, Mayor Young,

Governor John Blanchard, and Michigan Supreme Court justice Dennis Archer. Cockrel, Hamlin mused, was driven by intent— great conviction and commitment—and that drive may have been "responsible for his death."[24] His wife often heard friends and associates say, "We feel cheated. He should have become our mayor."[25]

A year later, in the summer of 1990, Nelson Mandela toured the United States after spending twenty-seven years in prison. One of the sites he visited was Tiger Stadium. It's doubtful that Cockrel would have been invited to share the rostrum at Tiger Stadium with the South African leader, since Mayor Young was calling the shots. To have Cockrel at the event would have riled a few of the other dignitaries, possibly even Judge Damon Keith, whom Young chose to deliver the opening remarks. On the morning of the event, Keith noticed that Rosa Parks had not been invited, which to him was a grievous oversight. Keith quickly contacted Parks's aide, Elaine Steele, and said that he would pick her up. When Mandela and his wife, Winnie, emerged from the plane, one of the first people they recognized was Rosa Parks. "Nelson Mandela stated that Parks had been his inspiration during the long years he was jailed on Robben Island and that her story had inspired South African freedom fighters."[26]

The meeting between Parks and Mandela brought the civil and human rights struggles to an exciting pinnacle. Parks appeared overwhelmed by the moment, as exhilarated as she had recently been in Washington, DC, for her seventy-seventh birthday celebration at the Kennedy Center.[27] Detroiters will never forget the two days Mandela spent staying at the Westin Hotel in Renaissance Center, walking along Atwater Street, traversing Hart Plaza, and visiting Ford's Dearborn Assembly Plant. "I am your flesh and blood," he told the awed workers. "I am your comrade." Black nationalist activist the Rev. Milton Henry, formerly

of the Republic of New Afrika, was part of the welcoming committee and regaled Mandela with an excerpt of biblical scripture.

That evening fifty thousand people jammed Tiger Stadium to
see Mandela and to hear Stevie Wonder, Aretha Franklin, and
local blues diva Ortheia Barnes serenade the great leader. After
shouts of "Amandla!" which means "freedom" in Xhosa or Zulu,
Mandela told the crowd, "Right now I wish I could climb down
the stage and join you in the stands and embrace you one and
all." He stunned Detroiters when he told them that the songs
of Motown had helped him survive the prisons of South Africa. "Brother, brother, there's far too many of you dying," he
sang, mimicking Marvin Gaye, much to the amazement of the
crowd.[28]

Parks had also been deeply committed to Detroit's survival. She was
particularly devoted to the *Michigan Chronicle*, a treasured institution. Near the end of the decade, the *Chronicle*, celebrating
its fiftieth anniversary, was still recovering from the loss of two
stalwarts—the publisher and editor in chief, Longworth Quinn,
and a highly respected columnist, Albert Dunmore, who at one
time was the paper's managing editor. Quinn, who arrived at the
paper in 1944 as the business manager, moved steadily upward
until he was the helmsman, proving that he had the leadership
skills to keep the paper afloat. "His unique contribution to the
birth and growth of our annual Fight for Freedom Fund Dinner
was published in the *Chronicle* week after week in every name
of each dinner subscriber," remembered Arthur Johnson, then
executive secretary of the Detroit branch of the NAACP. "He
also handled special publicity for the dinner from the beginning
up to his death."[29]

Like his colleague Quinn, Dunmore was a graduate of Hampton Institute, as well as a journalist and civil rights activist fully

aware of the paper's importance as an alternative to mainstream media. He had spent twenty years at the *Pittsburgh Courier* before reuniting with Quinn at the *Chronicle* in 1961. In 1968, Dunmore was hired by Chrysler as a specialist in urban affairs. But the ink in his blood brought him back to the *Chronicle* in 1988, where until his death he worked as a consultant.

24

A MAYOR AND MALICE

By 1990, Detroit's population was just over a million and predominantly black. Since the end of World War II, nearly a million and a half whites had left the city. The suburbs, Mayor Young lamented, ". . . had surpassed Detroit not only in population but in wealth, in commerce—even in basketball, for God's sake."[1] He was saddened, too, to learn that on January 5, Judge Longworth Quinn Jr. had apparently put a pistol to his head the night before and was found dead in a bedroom at his mother's house. Judge Quinn, forty-six, left a suicide note, but it was not disclosed by the police. Even the headline story in the *Michigan Chronicle*, where his late father had been editor for many years, could provide only a modicum of information about the tragedy. It was probably Danton Wilson, the executive editor, who penned the editorial that recounted Quinn's varied career as an activist, teacher, lawyer, and chief judge of Detroit's Thirty-Sixth District Court without any mention of possible despondency over the death of his fiancée, who leaped from the twenty-third floor of their apartment in Trolley Palace in 1984. "Those closest to him," the editorial stated, "say his most important legacy was as a humanitarian. He was a superior judge, handling with mental dexterity lofty judicial concepts and legal ideas. His writing on even the most complicated and technical and legal matter was lucid."[2]

Quinn's gifts could be thought of in musical terms. As the jazz musician Dox, portrayed by Von Washington in Bill Harris's play *Coda* that opened in the spring of 1990 at the Attic Theater relates, "I think everybody, like, gets a gift." He's explaining to Theresa, his daughter, an aspiring musician, the unique sound that differentiates one musician from all others.

Everybody don't realize it, or get the chance to develop it. But some—lucky ones do.

Now, don't ask me how it's decided, and it's sad when they don't, but it's even sadder when that gift is just pushed aside, out of anger, or ignorance, or fear or— Anyway, like I was trying to tell you before, for a musician, your sound is the only thing that's yours.

That very first sound you make is how they know you're alive, and they say "Yeah, baby, welcome to the world." And when it's all over, they bury you, by yourself, no lover, no money truck, no dope man, just you; barefoot, and with a split up the back to your dress.

But what lives is the story you told. And the way you told it. And the sound you told it with. That's it.[3]

One of the performers in the play was Thomas "Beans" Bowles, who certainly possessed a unique sound on the baritone saxophone and flute. He was popularly known as Dr. Beans Bowles and few Detroit musicians bridged the worlds of jazz and Motown as well as he did. That bridge began in Arkansas, extended to Indiana, to Saint Louis, and on to the navy before Bowles found his home in Detroit. He was a mainstay on baritone saxophone in bands led by Lionel Hampton, Bill Doggett, and Illinois Jacquet, but most visibly with Maurice King and his band at the Flame Show Bar, where the Gordy family, including Berry, was holding forth. King's résumé was also impressive; he had replaced the venerable Jesse Stone as the leader of the Sweethearts of Rhythm, the first integrated all-women's jazz band. As he was with the King ensemble, Bowles was Gordy's aide-de-camp and soon an all-purpose member of the company—playing in the band and coordinating with the Motor Town Revue, and his flute solo is featured on "Fingertips," a hit tune recorded by Stevie Wonder in 1963. There was even a stint as musical director for comedienne Joan Rivers. Bowles finally got his own ensemble and a venue of the same name when he became musical director for the Graystone Jazz Orchestra. By July 1991, the Graystone International Jazz Museum, no longer at its original location on Woodward (it was demolished in 1980) but on Broadway in downtown Detroit, was guided by James Jenkins, who founded the museum in 1974. After Jenkins died, Bowles was forced to function in a dual capacity to keep the museum afloat, which was largely supported by funds from white donors.[4]

White patronage of jazz was nothing new, and for the Graystone it went back to the 1920s, when Jean Goldkette and his orchestra commanded the house. Back then, many black musicians called it the Stone Gray for its policy of permitting blacks to attend on Monday nights only. Cover charges were also readily paid by white patrons of Baker's Keyboard Lounge, the city's oldest continuously active jazz club. Their money supported white-owned establishments but seldom black-owned businesses and merchants such as Ed Vaughn, a state representative and entrepreneur, whose bookstore was destroyed by the police during the 1967 rebellion. They claimed they raided the store because of reports that weapons were there. Thirty years later, in 1990, Vaughn showed the same ambition for private enterprise but this time on a larger scale. Yourland Mall was Vaughn's response to the malls surrounding Detroit that were siphoning off black dollars. "It's all part of what I call the 90-percent solution to economic freedom, which is to get Black folk to spend 90 percent of their consumer dollars in the Black community," he told a reporter. "We're trying to instill this idea in the African American community so that our dollars turn over in our community at least once before leaving it."[5]

In the 1990s, black businesses in Detroit, as Vaughn inferred, were troubled and in decline. The institutions they depended on to feed them a steady supply of personnel and potential entrepreneurs, such as Lewis Business College, was clogged and struggling with its own set of peculiar challenges. Founded in 1928 by Violet T. Lewis in Indiana, by 1941 Lewis was incorporated in Michigan, becoming the first historically black college in the state. It was during the tenure of Dr. Marjorie Harris as president that the college began its pursuit of junior college status. In 1975, under the name Lewis College of Business, it received accreditation from the North Central Association of Colleges and Schools (NCA). That status was reaffirmed in 1990, though like much of the city, the school was feeling the onslaught of a budget crisis that hampered enrollment and dreams of expanding the curriculum and staff.[6] There were rumors that the school would soon be relocating to the far west side of the city.

Even the Bing Group, a steel processing and distribution company founded by basketball legend Dave Bing, experienced a dip in profits in 1990 when it posted sales of $61 million, down 17.44 percent from 1989. Meanwhile the profits at Bing's other company, Superb Manufacturing, increased by 40.49 percent, roughly an $8 million increase from $20 million the year before. "It was a bad year for profits," an automotive analyst concluded,[7] though one of Bing's companies appeared to do well. In any case, it may not have been a banner year for Bing on the business steel front, but he picked up many commendations and honors. During the NBA All-Star Game in 1990, he was given the Schick Achievement Award for his work after his outstanding basketball career. He was also inducted into the Naismith Memorial Basketball Hall of Fame that same year.

Noted Detroit painter Bennie White Ethiopia, his locks long and gray, stood admiring his depiction of Malice Green on a wall. In contrast to Ethiopia's hair, Green's was coifed in an Afro that surrounded his young, handsome face like a black halo. This was Ethiopia's tribute to the fallen Green, thirty-four, who had been killed at this spot by two white policemen on November 5, 1992, outside a suspected crack house on West Warren Street. When Green's car stopped in front of the alleged crack house, the officers, Larry Nevers and Walter Budzyn, ordered him to get out of the vehicle. When Green refused, they radioed for backup, and meanwhile removed him from the car by force. They noticed that Green kept one of his fists clenched, and they ordered him to open it. Again he refused, and they began banging his fist with their heavy metal flashlights. "While the policemen were beating Green, five additional officers arrived in response to the backup call," according to an account by the police. "By then, it was later alleged, Nevers and Budzyn were hitting Green on the head with their flashlights. One of the five, a white officer named Robert Lessnau, was alleged to have joined in the beating. Sergeant Freddie Douglas, who was black and the ranking officer at the scene, allegedly did not participate in the beating, but neither did he intervene to stop it."[8]

Malice Green died that night, and the anger in the community spread faster than the details of his death. Unlike the outrage that had followed the beating of Rodney King in Los Angeles a few months before, no riot occurred in Detroit. Community activists and civic leaders, alarmed by the tragedy, demanded that the officers involved be immediately suspended. Within two weeks, Wayne County prosecutor John D. O'Hair handed down second-degree murder charges on Nevers and Budzyn. Sergeant Douglas was charged with involuntary manslaughter and willful neglect of duty for failing to halt the beating. This charge was later dismissed by another judge on the grounds that the beating was already under way when Douglas arrived. Officer Lessnau was charged with aggravated assault. They all pled not guilty.

For more than three months in the summer of 1993, the trial raged before Judge George Crockett III, whose father was the legendary legal genius. The fact that the trial was aired via Court TV may have helped to reduce the possibility of a riot. Two separate juries were impaneled. The Nevers jury was composed of ten blacks and two whites; Budzyn's had eleven blacks and one white. Officer Lessnau had a bench trial before Judge Crockett. The community watched with interest, their eyes glued on Kym Worthy, whose track record as a prosecutor was remarkable. She was flamboyant and never shy when it came to dramatics. Nevers told the court that he feared for his life during the altercation and confessed that he had hit Green several times with his flashlight. Budzyn denied ever striking Green and said he had not seen anyone else hit him. "That testimony [prompted] one of the highlights of Prosecutor Worthy's presentation. She pulled a tape measure from her pocket and stretched it out two feet. 'You were this far away from Malice Green and didn't see him being pummeled to death?' she demanded. 'You couldn't smell the blood?'"[9] Another gripping moment occurred when Scott Walsh, an emergency medical technician who had tried to help the injured Green, took the stand. He testified, "There was so much blood on his head that our bandages just slid right off."[10]

On August 16, with the same emotionless delivery as his father's, Judge Crockett announced his decision in the case of Officer Lessnau, finding him not guilty of assault with intent to cause bodily harm. Five days later, the jury reached a verdict in the Budzyn case, but it was sealed until the Nevers trial ended. A few days later, both Budzyn and Nevers were found guilty.

Before they were sentenced, both Nevers and Budzyn apologized to Malice Green's family in the courtroom. Then Judge Crockett pronounced sentence. Larry Nevers, 53, was given 12–25 years in prison, with no parole permitted until he served at least nine years and eight months. Walter Budzyn, 47, was sentenced to 8–18 years, with a minimum of six and a half years. Before they were led from the courtroom, both former police officers asked that they be sent to out-of-state prisons. They said that, as new prisoners, they wanted to dodge any chance of cell block confrontations with prisoners whose incarceration was the result of their work as Detroit policemen. The Michigan Department of Corrections made arrangements for both men to serve their time in Texas.[11]

Mayor Young felt that the officers had committed murder (a politically incorrect thing to say at the time but typical of Young). Meanwhile, Dennis Archer, his successor, maintained silence on the case before, during, and after his mayoral triumph in 1993.[12]

From a humble background, Dennis Archer had diligently worked his way up the ladder of success to become the city's mayor. He was always grateful to Mayor Young for his support and encouragement. After working his way through college in a succession of menial jobs, Archer earned his teaching degree from Western Michigan University, and then after he spent several years in night classes at the Detroit College of Law, the parchment was his and he was ready for the legal arena. He moved in steady progression from an outstanding career as a lawyer to become the president of the predominantly black Wolverine Bar Association in 1979. Four years later, he was the leader of the National Bar Association. In 1985, Governor James Blanchard appointed him to fill a vacancy on the Michigan Supreme Court. A year later, he was elected to an eight-year term on the bench, the first African American to hold the position in twenty years and the second in the state's history. Otis Smith had been appointed to the position in 1961 by Governor John Swainson.

What appeared to be a terminal success for Archer turned out to be just another momentary plateau. In 1990 he resigned from the bench, leaving a guaranteed annual pension of $50,000 on the table, to pursue the elusive office of mayor. "When Archer decided to run for mayor in 1990," Joe Darden and Richard Thomas wrote, "he had a private meeting with Mayor Young and told him he would like to 'emulate' what the mayor had done. Young, who was very ill and in his seventies, refused to commit himself to his onetime reelection campaign manager, no doubt because he was contemplating running for a sixth term."[13] In his autobiography, Young mentioned Archer only once in passing, devoting his most caustic response to his longtime political ally, former congressman George Crockett, who had introduced Archer's candidacy. The split between Young and Crockett had been two years in the making, going back to 1988, when Crockett approached Young to be his successor in Congress. Young told him he didn't want to be a congressman, "didn't consider it a promotion, and in fact didn't like a goddamn thing about Washington."[14]

The rejection of the offer apparently upset Crockett, according to Young, because after the election in which Crockett won, he claimed that Young had supported his opponent, Council member Barbara Rose-Collins. Young vehemently disputed the allegation, though two years later, in 1990, he did back the candidacy of Rose-Collins, who was victorious. As for the mayoral race in 1993, Young, his health showing no signs of improvement, decided not to pursue reelection and threw his support to the city's general counsel, Sharon McPhail. While she did well, coming in second in the crowded primaries, she failed in the general election, losing to Archer by 56 or 57 percent to 43 percent, depending on the source. Seven years later, she once more waged a vigorous campaign and became the Wayne County prosecutor in a race against future mayor Mike Duggan. She charged that Duggan was really a stalking horse for county executive Ed McNamara to prevent a federal investigation of McNamara and his cronies. McPhail's supporters were convinced she had defeated Duggan, but the out-county votes, particularly from Duggan's hometown of Livonia, were difficult to recount, and therefore the victory was Duggan's.

Archer took office promising to uphold his campaign pledges to build bridges between the city and the suburbs, between downtown Detroit and the surrounding neighborhoods, and between blacks and whites, pledges diametrically opposed to the outlook of his predecessor. Unlike Young, who often expressed his disgust with Washington, Archer forged a friendship with President Bill Clinton that gained him entrance to the White House in January 1994 and a night sleeping in what he thought was Abraham Lincoln's bed. "At the root of [Archer's] vision for Detroit was adherence to a view that to stabilize and revitalize the city required bridge-building, negotiation and compromise with the suburbs and the white business elites. It is a vision that sees cultural separatism as an economic dead end for African Americans."[15] Although Archer took exception to many of Young's policies, he nonetheless continued many of them, particularly the development of downtown Detroit. He would learn, as Young clearly realized, that "the forces of economic decay and racial animosity were far too powerful for a single elected official to stem."[16] The crisis too much for even two elected officials to stem. In effect, Archer inherited an illusion of sufficiency and well-being, one that had begun to unravel before Young took office and fully accelerated under Archer's watch. The depletion of financial reserves, a dwindling tax base, a steady decline in population due to white flight, and corruption lurking vulture-like on the horizon presaged the future chapters of a doomsday scenario.

Under Archer, there may have been relative improvement in race relations. He certainly did a good job enticing new corporations to the city, but there were still some troubling social and political issues that seemed impossibly tough to gauge and remove.

Black-on-black violence continued to gnaw at the city, and no incident symbolized this problem more than the attack on Rosa Parks. "On August 30, 1994, at the age of 81, Parks was mugged in her home by Joseph Skipper, a young black man," recounted Jeanne Theoharis. "Skipper broke down her back door and then claimed he had chased away an intruder. He asked for a tip. When Parks went upstairs to get her pocketbook, he followed her. She gave him three dollars he initially asked for, but he demanded more. When she refused, he proceeded to hit her."[17] Despite her age, Parks tried to ward off his blows, showing the resolve acquired during her days of activism. However, the volley of blows were too much and, at last, she relented and gave him all of her money—$103. After he departed, she called her good friend Elaine Steele, who had become a constant caretaker. She phoned the police, and a half an hour later, they arrived to see a battered civil rights icon. The irony of the attack was inescapable. Here was a woman who had risked her life to bring an end to a segregated society, an avowed nonviolent opponent of racism and discrimination, now waylaid by one of her own. It was a horrible moment that circulated around the globe but with a particular resonance of despair in Detroit. But Parks refused to see her tragedy as a sign of community dysfunction, Theoharis observed. "Many gains have been made. . . . But as you can see, at this time we still have a long way to go." Skipper was sentenced to eight to fifteen years, to be served in an out-of-state prison for his own safety.[18]

Matel Dawson, seventy-eight, a longtime employee of the Ford Motor Company, was in 1980 beginning his donations to the United Negro College Fund, the NAACP, and other charitable organizations, which by a decade or so would amount to more than a million dollars. Dawson, a native of Louisiana and a forklift operator at Ford's Dearborn assembly plant, said he established the scholarship funds in his name and grandparents' names at Louisiana State University. His reason for giving, he said, originated with his parents. Plans were under way to set up a scholarship in their names as well. That he was able to donate such a large sum of money from his salary of $23.47 an hour and from fifty years of working overtime earned him national attention, something that he was proud to proclaim. When he's gone, he said, "I want people to say good things about me."[19]

During his long association with Ford and the UAW, Dawson admired the work of labor leader Horace L. Sheffield Jr. and, like his fellow workers, mourned the passing of the great labor leader. For more than a half century, Sheffield, seventy-nine, had been an indomitable fighter for workers' and civil rights. He died on March 1, 1995, of congestive heart failure at Receiving Hospital. The Sheffield family had made its trek from Vienna, Georgia, to Detroit in 1919, when Horace was three years old. At eighteen, he began working at Ford and by 1941 was among the coura-geous union officials in the United Automobile Workers Local 600. He was a key organizer in a strike against Ford demand-ing an end to discrimination. Sheffield extended his activism as president of the Detroit Coalition of Black Trade Unionists and was a founder of the radical Trade Union Leadership Council (TULC). The same energy for self-determination that he com-mitted to labor was applied during his tenure as director of the Detroit branch of the NAACP. He marched with Dr. King and met with Henry Ford II. Whether speaking to a crowd at a union rally or composing words for the various columns that he wrote, Sheffield was a thoughtful and deep thinker who was unsparing in his critique of what he felt was wrong in the world of labor and organizing. "During my three terms as president of the De-troit branch of the NAACP," said Arthur Johnson, "we launched with the active support and participation of Horace Sheffield the campaigns to achieve fair banking practices, nondiscriminatory insurance rates in Detroit, and the 'Buy Detroit' campaign. He helped to shape our strategies and to sustain our will in these battles."[20] Sheffield's son, Horace Sheffield III, has extended his father's legacy and social resolve through his personal commit-ments and his leadership in the Detroit Association of Black Or-ganizations.

A hale and hearty Sheffield Jr. would have been involved in the newspaper strike of 1996 and probably a member of Readers United, a coalition of community activists and concerned clergy who were instrumental in giving the strike wider exposure as well as helping to raise benefit funds for the workers. Perhaps he would have also weighed in on the announcement by Mayor Ar-cher concerning the creation of casinos in the city with an inter-est in the proposal that 50 percent of the workers be residents. In the meantime, black workers in Detroit, no longer receiving compensation or willing to deal with rejection, made fewer and fewer trips to the unemployment office. One look at the labor index of the day reflected their disappointment. In 1995, Detroit had 55 jobs per 100 persons, compared with Bloomfield Hills, a wealthy outlying suburb, with 272.7 jobs per 100 residents.[21] Moreover, the report adds, the high-paying blue-collar jobs that had created and then sustained the black middle class had moved out of the city. What remained were a limited number of low-paying positions and white-collar jobs that were customarily out of the reach of prospective black workers. In short, the process of deindustrialization, the disappearance of the manufacturing jobs that were part and parcel of the Detroit experience, was a terrible fact of life, and more and more people looked to the underground market to satisfy their needs. There were cynical reports that Detroit resembled a Third World country with its concentration of poverty compounded by a declining tax base, spreading squalor, inadequate health facilities, and high infant mortality.

Detroit's daunting Third World circumstances did not stop Dr. Charles Wright and his cohorts. They forged ahead with their plans to celebrate the new site of the Museum of Afro-American History, including a brown-bag lunch for the local taxi and limousine drivers. On Saturday, April 12, 1997, the public was invited to the ribbon cutting and dedication ceremony performed by Mayor Archer. A week later, the expansive rotunda was filled with authors from around the country, including Yolanda Joe, Elza Dinwiddie-Boyd, Jonell Nash, Cheryl and Wade Hudson, and Dr. Wright, promoting his new book, *The National Medical Association Demands Equal Opportunity*.[22]

It had been four years since the ground was broken for the museum's third site on Warren Avenue and Brush Street. The building, 120,000 square feet, was designed by black architect Harold Varner of Sims-Varner, Inc. He had been influenced by the buildings that he had visited in Africa. The rotunda was constructed with superbly balanced acoustics that allowed a person to whisper at the center and be heard clearly throughout the expansive room. Varner also designed the expansion of the Cobo Center, the remodeling of Martin Luther King High School, the overhead bridges that connect the Millender Center to the Renaissance Center, and the Coleman A. Young Building at the Millender Center.[23] Dr. Wright explained that the museum's core gallery "was complemented by two exhibition galleries devoted to the arts, history and technology."[24] Wright employed the historian Norman McRae and Robert O. Bland, both renowned educators, to keep the historical record accurate and up to date. McRae, who was among the city's foremost historians, taught at Wayne State University. Bland was the vice president and dean at Lewis College of Business.

In the fall of 1997, black Detroit was dealt a triple punch of despair. First there was the death of Judge George Crockett Jr. He was being mourned when Joyce Garrett and then Coleman Young died. Crockett's death on September 7 did not come as a shock to Detroiters. He had suffered a stroke and spent the last five days of his life in a hospice in Washington, DC. Crockett was eighty-eight when he died. Twenty days later, on September 27, Joyce Garrett made her transition at sixty-six in Bloomfield Hills, Michigan. Of the three notables, Garrett, who had a string of accomplishments before becoming "the first lady of Detroit," was the least known to a national audience.

Born Joyce Finley in Detroit in 1931, she established her intellectual acumen and brilliance when she passed the Foreign Service Examination and became the first African American female Foreign Service officer. She was on a diplomatic track when she decided to return to Detroit, where she resumed her education, earning a master's degree in political science from Wayne State University in 1966. Over the course of the two years that followed, she held several important civic offices, including assistant director of the Michigan Civil Rights Commission. By 1968, Finley, now Joyce Garrett, was a loyal companion to Mayor Young and was chosen as his aide-de-camp. Later she supported her daughter, Shahida Mausi, as she rose in the ranks of city government.

Coleman Young's passing at seventy-nine on November 29, 1997, was as newsworthy as his tumultuous life. A huge photo of him dominated the front page of the *Michigan Chronicle*, where his legacy was exhaustively recounted by Patrick Keating. The combative civil servant died of respiratory failure at Sinai Hospital almost two months to the day after the departure of his companion. On December 5, live coverage of his funeral services from Greater Grace Temple was carried on all the major local television outlets as well as nationally on C-SPAN. The Rev. Charles Butler conducted the services, moderated by radio maven Martha Jean "the Queen" Steinberg, with practically every elected official of significance in the state in attendance, including Governor John Engler, Senator Carl Levin, and Mayor Dennis Archer parading to the podium. Aretha Franklin closed the services with a powerful version of "The Impossible Dream," from the Broadway musical *Man of La Mancha*, her voice exceeding one plateau after another as she sang of the "unreachable stars."

At the same time that the city's first African American mayor was being laid to rest, Wayne State University was swearing in its first black president. Dr. Irvin D. Reid came to Wayne from Montclair State University in New Jersey and placed his expertise in applied economics to work almost immediately. The first thing he did was increase the $27 million annual budget to $80 million. He oversaw the expansion of the university, especially its research capability and its spinoff businesses in the midtown sector. A black president, however, didn't mean that the student body would undergo a similar dramatic change in color. Since its inception in 1868, the school has maintained a lopsided ratio of white to black students which has always struck many residents as odd since the city became predominantly black. Even more distressing, only 10 percent of the black students admitted earn a degree within six years. One problem may be that the educational pipeline from Detroit's public school system has not adequately prepared students for a college curriculum. Many of the black students receive remedial and tutorial assistance. Of course, there were a number of exceptions, and the Rev. Dr. Wendell Anthony was one. Long before he gained national attention in 1998 when he was arrested outside the US Supreme Court building for protesting the Court's failure to hire African American clerks, Anthony's activism bona fides were very impressive. Political activism began for this native of Saint Louis during his days at Central High School, which gave him a leg up on the other students at Wayne State. A black studies major, he was a campus leader who was well-grounded in the liberation movements in Africa. This was the fodder and training he needed after he left the academy, entered the ministry, and by 1993 was at the helm of the local branch of the NAACP, the organization's largest affiliate. He was often at the forefront of marches and demonstrations, and he was just as formidable in the pulpit. Soon he had his own church with a congregation to shepherd. "For how long can the court judge diversity and equity, if in fact it lacks the diversity and equity it claims to judge," he told a reporter during the 1998 demonstration at the Supreme Court.[25]

Few congressmen were as adept and knowledgeable about the affairs of Washington, DC, as Representative Charles C. Diggs. By the time he died, on August 24, 1998, he had brushed up against or angered just about every branch of the federal government, including the Supreme Court, which he had to deal with directly after he was censured in 1979 by a House committee for taking some $60,000 in kickbacks from his congressional staff and the Court refused to review his conviction. He claimed he was being unfairly prosecuted because of his race but was eventually sentenced to three to five years, of which he served only seven months in a minimum-security prison in Alabama. "I considered myself a political prisoner during my incarceration," he told a reporter. "I was a victim of political and racist forces. I will go to my grave continuing to profess my innocence."[26]

During his twenty-five years in Congress, Diggs stretched his influence and commitment from Mississippi to Zimbabwe, or Rhodesia, as it was called when he was a member of the House Foreign Affairs Committee. His knowledge of African Affairs in Congress was peerless, so much so that he was called Mr. Africa. Diggs endeared himself to black activists who were dedicated to the liberation of Africa from European colonialism. His comprehensive understanding of the liberation movements in Angola, Mozambique, and Guinea-Bissau, all under Portuguese domination, made him welcome among such African revolutionaries as Samora Machel, Eduardo Mondlane, Marcelino dos Santos, Amilcar Cabral, and Agostino Neto. He was consistent in his demand that the United States stop opposing resolutions condemning Portugal's oppressive policies. When colonialism ended, a civil war erupted among the various liberation movements. When Diggs learned that the CIA was covertly supporting UNITA (the National Union for the Total Independence of Angola), he used his influence as chairman of the African Subcommittee to cut off funding for the operation.[27]

By the time of his death in 1998, Diggs's accomplishments had long been obscured. He was living in Washington, DC, when he died, and he is buried in Warren, Michigan. His legacy continues in Detroit in the various funeral homes in the city that bear his name, though they are now known as Stinson-Diggs Chapel, Inc.

While many Detroiters recalled Diggs's achievements and mourned his passing, in the late 1990s, they were mainly concerned with the problems in the school system. In 1999, Governor John Engler began paving the way to take over the city's duly elected school board. By the first of April, the deal was done, and the Michigan House of Representatives passed Public Act 10, a final version of the so-called school reform bill, putting Detroit's school system under the mayor's control. Mayor Dennis Archer immediately acceded to the takeover and demanded the resignation of the defunct board, replacing them with several prominent officials, many of whom were notable educators, including Detroit deputy mayor Freman Hendrix; William Beckham, president of New Detroit; Dr. Glenda Price, president of Marygrove College; Frank Fountain, vice president of Daimler-Chrysler; Pam Aquirre, CEO of Mexican Industries of Michigan; and Marvis Coffield, director of Operation Get Down, a social agency on the city's east side with an excellent reputation. The key member of the board was Arthur Ellis, the state superintendent of education and Engler's close associate. His vote was crucial to whomever was installed to head the school system.[28]

This decision was as hotly contested in Lansing as it was in the neighborhoods of Detroit, but most agreed that something drastic had to be done if it was true that, of the nearly two hundred thousand students in the system, only 30 percent were graduating on time, that the district's academic performance was subpar, and that enrollment was steadily declining. Given the wretched conditions, it was understandable that complaints were coming from all quarters. The business community, a major player in the takeover, charged that the school system was not doing its job and that too many of their employees couldn't read or write and were desperately in need of remedial education if they were to be hired and function successfully in the workplace. Members of grassroots organizations were vehemently opposed to the takeover "on the grounds that it disenfranchised Detroit residents, the vast majority of whom were black."[29] Their resentment was, to a great degree, muted because Archer's new appointees were accepted by parents, teachers, and the students. Even so, a new board was only seven individuals, but it was with the twenty thousand school employees and their union that the rubber met the road. The differences about control may have been momentarily resolved, but the struggle was far from over. It clearly was not over for such community sentinels as Dr. John Telford, who as a former Detroit school superintendent, had a bird's-eye view of the turmoil surrounding the takeover. In a column he wrote some years later, he stated:

At the time of its unjust state takeover, Detroit Public Schools boasted a $93 million surplus and its test scores were at the state midpoint and rising, despite the city's chronic social problems engendered by what nationally recognized urbanologist john a. powell and I described in a May 5, 1999, *Detroit Free Press* column as "concentrated poverty" by race and by residence. However, Detroit voters had recently passed a $1.5 billion construction-bond millage, and Governor Engler and those close to him were hungrily eying the potential contract bids, so they took DPS over and supplanted the democratically elected Detroit Board of Education with an appointed "reform" board simply because they could.[30]

Only time would tell if the takeover would prove effective, but in the meantime the city's workforce was still waiting for a similar move that might alter what had become an unrelieved, unchanging state of unemployment.

Weeks before classes in the city were set to resume, there were intimations that the teachers were not exactly satisfied with the way things were going. As Labor Day approached, rumors of a possible strike began to make their way through the union. Signs in the holiday parade, like NO CONTRACT, NO WORK, signaled even stronger that a stoppage was imminent. At the end of the Labor Day weekend, the teachers went on strike. They spurned their negotiators' recommendations and expressed their grievances about a longer school day, merit pay, class size, and other reforms proposed by the district's new interim chief executive, David Adamany, who had been president of Wayne State University from 1982 to 1997.[31] The walkout, which was in violation of a 1994 law barring teachers from striking, was a brief one; within a week it was over, and a tentative agreement was reached. "We consider it to be not only a victory for the teachers," said John Elliott, president of the Detroit Federation of Teachers, "but for the students we teach. We're not where we want to be, but we have moved up considerably if this agreement is approved." He said the increase in wages was competitive, but the agreement was left for his members to ratify.

Teacher ratification apparently didn't necessarily mean satisfaction, particularly for the rank-and-file members, many of whom were still in the dark about the actual content of the contract. "On November 18, an estimated 5,000 students marched on the school center building, demanding not merely protection [from the large number of reported rapes in schools], but 'books, supplies, lower class size.' On December 2, about 75 teachers and students marched together to the school center building, echoing the same chant, and demanding to be informed of the contents of the teacher contract."[32] Because there was no demographic or racial breakdown of union representation available at that time, there is no way to determine how many of the teachers were African American.

Somehow Mayor Archer, who had earlier failed to mediate the differences between the workers and the newspapers, was able to steer away from the wreckage of the conflicts, and in 2000 he was named Public Official of the Year by *Governing* magazine. The magazine didn't discuss the fact that Archer was governing a rapidly changing demographic in which black middle-class flight from the city now exceeded white flight. There were other signs that the middle class was unsettled by the socioeconomic trends in the city, none more disturbing than the appreciable drop in median household income. "The folks with the wherewithal to leave, the folks with the jobs . . . those are the people [who] have the ability to exercise voting with your feet," said David Martin, a professor of public policy at Wayne State University.[33] And flight from the city was given additional impetus with the state's repeal of a residency law for city employees in 1999. Without the residency requirement, as was predicted, the city would see its annual revenue reduced by more than $20 million. Much of the loss is attributed to the fact that nonresidents who work in the city pay half the city income tax rate of residents. "But many Detroiters believe the actual impact has been far greater, because many of the public employees who have left are police officers and firefighters whose departures have decimated formerly middle-class neighborhoods."[34]

But it wasn't only police and firefighters in flight to the suburbs. Many African Americans, disappointed by service cutbacks and an increasingly decimated school system, sought better communities to raise their children, where there was more attention from the municipal government. On the other hand, the outflow was matched by a steady but lava-like influx of young white boys and girls from exurbia, gathering around the Fox Theatre and the Fillmore in the hopes of seeing Eminem. Just when everything south of Eight Mile Road was getting darker and darker, a white rapper emerged, and by the end of the year and the decade, his album *The Slim Shady*, his alter ego, would go platinum. He was the iconic entertainer on his way to commanding a considerable portion of the growing hip-hop flow of cash, at the same time presenting the first sprigs of gentrification. Not too far away from the neighborhood where Eminem was giving the city a fresh breath of recognition was a six-foot-high wall, now festooned with colorful images, that once stood as a dividing line between the black and white residents.

Gentrification was one thing to worry about, but police brutality was a far more menacing immediacy for young black Detroiters. They were keenly aware there was little mercy awaiting them from the police, nor from school counselors or employment agencies, and certainly not from the drug dealers. Amid a dysfunctional educational system, library closures, and inadequate funding of other community institutions, young black Detroiters were marooned in a poverty of culture that forecast a culture of poverty. They could expect very little wiggle room between a rock and a hard place in a city devoid of guidance and direction.

25

EMERGENCY, RESURGENCY

As bleak as the outlook was for young black Detroiters at the start of the new millennium, they might have found some inspiration in the appearance of Ahmed Kathrada in the city to promote his book *Letters from Robben Island*. Kathrada was Nelson Mandela's cellmate in prison and, like his esteemed comrade, was incarcerated for his refusal to abide the draconian system of apartheid that strangled black opportunity. He was invited to Detroit by state senators Joe Young Jr., Virgil Smith, and Jackie Vaughn, all of Detroit and each significantly involved in the divestment movement that helped to cripple South Africa's economy and aided the struggle to free its political prisoners. By sponsoring Kathrada's trip to Detroit, the politicians were not only honoring the freedom fighter, but also renewing the memory of Mandela's visit ten years earlier. "When we divested the state pension funds we saw the money start to come out of South Africa," Smith said, during the celebration at the Charles H. Wright Museum of African American History. Young added, "We were able to change the world with a few pieces of legislation. Many didn't believe it could work but it did."[1] Kathrada explained that his book was basically a compilation of his letters that he retrieved from guards after he was released in 1989, one year before Mandela. While they were in prison, he said, he also helped Mandela write his autobiography, *Long Walk to Freedom*. Senators Young, Smith, and Vaughn had expended great time and energy toward ending apartheid in South Africa, but vestiges of a similar discriminatory system remained right in their own districts.

As for black workers' experiences in the various unions, there was nothing new. Race relations within the UAW were often a very conflicted issue. One would have thought that by the year 2000, years after the turbulent strikes and the relative successes of the civil rights movement—in which the UAW had played a vital role—that race relations would have been much better. Yes, there were three African Americans on the fifteen-member executive board, but less than 1 percent of the skilled tradespeople covered by the DaimlerChrysler AG–UAW national labor contract were black. On the other hand, according to Joseph Szczesny, author of *African Americans on Wheels*, black workers accounted for more than 40 percent of the automaker's unskilled laborers. The situation was no better for blacks at Ford and General Motors.

Racial diversity was much better at Comerica Bank, where Louise G. Guyton had recently been promoted to vice president in the Public Affairs Department. Guyton was the founder of the Greater Work Foundation. The mission of the foundation is to create positive community change through collaborative efforts by focusing on transforming neighborhoods and strengthening individuals and families—a difficult task indeed. For her tireless pursuits and commitment to the city, in 2000 she was the recipient of the Spirit of Detroit Award from the City Council. Like the Rev. C. L. Franklin and Martha Jean "The Queen" Steinberg, Guyton was a native of Memphis, and through her affiliation with a number of civic and civil rights organizations, there were opportunities to connect with them. Steinberg's clarion calls were a popular staple of the city's media, particularly radio. Her voice was stilled forever on January 29, and it was a sad day for her listening audience, who relied on her information and trusted her as "the town crier."

Mourning the loss of the Queen had not concluded for the city when almost a month later, on February 20, Jaramogi Abebe Agyeman, eighty-eight, formerly the Rev. Albert B. Cleage Jr., made his transition. More than five hundred people attended his funeral services, and Menelik Kimathi, the second holy patriarch of the Shrine of the Black Madonna, said "For what he was able to do, we stand in awe."[2]

Despite the emotional setback of the loss of such inspirational personalities as Steinberg and Agyeman, there were signs of resilience and resurgence on the artistic front in the works of Tyree Guyton. Guyton was the subject of an HBO Films documentary, *Come Unto Me: The Faces of Tyree Guyton*. The film was the recipient of several honors, including an Emmy Award for editing in 2000 and an honorable mention at the Sundance Film Festival for director Nicole Cattell. Guyton calls his artistic efforts The Heidelberg Project, in which he uses discarded and found objects from within and outside abandoned buildings on Detroit's east side. Since the project's inception in 1986, it has been a source of controversy. Some neighbors appreciate his attempt to beautify the dilapidated buildings and squalid area, while others view his efforts as no more than a continuation of the detritus, a heap of garbage. Whatever the opinions of neighbors, the project has become a tourist attraction, even more so when several of his buildings were set aflame. The intentions of the project are best expressed on its website, which notes that it "offers a forum for ideas, a seed of hope, and a bright vision for the future. It's about taking a stand to save forgotten neighborhoods. It's about helping people think outside the box and it's about offering solutions. It's about healing communities through art—and it's working!"[3]

Similar artistic endeavors to uplift the community—and a far less controversial project of resurgence—were under way at the Plowshares Theater. Since the theater company was launched in 1989 by Gary Anderson and Michael Garza, it has more than fulfilled its mission of breaking new ground—in keeping with its name—nurturing aspiring actors, writers, and directors and presenting works that are fresh and innovative. Over the last decade, the company has been the recipient of both critical and popular acclaim, earning numerous awards in nearly every theater category, including rave reviews from area critics. Currently, it is the city's only professional African American theater company and is gradually being recognized nationally. In 2000, Anderson received the *Detroit Free Press*'s Lawrence DeVine Award for outstanding contribution to the theater. "Ten years ago we couldn't give away tickets," Anderson said as the company prepared to celebrate its tenth anniversary with a production of *Ain't Misbehavin'*. "We wanted to begin our tenth anniversary season with a bang."[4]

Diana Ross's Return to Love tour was another sign of possible Detroit resurgence. The tour was designed primarily as a reunion of the Supremes. Ross had the best intentions, but the tour failed to ignite, and fans were particularly disappointed when the planned "reunion" didn't include Mary Wilson in the concert engagements. They were not prepared to witness Scherrie Payne and Lynda Lawrence alongside Ross in the June date, though apparently some had been tipped off that the tour was not as advertised. By July the promoters pulled the plug on the Return, and die-hard Ross fans were left to wonder, where did their love go? "People in this town," wrote Susan Whitall, a reporter for the *Detroit News*, "have long memories. The black community in Detroit has an intense belief they've been done wrong by Diana."[5] Whatever the reason for the poor turnout and the canceling of the tour, it was another dark moment for Motown and its fans, many of whom were still grieving over the loss of Gwen Gordy Fuqua, Berry's sister, who died in November 1999 in San Diego at seventy-one. But she was more than just Berry's youngest sister, according to folks such as Maxine Powell, who had tutored the young men and women of Motown in the fine arts of decorum and etiquette. "When I think of Gwen," Powell wrote in an article for the *Michigan Chronicle*, "I think of a person who always reached out to others . . . she embraced all of the positive qualities of life. She also took pleasure in inspiring, uplifting and coordinating wardrobes for others. . . . She lives on, especially through those whose lives were intertwined with hers."[6] And that would be practically everyone who came anywhere near Motown and experienced her genius in business and songwriting, for which she was never properly credited by her co-composers.

Another portent of resurgence was delivered during the Motor City Music Foundation 2000 awards ceremony, sponsored by the *Detroit Metro Times*, an alternative newspaper with a number of African American employees. Along with awards for nationally acclaimed artists with Motown roots, including Stevie Wonder and CeCe Winans, numerous local artists were also saluted for their achievements. Among the nominees were jazz vocalist Ursula Walker, blues singer Alberta Adams, and saxophonists George Benson and David McMurray. Twenty years was a time to celebrate, particularly at the beginning of century, and that's what the *Metro Times* was doing for several weeks after a score of years as the city's leading alternative paper. It was also a time to look back and get a bead on the future, as the paper's former editor Larry Gabriel did in September. "We've been celebrating this 20th anniversary over the past month and going over many of the things that have made the *Metro Times* what it is," he wrote. "All of this seems to beg the question of what the future holds. You can make a lot of predictions and most of them will be wrong. Trust me on that. But you can wonder and dream."[7]

Predictions and looking to the future are always at the core of a mayor's State of the City Address, but by the end of the year, much of what Mayor Archer hoped for to rejuvenate the flagging revenue was still stuck in the pipeline. In January 2001, Archer was enthusiastic about the prospects ahead as he began his seventh year in office. He was especially proud to announce that the homicide rate was the lowest since 1968. He was equally effusive about Comerica Park, the new home of the Detroit Tigers. His praise for African American investor Bill Brooks, who had laid plans to renovate the long dormant neo-renaissance-style David Whitney Building, was well-intended but rather myopic. Brooks's dream, as well as the mayor's hopes for Belle Isle and the city's incredibly sclerotic educational system, were still dormant on the drawing board. The mayor's rose-tinted glasses merely reflected the tangle of red tape that kept him from realizing his most cherished prospects.

If Archer needed a businessman to single out for accolades, George Hill may have been a better choice. Hill was the president of Adhesive Systems. This black-owned, Detroit-based company had for seven years produced thirty types of adhesives and sealants for Kraft Foods. Black shoppers who purchased Velveeta pasteurized prepared-cheese product and Stove Top stuffing were most likely unaware that they were helping a local black entrepreneur and his employees. Adhesive Systems has been in business since 1987 and has annual sales of approximately $15 million and a diverse forty-seven-person staff that includes chemists, engineers, and factory workers. But more than sealing Kraft packages, Hill and his company play a key role in holding the community together. "We've been responsible for anchoring this industrial park and not letting it go to ruin," Hill said. "We have provided employment, tax revenues, education and training and a whole host of things to the neighborhood to stabilize it."[8]

No revitalization of black Detroit has been done without the stabilizing role of the city's churches. A solid indication of this fact occurred when the churches, led by the Rev. Jim Holley of Little Rock Baptist Church, launched an Adopt-a-School initiative, an offshoot of the Detroit Safe Streets Program, which began after a rash of schoolgirl rapes. The goal, according to Bernard Parker, the Detroit Public Schools' deputy CEO of community responsibility, was to get all 263 schools formally adopted by one or more churches. "By doing so," Parker told the press, "people and resources can be organized around making the school a success." The pairing of churches with schools combined a large swath of the city's spiritual and intellectual capital—Little Rock Baptist and Mount Zion New Covenant Baptist Church adopted Northern High School; Galilee Baptist Church adopted Osborn High; historic Second Baptist embraced Duffield Elementary, which so many of Detroit's notables had once attended; Bethel AME locked hands with Golightly Educational Center, named after Cornelius Golightly, the esteemed educator; Hartford Memorial Baptist Church, famous for hosting appearances of such legends as Paul Robeson, was linked with Mumford High School.[9] In 1985, thanks to Eddie Murphy and his role as detective Axel Foley in *Beverly Hills Cop*, in which he wears a Mumford sweater, the school received national attention. Any mention of the three

Beverly Hills Cop films without citing Gil Hill, who portrayed Foley's boss, Inspector Todd, would be a serious oversight, given Hill's importance to the city's history as a real-life police detective and president of the City Council.

Setting aside his badge for a while and taking a break from Hollywood, Hill sponsored a testimonial resolution for Maxine Rayford Taylor by Councilmember Kenneth K. Cockrel Jr. Taylor was being saluted for her thirty-three years as a teacher in the public school system, including stints at Jamieson, Joseph Campau, Bennett, Fannie Richards, and Maybury, and her favorite post, according to Cockrel, McMillan Dual Multicultural School. The resolution was adopted unanimously by the nine council members, and they wished Taylor a happy retirement and time to devote to her hobbies of dancing and playing the piano and flute.[10] Such a measure was a daily routine for Hill, though his mind was probably preoccupied with campaign matters after earlier in the year announcing his intention to run for mayor in 2001.

Hill, like many other leaders in the city, and none more so than Mayor Archer, were concerned about another alarming increase in fatal shootings by the Detroit police. Detroit, according to reports from several local papers, had the highest number of fatal police shootings among the nation's largest cities. This was not news to Archer, who in September announced that he would ask Attorney General Janet Reno to investigate every fatal Detroit Police Department shooting, an inquiry welcomed by Police Chief Benny Napoleon.[11] Reno had already been approached about such an investigation earlier in the year when she met with Arnetta Grable regarding the killing of her son Lamar Grable and two others in 1996 by Officer Eugene Brown. Through her attorney, David Robinson, she had initiated proceedings leading to federal consent decrees. Police Chief Napoleon, following a public outcry about the number of civilians being shot by the police, ordered that the department reinvestigate Brown, who had been cleared by the Wayne County Prosecutors' Office of any wrongdoing. Brown, during his seven-year career, had shot nine people, three of them fatally.[12]

In the spring of 2001, when Mayor Archer announced that after seven years in office he would not be seeking another term, the candidates for the position assembled at the starting line— Councilmember Nicholas Hood III, businessman Charles Beckham, and Bill Brooks, a former GM executive, were there before Archer voiced his intentions. Another contender was Police Chief Benny Napoleon. The local pols began to toss in a slew of other candidates, including Sharon McPhail, whom Archer had defeated in 1993; Geoffrey N. Fieger, who had been the Democratic candidate for governor in 1998; and Kwame Kilpatrick, the offspring of two political notables, one a minority leader in the State House, the first African American to hold the position. At this early stage, no mention was made of Gil Hill, who with Kilpatrick was a finalist after the September nonpartisan primary was over. In physical terms, if not financially, it was Hill's David versus Kilpatrick's Goliath. It was also the old man (Hill would be seventy on November 6, Election Day) against the young man, Kilpatrick, thirty-one.

"For a long time [Hill] ran far ahead in the polls. . . . But Kilpatrick . . . [grabbed] a ten-point lead," wrote political analyst Jack Lessenberry. "Mr. Kilpatrick creamed the favorite in the primary, winning an absolute majority in the crowded field, with just over 50 percent to Hill's anemic 34.5 percent."[13] Assessing the results of the primary, it didn't look good for Hill, who was bulldozed by the former college football tackle. Kilpatrick won virtually every demographic group except the oldest voters. He took the majority of the absentee ballots, which Hill had believed would be his. Hill had clearly underestimated his opponent's charisma, his oratorical skills, and the financial clout he had quietly and cleverly amassed. It was clearly going to be an uphill battle, but the veteran officer had no quit in him and promised to mount a more formidable campaign than he had mustered in the primary.

It would be for naught.

26

KWAME TIME!

Gil Hill took to the hustings and began stumping like never before, but it was too little and much too late. Kwame Kilpatrick, bolstered by the acclaim received during his speech in Los Angeles at the Democratic National Convention the previous year and by the largess of corporate bucks, won impressively, 54 to 46 percent, according to the election results from several media outlets. Still in his thirties, Kilpatrick had no compunctions about being dubbed the Hip-Hop Mayor. The diamond stud in his ear, much in the manner of the late Prophet Jones, gave the title additional cachet.

As early as the summer of 2001, the *Detroit Free Press* reported that Kilpatrick, then a state representative in the previous year, had solicited a $50,000 contribution to his civic fund from the president of a homeless shelter. Later that year, he urged the Detroit–Wayne County Mental Health Board to award the director of the shelter a $22.7 million contract. The move sparked an Internal Revenue Service inquiry and possibly marked the beginning of his pay-for-play political machinations. It didn't hurt to have the backing of Ed McNamara, the Wayne County executive, whose chief of staff was Kwame's father, Bernard Kilpatrick. The confederacy of collusion was taking shape; the surface of Kwame Kilpatrick's ultimate downfall had been scratched.[1]

At his inaugural ceremony at the Fox Theatre, Mayor Kilpatrick, with his family occupying the front-row seats, announced, "I stand before you as a son of the city of Detroit and what that represents. This position is personal to me. It's much more than just politics. I want you to understand that." The speech underscored a promising beginning, and the deal was sealed when the Winans singers asked the audience to join hands, as Kilpatrick and former Mayor Archer did, and sing along: "Together we stand, divided we fall. Let's build a bridge, tear down the walls."[2]

But owning up to a hip-hop lifestyle may have been detrimental to the young, flamboyant mayor. He was hardly in office before he was besieged by a flurry of rumors about wild parties at Manoogian Mansion. While none of them was confirmed, they were enough to fuel the media and public perception of a mayor less than serious about his comportment. The rumors and innuendoes reached a critical mass, and when some of the allegations were confirmed, there was no way for him to tamp down the furor or hold back the tide of incrimination.

When Kilpatrick moved into the mayor's mansion, he couldn't see from his window a city simmering in discontent, a gloomy, opaque future that all of his high-sounding rhetoric about a "Motor City makeover" could not brighten. "You need to come back to the people who helped raise you," he told a graduating class of Detroit's Renaissance High School in a speech in the summer of 2002. He stressed the "awesome responsibility" that those fortunate enough to attend college had to those who could not.[3] During moments like this, the mayor seemed to be headed in the right direction, his moral compass fully functional, homed in on rebuilding the crumbling neighborhoods.

Along with the concern about Kilpatrick's morality, the city residents should have been equally concerned about the neglect from the state's capital. In 2002, the state of Michigan shared revenues with the city of about $333 million a year, but from that apex the number gradually began to dwindle. The dial on Detroit's economic meter dipped precipitously, and in nearly every category, from employment to housing startups, the outlook was increasingly dreary. As white workers moved to the suburbs, along with them went a considerable percent of the city's revenue base, a factor that would become even more critical by 2005. Some of this shortfall might have been foreseen and forestalled, but Kilpatrick and his colleagues were dealing with other pressing problems.

Mayor Kilpatrick was not the only prominent black man in the city snared by luxury and excess. In 2003, La-Van Hawkins, a native of Chicago, owned more than a hundred Pizza Hut franchises in Michigan, as well as Sweet Georgia Brown, a posh new restaurant in Greek Town. His sales numbers—$300 million—were almost as gargantuan as his nearly three-hundred-pound body. His earnings made his franchises the twelfth largest black-owned business in the United States. When he was not relaxing at one of his lavish mansions or flying high in his private jet, he was tooling about town in his Bentley convertible, presenting an obvious appearance of wealth and prestige. He was the darling of Detroit's nouveau riche and a posse of clamoring political aspirants, all hoping to get his attention and his financial backing.

"I'm proof that you can do anything," Hawkins boasted in a profile in *Ebony* magazine. "I've succeeded against all odds because I refused to be denied. . . . From rags to riches, I did it my way; from the projects to the boardroom, I did it my way."[4] It was perhaps inevitable that the mayor and the mogul would meet. That happened over a lunch at Sweet Georgia Brown. Kilpatrick said he was glad to have an entrepreneur like Hawkins "infusing new energy into our business community. . . . He is not the blue suit, blue shirt, red-tie wearing business-person from the traditional type of business community. That has inspired a totally new group of people."[5] The two men exchanged their ideas about success, then went their separate ways to decline and disappointment.

When a referendum vote reestablished an elected school board, it was not a happy development for Mayor Kilpatrick. He had his own plan to prevent a fully elected school board, which might minimize his control. This setback, however, was not enough to cause him to lose his reelection bid in 2005. In fact, he used the turmoil around the referendum as a weapon against Freman Hendrix, his challenger. He depicted him as a tool of the rich white suburbs. His campaign team aired dramatic footage in an ad reminding voters that when Hendrix was deputy mayor under Archer, he ordered the police to forcibly remove protesters, including a female senior citizen, from a meeting of the state-appointed school board takeover.[6]

This ad, along with sizable monetary contributions from a third-party group for Kilpatrick named The Citizens for Honest Government, was successful in reversing a lot of the negative reports alleging that Kilpatrick had charged over $200,000 on his city-issued credit card for travel, meals, and entertainment during his first thirty-three months in office. At the same time, his father's defense refuted allegations of a raucous party at Manoogian Mansion. It was all a lie, he said, comparing it to the falsehood that the Jews were to blame for the Holocaust. He later apologized for this statement. According to Kilpatrick's spokesman, Howard Hughey, the mayor's expenses were part of his effort to attract business to the city, which had struggled with a steep population decline since the 1950s and the resulting erosion of the tax base.[7]

The run-up to the general election had Hendrix, who charged that Kilpatrick's platform was nothing more than "smoke and mirrors," a clear winner. The media were ready to make that announcement of his victory. Fortunately, they didn't make the mistake that the *Chicago Daily Tribune* did in 1948, with headlines declaring that Thomas Dewey had defeated the incumbent president, Harry Truman. The Kilpatrick campaign was given a boost by the turnout of young voters as well as his warm words of compassion and an expression of renewed maturity at Rosa Parks's funeral. She died October 24, 2005. One paper called his 53 to 47 percent margin of victory over Hendrix as "stunning," but it was no surprise to *Detroit Free Press* columnist Desiree Cooper. "Perhaps it was the Rosa Parks factor," she wrote. "Her funeral last week was a marathon of speeches exhorting blacks to remember the hard-won civil rights battles, especially voting rights. . . . If there's one thing we've learned from the state takeover of the Detroit school board: You don't mess with the right to vote. What happened during Tuesday's election? The black bourgeoisie was pitted against the working poor, the darks against the lights, the intellectuals against the street fighters. It might have been a lot of things, but it wasn't a surprise."[8]

Rosa Parks had been ailing for several years, confined to a wheelchair and reportedly suffering from dementia before she passed away. More than four thousand mourners packed Greater Grace Temple, and hundreds more stood outside the church that late October morning for Parks's funeral, which capped a week of services in tribute to the civil rights icon, including one in the nation's capital at the Capitol Rotunda, where a woman renowned for refusing to relinquish her seat was the first to lie in state at this hallowed space. As expected, there was chorus after chorus of "We Shall Overcome" before the church's bishop, Charles Ellis III, who led the service, bade the great lady farewell. "Mother Parks, take your rest. You have certainly earned it."[9] The line of dignitaries filing past her casket was endless, all of them deeply moved when Aretha Franklin, as she did at Coleman Young's funeral, filled the church with a magnificent rendition of "The Impossible Dream."

Having laid the "mother of the civil rights movement" to rest, the city and its leaders had to get back to work, many of them carrying a renewed sense of energy and dedication to doing the right thing and ensuring the continuance of Parks's indomitable spirit and commitment. Franklin, the diva, had to keep to her busy schedule and travel to Washington, DC, and accept the Presidential Medal of Freedom from George W. Bush. The defeated Hendrix had to find another way to continue as a public servant. Cooper, the reporter, had to deal with a huge number of letters and e-mails from her readers. One even took umbrage at her analysis of Kilpatrick's victory, declaring it was "simplistic." He wrote that "Cooper suggests that Kilpatrick won because he played the race card before a poor, uneducated electorate. I'm a white philosophy professor who lives in Sherwood Forest. I, reluctantly, voted for Hendrix, but I have many educated, affluent, sensible and even white friends who voted for Kilpatrick, for reasons I understand and respect." Furthermore, he added, "Hendrix was an uninspiring candidate . . . he was arrogant on the campaign trail, he lacked details . . . and he ultimately couldn't match Kilpatrick's intelligence and charisma."[10]

Kilpatrick's intelligence and charisma were showcased again on January 5, 2006, during his second mayoral inaugural address at the Fox Theatre, still glowing from the marvelous renovations of metalsmith Carl Nielbock. Local radio commentator Frankie Darcell served as moderator and brought David Baker Lewis, Kilpatrick's reelection campaign chairman, and his campaign's chief political strategist, Art Blackwell, to the stage to introduce the city's sixtieth mayor. Standing beside his wife, Carlita, who held the Bible, with his three boys nearby, Kilpatrick was sworn in by Judges Damon Keith and Karen Fort Hood. Change is usually a typical topic of such speeches, and Kilpatrick devoted considerable time to it, noting that it was "a chance to change the image of Detroit." He told the packed theater and distinguished guests, including Governor Jennifer Granholm, Council President Maryann Mahaffey, Erma Henderson, and Congressman John Conyers, that his administration would not be about "fixing things, it will be about transformation." Inevitably, race and regional cooperation were dominant themes, and he cited the prominence of those factors in the city's history. The Detroit Pistons' teamwork was the example he used to stress how the city could succeed. It should not be about who scores the most points, but about winning, he explained, "like the Pistons." Toward the close of the nearly hour-long ceremony, which was broadcast nationally on C-SPAN2, Kilpatrick began a humorous recitation of why he loved the city and what Detroit love is. "Going to the corner store and getting a Faygo and some Better Made hots, that's Detroit love." He drew the loudest response when he said, "Ice Skating at Campus Martius Park with some brothers from Linwood and Dexter who have never put on a pair of skates, that's Detroit love." But most striking was his fragment of lyric about cars: "Diamond in the back, sun-roof top, making the scene in a gangster lean, uh-huh, that's Detroit love!"[11] The image he evoked was prophetic, later applied to him.

It may not have been a key item on his list of things to highlight during his inaugural address, but Mayor Kilpatrick did give a nod to the upcoming Super Bowl XL and what it could mean to the city's economy. The event also presented a grand opportunity for promoters of a national monument to Dr. Martin Luther King Jr. in Washington, DC, to do some backslapping, handshaking, and schmoozing with the local bigwigs with healthy bank accounts.

Columnist Cooper, ever alert for ways to tie sports into civil rights, featured a story on former football great Kellen Winslow, a business-development director for Disney's Wide World of Sports Complex in Orlando, who was in town representing those proposing a King memorial. She couldn't catch up with the still fleet-footed former tight end, but there was a comment from Harry Johnson, president of the Memorial Project Foundation. "The goal is to raise about $300,000 in Detroit at the beginning of Black History Month," he said. "Despite its hardships, Detroit has always been a giving community."[12] Black history, Super Bowl, Kellen Winslow, and Dr. King—it sounded like a perfect mix to get the ball rolling, and if Winslow and the King coordinators could have gotten $5 from each of the nearly seventy thousand spectators at Ford Field for the game on February 5, exactly a month after Kilpatrick's speech, that would have been a splendid kickoff for the fund-raising initiative. But that idea was not part of the plan. The money would come from a series of other Super Bowl–related events, the proceeds of which would be added to the $50 million already in the coffers for the monument.

27

A SPARK OF REDEVELOPMENT

Two years after Mayor Kilpatrick launched the Detroit Economic Development Organization to spur employment and training in various industries, the plan was beginning to take effect. Ford Field had been packed to the rafters for the Super Bowl, and similar crowds were expected in the summer at Comerica Park, where the Tigers play. At both venues, whites were the majority of the attendees, most of them from the suburbs. A bustling arts scene is a better barometer of diversity in the city. Indicative of this hopeful sign was the annual Ford Freedom Award gala at the Charles H. Wright Museum of African American History in May. Woodie King Jr. was at the center of the festivities at the Museum. King, a former Detroiter now living in New York City and cofounder of the Concept East Theater, was saluted along with Morgan Freeman and the late Ossie Davis. King was given a special Ford Freedom Pioneer Award for creating numerous opportunities in the performing arts for African Americans.[1] Some of those in attendance for this gala and other events were among the seventy thousand paid admissions and the twenty thousand paid memberships for the year, thereby meeting the goals established in return for the $2.5 million grant from the Kresge Foundation Challenge. While the grant saved the museum, the goals were not sustainable, according to the museum's chief communications officer, Tony Spearman-Leach. "Many of the new memberships and admissions were one time and many of the members did not renew."[2]

A sizable number of Detroiters who love art and perhaps visited the museum from time to time assembled outside the six-foot-high concrete wall that ran a half mile from Eight Mile Road to Pembroke Avenue. It was called the Birwood Wall because it ran between that street and Mendota. It was built in the 1940s as a barrier separating black and white residents. Children who lived nearby played ball against the wall in the early fifties and would often mount it to see who could walk atop the narrow strip the farthest. The folks who gathered there in May 2006 were black and white, urban and suburban, and rather than putting a sledgehammer to the wall and tearing it down, they were there to help the artist Chazz Miller convert a symbol of racism into one of unity and inspiration. The huge, colorful mural with all sorts of insets and bubbles, resembling in many ways the illustrations on parts of the Berlin Wall, was a continuation of Miller's efforts with the Public Art Workz, which he founded and directed. The project was part of the Motor City Blight Busters program. As one reporter noted, it is impossible to take the entire mural in all at once, because of its length. "But certain images pop out in a slow pan: Rosa Parks boarding a bus that would make her a household name in the civil rights strug-

gle, followed by a man carrying a sign that says, 'Fair Housing.'"
There is a proliferation of children blowing bubbles, within each
of which is contained a painting of an auto plant or a word, such
as *peace* or *flowers*. Miller explained that the "bubbles are a form
of creation. Children's imaginations create the future," he said.
"Also, bubbles capture images and distort them and give you a
new perspective."[3]

A coterie of black business leaders came together in the fall
of 2006 with the objective of improving Michigan's dismal economic outlook. Included in the network of organizations, tenta-
tively called the African American Business Alliance, were the
longstanding Booker T. Washington Business Association, the
National Association of Black Automotive Suppliers, the Detroit
Chamber of Commerce, and the Black Women Contracting Association. All told, they represented more than five hundred
companies in the Detroit metropolitan area. Among the group's
objectives was to promote black-owned firms (of which there
were nearly twenty thousand in the state with almost $2 billion
in sales), bridge gaps in access to capital, and influence politics to
the benefit of the member organizations and their constituents.
Bill Brooks, chief executive officer of United American Health
Care Corporation, was selected to lead the alliance. "The time,
therefore, is particularly great because of what Detroit is doing
and its attempts to revitalize its economy," said Geneva Williams, one of the organizers of the alliance and president of City
Connect Detroit, a nonprofit that specializes in fund-raising.[4]

It's debatable what impact the alliance may have had on James
Hooks, the sole proprietor of the only African American–owned
grocery store in the city, or even if his was among the five hundred
companies earmarked for assistance. His store, Metro Foodland,
is located at Southfield Freeway and Grand River Avenue, where
it's been since he left his job at Kroger's in the mid-eighties. Despite thefts and security problems, he said his business—with

sixty employees—is doing very well, especially during the first part of the month. Residents who live within walking or short driving distance of his store have an advantage that more than a half million other Detroiters do not have—those who live in "food deserts," vast stretches of the city where residents have little or no access to affordable, nutritious food. But there are researchers who contend that the city is not a food desert. "Detroit's food issue does not come from a lack of physical stores . . . it is rooted in an unequal racial and economic system that [creates] the necessity for self-determined communities."[5]

Self-determination has been a watchword for Malik Kenyatta Yakini for years and was a motivating factor in February 2006 when he, along with several residents, founded the Detroit Black Community Food Security Network (DBCFSN). For his work in educating the children of the city, he was honored as Administrator of the Year by the Michigan Association of Public School Academies. The first plot of land acquired by the DBCFSN was on the city's east side, and there they began with the "lasagna method," in which they planted vegetables and herbs and developed work schedules, layering new activities as they became achievable. Eventually they became one of the treasured stops on the Detroit Garden Tour. When the quarter acre of land was purchased by a developer, they relocated to the city's west side on property owned by the Pan-African Orthodox Christian Church, founded by Jaramogi Abebe Agyeman. They revitalized land that had grown fallow, renaming it the D-Town Farm. On its website, the group stated:

> We observed that many of the key players in the local urban agricultural movement were young whites, who while well-intentioned, nevertheless, exerted a degree of control inordinate to their numbers in Detroit's population. Many of those individuals moved to Detroit from other places

specifically to engage in agricultural . . . work. It was and is our view that the most effective movements grow organically from the people whom they are designed to serve. Representatives of Detroit's majority African-American population must be in the leadership of efforts to foster food justice and food security in Detroit. While our specific focus is on Detroit's African-American community, we realize that improved policy and an improved localized food system is a benefit to all Detroit residents.[6]

By 2007, the organization, with an emphasis on creating garden beds, walkways, and an irrigation system, had grown considerably, gathering additional resources, tools, and outlets for their products, including space at the city's renowned Eastern Market. That summer, plans were under way for a Harvest Festival in the fall.

From the Food Security Network or D-Town Farm came the vegetables to complement the meat being cooked and served at Bert's Marketplace, within walking distance of the urban farmers' site at Eastern Market. No matter where you roamed in the market, the aroma from the huge outdoor barbecue pits wafted your way, enticing you to sample the spareribs, burgers, sausages, and hot dogs being prepared by Jai-Lee Dearing, the son of Bert Dearing, one of the city's most industrious African American entrepreneurs. Many of the patrons at the pits and the nearby club were also regular customers at Dearing's blues club not too far away downtown. From his father, Jai-Lee, thirty-four, was learning the intricacies of running his own business, which will undoubtedly buttress the nearby music and live theater venue under the Dearing name. In an interview with reporter Cassandra Spratling, Jai-Lee elaborated on the family's history, noting that his father's was the only black-owned business in the Eastern Market. Shoppers in the market were often lured to Dearing's restaurant, where the smell of barbecue filled the air. When she asked him the most important lesson he had learned thus far from his father, he said: "When things are great, you need to know how to save. When times are tough, you need to know how to stretch what you have. . . . I'm the fourth generation to be in business, and I'm teaching my children to be involved in the business."[7]

What Bert Dearing was trying to do and succeeding so well at in the city's hub, Mark Douglas was doing on the outer rim of metropolitan Detroit with his auto dealership. Douglas was the son of Walter Douglas, a former vice president of New Detroit, Inc. and an advisor to Coleman Young. In 1985, Walter Douglas entered a minority training program hosted by the Ford Motor Company. A year later, he purchased a share of Avis Ford in suburban Detroit. He became a majority owner in 1992. In 2006, he turned over the business operation to his son, Mark.

It should be noted that prior to Douglas's ownership in 1992, there were a number of black-owned automobile dealerships, most notably those of Porterfield Wilson; Nathan Conyers, the brother of Representative John Conyers; Pamela Rodgers; Mel Farr, a former running back for the Detroit Lions; and Ed Davis, the pioneer in this business. By the time Davis retired from selling new and used cars in 1971, designer Ed Welburn, a native of Philadelphia, was completing his bachelor's degree in fine arts at Howard University. In 1972, the same year of his graduation from Howard, he began working at GM as an associate designer. A year later, he joined the Buick Exterior Studio, lending his creativity to the Buick Riviera and Park Avenue. Within a few years, he was director of GM's Advanced Design in Warren, Michigan. His talented team was responsible for the development of new and innovative vehicles for all GM models. In 1975, he was assigned to the Oldsmobile Exterior Studio and was subsequently named chief designer of the studio in 1999. Seven years later, in 2006, he began a two-year stint at Saturn, which culminated in a prize overseas assignment in Germany, where he worked on future global design programs.

By 2007, Mark Douglas was among the last of the black car sellers. His dealership is located on the outskirts of the city at Twelve Mile Road and Telegraph. "Ultimately to be legacy and to have the opportunity to pass on a legacy type business, like the one I'm fortunate enough to be in, is really the blessing," Douglas said. "Not so much that I'm an African American business owner, but more so the fact that I'm an African American business owner who just happens to be a Ford dealer, that just happens to be on one of the most successful corners in Southeast Michigan."[8]

There were other thriving corners in the city. One in the Cass Corridor belonged to Janet Webster Jones, the owner of Source Booksellers. Jones, whose mother was a librarian, has been in the book business for more than twenty years, opening her store in 1989. She is also a living repository of Detroit and Michigan history, elements of which are invariably interwoven in any discussion with her. "We've had about forty years of loss of population, loss of jobs, income," she told an interviewer. "Our social fabric has been shredded in a lot of ways." But there is always a glimmer of optimism in her discussions. "So I look at Detroit and it is huge, huge. And what it will be, how it will look is all going to depend on the people. Because it's always the people and not the place."[9]

This chapter opened with a discussion of black Detroit's evolving art scene, and there is no better way to begin its conclusion than by profiling George N'Namdi, an art dealer and educator, who has been a resident of Detroit for more than a generation. A native of Columbus, Ohio, he earned his master's degree in education from Ohio State University and a PhD in psychology from the University of Michigan in 1974. But his passion was art, which he began collecting while a student in college. In 1978, he and his wife, Carmen, founded Nataki Talibah School House, an independent grade school they named after their late daughter. While his school prospered, N'Namdi continued to collect art, and by 1989 he opened his gallery in Detroit, relocating to the city from Birmingham, Michigan. He also has galleries elsewhere, including one in New York City.

"Relocating back to Detroit, there were a lot of complexities to it," he said. "We decided to establish an art center, as opposed to remaining a gallery. The challenge of funding the renovation of the building was complex and took longer than expected."[10]

A Detroiter or Highland Parker for many years, Marian Kramer had no need to relocate. What was new and invigorating for this activist, who was a prominent member of the League of Revolutionary Black Workers, was her role as director of New Chances JET. In many respects this new program is an extension of what she had done for many years as a leader of the Michigan Welfare Rights Organization. Kramer has a reputation of being a thorn in the side of the status quo, the movers and shakers whom she feels compelled to irritate to action. She and her colleagues have always tried to "afflict the comfortable and comfort the afflicted," as newspaperman Finley Peter Dunne once put it, particularly in helping those on welfare and ignored by bureaucrats and policy makers.

When Kramer was honored by the *Michigan Chronicle* in 2007 as one of the city's leaders, it could not have saluted a more determined and uncompromising activist. "The fire that burns in the hearts of such activists keeps the powerful in check," the *Chronicle* said of Kramer, and that fire shows little sign of dimming or being extinguished.

Another spark of redevelopment has long been flickering at the Northwest Activities Center (NAC), where Ron Lockett has been the executive director since 2002. A lifelong Detroiter with many years working as a counselor in youth affairs, Lockett found his niche at NAC. It was a very propitious moment recently when Dave Bing showed up at the center for the inauguration of a new gymnasium there. "None of this renovation could have been done without the financial support of the Fifth Third Bank," Lockett said. "They have been indispensable and unstinting in helping the center become the axis of a thriving community."[11]

The center is merely continuing a tradition that began in 1955, when it was the Jewish Community Center, but with the radical demographic change in the neighborhood, a fresh approach has been applied. "We are offering the same services and outreach that the Jewish Center did years ago," Lockett said. "It's just with new residents. I think what we are doing could be a model for the rest of the city, particularly the working partnership with the banks."

28

DHAKA IN DETROIT

No matter how bright and promising Detroit has appeared from decade to decade, there is the inevitable dark side, a depressing stage of stagnation and apparent hopelessness. The focus in the previous chapter on the "talented tenth," the city's black elite, is but a glimpse of the possible that provides relief from the notion that Detroit is beyond salvation. It's hard to ignore the misery index of a city where more than 70 percent of black children live below the poverty line. Many of them in single-parent households.

But despite their circumstances, they are alive, which is not like so many, who are among the 15 out of 1,000 blacks in the infant-mortality statistics, a ratio almost three times that of white babies and comparable to many Third World countries.[1]

Obviously, poverty and the lack of nourishment and medical care are factors in low birth weight and infant mortality, and this problem is exacerbated by the decrease in funds for family planning and contraceptives.

In several dramatic ways, Detroit compares to Dhaka, Bangladesh, where there is very little left of a once prosperous manufacturing base, where residents purchase most goods from other countries and seldom own or control the means of production. Securing loans, obtaining the often required collateral and/or credit, and family wealth are all key factors in owning one's own business, but few aspiring black entrepreneurs in Detroit have possessed these requisites. When they have—and black businessmen and women in Detroit vary little from their counterparts in other states—four in ten of them operate in the health care, social assistance, repair, maintenance, laundry, and personal services sectors. New York City had the most black-owned businesses in 2007 with 154,929 (or 8 percent of all the nation's black-owned businesses), followed by Chicago with 58,631 (or 3.1 percent), Houston, with 33,062 (or 1.7 percent), and Detroit with 32,490 (or 1.7 percent).[2]

Black businesses were enduring their usual dismal prospects, and given that the city's population was becoming more African American by the day, it's little wonder that the overall forecast for the city was doom and gloom. The New Year, 2008, was hardly under way before a grim report from *Crain's* indicated that nothing had changed in the last several months in Detroit. "Imagine living in a city with the country's highest rate of violent crime and the second-highest unemployment rate." This was just the opening salvo describing the nightmare scenario as the article went on to conclude that "the Motor City grabs the top spot on *Forbes'* inaugural list of America's Most Miserable Cities."[3] For Detroit to earn this inglorious notice, economists took the aggregate sum of several indicators, indices, and measures—

each prefixed with the word *misery*—of 150 major metropolitan areas with a minimum population of 371,000, and Detroit came out on top, with Flint in third place. This comes as no surprise if unemployment is a chief factor, because both Detroit and Flint have for years been at the mercy of whatever happens in the automobile industry, and during this period, downturn was the direction both cities experienced. An even more disturbing omen and indication of Detroit's future was forecast by native son Mitt Romney, who in the *New York Times* wrote an op-ed titled "Let Detroit Go Bankrupt." At the time, Romney had lost the Republican presidential nomination to Senator John McCain of Arizona, and his bid for the land's top office was in no better shape than the automobile industry, which he believed needed a turnaround, not a bailout.

"I was born in Detroit," Romney wrote, "the son of an auto chief executive. In 1954, my dad, George Romney, was tapped to run American Motors when its president suddenly died. The company itself was on life support—banks were threatening to deal it a death blow. The stock collapsed. I watched Dad work to turn the company around—and years later at business school, they were still talking about it. From the lessons of that turnaround, and from my own experiences, I have several prescriptions for Detroit's automakers." He proposed that labor agreements be aligned in pay and benefits to match those of workers at the foreign car companies, that retiree benefits be reduced, and that the management teams and sales forces be replaced. "A managed bankruptcy may be the only path to the fundamental restructuring the industry needs," he concluded.[4] This was mainly his prescription for the auto industry, though in a way, he was prescient as to what would arrive for the city in a few years. There was a young man in the other party with his own ideas about how to handle the problems Detroit was facing, and how Romney's own words would come back to haunt him.

That young man was Barack Obama, a one-term senator from Illinois who gained national attention in a speech at the Democratic Convention in 2004 and rocked the nation four years later when he defeated Hillary Clinton in the primaries and went on, with Joe Biden as his running mate, to win the presidential election. During Obama's campaign appearance at Joe Louis Arena in Detroit in the summer, Katherine Brown was among the twenty thousand clamoring to see him. "I stood in a long line that stretched along the waterfront," she told a reporter. "He was fantastic and the cheering was so loud and constant there were times when you could hardly hear what he was saying."[5]

What he said there was similar to his remarks earlier at an unscheduled stop outside an engine plant in Flint. "Flint, this is our moment," Obama said. "This is our time to unite in common purpose, to make this century the next American century. . . . And if you'll vote for me, if you'll work with me, if you'll organize with me, we will win Michigan, we will win this election, and you and I together will change the country and change the world." And possibly change Detroit's Third World status?

A portion of the world was changed on November 4 when Barack Obama became the nation's first black president. Obama won despite the early setbacks when he removed his name from the ballot after Michigan moved up its primary. His Republican adversary, John McCain, saw this as an opening, but the polls showed him the error of his ways, and he eventually conceded the state to his opponent; and Obama and Biden took Michigan by a double-digit margin, compiling a three-to-one margin in Wayne County. Some of Detroit's old-timers compared the celebration of Obama's victory to the ones from their youth when Joe Louis knocked out Max Schmeling. "I never thought I'd live to see the day a black man would be in the White House in the Oval Office and not be a servant," said Addie Thompson, an eighty-eight-year-old woman who first voted for Franklin Delano Roosevelt. She celebrated the moment with her family on the city's west side. "When I heard the news I couldn't believe it. I broke down in tears."[6]

A more official celebration occurred at the Renaissance Center in downtown Detroit, where practically every political bigwig in the Democratic Party lined up for an opportunity to address the overflow crowd. "This is a great day to be a resident of Detroit," said interim mayor Ken Cockrel Jr. "It's a great day to be a Michigander, it's a great day to be an American. Not only have we made history, but we have begun to chart the course for a new direction in this country."[7]

A new direction for the city, too, was probably on Cockrel's mind that evening. Two months earlier, in September, he was given the reins of the city when Mayor Kwame Kilpatrick, after pleading guilty to felony charges, resigned. His fall was another reminder of the city's Third World circumstances. Cockrel, formerly the president of the City Council, Governor Jennifer Granholm, and even a rather contrite Kilpatrick talked about the city "moving forward," despite the embarrassing setback. It all began with Kilpatrick's extramarital affair with his chief of staff Christine Beatty. To keep the affair secret, the mayor fired three police officers; they sued the city. Kilpatrick then fraudulently used more than $8 million to settle the lawsuit before it went to court. But the *Detroit Free Press*, through the Freedom of Information Act, was able to secure steamy text messages between the lovers from their cell phones, which contradicted their testimony under oath that no such affair existed. Beatty had already resigned when the affair became public, and Kilpatrick was hit with eight felony charges, plus two more after investigators said he interfered with the police officers in their attempts to serve a subpoena related to the text messages. "Mr. Kilpatrick's lawyers tried unsuccessfully in recent days to negotiate plea agreements that would not involve jail time, but prosecutors were adamant. Mr. Kilpatrick will serve 120 days in county jail for the guilty pleas to two felony counts of obstruction of justice. He also pleaded no contest to one of the assault charges. The others were dismissed."[8] Kilpatrick had entered the political arena with great pizzazz and promise, but was apparently unable to set aside those youthful impetuosities, the often fatal temptations of love. When the charges first seeped out, he vehemently denied them, declaring that his accusers, including the city's media, were imbued with a "lynch mob mentality." Later, he said, "I take full responsibility for my actions. I wish with all my heart that we could turn back the hands of time and tell that young man to make better choices. But I can't. Our challenge now is to put the anguish and turmoil of recent months behind us and join in a common cause to love our city, to love one another, and move forward together."[9]

Moving forward would be done without Kilpatrick, but it would involve a tonnage of sludge and criminal charges against Monica Conyers, the congressman's wife, who assumed the helm at the City Council after Cockrel became the interim mayor. A year later, the often embattled councilwoman pled guilty to accepting a bribe in the Synagro sludge scandal. While black America was still excited about the prospects of the Obama administration, Detroit was enduring one scandal after another.

To expunge the grime of corruption that smeared the city required a squeaky-clean personality, someone who could push the scandals to the back pages and command the front pages with panache. Dave Bing may not have been the white knight the beleaguered wished for, but at least he was not mired in controversy and had brought Detroit a certain amount of fame and prestige as a Piston and as a very successful businessman.

In the middle of October 2008, alerted to the shenanigans at Manooghian, Bing announced that he was a candidate to become the next mayor of Detroit. Used to being at the top of the heap, Bing finished first among fifteen candidates in the nonpartisan primary. Still, there was another round before the fight was over—a runoff against Cockrel, who amassed the second highest number of votes.

Once again Bing was the winner, rewarded with the task of completing Kilpatrick's term, slated to end on December 31, 2009. Almost immediately upon taking office, Bing set about dealing with the city's pressing union issues. He placed the city's outrageous total of 51 union contracts in the crosshairs, wrote Drew Sharp in his biography of Bing, at which his subject took umbrage. "He terminated 16 of those contracts, quickly developing a reputation as a union basher. He eliminated 400 city employees off the books."

Later, Bing would say that these were moves he had to make because the city was stuck in such a deep economic abyss that it should have filed for bankruptcy then. Moving the city forward meant paring down the payroll and sending a number of Detroiters to the unemployment line.[10] Such drastic moves could have destroyed any hopes of his winning the full-term election in November 2009, but he won handily, defeating perennial candidate Tom Barrow. Now it was his turn to take the stage at the illustrious Fox Theatre for his inauguration. Bing said, "We will no longer be defined by the failures, divisiveness, and self-serving actions of the past. We are turning the page to a new time in Detroit, focused not just on the challenges we face, but the opportunities we have to rebuild and renew our city."[11]

Mayor Bing was slowly warming to his new position when he was confronted by the cold reality of gun violence. Throughout the nation over the previous decade, from 1999 to 2009, gun violence had taken the lives of thousands of young black men and women, and hundreds of them were unarmed victims of unwarranted police violence. Few of these terrible tragedies were as heart-wrenching as the killing of seven-year-old Aiyana Jones by a police officer in May 2010. It was around midnight, and Aiyana was asleep on the couch with her grandmother nearby watching television. Neither of them had time to react to the thud at the door nor the flash-bang grenade tossed into the living room by the police at the start of the raid. Officer Joseph Weekley immediately began firing his MP5 submachine gun blindly through the window into the smoke and chaos. One of the bullets entered Aiyana's head and exited through her neck. She was killed instantly. The SWAT team had come looking for a murder suspect who lived upstairs but left with only a dead child. The entire horrendous episode was caught on camera by a television crew working on *The First 48*, a true-crime program for A&E. It was hard to dispute the filmed evidence, but the police tried, even suggesting that Weekley's gun discharged accidently after he was bumped by the grandmother.

"There is no question about what happened because it's in the videotape," said Geoffrey Fieger, the attorney for the family. "It's not an accident. It's not a mistake. There was no altercation." Aiyana was shot from outside on the porch. The video showed the officer throwing the stun grenade through the window and within milliseconds firing from outside the home.[12] Despite the conclusive evidence, two trials ended in mistrials, and the prosecutor dismissed the remaining charge. Weekley was not punished in any way—justifiably, it was argued, because his actions were and are standard operating procedure for SWAT raids.

Mayor Bing's response to the tragedy was much too slow, and the media and a number of residents took him to task for this. His reaction was methodical, his remarks measured, as if choosing to err on the side of caution. "I want the facts to prove what happened," he told a reporter. "You have a lot of people who get very emotional and I understand that. [But] you've got to control emotion and you can't just jump off the deep end because a tragedy happened. And this is obviously a tragedy."[13] Where was Police Chief Warren Evans, who had up to this point done a fairly commendable job reducing crime in the city? According to one report, he was overseas while his mayor was in over his head, flummoxed and bewildered by the entire situation. Bing would be even more flustered and upset when he learned that Evans had given the producers of the show permission to film the police for their cinema verité. Nor was he aware that Evans was involved in the creation of a reality series pilot called "The Chief" for A&E. "Evans was seen sporting an assault weapon strapped around him as he made arrests." Two months later, he was fired.[14]

Although troubled by the child's senseless death, Mayor Bing turned his attention to another pressing dilemma—the city's public school system's declining attendance and a $300 million annual city deficit. The public schools of Detroit were always a key concern of the mayor. Four years before, in 2005, he had invested money in the development of charter schools. That action precipitated a confrontation with the Detroit Federation of Teachers. By 2009, the problem in the public schools remained as pressing as ever, but Bing now had the expertise of Robert Bobb to help him through the educational quagmire. With more than thirty years of executive management experience helping governments, businesses, and schools find funding and operational solutions, Bobb appeared to be perfectly suited to navigate Detroit's troubled waters. In four cities he had served as a city manager. He'd been president of the Washington, DC, Board of Education before accepting Governor Granholm's appointment as emergency financial manager of the Detroit Public Schools (DPS). Exercising severe cost-cutting measures, Bobb reduced the deficit to $86.8 million by the summer of 2009.[15] He and Bing were newsmakers of the year in 2010, and Bobb was on a roll, appearing on *Meet the Press* along with Secretary of Education Arne

Duncan, who had said on one occasion that Detroit has "arguably the worst urban school district in the country."[16]

Bobb was a strict and forceful manager, and with an almost drill-sergeant mentality, he told the school's principals that they had a year to turn things around at the lagging schools. When they didn't, he applied his take-no-prisoners attitude, closing fifty-nine schools, firing central office staff, and selling off idle assets in order to trim the budget deficit. He "expanded Advanced Placement offerings, more than doubled reading and math lesson time for younger students, obtained contract concessions from the teachers union, launched a $500 million school rebuilding campaign (with voter approval) and upended a culture of inertia and waste."[17]

A day or so after Aiyana was shot and killed, Bing asked Rochelle Collins, his government liaison officer, to resign, allegedly while she was on sick leave. She filed a lawsuit charging wrongful dismissal in the workplace with Bing and Karen Dumas, his chief communications officer, as the defendants. Even more seriously, she accused Bing, Governor Rick Snyder, Bobb, and Kirk Lewis, the chief mayoral adviser, of "concocting a covert scheme in February 2011 that would have put Bing unilaterally in charge of all city financial affairs."[18] The showdown between Collins and Dumas was resolved when the City Council voted 6–3 to approve a $200,000 settlement to Collins (Joann Watson, Kwame Kenyatta, and Brenda Jones voted against it).

Soon afterward, Dumas resigned, and another potentially damaging city scandal was nipped in the bud. The always resourceful Dumas told reporter Jim McFarlin that she continues to meet with Bing to discuss various business matters. Bing's biggest problem, she said, was that "he's too nice."[19]

With his administration reeling and muddled with controversy, Bing received another blow when he learned his good friend Sam Logan had died. Logan, a native of Louisiana but a product of Detroit schools, including Commerce High School and the University of Detroit, died three days after Christmas in 2011. He was best known for his stewardship of the *Michigan Chronicle*; during his forty years there, he rose through the ranks, mainly in advertising, and eventually facilitated the sale of the paper to Real Times Publishing, Inc.

To Mayor Bing, Logan "was more than a Detroit icon, he was a respected pioneer in black journalism who championed the need for coverage of a community not totally served by the mainstream media."[20] Bing was among the hundreds who attended Logan's funeral at Greater Grace Temple. He mourned the passing of his friend, and funeral director O'Neil Swanson's encomium was thoughtfully composed, but he knew there would be more gloom for the city in a couple of months when he delivered his State of the City speech. By then Detroit would be completely broke, and there would be more serious talk about an emergency manager to take over the city, something Mayor Bing had sworn not to ask for, though the governor had earlier signed legislation into law with provisions allowing the state to intervene in distressed cities such as Detroit.

Gradually, the murmurs of bankruptcy began to swell into a crescendo that echoed from the Renaissance Center to the Fisher Building, a reality residents experienced years ago in the surrounding neighborhoods. Bing said that one of the mistakes the newly appointed emergency manager, Kevyn D. Orr, made was "that he got too heavily involved in city government . . . when his job was to help get our finances straight. It's hard enough doing one job and he was trying to do two."[21]

29

A LOOMING CHIMERA

Amid the rumors of bankruptcy there were seeds of hope, at least for downtown Detroit, with the arrival of Dan Gilbert's Quicken Loans and Compuware, whose financial pledges to help employees find homes nearby were matched by Blue Cross/Blue Shield of Michigan and other companies. Similar efforts had been launched years before in midtown, where the expansion of Wayne State University and Detroit Medical Center and the subsequent development in the area spurred development along the waterfront. Although wealth is concentrated downtown, there are pockets of black prosperity from Palmer Woods, in the city's north, to Grayhaven, on the far east side. These neighborhoods recall some of the vistas of beauty and promise once prevalent in Detroit. They are reminders of the glorious boulevards of dreams and enchanting cottages that black Detroiters purchased and refinished with homeowners' unbreakable love. Now there were only vestiges of the splendid streets, well-kept manicured lawns, and homes brimming with hope and possibility. This was a time when the city had the largest percentage of black homeowners and the highest comparative wages in the nation.

Many black residents were upset that reporters deployed to the city excluded them from discussion when they wrote about the "good things," mostly downtown. Yes, the ruins are extensive—and none more bleak and devastated than Highland Park. A Sherwood Forest, Indian Village, and Lafayette Park may not be beautiful, but they are a far cry from the reports about a city resembling Dresden after the bombings of World War II.

During a visit to the city in the summer of 2015, Darren Walker, President of the Ford Foundation, was given a tour, and he noticed the contrast. He passed through Sherwood Forest and then into the blighted areas near Woodward and Seven Mile Road. "We're used to seeing this in India and other locations, but to see it in our neighborhood is disturbing," he said. "What continues to inspire me is the optimism in the city. People in Detroit have a boundless capacity to be the best and look to the future."[1]

Over the last three or four years, with bankruptcy a reality and the emergency manager in place, the city continues to alternate between positive signs of development below Grand Boulevard and ceaseless decay beyond. Even so, there is an interesting plan on the drawing board that would combine Dan Gilbert's Bedrock, Jim Jenkins's construction company, and Rheal Capital Management, founded and led by John Rhea, the former chairman and CEO of the New York City Housing Authority (NYCHA). With Rhea at the throttle, the nexus of companies—with these three as the putative core—would, as he views it, be able to provide the capital, incentive, and know-how to rebuild the city. Unlike the squadron of reporters who parachuted in, got their stories, and departed, Rhea was born and raised in the city, a successful product of the DPS and a graduate of Detroit Jesuit High School. He earned his bachelor's degree in economics and government from Wesleyan University before being hired at PaineWebber. He earned his MBA from Harvard Business School. His background in investment banking, corporate strategy, and financial management prepared him for the task of revitalizing Detroit. All was not rosy in New York City under the Bloomberg administration, and it was widely reported that Rhea resigned before Mayor Bill de Blasio could fire him. After four years at NYCHA, whatever the reasons for his departure, administering the largest array of public housing in the nation has endowed him with a perspective he could not have acquired otherwise. "Detroit is very attractive," Rhea said during an interview with *Michigan Chronicle* reporter Donald James. "This is the first time in decades that I've seen a broad coalition in Detroit across such entities as government agencies, private sectors, foundations, philanthropic groups, banks, and local residents, all joining together and putting together a blueprint as to what role they will collectively play to move Detroit forward."[2]

Rhea's plan and one proposed by Chris Ilitch—his "transformational initiative" to create more than eight thousand construction-related jobs—are what thousands of unemployed Detroiters are hoping for. Proof of their desire to work was demonstrated in the spring of 2013, when a multitude of job seekers showed up for a job fair at Quicken Loans, which was looking to recruit about five hundred people.[3]

In November 2014, less than sixteen months after Detroit became the largest city in the nation ever to file for bankruptcy, federal judge Steven W. Rhodes approved a plan for the city to rid itself of $7 billion in debt and invest $1.7 billion in city services. "What happened in Detroit must never happen again,"

Judge Rhodes said. "This must never be repeated anywhere in this state."[4]

A sigh of relief echoed from the city's riverfront all the way to Eight Mile Road, especially in parts of Detroit suffering most from the financial calamity. Now that the "grand bargain"—which saved the valuable collection at the Detroit Institute of Arts as well as providing money to salvage workers' pensions—is a done deal, there are still a number of details to be worked out. The path toward solvency remains tricky. Emergency manager Kevyn D. Orr has done his job and moved on, but too much of the emergency continues to strain the city's delicate fiscal condition.

Even so, the city is no longer on life support, no longer in danger of a fiscal meltdown, and there's a stronger economic pulse with the arrival of new companies and industries. One of the more impressive ventures to Detroit is that of Shinola (not the defunct shoe-polish company). Watches are the company's main product, but it also manufactures bicycles, leather goods, and an assortment of other items. Most meaningful for Detroiters are the job opportunities, and it was certainly encouraging to see African American men and women, presumably employees, in the company's recent nationwide advertising campaign. If the ad is representative of black employees at the company, then it's a hopeful sign, not only of the city's business rejuvenation, but also of job opportunities for its residents, particularly for those who now comprise the bulk of the unemployed.

When Shinola was launched in 2012, it was part of a wave of new enterprises seeking traction in a city still reeling from bankruptcy. Many questioned the decision to locate in Detroit, but the company's explanation was enthusiastically received. "We know there's not just history in Detroit, there is a future," the company stated. They were bringing back Detroit's "glory of manufacturing"—good news for the economically depressed residents, those already in flight, and those on the verge of departure. "We felt like this is our fourth year, and we have a lot of things to celebrate, but especially over 500 employees in the U.S. now," said Bridget Russo, Shinola's chief marketing officer. "The campaign is highlighting not only the brand, but the job creation and ultimately the people, because they're the fabric of what we do."[5]

It is not disclosed how much of that "fabric" of 500 employees is African American, but almost 400 of the workers live in Detroit. About 240 of them work in manufacturing; others work on e-commerce, marketing, and the company's website.

Shinola could be a harbinger of the city's recovery. It is certainly welcomed with optimism by those working there as well as the thousands of others hoping for jobs in the near future. That optimism is enhanced by Shinola's plan to expand its operation in the city beyond its manufacturing center in the Cass Corridor and its headquarters in the College of Creative Studies in the historic Argonaut Building in midtown.

"I've been working at Shinola for more than three years," one employee said. There's a "good employee discount, friendly coworkers (some)," and "most managers while being focused on the business can still be fairly nice and respectful to employees."[6]

It remains to be seen what impact the "grand bargain" will have on black Detroiters, though pensioners should be relieved. The economic collapse did not happen overnight. Like so much of Detroit's history, good or bad, it was the result of a cumulative process, a steady interaction of social, political, and economic elements that collided and often tumbled to unpredictable outcomes. Long before the current crisis, there were indicators, portents of disaster in the same way that decay and erosion forecast devastation. Sometimes, if remedies are applied promptly, the crash can be averted. In Detroit's case, the changing demographics, a shrinking revenue base, the onset of deindustrialization, corporate indifference, inadequate management, and corruption eviscerated a metropolis already struggling for stability. I leave it to the social scientists and economists to assess the damage, how it got there, and what can be done to restore and sustain the city. Let them quibble over the water and sewage flow of revenue at the core of the argument about regional government, whether the bankruptcy was inevitable, the actual worth of the "grand bargain," what agency or entity will control the city's financial future, and most important, the pertinence of race in the whole shebang. It's hard to analyze and evaluate anything in America without carefully considering the race factor; for that reason, Detroit, with its black majority, could be a test case for many aspects of social, political, and economic control of municipalities. But at this stage of Detroit's history, Councilman James Tate feels that class is equally important in understanding the city's dilemma. He's not about to dismiss the race factor, but it's not as pronounced in a city that's predominantly black. "What I hear more than anything among my constituents is renters versus homeowners," he said.[7]

It is no easy assignment to pinpoint when and how the race, class, and gender factors were in play when the city began its downward spiral. Doing so will challenge even the best historians and social scientists. In his book *The Unwinding: An Inner History of the New America*, George Packer wrote that no one can say when the country began to unravel, because "it began at countless times, in countless ways." Such is the unraveling of Detroit, and its reassembling may occur with a similar sense of mystery, the indicators of renewal no less baffling than the first trace of "rust on the belt."

In July 1701, Detroit came into existence. In July 2013, Detroit reached the nadir of decline. In July 2015, Mike Duggan took the wheel, the first white mayor since Roman Gribbs (1970–74). He won because he earned the black vote and now, as

the late James Boggs once warned, he has the awesome responsibility of leadership. One glorious thing in his favor is the city's
history, a tradition of getting up off the floor, coming back in the
same way Joe Louis came back on June 22, 1938. Like Detroit,
there was no place for him to go but up, after hitting rock bottom. But bottom without "Black" attached is meaningless for
poet jessica Care moore, who moved back to Detroit from New
York City, looking for the "old city" that she prefers rather than
all the talk about a "new Detroit." Her energetic enthusiasm for
her hometown is undiminished by all the negative reports. "I
grew up in Detroit with a father who had his own construction
company, he was a hardhat," she remembered, noting that he
helped build Wonderland Mall. "His name was Tom Moore and
he had a Cadillac and I would ride in the front with him." Moore
has her own publishing company, and her new book, *Sunlight
Through Bullet Holes*, is an homage to Detroit. She explains that
the book and its title are emblematic of a resurgent Detroit and
says, "Despite the attacks on us we find the light."[8] "The integrity and heart of our people are not bankrupt," one of her poems
declares. "We are rich with history. Raised on tradition. Our
Daddy's lessons / Our Momma's intuition."

Another renowned Detroit poet, from far away Oaxaca,
Mexico, echoes her colleague:

From Now On

and put your ear here:
the sound of our soul
is felt no more
in the punishing piston's drive
but the straight ahead free flight
of 2 am jam sessions
supplanting the song of the slave.

in the Eastern region
farmed by Yusef Lateef
and legions of others
we thrive.
tonight
geri allen, marian hayden, regina carter, and gaylynn
mckinney
play us into the dawn
and here come
james carter, craig taborn, jaribu shahid, rayse
biggs, david macmurrary
tani tabal, pam wise, rodney whitaker, shawn
thunder wallace . . .
the line at the bandstand is long
with depth and reach
to vault this river
in one wide stride rhythm
swingin'
from now on.

—Michele Gibbs, from *Spare Parts: The Detroit Suite* (Shango Fireside Publishing, Highland Park, MI, 1998)

AFTERWORD

By Ron Lockett, Executive Director of the Northwest Activities Center

From my current position as the executive director of the Northwest Activities Center, having lived many years on the city's east side and attended school in midtown and elsewhere—to say nothing of my six decades working in and around Detroit—I think I can speak with authority about my hometown. In *Black Detroit: A People's History of Self-Determination*, Herb Boyd has done a marvelous job of research and discussion, and many of the incidents and personalities he cites are inextricably connected with my experiences.

At the moment, Detroit is a city on the rebound, with numerous new economic developments in the downtown and midtown areas. Midtown, though it now encompasses more territory, was once known as the Cass Corridor. Its hot real estate now includes Wayne State University, Tech Town, the Cultural Center, and many renovated living quarters with soaring rents. The area literally has its own transportation service, the Q Line, a streetcar system named after one of its benefactors, Quicken Loans, owned by billionaire Dan Gilbert. Little Caesars Arena will host both the Red Wings and the Pistons. Sadly, the arena developers have been unable to meet the goal of hiring 50 percent Detroiters to work on this $700 million project. The penalty is a fine that goes into a fund for training city residents to become job ready. Somehow it seems that Detroiters are missing out on a major event that occurs every generation or two.

Most Detroiters live in neighborhoods, and in these areas, development is uneven. There are some flashes of improvement, but by and large, communities are still struggling with unemployment, crime, and low-achieving schools. Detroit is a city with large expanses of uninhabited land and is sprinkled with thirty-one thousand vacant and dilapidated houses. In various pockets throughout town, community-based organizations have worked tirelessly to maintain their respective areas against a tide of neglect and disinvestment. The current mayoral administration has tried to use an assortment of methods to arrest the decline of the neighborhoods, with moderate success. This gargantuan task has been assisted with massive aid from the Obama administration, but the city still has major hurdles ahead with a large poor, unskilled, and semiliterate population.

There are several African American–led organizations aiding the "New Detroit" culturally. These groups include the Wright Museum, Chene Park, and N'Namdi Gallery. The Carr Center, a social-cultural venue, was unable to keep its site in the new Paradise Valley development (Harmonie Park) and is looking for a new permanent home. The terrain is difficult and perilous for cultural groups without large endowments and corporate sponsors. Many organizations with wonderful visions have been unable to survive.

For Detroit to improve the quality of life for all its residents, a mechanism for them to share directly in the governance of the city must be created. Political power and self-governance has been severely weakened by the State of Michigan by its toxic tools of bankruptcy and emergency management. Lansing has a very paternalistic view of Detroit, the city that essentially built the state. For the improvement of schools, public transportation, and human services and for the rebuilding of its aging infrastructure to occur, Detroiters must retake total control of their institutions. This power must be seized in what is a protracted battle for survival of the soul of the city. Most residents in struggling neighborhoods can't move away and have limited options for improving their condition. There is plenty of ferment for change in the neighborhoods.

Northwest Activities Center (NWAC) is a pillar of stability. As one of the largest community centers in Southeast Michigan, the NWAC provides an array of services to Detroit residents from the dawn of their existence to their twilight years. However, the status quo was anything but clear in the intervening years before the historic Detroit municipal bankruptcy. As a nonprofit corporation focused on uplifting its residents, it had to search for a corporate partner committed to its historic mission. In the years before bankruptcy, the annual city allocation provided to NWAC plummeted to zero, and the organization had to rebrand itself as a unit bringing the community together within its walls to fill the various service-delivery vacuums in northwest Detroit. Enter Fifth Third Bank, providing a $2 million lifeline to NWAC for capital building improvements and employee back pay. NWAC was built in 1955 as the Jewish Community Center and bequeathed to the City of Detroit in 1974. The 1967 rebellion hastened the departure of Detroit Jews from the area. The Center was part of the Jewish community for only nineteen years, while the African American community has been served by it for the past forty-two years. Today NWAC has over three hundred thousand visitors annually.

As Detroit enters a new phase of growth after so many fits and starts, its future looks mixed. Ideas abound—for urban farms, bike paths, mixed residential/commercial developments, etc. But the city can achieve its true greatness only when the majority population shares in the incredible growth downtown and this same material energy is duplicated in the neighborhoods. One major dilemma facing young African American Detroiters is whether to stay in Detroit or go elsewhere to start careers and pursue business dreams. Many parents fret that their kids will not return home after college.

One part of the city is being revitalized by several entrepreneurs pulling together to fill shopping and service voids. The Avenue of Fashion on Livernois Avenue is the prototype of what should be replicated in neighborhoods throughout the city. Residents now eat in new restaurants and shop for quality merchandise in upscale stores owned by local entrepreneurs. This type of synergy is vital for a city with vestiges of its historical legacy of political and economic inequality still very tangible.

Our spirits were uplifted when two of our high schools, Cass Tech and Martin Luther King Jr., brought home state championships in football in 2016.

Detroit is a city of survivors who have endured highs and lows throughout its storied history. We have gone from the riot in 1943 and the rebellion in 1967 to the Pistons' world championships in 1989, 1990, and 2004, from Martin Luther King's first "I Have a Dream" speech in 1963 to the election of our first African American mayor, Coleman A. Young in 1974, from a population of 1.8 million in 1950 to 670,000 today. Detroit will find a way to survive by rebranding, retooling, and rediscovering itself. I'm proud to be a Detroiter.

AUTHOR'S AFTERWORD

Since its publication, *Black Detroit: A People's History of Self-Determination* has received bountiful praise from reviewers in journals, magazines, and newspapers, including *Publishers Weekly*, *Kirkus Reviews*, the *New York Times*, *Washington Post*, and *Detroit Free Press*. The response from its diverse readership has been exceptionally gratifying and greatly appreciated; none more approving than the residents of Detroit.

It has been heartwarming to receive calls like the one from a reader overflowing with joy that her family was included.

On many occasions, I have acknowledged that this has been a most remarkable journey based on my experience doing research in Detroit's impressive archival collections, excavating recollections from my years growing up, attending schools, and working in various fields in Detroit, and equally important accessing decades of my mother's resourceful and remarkable memories. There were the productive sessions with my wife, Elza Dinwiddie Boyd, and my agent, Marie Dutton Brown.

As they often remind me, *Black Detroit* really belongs to the people; the early migrants fleeing slavery and the impositions of Jim Crow and the succeeding generations who worked in the plants, taught in the schools, challenged the social, political, and economic inequities, and through their genius, ingenuity, and commitment, helped to build this great city. Compressing more than three hundred years of history in one volume was a challenging and daunting task. From the beginning, I knew that there would be individuals, issues, incidents, and episodes that would not make the cut. Those chapters I leave for future writers imbued with a similar passion about the city's history.

Upon publication of the book, there were sections where I realized could have been more expansive, more insightful. Inevitably there would be several omissions and oversights that I am acknowledging in this and future editions of *Black Detroit*. One significant oversight was the failure to include mention of the pioneering role of black radio, especially the combined vision of Dr. Wendell Cox and Dr. Haley Bell, the founders of WCHB-AM. The station's call letters were the doctors' initials, and it was the first American black-owned station. Founded in 1956, the station provided a platform for a host of enterprising and creative broadcasters. In a similar vein, the early ventures in the city's black television market and the role of Gil Maddox and Tony Brown in this endeavor is herewith acknowledged. Moreover, the recognition of Joe Von Battle and his music store on Hastings Street and the work of his daughter, Marsha Music, to ensure his legacy is critical in the discussion of Detroit's music history.

During a recent visit to NYU Abu Dhabi, where Michael Dinwiddie teaches, I read that Jeff Mills, a DJ and techno collective innovator, was also visiting the United Arab Emirates to lecture and perform in Dubai. It seems that Detroit and Detroiters have no boundaries, and no matter where I roam the city and its natives have a significant presence.

Many people's contributions such as Gerald Simmons (Kwadwo Akpan) are mentioned in the notes and the acknowledgements. And many others are included in the book, even if they do not appear in the index. My friends in Detroit have asked why the tireless commitment of Peggy Moore, Herbert Metoyer, and the Detroit Writers' Guild were not mentioned. They nurtured a coterie of aspiring writers and while they may not have been part of the Guild, young writers such as Tiya Miles (*The Dawn of Detroit*) and Angela Flournoy (*The Turner House*) have respectively enshrined segments of Detroit's distant past and highlighted the contemporary issues that keep the city's history and literary legacy alive. I have received requests to mention Dr. Murray Jackson, the Boggs Center, and the ongoing dedication of activist Helen Moore.

I wish I had known more about the life and contributions of Richard Maurice, the pioneering black filmmaker. Recently, while writing an obituary on a photographer Don Hogan Charles, I came across a photo in *Ebony* magazine of Carolyn and Arthur Reese in Hattiesburg, Mississippi in 1964. Both were phenomenal Detroit school teachers and, at that time, were there working on the voting registration drives across the South. Like the parents of Michael Simanga, the Reese's escaped my memory, but their fight for freedom and justice should not be forgotten.

As we look back and face forward, in the tradition of the Sankofa bird, there is a plethora of promising developments around the city. On the cultural front gallery-owner George N'Namdi envisions an art district, a specific section of the city where artists can gather to present, perform, and share their creativity. The enterprising Dan Aldridge has assembled many notable musicians with Detroit roots for a historic recording that will complement what musician, composer, and teacher Mike

Monford is doing with aspiring young musicians at the Chandler Park Academy of Music. What Mike is doing is similar to the many years of music education offered by pianist/composer James Tatum, and how wonderful to learn of the success of one of his students, Jherrad Hardeman, who composed the music for Dr. Henry Louis Gates's documentary *Many Rivers to Cross*.

By now, I think my point should be clear, and I could go on for several more pages, if not another volume, on the significant folks who are not between these covers. More than anything that is a testament to the multitude of black Detroiters, who I hope are given wider exposure in future books about the city's history.

In effect, *Black Detroit*, is an effort to make sure that many of the city's African American citizens are not omitted—as they often are—when the books about Detroit continue to be published. And in a broader context, it is my hope that this book inspires other black writers to document their communities and thereby add to the rich history of the black experience in America.

It's very easy not to document the stories of those whose blood, sweat, and tears cleared the land, broke the sod, and, too often without compensation, erected the first edifices in the city. Today, there is a flurry of development in downtown and midtown Detroit, and now the city is receiving more attention than it did during the bankruptcy phase. But revitalization of the city should not exclude the outer regions, those neighborhoods where my mother lived and raised her children.

Finally, I am greatly appreciative and proud of the awards, nominations, and recognition *Black Detroit* has receive since its first publication, and now I am even more aware of the work still to be done to keep the record straight and guarantee our rightful place in world history. Let the blessings now showered on Black Detroit be extended and shared with all who have endured the good and bad of the city's history.

AUTHOR'S NOTE: A SON REMEMBERS

Here and there throughout *Black Detroit* I have mentioned Katherine Brown. That is my personal pride, because she is my mother. Now you can go to the index and see how she is inextricably woven into the narrative. I could not have done this book without her sharing her story, her memories, with me. And what a memory! Only on a couple of points did we differ, mainly in counting the number of places where we've lived in this city.

I deliberately refrained from including every historical incident in which she was present or which she vividly recalled. However, I found it impossible to exclude my deepest impressions of her, when I was four and she brought my brother Charles and me from Alabama to Detroit, just in time for me to experience the race riot of 1943.

From her early reconnaissance trips to Detroit before moving here, down to her apartment in the LaBelle Towers in Highland Park, most of her ninety-six years have been in her beloved Motown. I think I was about five or six when I began badgering her with questions about my father, asking why he wasn't with us in Detroit. It took me years to unravel that she and my father had different views about how and where the children should be raised. As a farmer, my father was a man of the soil; my mother was a dreamer and wanted something more than the limitations of Jim Crow.

She had only an eighth-grade education, but my mother was extremely resourceful. During World War II, she was among a fortunate few black women to gain employment in the "arsenal of democracy." When that ended, I remember the succeeding years when she would leave the house at the break of day and return as the sun went down. It took a full day for her to travel to the suburbs and then come home after her job as a domestic was done. Her native abilities were phenomenal, stuff no classroom could have taught her.

She shared these things with me, teaching me to read and write, to prepare my breakfast, to handle her precious shellac records—and she was the best bid whist partner I've ever had. Imbued with her lessons of life, I was never without confidence, never without her encouragement to excel.

When I was nineteen, she managed the kitchen at Hall's Department Store on Schoolcraft and Wyoming. It wasn't long before she convinced the owner to give me a job chasing stock and working in the warehouse. But neither of us lasted very long at the store, and soon she was back doing "day work." Because of the thorough way she cleaned a house, she was always in demand in the suburbs, primarily working in Jewish homes, where she learned their culture and taught me a smattering of Yiddish. She acquired additional familiarity with Jewish rites and rituals during her many years working in the kitchen at Shaarey Zedek, one of the nation's largest synagogues.

I should note that Cat Boyd became Katherine Brown after marrying my stepfather, Willie, whose most memorable gift to us was my sister Corliss and my brother Russell. When their marriage ended, her sense of independence was renewed. Now on her own with four children, her determination to provide for them was given a fresh round of stress, another test she passed with flying colors.

Over the years, Katherine Brown, like her children, grew up with the city, rolled with its punches, and cheered its victories, ever ready to meet each challenge with imagination and ingenuity. I sat next to her one day at Briggs Stadium and watched as she rooted for Charles, the captain of the Northwestern High School baseball team, as they defeated Cass Tech for the city championship. She had every reason to be proud, for it was she who taught us how to catch and hit the ball, as well as the intricacies of the game. I know few women who can rattle off information about sports as knowledgeably as she can.

She was also an indispensable fount of news when I wasn't in the city. I was in the army in 1963 when Cynthia Scott was killed, but my mother filled in the blanks for me on this tragedy because Cynthia, or Bay-Bay, as we called her, had lived upstairs over us on Cardoni Street when she was a little girl.

My mother's ability to relate and discuss current events in Detroit was the real bounty for her son. How blessed I was to share in her wisdom and knowledge, particularly about how to be a good person. Sometimes I wish more of her good sense would have rubbed off on me. I would consider myself lucky to possess more of her Christian charity, her sense of community. When I tell people that at ninety-six, she drives to the various food pantries around the city, gathering items that she then shares with the seniors in her building, they are flabbergasted.

What I know about Detroit I learned following her path, talking to her friends, listening to her recollections about Black Bottom, Paradise Valley, Little Rock Baptist Church, the Jeffries Projects, and the changing aspects of the city.

I can expect a wave of criticism when she reads this book—things I left out, people I didn't mention, events I've forgotten. Then with her typical praise, she'll tell me how wonderful it is, and maybe next time I'll do even better.

No matter her judgment, my one wish is that the book is finished before she joins the ancestors, because it was so often her words and guidance that led me to them and their stories.

ACKNOWLEDGMENTS

As Captain Renault did in *Casablanca*, I've rounded up the usual suspects for another one of my literary journeys, and these suspects are informants in the best sense of the word. Some of these informants are no longer with us, but what they taught me about the history of Detroit are lessons of lasting memory, and I hope I've given them the truth and insight with which they were delivered.

The alpha and omega of this book is my mother, Katherine; she blessed me with a passion for life, an infinite curiosity, and as she has collected a home overflowing with whatnots, knick-knacks, photos, and memorabilia. I've inherited that spirit in gathering friends, all of them repositories of black history and culture. There is an affectionate circle of griots who have been indispensable to all of my books, and their impressions abound on the pages here. That circle includes Dan Aldridge, Malik Chaka, Ron Lockett, George Gaines, Michael Dinwiddie, Don Von Freeman, Dorothy Dewberry, Imhotep Gary Byrd, Lloyd Williams,

Voza Rivers, Elinor Tatum, Nayaba Arinde, Jules Allen, Robert Van Lierop, Haki Madhubuti, Ralph "Buzzy" Jones, Ron Daniels, Ron Williams, Fred Beauford, Keith Owens, Eddie Harris, Keith Beauchamp, Gloria Aneb House, Larry Gabriel, Kim Heron, Jeff Santos, Rae Alexander Minter, Dan Coughlin, Don Rojas, Christopher Griffith, Gene Cunningham, Geri Allen, Barbara Cox, Leni Sinclair, Reggie Carter, Ruben Wilson, jessica Care moore, JoAnn Watson, Billy Mitchell, Woodie King Jr., Cliff Frazier, David Ritz, and Hakim Hasan.

This is the immediate circle, and I have called on them and relied on them in one way or another in all of my writing assignments, and those on the list know exactly the wisdom they have dispensed. Each one of the several neighborhoods in Detroit, from Black Bottom to Eight Mile Road, possessed a reservoir of storytellers, folks eager to bend my ear with gossip and tall tales. I met the late Cleophus Roseboro on the North End, and over the years he was a boundless resource of information, particularly about downtown Detroit and how the city operates. His almost weekly letters to the *Free Press* kept me abreast of municipal shenanigans and issues of importance to ordinary citizens.

From Cardoni, we took flight to Pinehurst where the Binion brood were my companions, none more enduring than John, McArthur, and Tom. They helped me navigate the tricky racial terrain, giving me the support I needed as we integrated an all-white territory. I wasn't long enough in the vicinity to gather the lessons I learned at Moore School, McMichael, and Northwestern High School. A few of those teachers and counselors, particularly Ms. Johnson, Mr. Sweetini, Ms. Vyn, and H. P. Brown, prepared me for the research, and instilled in me a pursuit of excellence that was extended during my fifteen years at Wayne State University, where the loss of Malcolm X had sent me.

From Professor Norman McRae at Wayne State, I got my first dose of Detroit's history, and his inspiration dovetailed nicely with a coterie of students and associates guiding me deeper into the city's historic precincts. Lonnie Peek, Ozell Bonds, Bruce Williams, Susan Cooper, Gerald Simmons (Kwadwo Akpan), and Kathy Gamble were my comrades when we launched the Association of Black Students and the seminal seeds of black studies. Most of them came of age in the city, and their varying paths instructed me in ways they will never know. Geneva Smitherman, David Rambeau, Ernie Allen, Art Blackwell, Richard Simmons, Conrad Mallett Jr., Charles Simmons, Edward Simpkins, Hubert Locke, Woodburn Ross, John Sinclair, Charles Moore, Bob Mast, John Watson, Harry Clark, Ron Hunt, Queen Dooley, and Alice Tait were on campus enhancing my academic and intellectual compass.

Several institutions, their administrators, and staff deserve thanks, including the Burton Historical Collection and the E. Azalia Hackley Collection at the Detroit Public Library; the Walter Reuther Collection, especially Louis Jones; the stacks at Wayne State University Library; and the Dr. Charles H. Wright Museum of African American History, particularly Juanita Moore, Charles Ezra Ferrell, and Yolanda Jack; the Detroit Institute of the Arts; the Detroit Historical Society; and the Skillman Branch of the Detroit Public Library.

Working at the *Detroit Free Press*, the *Michigan Chronicle*, the *Detroit Sun*, and the *Metro Times* afforded me access to reporters, editors, and the papers' archives—and the early stewardship of Longworth Quinn, Jim Ingram, and Nadine Brown was vastly rewarding

Of service to me were a number of critical players—Doug Bretz provided living accommodations during two month-long stays in the city; members of my family, such as Thelma and Odell Dinwiddie, and Taylor and Michelle Segue, opened their doors and hearts to a couple of vagabonds. My daughters, Rhonda, Almitra, Catherine, and Maya; my son, Johnny; and their mothers reminded me that my Detroit roots are more than words but blood and marrow.

And then there are the scholars and civic leaders who took time from their busy schedules to give additional ballast to the project, and a few of them—Heather Ann Thompson, David Levering Lewis, Peniel Joseph, Betty DeRamus, Rep. John Conyers, and Ta-Nehisi Coates—even contributed very thoughtful blurbs. Photos by Dale Rich present empowering images that more than complement the narrative. Recently, this group has been enlarged by the arrival of Errol Henderson, Cheryl Sterling, Fred Logan, Sabira Bushra, Shimon Mercer-Wood, Cinque Brath, Bob Gumbs, Glenn Hunter, Suzanne Smith, and Michael Stauch.

There is a confederacy of black women who forged and developed this book: My editor Tracy Sherrod meticulously combed the manuscript, and I hope I have sufficiently answered many of her queries; Marie Brown, my agent and guardian angel, watched over the book with a deep love and attention; and my wife, Elza, completes this triumvirate of talent that gives the book a special balance of meaning and gravitas. Since my wife has been joined at the spine with me and of such immeasurable value in all my books, praising her is like patting myself on the back. We have been an inseparable duo, and nothing I've done in the classroom, in my journalism, and certainly as an author has been finished without her approval—and of course that would mean approving her own indivisible contribution.

But in the end, no matter the competence and intelligence of your "suspects," the book belongs to the author, and I am ready and willing to take the blame for the shortcomings and charge the suspects for its accomplishments.

Black Detroit was a lifetime in the making and, like the city, it remains a work in progress, a progress that only its denizens and readers can complete.

NOTES

Chapter 1: Cadillac, "The Black Prince"

1. "Cadillac Papers," ed. Clarence M. Burton (Michigan Pioneer and Historical Society Collections 33, 1904), 96–101.
2. Agnes C. Laut, *Cadillac: Knight Errant of the Wilderness* (Indianapolis: Bobbs-Merrill, 1931), 45–47.
3. C. M. Burton, *The Building of Detroit* (1912), 10.
4. Scott Martelle, *Detroit: A Biography* (Chicago: Chicago Review Press, 2012), 4.
5. C. M. Burton, *Cadillac's Village; or, Detroit under Cadillac with List of Property Owners and a History of the Settlement, 1701–1710* (Detroit, 1896), 70. Among the slaves owned by Joseph Campau was a young one named Crow, who was quite a favorite of Mr. Campau. He was often dressed in scarlet in stark contrast to his color. To amuse townspeople, Crow would climb to the top of Sainte Anne's steeple, and like Quasimodo, the hunchback of Notre Dame, perform gymnastic tricks. He was as supple and elastic as a circus rider. He had been purchased from Montreal and later drowned in the Campau swimming pool. See General Friend Palmer, *Early Days in Detroit* (Hunt & June, 1906), 105.
6. Norman McRae Jr., *Blacks in Detroit, 1736–1833: A Search for*

Community on the Western Frontier (Ann Arbor: University of Michigan Press, 1982), 52.

7.   Marcel Trudel, *L'esclavage au Canada François: Histoire et conditions de l'esclavage* (Les presses de l'Université Laval, 1960), 188.

8.   Jorge Castellanos, "Black Slavery in Detroit," *Detroit in Perspective: A Journal of Regional History* 7, no. 2 (Fall 1983): 43. This also appears as a chapter in *Detroit Perspectives—Crossroads and Turning Points*, ed. Wilma Wood Henrickson (Detroit: Wayne State University Press, 1991).

9.   Tiya Miles, National Public Radio with Michel Martin, Jan. 30, 2012.

10. McRae, op. cit., 54. F. Clever Bald explained: "Some of the Indians at Detroit were slaves. They were captives who had been taken in wars between hostile tribes and sold to whites. These people were known as Panis, phonetic spelling of Pawnee, a tribe considered by more warlike savages to be degraded and fit only for servants. Visitors to Detroit reported that there were none better." *Detroit: First American Decade 1796–1805* (Ann Arbor: University of Michigan Press, 1948), 40.

11. Brian Leigh Dunnigan, *Frontier Metropolis: Picturing Early Detroit, 1701–1838* (Detroit: Wayne State University Press, 2001), 50.

12. Milo Milton Quaife, ed., *The Siege of Detroit in 1763: The Journal of Pontiac's Conspiracy and John Rutherford's Narrative of a Captivity* (Chicago: Lakeside Press, R. R. Donnelly & Sons, Christmas, 1958), 27. Not only is there an alternative version of Pontiac's plan, but also there are different spellings of Gladwyn's name and Catherine's tribal background. Howard Peckham in *Pontiac and the Indian Uprising* (Princeton, NJ: Princeton University Press, 1947) cites an account by Henry Connor, "son of the first permanent settler of St. Clair County, and himself as interpreter at Detroit in the early nineteenth century, related that he was acquainted with Catherine; that she was young (in 1763) and in love with Gladwin; and that she unromantically perished long afterward by falling while drunk into a vat of boiling maple syrup." See Quaife, 31.

13. Robert E. Roberts, *Sketches and Reminiscences of the City of the Straits and Its Vicinity* (Detroit: Free Press Book and Job Printing House, 1884), 24. Many residents of Black Bottom recall a yellow frame house with a turret-like arrangement at the top

that might have served as a lookout during the battle. If you dug deep enough, local wags said, the earth was bloody red from the wounded and the dead, and that's why a cemetery was established at this location.

14. Clarence M. Burton, *The City of Detroit, Michigan, 1701–1922* (Detroit: S. J. Clarke, 1922), 193.

15. Ibid., 24. This incident is reminiscent of one that occurred in New York City in January 1641, when an overweight Manuel de Gerrit de Reus broke the hangman's ropes. He had been tried and convicted of killing another company slave, Jan Premero. He and nine other company slaves confessed to the murder, knowing it was a capital crime in New Amsterdam but relying on the reluctance of the company to execute nine of its thirty slaves. Since no individual confessed to inflicting the lethal blow, the Provincial Council (acting in a judicial capacity) ordered the drawing of lots to determine who would be punished. "They believed that the hand of God would intervene to help identify the perpetrator. Manuel drew the short straw and was sentenced to death by hanging. But when Manuel was pushed off the ladder, both ropes broke and he fell to the ground. The crowd shouted for mercy, convinced that a failed execution was an act of God. The Provincial Council agreed and pardoned all nine slaves on condition of good behavior and willing service." See www.newamsterdamhis torycenter.org/bios/manuel.html.

16. General Friend Palmer, *Early Days in Detroit* (Hunt & June; repr. Detroit: Gale Research Co., 1979), 105.

17. *Michigan Historical Society Journal* 9: 395; and https://archive .org/details/michiganhistoric09michuoft.

18. Thomas Meehan, "Jean Baptiste Pointe du Sable, the First Chicagoan," *Journal of Illinois State Historical Society* 56 (Autumn 1963), 451.

19. Burton, op. cit., 227.

20. Harley Lawrence Gibb, "Slaves in Old Detroit," *Michigan History* 18 (1934), 145.

21. Ibid., 146.

22. William Renwick Riddell, "The Negro Slave in Detroit When Detroit Was Canadian," *Michigan History* 18 (1934), 48–50. Mr. Kenny was responding to a letter from McKee that was listed as an auction item at Swann Galleries in New York on March 21–26, 2015 for $800–$1,200. Here's how McKee, writing to

his brother James from Fort Detroit, expressed his exasperation about his runaway slave: "I sit down hastily to inform you that Bill [Kenny], Hannah's son, ran away to General Wayne's camp while I was lately in Lower Canada. I have since heard that he intends to go to see his mother in Pittsburg[h]. I beg therefore if you can find him that you will take him & send him to be sold, if you can get a good price for him at some considerable distance from Pittsburg[h] or this country. Be perfectly on your guard & do not trust to one word of what he may say. He was left in charge of my house here on my going to Quebec & took the opportunity of my absence to go off with many things belonging to me." A note in the brochure adds: "As both Upper Canada and Pennsylvania had passed gradual abolition acts, the handling of the sale was a delicate matter, so brother James would not have been able to make the sale in Pittsburgh. Slavery documents from the Western Frontier are scarce, and McKee's involvement adds to the interest." See Swann Galleries catalog, Mar. 21, 2015, p. 15.

23. McRae, op. cit., 82.
24. Tiya Miles, "Slavery in Early Detroit," *Michigan History*, May–June 2013, 33–35.
25. Martelle, op. cit., 15.
26. See www.daahp.wayne.edu/biographiesDisplay.php?id=97.
27. Gail Buckley, *American Patriots: The Story of Blacks in the Military from the Revolution to Desert Storm* (New York: Random House, 2001), 47; and Bernard C. Nalty, *Strength for the Fight: A History of Black Americans in the Military* (New York: Free Press, 1986), 21.
28. Ferris E. Lewis, *Michigan Yesterday and Today* (Hillsdale, MI: Hillsdale Educational Publishers, 1980), 231.
29. David M. Katzman, *Before the Ghetto: Black Detroit in the Nineteenth Century* (Urbana: University of Illinois Press, 1973), 6.
30. Ibid., 7.

Chapter 2: The Blackburn Affair

1. Karolyn Smardz Frost, *I've Got a Home in Glory Land: A Lost Tale of the Underground Railroad* (New York: Farrar, Straus & Giroux, 2007), 159.
2. Ibid., 160.

3. George B. Catlin, *The Story of Detroit* (Detroit: Detroit News, 1923), 321.

4. Ibid., 167.

5. *Detroit Journal and Advertiser,* July 19, 1833; and Frost, 167.

6. Frost, op. cit., 168.

7. Betty DeRamus, *Forbidden Fruit: Love Stories from the Underground Railroad* (New York: Atria Books, 2005), 66. This may not be exactly correct, according to an interview with Frost, since Willoughby was freed in Kentucky on August 1, 1817, but one of his daughters was born in Ohio in 1824 (recorded in the 1850 census in reference to Julia Willoughby Lambert, wife of William Lambert and the younger daughter of Benjamin and Devorah Willoughby). It was shortly after Julia's 1824 birth in Ohio that the Willoughby family moved to Detroit.

8. Ibid., 67.

9. DeRamus, op. cit., 68.

10. Peter Gavrilovich and Bill McGraw, eds., *The Detroit Almanac: 300 Years of Life in the Motor City* (Detroit: Detroit Free Press, 2001), 515.

11. Norman McRae, "The Thornton Blackburn Affair," in *Detroit Perspectives: Crossroads and Turning Points,* ed. Wilma Wood Hendrickson (Detroit: Wayne State University Press, 1991), 96.

12. DeRamus, op. cit., 73. Later it was reported that Lewis or Louis Austin, who had bravely assisted in Thornton's escape, was shot and died two years later from his wound. See Frost, 179.

13. *Pioneer Society of the State of Michigan,* 2d ed, vol. 12 (Lansing, 1908), 592.

14. Frost, op. cit., 189.

15. See   www.nytimes.com/2007/06/17/books/review/Reynolds-t .html?pagewanted=print&_r=0. "Upper Canada (now Ontario) had just passed the Fugitive Offenders Act to allow for the extradition of criminals to the US, but they had to have committed a felony, or capital crime such as murder, horse theft or rape in order to qualify," Frost advised me in an e-mail. "This was the first test case of the new law, and just running away from slavery did not qualify, since slavery was just about to be abolished in the British Empire, but inciting a riot and trying to kill the Sheriff did, which is why the Blackburns were accused of the two crimes by Mayor Chapin."

16. Frost, op. cit., 149.

17. Frost, e-mail, June 16, 2015.
18. See http://detroithistorical.org/learn/encyclopedia-of-detroit.
19. Silas Farmer, *The History of Detroit and Michigan* (Silas Farmer & Co., 1889), p. 345.
20. Robert E. Roberts, *Sketches and Reminiscences of the City of the Straits and Its Vicinity* (Detroit, 1884), 111.

Chapter 3: Black Abolitionists

1. David M. Katzman, *Before the Ghetto: Black Detroit in the Nine-teenth Century* (Urbana: University of Illinois Press, 1973), 13; and W. B. Hargrove, "The Story of Maria Louise Moore and Fan-nie M. Richards," *Journal of Negro History* 1 (Jan. 1916), 23–33.
2. Katzman, op. cit., 13.
3. Silas Farmer, *The History of Detroit and Michigan* (Silas Farmer & Co., 1889), 346.
4. Cara L. Shelly, "Bradby's Baptists: Second Baptist Church in De-troit, 1910–1946," *Michigan Historical Review*, 17, no. 1 (Spring 1991), 3. The departure may have been precipitated also by the desire of a church location closer to the Underground Railroad station.
5. Charles L. Blockson, *The Underground Railroad: First Person Nar-ratives of Escapes to Freedom in the North* (New York: Prentice Hall, 1987), 197.
6. Ibid., 198. The elaborate rituals of the Order were spelled out by Lambert. In the first chapter, there are three degrees: Captives, Redeemed, and Chosen; another one was listed as Confidence, and all were used on the Underground Railroad. When a con-ductor or passenger gave the word "cross," the correct reply was "over." Another sign included the placing of the right forefinger over the left forefinger.
7. Henry Bibb, *Narrative of the Life and Adventures of Henry Bibb, an American Slave, Written by Himself*, ed. Litwack, Leon, and Meier, intro. Lucius C. Matlack (New York, 1859; Black Leaders of the Nineteenth Century, Urbana: University of Il-linois Press, 1988), 195–96. A rare copy of the narrative is at the Swann Galleries in New York City for auction, priced at $2,000–$3,000. It includes ten pages of testimonials preceding chapter 1, and features a copper-engraved frontispiece portrait

by Patrick Reason, eleven full-page engravings, and seven half-page head-and tail-pieces.

8. Ibid., 90.
9. Katzman, op. cit., 13.
10. Wilma Hendrickson, ed., *Detroit Perspectives: Crossroads and Turning Points* (Detroit: Wayne State University Press, 1991), 179.
11. Frank Angelo, *On Guard: A History of the Detroit Free Press* (Detroit: Detroit Free Press, 1981), 58.
12. Ibid., 72
13. See   http://ugrr.mmaps.magian.com/media/Pdf/William_Lambert_People_UGRR_Final_1.pdf.
14. Farmer, op. cit., 347.
15. David S. Reynolds, *John Brown: Abolitionist* (New York: Knopf, 2005), 299.
16. Ferris E. Lewis, *Michigan: Yesterday and Today* (Hillsdale, MI: Hillsdale Educational Publishers, 1980), 249.

Chapter 4: Faulkner and Flames

1. Tobin T. Buhk, *True Crime in the Civil War: Cases of Murder, Treason, Counterfeiting. Massacre, Plunder, and Abuse* (Mechanicsburg, PA: Stackpole Books, 2012), 75–76.
2. Ibid., 78.
3. Ibid., 79.
4. *A Thrilling Narrative from the Lips of the Sufferers of the Late Detroit Riot, March 6, 1863, with the Hair Breadth Escapes of Men, Women and Children, and Destruction of Colored Men's Property, Not Less Than $15,000* (Detroit, 1863).
5. Ibid., 1.
6. Ibid., 2.
7. Buhk, op. cit., 85–86; and Melvin G. Holli, *Detroit: New Viewpoints* (New York: Franklin Watts, 1976), 86. Faulkner, according to Arthur M. Woodford, was found innocent of the charges "when the two girls confessed that they had perjured themselves." See Arthur M. Woodford, *This is Detroit: 1701–2001* (Detroit: Wayne State University Press, 2001), 71.
8. Ferris E. Lewis, *Michigan Yesterday and Today* (Hillsdale, MI: Hillsdale Educational Publishers, 1980), 250.
9. Ibid.

10. Ibid.

11. James M. McPherson, *The Negro's Civil War* (New York: Ballan-tine, 1991), 201.

12. Peter Gavrilovich and Bill McGraw, eds., *The Detroit Almanac: 300 Years of Life in the Motor City* (Detroit: Detroit Free Press, 2001), 41.

Chapter 5: Early Years of the Black Church

1. Norman McRae, *The History of Second Baptist Church, 1836–1986* (Second Baptist Church of Detroit, 1986), 55.

2. Betty DeRamus, *Freedom by Any Means: Con Games, Voodoo Schemes, True Love and Lawsuits on the Underground Railroad* (New York: Atria Books, 2010), 130.

3. McRae, op. cit., 55.

4. Ibid., 60.

5. "Chronology and Outlines of the Episcopal Church," Papers of the Protestant Episcopal Church of Michigan, Michigan Histori-cal Collection; Katzman, op. cit., 43; and www.pluralism.org/profiles/view/71797.

6. David M. Katzman, *Before the Ghetto: Black Detroit in the Nine-teenth Century* (Urbana: University of Illinois Press, 1975), 21.

7. McRae, op. cit., 61.

8. Nathaniel Leach, *The Sesquicentennial Chronological History of Second Baptist Church, 1836–1986*, 41.

9. Cara L. Shelly, "Bradby's Baptists: Second Baptist Church in De-troit, 1910–1946," *Michigan Historical Review* 17, no. 1 (Spring 1991), 4.

10. Robert A. Rockaway, *The Jews of Detroit: From the Beginning, 1762–1914* (Detroit: Wayne State University Press, 1986), 40.

11. Ibid., 26, 34.

12. Ibid., 40.

13. John B. Reid, "A Career to Build, a People to Serve, a Purpose to Accomplish: Race, Class, Gender, and Detroit's First Black Women Teachers, 1865–1916," *Michigan Historical Review* 18, no. 1 (Spring 1992), 11. Although Richards is the primary teacher in the essay, others include Delia Pelham Barriers, Meta E. Pelham, E. Azalia Smith Hackley, Theresa Smith, Etta Edna Lee, Lola Gregory, Sarah Webb, Clara Shewcraft, and Florence Frances Cole, whose father, James Cole, was considered the wealthiest black man in Detroit.

14. McRae, op. cit., 80.
15. *Detroit Plaindealer,* May 2, 1890, p. 1.

Chapter 6: Black Arts in the Gilded Age

1. Wilma Hendrickson, *Detroit Perspectives: Crossroads and Turning Points* (Detroit: Wayne State University Press, 1991), 194.
2. "Theodore Finney," in Fred Hart Williams and Hoyt Fuller, "Detroit Heritage," typewritten manuscript in Fred Hart Williams Papers, Burton Historical Collection, Detroit Public Library; also cited in Herb Boyd and Leni Sinclair, *Detroit Jazz Who's Who* (Detroit: Detroit Jazz Institute, 1984), 78.
3. Peter Gavrilovich and Bill McGraw, eds., *The Detroit Almanac: 300 Years of Life in the Motor City* (Detroit: Detroit Free Press, 2001), 105.
4. David Katzman, *Before the Ghetto: Black Detroit in the Nineteenth Century* (Urbana: University of Illinois Press, 1973), 171.
5. "John W. Johnson," Fred Hart Williams Papers.
6. Samuel R. Charters, *Jazz: New Orleans 1885–1963* (New York: Oak Publications, 1963), 2.
7. Rachel Kranz, *The Biographical Dictionary of Black Americans* (New York: Facts on File, 1992), 98.
8. "Harry Guy," Fred Hart Williams Papers, Burton Historical Collection, Detroit Public Library.
9. W. C. Handy, *Father of the Blues* (New York: Macmillan, 1941), 64.
10. Herb Boyd and Lars Bjorn, interviews with the musicians for the Jazz Research Institute in 1978. Trafton was in his seventies when he returned to school at Wayne State University to complete his degree and was a student in two of my classes.
11. Fred Hart Williams and Hoyt Fuller, "Theodore Finney Papers," Detroit Heritage, typewritten manuscript in Fred Hart Williams Papers, Burton Historical Collection, Detroit Public Library.
12. Robert Hayden, *American Journal 1913–1980* (New York: Liveright, 1978).
13. Albert McCarthy, *Big Band Jazz* (Berkeley, CA: Berkeley Pub. Corp., 1974), 22.
14. See www.daahp.wayne.edu/biographiesDisplay.php?id=21.
15. Gene Fernett, *Swingout! Great Negro Dance Bands* (Midland, MI: Pendell Pub. Co., 1970), 25. John Chilton, *Who's Who of Jazz:*

Storyville to Swing Street (Chilton Book Publishing Co., 1978), offers some different facts about Cook's life. For example, he contends that Cook obtained a doctorate from the Chicago College of Music.

16. Fernett, op. cit., 27.
17. *Detroit Tribune*, Feb. 11, 1939, www.ipl.org/div/detjazz/Stompin .html.
18. Francis H. Warren, compiler, and John M. Green, ed., *Michigan Manual of Freedmen's Progress* (Detroit: John M. Green, 1915), 69.
19. Ibid., 3.
20. Ibid., 92.
21. See www.blackpast.org/aah/hackley-emma-azalia-1867–1922.
22. M. Marguerite Davenport, *Azalia: The Life of Madame E. Azalia Hackley* (Boston: Chapman & Grimes, 1949), 157.
23. See https://www.nytimes.com/books/first/k/keiler-anderson .html; and Allan Keiler, *Marian Anderson: A Singer's Journey* (New York: Scribner, 2002).
24. Lisa Pertillar Brevard, *A Biography of E. Azalia Smith Hackley, 1867–1922, African American Singer and Social Activist* (Lewiston, NY: Edwin Mellen Press, 2001), 122.
25. *Detroit Plaindealer*, Jan. 9, 1891, p. 4.
26. Katzman, op. cit., 160; M. A. Majors, *Noted Negro Women: Their Triumphs and Activities* (Chicago: Donohue & Henneberry, 1893), 335; and Mrs. N. F. Mossell, *The Work of the Afro-American Woman* (Philadelphia: Ferguson, 1908), 15. Mrs. (Gertrude) Mossell was married to Dr. Nathan Francis Mossell, the first black graduate of the University of Pennsylvania School of Medicine, and was the sister of Maria Louisa Bustill, who was married to William Drew Roberson, the father of Paul Robeson. A fairly detailed history of the genealogy of the Bustill, Mossell, Robeson, and Tanner families (Dr. Mossell's brother, Aaron, married Mary Louise Tanner, the aunt of Henry Ossawa Tanner, the great painter) is in Martin Duberman's *Paul Robeson* (New York: Knopf, 1988), 5, 8. And Lambert's connection with the *AME Church Review* put her under the guidance of Bishop Benjamin Tucker Tanner, the founder and first editor of the publication from 1884–88. See William Seraile, *Fire in His Heart: Bishop Benjamin Tucker Tanner and the AME Church* (Knoxville: University of Tennessee Press, 1988), preface, i. Bishop Tanner was Mary's brother and Henry's

father. And though Lambert didn't make it into the inaugural edition of the *Review* in 1884, D. A. Straker did.

27. Jessie Carney Smith, ed., *Notable Black American Women* (Detroit: Gale Research, 1992), 230.

28. *Detroit Plaindealer*, Apr. 14, 1893, p. 5. Either she had returned from Omaha, or her job in charge of the *Mission-Monitor*, published in Nebraska, didn't require her to be out there. She was given that assignment in January, according to the *Plaindealer*, and Dunbar's recital was in April. Dr. James Ames, running for the state legislature, benefited from Pingree's campaign and was the last black elected to the lower house until 1920.

29. *Detroit Plaindealer*, May 12, 1893, p. 5.

30. Alma Forrest Parks, "Survey of Detroit," *Negro Digest*, Nov. 1962, p. 88.

31. Warren, op. cit., 65.

32. Randall Kenan, ed., *James Baldwin: The Cross of Redemption, Uncollected Writings* (New York: Pantheon, 2010), 126.

Chapter 7: The Pelhams and the Black Elite

1. *Detroit Plaindealer*, Apr. 11, 1890, p. 8.

2. Francis H. Warren, compiler, and John M. Green, ed. *Michigan Manual of Freedmen's Progress* (Detroit, 1915), 91. It's in Warren's manual that Pelham is said to be the second son and the fifth child.

3. *Cleveland Gazette*, Saturday, Feb. 16, 1895, 2.

4. Ibid., 3.

5. Warren, op. cit., 92.

6. See www.blackpast.org/aah/national-afro-american-league-1887 –1893.

7. Ibid. Other sources include: Benjamin R. Justesen, *Broken Brotherhood: The Rise and Fall of the National Afro-American Council* (Carbondale: Southern Illinois Press, 2008); Nina Mjagkij, *Organizing Black America: An Encyclopedia of African American Associations* (New York: Garland, 2001); and Jack Saltzman, *Encyclopedia of African-American Culture and History: The Black Experience in the Americas* (Detroit: Macmillan Reference USA, 2006.) See also David Levering Lewis's *W.E.B. Du Bois (1868–1919): Biography of a Race* (New York: Holt, 1993), 230. Lewis contends that the Council, which attempted to pick up

the struggle where the League left off, did very little and was basically ineffective before it faded completely. Moreover, he disparaged Fortune as an alcoholic. But this didn't seem to bother Booker T. Washington, who kept him among the executives at the National Negro Business League, and Fortune was a loyal, unwavering supporter of Washington's policies, all of which were widely publicized via his paper, the *New York Age*.

8.   Warren, op. cit., 91.

9.   Peter Gavrilovich and Bill McGraw, eds., *Detroit Almanac: 300 Years of Life in the Motor City* (Detroit: Detroit Free Press, 2001), 107.

10. Louis R. Harlan, *Booker T. Washington: The Wizard of Tuskegee, 1901–1915* (New York: Oxford University Press, 1983), 15.

11. J. R. Hamm, "Proceedings of the National Negro Business League," Boston, August 23–24, 1900. Could this be the same Susie Smith whom David Katzman describes as the daughter of AME Bishop C. S. Smith who taught music and harmony at the Michigan Conservatory of Music? Such was her prowess at the keyboard that she was invited to perform a recital at President Roosevelt's inauguration in 1905. See Katzman, 160.

12. Gavrilovich and McGraw, eds., op. cit., 43; and Harlan, 142.

13. Richard W. Thomas, *Life for Us Is What We Make It: Building Black Community in Detroit, 1915–1945* (Bloomington: Indiana University Press, 1992), 15.

14. Ibid., 13.

15. Ibid., 16.

16. Warren, op. cit., 86.

17. David M. Katzman, *Before the Ghetto: Black Detroit in the Nineteenth Century* (Urbana: University of Illinois Press, 1973), 95–96.

18. Ibid., 97.

19. Ibid.; and *Cleveland Gazette*, Apr. 7, 1900, p. 2.

20. *Detroit Plaindealer*, June 19, 1891, p. 1.

21. James A. Riley, *The Biographical Encyclopedia of the Negro Baseball Leagues* (New York: Carroll & Graf, 1994), 810–11.

22. *Cleveland Gazette* 5, no. 21 (Jan. 7, 1888), 1.

23. Ibid.

24. See http://strakerlaw.org/History.html.

25. Willard B. Gatewood, *Aristocrats of Color: The Black Elite, 1880–1920* (Fayetteville: University of Arkansas Press, 2000), 127–29.

26. *Detroit News-Tribune*, Apr. 27, 1902.

27. Gavrilovich and McGraw, eds., op. cit., 43.

28. See www.detnews.com/history/ames/ames.htm.

29. Wilma Hendrickson, ed., *Detroit Perspectives: Crossroads and Turning Points* (Detroit: Wayne State University Press, 1991), 254.

30. Katzman, op. cit., 104–5.

31. Richard Oestreicher, *Solidarity and Fragmentation: Working People and Class Consciousness in Detroit, 1875–1900* (Urbana: University of Illinois Press, 1989), 35.

32. M. Marguerite Davenport, *Azalia: The Life of Madame E. Azalia Hackley* (Boston: Chapman & Grimes, 1947), 23–29.

33. *Detroit News*, May 16, 1907, in Burton, Scrapbook, vol. 27, p. 126; and Katzman, op. cit., 131.

34. Howard Zinn, *A People's History of the United States, 1492 to the Present* (New York: HarperCollins, 2003), 315. Many American troops in the Philippines were brutally gung-ho. Once soldier wrote that killing Filipino "niggers" was better than coon hunting back home.

35. Lewis, op. cit., 298.

36. Gavrilovich and McGraw, op. cit., 165.

37. W.E.B. Du Bois, ed., *Proceedings of the Seventh Annual Conference for the Study of Negro Problems* (Atlanta University Press, 1902). Paradoxically, the closing remarks at the conference were delivered by Booker T. Washington, who praised Du Bois lavishly, noting, "The work that Dr. Du Bois is doing will stand for years as a monument to his ability, wisdom, and faithfulness." A year later, Du Bois in his book *The Souls of Black Folk* excoriated Washington in one of the most famous essays in American literature. But Du Bois's criticism was mild compared to that of William Monroe Trotter, who militantly opposed Washington's ideas of accommodation and conciliation.

38. Ibid., 171.

39. Ibid., 167.

40. John Hope Franklin and Alfred A. Moss Jr., *From Slavery to Freedom* (New York: McGraw-Hill, 2000), 310.

41. Howard Brotz, ed., *African American Social & Political Thought, 1850–1920* (New Brunswick, NJ: Transaction Publishers, 1996), 449.

42. Ibid., 535.

Chapter 8: Detroit and World War I

1. Lars Bjorn with Jim Gallert, *Before Motown: A History of Jazz in Detroit, 1920–1960* (Ann Arbor: University of Michigan Press, 2001), 11.

2. Carole Marks, *Farewell: We're Good and Gone* (Bloomington: Indiana University Press, 1989), 3.

3. Emmett Scott, "Letters of Negro Migrants of 1916–1918," *Journal of Negro History* 4, no. 3 (July 1919), 290–340.

4. Alferdteen Harrison, ed., *Black Exodus: The Great Migration from the American South* (Jackson: University Press of Mississippi, 1991); and Carole Marks, "The Social and Economic Life of Southern Blacks During the Migration," 46.

5. John C. Dancy, *Sand Against the Wind* (Detroit: Wayne State University Press, 1966), 103.

6. John M. T. Chavis and William McNitt, *A Brief History of the Detroit Urban League, and Description of the League's Papers in the Michigan Historical Collections* (Ann Arbor: University of Michigan Press, 1974), 5.

7. George Edmund Haynes, *Negro New-Comers in Detroit, Michigan: A Challenge to Christian Statesmanship, a Preliminary Study* (New York: Home Missions Council, 1918), 14. Most of the workers listed here were men, and the tabulation was compiled from a house-to-house canvass of 407 heads of families, of whom 362 were men. Of the 45 women, 12 were doing day work; 10 were housekeepers taking in roomers; and among the others there were 6 laundresses, 2 hairdressers, 1 nurse, 1 unspecified, 1 seamstress, 1 cook, 1 receiving a pension, 4 miscellaneous, and 7 unknown. Black women were also showing increased numbers among theater ushers and in the garment trades, particularly with the A. Krolik Company.

8. Victoria Wolcott, *Remaking Respectability: African American Women in Interwar Detroit* (Chapel Hill: University of North Carolina Press, 2001), 53.

9. Richard W. Thomas, *Life for Us Is What We Make It: Building Black Community in Detroit, 1915–1945* (Bloomington: Indiana University Press, 1992), 63–63.

10. Dancy, op. cit., 99.

11. Ibid., 56.

12. Charles E. Cobb Jr., *This Nonviolent Stuff'll Get You Killed: How*

Guns Made the Civil Rights Movement Possible (New York: Basic Books, 2014), 241.

13. Horace Junior, ed., *Remembering Detroit's Old Westside, 1920–1950: A Pictorial History of the Westsiders*, 2nd ed. (Detroit: The Westsiders, 1997), 5.

14. Bill Harris, *The Hellfighters of Harlem: African American Soldiers Who Fought for the Right to Fight for Their Country* (New York: Carroll & Graf, 2002), 31.

15. Arthur E. Barbeau and Florette Henri, *The Unknown Soldiers: Black American Troops in World War I* (Philadelphia: Temple University Press, 1974), 79–81. The renowned poet Paul Laurence Dunbar wrote a poem that summarizes the role of the black soldier during that "great war." He wrote: "If the muse was mine to tempt it / and my feeble voice was strong / If my tongue were trained to measure / I would sing a stirring song. / I would sing a song heroic / of those noble sons of Ham / of the gallant colored soldiers / who fought for Uncle Sam."

16. Rachel Kranz, *The Biographical Dictionary of Black Americans* (New York: Facts on File, 1992), 181–82.

17. Dancy, op. cit., 122.

18. Gail Buckley, *American Patriots: The Story of Blacks in the Military from the Revolution to Desert Storm* (New York: Random House, 2001), 165.

19. Harry Haywood, *Black Bolshevik: Autobiography of an Afro-American Communist* (Chicago: Liberation Press, 1978), 59–60.

20. See www.findagrave.com/cgi-bin/fg.cgi?page=gr&GRid=3217.

21. Tony Martin, *Literary Garveyism: Garvey, Black Arts, and the Harlem Renaissance* (Dover, MA: Majority Press, 1973), 70–71.

22. Ibid., 71.

23. Thomas, op. cit., 196–98.

24. Dancy, op. cit., 146.

Chapter 9: Dr. Sweet and Mr. Ford

1. *Cleveland Gazette*, Nov. 28, 1925, p. 2.

2. Beth Tompkins Bates, *The Making of Black Detroit in the Age of Henry Ford* (Chapel Hill: University of North Carolina Press, 2012), 20.

3. Ibid., 21.

4. Richard W. Thomas, *Life for Us Is What We Make It: Building*

Black Community in Detroit, 1915–1945 (Bloomington: Indiana University Press, 1992), 273. Thomas misspells Sorensen's name and cites David Lewis's unpublished term paper as the source for this meeting. But as Angela Dillard observes in her highly informative book *Faith in the City* (p. 318), this term paper was based on interviews and materials subsequently removed from the Ford archives. While Dillard does not indicate it, the David Lewis here is David Levering Lewis, who submitted the paper as an undergraduate at the University of Michigan and later wrote the Introduction to Sorensen's *My Forty Years with Ford*. Dillard has his name as Sorenson too.

5. Shelly, Cara L., "Bradby's Baptists: Second Baptist Church of Detroit, 1910–1946," *The Michigan Historical Review*, Vol. 17, no. 1 (Spring 1991), p. 4.

6. Interview with Shahida Mausi, June 14, 2014.

7. Steven Watts, *The People's Tycoon: Henry Ford and the American Century* (New York: Random House, 2009), 491.

8. Kevin Boyle, *Arc of Justice: A Saga of Race, Civil Rights, and Murder in the Jazz Age* (New York: Holt, 2004), 26.

9. Phyllis Vine, *One Man's Castle: Clarence Darrow in Defense of the American Dream* (New York: Amistad/HarperCollins, 2004), 9.

10. See http://law2.umkc.edu/faculty/projects/ftrials/sweet/transcript excerpts.HTM#Opening.

11. Vine, op. cit., 112.

12. Ibid., 227.

13. See http://law2.umkc.edu/faculty/projects/ftrials/sweet/transcript excerpts.

14. Ibid.

15. Ibid.

16. Boyle, op. cit., 345.

17. Vine, op. cit., 244.

18. *Boston Herald*, May 14, 1926, p. 2.

19. *Broad Ax* (Chicago), May 22, 1926, p. 2.

20. Joyce Shaw Peterson, *American Automobile Workers, 1900–1933* (Albany: State University of New York Press, 1987), 131.

21. Bates, op. cit., 26.

22. Charles Denby (Matthew Ward), *Indignant Heart: A Black Worker's Journal* (Detroit: Wayne State University Press, 1989), 35. The explanation for the two names: just before the Depression, when Denby was fired by Graham Paige, he returned as a worker

under another name, claiming he had never worked at the company before.

23. Ibid., 36.

24. Horace Junior, ed., *Remembering Detroit's Old Westside, 1920–1950: A Pictorial History of the Westsiders*, 2nd ed. (Detroit: The Westsiders, 1997), 188.

25. Jayne Morris-Crowther, *The Political Activities of Detroit Clubwomen in the 1920s: A Challenge and a Promise* (Detroit: Wayne State University Press, 2013), 137.

Chapter 10: White Ball and the Brown Bomber

1.   Richard Bak, *Turkey Stearnes and the Detroit Stars: The Negro Leagues in Detroit, 1919–1933* (Detroit: Wayne State University Press, 1994), 125.

2.   Ibid., 125. Oddly, Bak fails to mention that Walker was himself a Negro Leagues star and was involved in a fracas in 1891 when he was attacked by a white gang while visiting friends in Syracuse. Later he was also part of the *Ferguson v. Gies* discrimination case in 1900. See chapter 6.

3.   Larry Lester, Sammy J. Miller, and Dick Clark, *Black Baseball in Detroit* (Chicago: Arcadia Publishing, 2000), 62.

4.   Ibid., 11.

5.   Ibid., 241.

6.   A recent book, *Ty Cobb: A Terrible Beauty*, by Charles Leerhsen (New York: Simon & Schuster, 2015) has a different take on the less than admirable accounts of the player's life, on and off the field. He writes that Cobb was not a racist and that many of the stories about his character and incidents in his life are either false or greatly exaggerated.

7.   Cheryl Wells, *Paradise Valley Days: A Photo Album Poetry Book of Black Detroit, 1930s to 1950s* (Detroit: Detroit Black Writer's Guild, 1998), 100.

8.   Ibid., 99. Two years before, Turpin had killed a Purple Gang member who, it was claimed, was involved in the killing of a police officer, Vivian Welsh, who allegedly was extorting money from the gang.

9.   Barney Nagler, *Brown Bomber* (New York: World Publishing/Times Mirror, 1972), 22.

10. Richard Bak, *Joe Louis: The Great Black Hope* (Dallas: Taylor Pub. Co., 1996), 24.

11. Nagler, op. cit., 27.
12. Herb Boyd with Ray Robinson II, *Pound for Pound: A Biography of Sugar Ray Robinson* (New York: Amistad/HarperCollins, 2005), 14.
13. Bak, op. cit., 199.
14. Lester, op. cit., 69.

Chapter 11: The Turbulent Thirties

1. Langston Hughes, *The Collected Works of Langston Hughes*, ed. Dolan Hubbard and Leslie Catherine Sanders, vol. 13 (Columbia: University of Missouri Press, 2002), 191.
2. Wilma Hendrickson, ed., *Detroit Perspectives: Crossroads and Turning Points* (Detroit: Wayne State University Press, 1991), 353–54.
3. August Meier and Elliott Rudwick, *Black Detroit and the Rise of the UAW* (New York: Oxford University Press, 1979), 42.
4. Richard W. Thomas, *Life for Us Is What We Make It: Building Black Community in Detroit, 1915–1945* (Bloomington: Indiana University Press, 1992), 96; and interview with Joseph Billups, Oct. 27, 1967, transcript, Archives of Labor History and Urban Affairs, Walter P. Reuther Library, Wayne State University, Detroit, p. 5.
5. Ralph Ellison, *Invisible Man* (New York: Vintage, 1947), 274–75.
6. Harry Haywood, *Black Bolshevik: Autobiography of an Afro-American Communist* (Chicago: Liberation Press, 1978), 345–46. Lengthy accounts of the League of Struggle for Negro Rights appear in a number of books by Gerald Horne, including *Black Revolutionary: William Patterson and the Globalization of the African American Freedom Struggle* (Urbana: University of Illinois Press, 2013), 47, 58. See also Earl Ofari Hutchinson, *Blacks and Reds: Race and Class in Conflict 1919–1990* (East Lansing: Michigan University Press, 1995), 141; Richard B. Moore, *The Collected Writings of Richard B. Moore: Caribbean Militant in Harlem, 1920–1972*, ed. W. Burghardt Turner and Joyce Moore Turner (Bloomington: Indiana University Press, 1992), 57–58; Mark Naison, *Communists in Harlem During the Depression* (New York: Grove Press, 1983), 42; and *The Encyclopedia of the American Left*, ed. Mary Jo Buhle, Paul Buhle, and Dan Georgakas (New York: Oxford University Press, 1998), 535. Interestingly,

the name Mary Dalton figures prominently in Richard Wright's novel *Native Son*.

7.   Coleman Young and Lonnie Wheeler, *Hard Stuff: The Autobiography of Mayor Coleman Young* (New York: Viking, 1994), 25.

8.   Ibid., 43.

9.   August Meier and Elliott Rudwick, *Black Detroit and the Rise of the UAW* (New York: Oxford University Press, 1979), 219.

10. Ibid., 45.

11. Beth Tompkins Bates, *The Making of Black Detroit in the Age of Henry Ford* (Chapel Hill: University of North Carolina Press, 2012), 197.

12. Tamara Barnes, "Buying, Boosting, and Building with the National Housewives' League," *Michigan History*, Mar.–Apr., 2013, p. 33.

13. Angela Dillard, *Faith in the City: Preaching Radical Social Change in Detroit* (Ann Arbor: University of Michigan Press, 2007), 70. The anti-union description is in direct contrast to the poetry of James McCall, and one wonders if by this time he is still the editor and publisher of the paper. His poem "The New Negro" is considered one of the seminal documents in the emergence of the Harlem Renaissance.

14. Meier, op. cit., 119.

15. Elijah Muhammad, *Message to the Blackman in America*, (Phoenix, AZ, Secretarius Memps Ministries, 1965) 17.

16. E. U. Essien-Udom, *Black Nationalism: A Search for an Identity in America* (Chicago & London: University of Chicago Press, 1962), 44. Searching for Fard's identity is no easy assignment, but here are few things that might be helpful for future scholars interested in such a pursuit. After 1934, very little is known about Fard's whereabouts. In his absence, the leadership role was assumed by Muhammad, and like his mentor, he too was known by various names, including Gulan Bogans and Mohammed Rassoull, and much earlier as Elijah Karriem. Among the lessons Fard taught his acolytes was not to participate in military matters since they are citizens of the Nation of Islam, not of the United States. Muhammad followed the letter and spirit of this advice.

In 1943, the FBI had entered the fray, if Fard and Muhammad weren't already in their crosshairs. It is clear from the blacked-out names in the redacted documents compiled by the FBI that one of their agents or an informant was among the small membership of the Nation of Islam, or Temple of Islam, as it was known at its inception. That informants were recruited and subsequently infiltrated the various organizations in Detroit and Chicago was confirmed in FBI documents during the period when Muhammad was interviewed and admitted that he hadn't registered with the Selective Service, resulting in his incarceration for four years (1942–46) in the Milan federal penitentiary in Michigan.

Overall, according to Clarence Kelley, director of the FBI, there were nearly fifty thousand pages of information pertaining to Fard and the Nation of Islam by 1974. Strangely, for all the snooping by law enforcement agencies, there is little evidence of correspondence between Fard and other members of the Nation of Islam, particularly between him and Muhammad and Burnsteen Muhammad, whose secretarial skills and good sense were absolutely indispensable for the founders of the NOI.

One of the few letters extant from Fard to Muhammad is not very coherent, perhaps merely a note in advance of a proposed future meeting in which points could be clarified. It was written at four in the morning, dated December 18, 1933, a year before Fard vanished, and mailed from the "South West Part of North America."

Fard begins by noting that he had received letters from Muhammad and from his brother, Kallatt. "I have been just getting over the terrible mistake and unofficial movements that you [sic] been taken not only one that you [sic] went to Birmingham but different time you have done minus things without saying anything before," Fard wrote, seemingly chastising his protégé. "I have numbers of records of charges against you; but I [sic] not brought them to enforce knowing you have taken these steps with good attentions. NOW MY DEAR BELOVED BROTHER, I will tell you again and again you have heard me from time to time that must not undertake the labor of Islam unless you do know it 100%."

Further along in the letter, Fard tells Muhammad that "the time is not ripe yet" for him to spread the word of his wisdom. Meanwhile, Muhammad is to study his assignments, particularly the complex math problems, to write down all the questions to ask when they meet, and to prepare for his trip to Chicago, of which he was to tell no one except his brother. In addition, he wrote, "you may promise some Ice Maker a big bone and get in with him and start arising [*sic*] the dead." An "ice maker" is a Christian minister, presumably someone who freezes his congregation with his sermons.

This letter may have been the last word from Fard, whose disappearance was as shrouded in mystery as his arrival. But perhaps, as noted scholar C. Eric Lincoln asserted in his book *The Black Muslims in America*, Fard had accomplished his mission and turned it over to an African American, Elijah Muhammad to lead. "Within three years," Lincoln wrote, "Fard had developed an organization so effective that he was able to withdraw almost entirely from active leadership."

Fard, Lincoln noted, had established a temple, developed a ritual and worship rules and regulations, founded a University of Islam—a combined elementary and secondary school—with an emphasis on mathematics, and created the Muslim Girls Training Class, "which taught young Muslim women the principles of home economics and how to be a proper wife and mother."

Furthermore, Fard left the seven thousand or so black Muslims with a new sense of identity, a new cosmology, a new eschatology, and a special place in the universe. To his way of thinking, African Americans were "Asiatic," the "original people" on Earth. He gave black men godlike status in relationship to the devil, whom Muhammad would transmogrify into white men.

17.   After Fard vanished into thin air, the door was open for Muhammad to elevate Fard himself from prophet to God incarnate, the Supreme God, "to whom was subordinated the commonplace godliness of the rank-and-file Blackman," Ernest Allen wrote in his essay included in *The Farrakhan Factor*, edited by Amy Alexander. "No more the worse for its indeterminacy than the idea of the Christian Trinity," Allen continued, "this dualistic notion of the divine would remain a pillar of NOI belief."

18.   Herb Boyd, *Amsterdam News*, May 11, 2011.

19.   G. Hubert, *The Detroit Riot of 1967* (Detroit: Wayne State University Press, 1969), 132.

Chapter 12: Boom Town

1.   Jeremy Williams, *Detroit: The Black Bottom Community* (Charleston, SC: Arcadia Publishing, 2009), 71. Mary Clarice McCauley

Cosey in Elaine Latzman Moon's *Untold Tales, Unsung Heroes: An Oral History of Detroit's African American Community, 1918–1967* (Detroit: Wayne State University Press, 1994), said the Brewster Public Housing Projects had just been built when she moved with her family in 1939.

2. Wilma Wood Henrickson, ed., *Detroit Perspectives: Crossroads and Turning Points* (Detroit: Wayne State University Press, 1991), 408–9.

3. Ibid., 410.

4. Angela Dillard, *Faith in the City: Preaching Radical Social Change in Detroit* (Ann Arbor: University of Michigan Press, 2007), 138.

5. Matthew Wilhelm Kapell, *Michigan Academician*, Sept. 22, 2009, and www.thefreelibrary.com/%22Miscreants,+be+they +white+or+colored%22%3A+the+local+press+reactions+to . . . -a0218112266.

6. Dillard, op. cit., 139.

7. Robert C. Weaver, *Negro Labor: A National Problem* (Port Washington, NY: Kennikat Press, 1946), 61.

8. Ibid., 68.

9. Ibid., 66.

10. Ibid., 77.

11. B. J. Widick, *Detroit: A City of Race and Class Violence* (Detroit: Wayne State University Press, 1972), 93.

12. Megan Taylor Shockley, "Working for Democracy: Working-Class African American Women, Citizenship, and Civil Rights in Detroit, 1940–1954," *Michigan Historical Review* 29, no. 2 (Fall 2003), 126.

13. Ibid., 142.

14. Interview with Katherine Brown, January 2014.

15. Thomas J. Sugrue, *The Origins of the Urban Crisis: Race and Inequality in Postwar Detroit* (Princeton, NJ: Princeton University Press, 1996), 28.

16. Stephen M. Ward, ed. *Pages from a Black Radical's Notebook: A James Boggs Reader* (Detroit: Wayne State University Press, 2011), 11. See Ernest Allen Jr.'s essay "Satokata Takahashi and the Flowering of Black Messianic Nationalism," *Black Scholar* 24, no. 1 (Winter 1994).

17. Ernest Allen Jr., "Satokata Takahashi and the Flowering of Black Messianic Nationalism," *Black Scholar* 24, no. 1 (Winter 1994), 39.

18. Ibid., 13.
19. Coleman Young with Lonnie Wheeler, *Hard Stuff: The Autobiography of Mayor Coleman Young* (New York: Viking Penguin, 1994), 49.
20. Ibid., 77.
21. Elijah Muhammad, *Message to the Blackman in America* (Phoenix, AZ: Secretarius Memps Ministeries, 1965), 179.
22. Allen, op. cit. 23.
23. Louis De Caro, *Malcolm and the Cross: The Nation of Islam, Malcolm X, and Christianity* (New York: New York University Press, 1998), 37.
24. E. U. Essien-Udom, *Black Nationalism: A Search for an Identity in America* (Chicago: University of Chicago Press, 1962), 68.
25. Ibid., 70.
26. Harvard Sitkoff, "Detroit Race Riot of 1943," *Michigan History Magazine* 53 (1969): 188.
27. Ibid., 189.
28. Interview with Katherine Brown, Jan. 11, 2014.
29. Interview with Sidney Barthwell Jr., Jan. 13, 2014.
30. Elaine Katzman Moon, *Untold Tales, Unsung Heroes: An Oral History of Detroit's African American Community, 1918–1967* (Detroit: Wayne State University Press, 1993), 78.
31. John Dancy, *Sand Against the Wind: The Memoirs of John C. Dancy* (Detroit: Wayne State University Press, 1966), 198.
32. Henrickson, op. cit., 423.
33. Williams, op. cit., 113.
34. Sitkoff, op. cit., 202.
35. Dancy, op. cit., 199.
36. James McGrath Morris, *Eye on the Struggle: Ethel Payne, the First Lady of the Black Press* (New York: Amistad/HarperCollins, 2014), 44.
37. Williams, op. cit., 76.
38. Young, op. cit. 85.
39. "25 African Americans You Need to Know," *Michigan History*, Jan.–Feb. 2001, p. 30; and www.blackpast.org/aah/brown-cora-mae-1914–1972.
40. Carolyn P. DuBose, *The Untold Story of Charles Diggs: The Public Figure, the Private Man* (Arlington, VA: Barton Pub. House, 1998), 7. This biography was originally published at Ann Arbor by the University of Michigan Press. According to Helen Nuttall

Brown, whose father was Dr. Harry M. Nuttall, the family didn't really rent the place to Diggs but allowed him to be the undertaker. See Elaine Latzman Moon's *Untold Tales, Unsung Heroes*.

Chapter 13: Breakthroughs

1. David Halberstam, *The Fifties* (New York: Villard Books, 1993), 128–29.
2. McArthur Binion, *Simplicism* (Detroit: G. R. N'Namdi Gallery, 2005), 1; interview with Binion, June 2, 2014.
3. Interview with Katherine Brown, Jan. 2014.
4. Halberstam, op. cit., 118–19.
5. Thomas Sugrue, *The Origins of the Urban Crisis: Race and Inequality in Postwar Detroit* (Princeton, NJ: Princeton University Press, 1996), 100.
6. Coleman Young with Lonnie Wheeler, *Hard Stuff: The Autobiography of Mayor Coleman Young* (New York: Viking, 1994), 146.
7. Suzanne E. Smith, *Dancing in the Street: Motown and the Cultural Politics of Detroit* (Cambridge, MA: Harvard University Press, 1999), 35.
8. Young, op. cit., 120.
9. See www.daahp.wayne.edu. Crockett was representing Carl Winter when he was cited for contempt of court and sentenced to four months in jail.
10. See http://hall.michiganwomen.org.
11. See www.usatoday.com/story/news/2013/07/01/john-conyers-korea/2480861.
12. Malcolm X with Alex Haley, *The Autobiography of Malcolm X* (New York: Ballantine, 1964), 220.
13. Simeon Wright with Herb Boyd, *Simeon's Story: An Eyewitness Account of the Kidnapping of Emmett Till* (Chicago: Lawrence Hill Books, 2010), 73–74. In this memoir, Wright dispels a number of myths and misconceptions about the incident, including whether Emmett actually whistled at Carolyn Bryant and what happened to the family after the trials.
14. Gayraud S. Wilmore and James H. Cone, eds., *Black Theology: A Documentary History, 1966–1979* (Maryknoll, NY: Orbis Books, 1979), 338–39. A much more definitive discussion of Cleage's ever evolving Black Christianity and the Shrine of the Black Madonna can be found in *Black Messiah* and *Black Christian Nationalism*.

15. Nick Salvatore, *Singing in a Strange Land: C. L. Franklin, the Black Church, and the Transformation of America* (Urbana: University of Illinois Press, 2006), 85.

16. Jeremy Williams, *Detroit: The Black Bottom Community* (Charleston, SC: Arcadia Pub. Co., 2009), 120.

17. See www.thehistorymakers.com/biography/shirley-ann-woodson -reid-40.

18. William R. Bauer, *Open the Door: The Life and Music of Betty Carter* (Ann Arbor: University of Michigan Press, 2003).

19. Herb Boyd and Kenn Cox, "Detroit Nightclubs," *The New Grove Dictionary of Jazz*, ed. Barry Kernfeld (New York: Macmillan, 1988), 206–7.

20. Miles Davis with Quincy Troupe, *Miles: The Autobiography* (New York: Simon & Schuster, 1989), 173.

21. Yusef Lateef with Herb Boyd, *The Gentle Giant: The Autobiography of Yusef Lateef* (Irvington, NJ: Morton Books, 2006), 71.

22. Dan Ouellette, *Ron Carter: Finding the Right Notes* (New York: Artistshare, 2008), 73.

23. Davis, op. cit., 171–75.

Chapter 14: From Motown to Showdown

1. August Meier and Elliott Rudwick, *Black Detroit and the Rise of the UAW* (New York: Oxford University Press, 1979), 219.

2. Ibid., 220.

3. Peter J. Hammer and Trevor W. Coleman, *Crusader for Justice: Federal Judge Damon J. Keith* (Detroit: Wayne State University Press, 2014), 68.

Chapter 15: A Brand-New Beat

1. Berry Gordy Jr., *To Be Loved* (New York: Warner Books, 1994), Kindle edition, chapter 2.

2. Ibid., 92.

3. William Robinson with David Ritz, *Smokey: Inside My Life* (New York: McGraw-Hill, 1989), 74.

4. Thomas J. Sugrue, *The Origins of the Urban Crisis: Race and Inequality in Postwar Detroit* (Princeton, NJ: Princeton University Press, 1996), 143.

5. Stephen M. Ward, ed., *Pages from a Black Radical's Notebook:*

A James Boggs Reader (Detroit: Wayne State University Press, 2011), 57.

6.   Ben Fong-Torres, ed., *The Motown Album: The Sound of Young America* (New York: St. Martin's, 1990), 30.

7.   Gordy, op. cit., 114.

8.   Robinson, op. cit., 103.

Chapter 16: Bing and Bang

1.   Nick Salvatore, *Singing in a Strange Land: C. L. Franklin, the Black Church, and the Transformation of America* (Urbana: University of Illinois Press, 2006), 237.

2.   Aretha Franklin with David Ritz, *Aretha: From These Roots* (New York: Villard Books, 1999), 99.

3.   Ken Coleman, *Million Dollars Worth of Nerve: Twenty People Who Helped to Power Black Bottom, Paradise Valley, and Detroit's Lower East Side* (Detroit: Coleman Communications, 2014), 54.

4.   Peter J. Hammer and Trevor W. Coleman, *Crusader for Justice: Federal Judge Damon J. Keith*, (Detroit: Wayne State University Press, 2014), 80.

5.   Coleman A. Young with Lonnie Wheeler, *Hard Stuff: The Autobiography of Mayor Coleman Young* (New York: Viking, 1994), 156.

6.   Dan Georgakas and Marvin Surkin, *Detroit: I Do Mind Dying—a Study in Urban Revolution* (Boston: South End Press, 1998), 16.

7.   An e-mail from Charles Simmons, Nov. 30, 2014. He elaborated on the organization and some of its activities: "We protested regularly at white owned and operated supermarkets which refused to hire Blacks. Or, we had our regular meetings in which we talked about a number of social justice leaders throughout history. These informal discussions always began a great debate about the person and the organization they represented. Our subjects included Critical Thinking; Education in Political Economy; African American and Labor History; Community Organizing; Social Justice History and Activism; U.S./Western International New Colonial and Military Policy; Leadership Training; Analysis of Corporate and Independent Media. And from studying the leaders of social justice and anti-colonial movements around the world, we learned about the need for study and courage to fight for change. Our development grew amidst the political and economic situation of de-facto segregation in commerce and official

segregation in housing; rising unemployment and discriminatory and unsafe working conditions due to the introduction of new technology into the auto industry sector, and a consistent level of Police Brutality against our community in 1963–65 Detroit. Four of the major confrontational activities we had included our opposition to the proposed Detroit Olympics in 1964; a major demonstration against Police Brutality; our travel to Cuba the same year; and General Baker's Call in 1965 'for support in Opposition to the Vietnam War draft.'" During his tenure at *Muhammad Speaks*, of which Malcolm X was the principal founder, Simmons filed numerous stories. He recounted his early days at the paper: "I began contributing articles to *Muhammad Speaks* Newspaper while I was working for the Associated Press in New York in 1969. I was hired by the Nation of Islam Leader, Mr. Elijah Muhammad to be the international correspondent after graduating from Columbia School of Journalism the following year. I continued writing for it through 1973 when I did a special assignment on the war in Angola. During that assignment, I was based at the United Nations and shared an office with a veteran journalist and editor of the *Harlem Daily Worker*, Abner Winston Berry. During the Fall, I would write about the discussions in the General Assembly by the Foreign Ministers, Presidents and representatives of the African Liberation Movements fighting against Apartheid and Colonialism, who came to the world body to share their views."

8.   David Goldberg, https://www.jacobinmag.com/2014/05/detroit-s-radical-general-baker. Luke Tripp recalled his days at Wayne State University: "I was attracted to socialist groups, which advocated struggle against racism and capitalism. It was through my contacts with these groups that I met young people who were interested in fighting racism through direct action. Together with a few of my Black friends whom I met on campus, we organized the Detroit Chapter of the Friends of the Student Non-violent Coordinating Committee in 1961 and participated in Civil Rights demonstrations in both the South and the North. However, most of us who were Black did not subscribe to the philosophy of nonviolence nor to the belief that racism and social inequality could be abolished within a capitalist system. Subsequently, we organized several radical student based organizations including the Black Action Committee and Uhuru. Our activities were

directed mainly against racial discriminatory practices of businesses in the Black community." See www.iww.org/history/documents/misc/Tripp, 2009.

9.   Thomas J. Sugrue, *The Origins of the Urban Crisis: Race and Inequality in Postwar Detroit* (Princeton, NJ: Princeton University Press, 1996), 195.

Chapter 17: March to Militancy

1.   Peter Gavrilovich and Bill McGraw, eds., *The Detroit Almanac: 300 Years of Life in the Motor City* (Detroit: Detroit Free Press, 2001), 113.

2.   Salvatore, op. cit., 256.

3.   See http://vault.fbi.gov/Malcolm%20X/Malcolm%20X%20Part%20 14%20of%2038/view.

4.   Nick Salvatore, *Singing in a Strange Land: C. L. Franklin, the Black Church, and the Transformation of America* (Urbana: University of Illinois Press, 2006), 266; and see the *New York Times*, Oct. 4, 1964, and the *Michigan Chronicle* from September through December.

5.   Coleman Young with Lonnie Wheeler, *Hard Stuff: The Autobiography of Mayor Coleman Young* (New York: Viking, 1994), 165.

6.   George Breitman, ed., *Malcolm X Speaks* (New York: Grove Weidenfeld, 1965), 171.

7.   Iyaluua Ferguson with Herman Ferguson, *An Unlikely Warrior: Herman Ferguson, the Evolution of a Black Nationalist Revolutionary* (Holly Springs, NC: Ferguson-Swan Publications, 2011), 144.

8.   Taylor Branch, *At Canaan's Edge: America in the King Years, 1965–68* (New York: Simon & Schuster, 2006), 194.

9.   Jeffrey Mirel, *The Rise and Fall of an Urban School System: Detroit, 1907–81* (Ann Arbor: University of Michigan Press, 1993), 302.

10.   Ibid., 316.

11.   Ibid., 321.

Chapter 18: The Motor City Is Burning

1.   Dan Georgakas and Marvin Surkin, *Detroit: I Do Mind Dying—a Study in Urban Revolution* (Boston: South End Press, 1994), 20.

2.   Interview with Conrad Mallett Jr., Apr. 26, 2106.

3. Van Gordon Sauter and Burleigh Hines, *Nightmare in Detroit* (Chicago: Henry Regnery, 1968), v–vi.

4. Arthur L. Johnson, *Race and Remembrance: A Memoir* (Detroit: Wayne State University Press, 2008), 102.

5. Martha Reeves with Mark Bego, *Dancing in the Street: Confessions of a Motown Diva* (New York: Hyperion, 1994), 147.

6. Peter J. Hammer and Trevor W. Coleman, *Crusader for Justice: Federal Judge Damon J. Keith* (Detroit: Wayne State University Press, 2014), 91.

7. Jeanne Theodaris, *The Rebellious Life of Mrs. Rosa Parks* (Boston: Beacon Press, 2013), 195.

8. Robert H. Mast, ed., *Detroit Lives* (Philadelphia: Temple University Press, 1994), 170–71.

9. See http://digital.wustl.edu/e/eii/eiiweb/ing5427.0527.070jimingram.html. Also see the television documentary series *Eyes on the Prize*, Henry Hampton, dir. (Two Cities, 1993).

10. Ibid., 41.

11. Joann Castle, from her unpublished manuscript, Nov. 29, 2014.

12. H. Rap Brown, *Die Nigger Die!* (New York: Dial Press, 1969), 137–38.

13. Dan Aldridge honored the author's request for his memory of the event, which he completed in September 2014. We offer it here in its entirety.

The Algiers Tribunal

Dan Aldridge

The Algiers Tribunal began on Wednesday, July 26, 1967, when Dorothy Dewberry of the Student Non-Violent Coordinating Committee informed me that she had received a telephone call from Margaret Cooper Gill and Omar Gill telling her that their son, Carl Cooper, and two of his friends had been shot to death by members of the Detroit Police Department at the Algiers Motel on Woodward Avenue near Virginia Park Street. They called Dorothy because they knew that she was involved in "the movement." I telephoned Mr. Gill seeking more detail, and he told me that he and his wife had been awakened from their sleep by a call from Lee Forsythe and James Sorter telling them that "Carl is dead." Gill explained further that when he called his son's room at the motel, the telephone was answered by what sounded like a "White policeman or detective," and when he said that he wanted to see the body of his stepson, Carl Cooper, the voice on the other end of the line told him, "You had better keep your black ass home. If you come over here, you'll get the same." It was about that time that he reported that Lee Forsythe and James Sorter burst into his living room, covered in blood almost head to toe and telling him that they witnessed the murder of Carl and saw Aubrey Pollard beaten so badly that he was almost unrecognizable. Gill ended the conversation by telling me that his son and his friends had been executed and that he wanted something done about it.

The next day, I contacted my friend, Lonnie Peek, and a photographer, Curt Slaughter. Later I contacted a Wayne State University law student and associate, Ken Cockrel, and Ken, Dorothy Dewberry, and I set about to interview the parents of the slain youth, plus Lee Forsythe, James Sorter, and a security guard who was employed by the Algiers Motel. All three were scared out of their wits, but they reported that they saw Carl Cooper get shot with a shotgun, while being forced to stand spread-eagle against the motel wall, heard Aubrey Pollard being shot in another room, and heard Fred Temple begging for his life in another room, prior to being shot. Forsythe and Sorter were only two of seven young black men who were badly beaten by Detroit police that early morning, in addition to the three who were murdered. It was not until later that we learned that the Detroit Police Department had first erroneously reported that Cooper, Pollard, and Temple were snipers who had been killed in a gun battle with police authorities. This lie was later retracted.

During our investigation, we learned that the *Detroit Free Press* had pictures of the crime scene and copies of preliminary autopsy reports, but they refused to grant us access to either.

Dorothy Dewberry and I were the co-directors of SNCC, and we had recently brought H. Rap Brown to Detroit to speak to what turned out to be a huge crowd at the Dexter Theater on Dexter Avenue. The crowd was so large that Rap had to speak from the roof of the theater. During that visit, I told Rap about the killing of the three young men and the fact that it appeared that the Detroit police officers who murdered these young men were not going to be prosecuted to the full letter of the law, and we concluded that a "people's tribunal" must be held to educate the public.

Sometime later, I approached John Ashby and his harpist wife, Dorothy Ashby, about holding the people's tribunal at the Dexter Theater. They said that the tribunal could be held there, but they asked us to try to obtain another venue because they had been threatened by the police because of the Rap Brown event. I agreed to search for another place to meet, because I knew that the police were not playing around and would probably be out to punish anyone whom they thought was connected to such a tribunal.

Lonnie Peek and I hid Forsythe and Sorter in a private location because we knew that some members of the Detroit Police Department were looking for them to eliminate them as witnesses. We had been informed by the "street communication system" that they were kicking in doors in the neighborhood and questioning/threatening people to surrender their location. Curt Slaughter and I attended every day of the preliminary examination/hearing for officers Ronald August and Robert Paille. We were told there and shown by members of the Detroit Police Department by slashing-of-the-throat signs that we would never live long enough to hold any "damn tribunal."

The preliminary examination was interesting, because Wayne County Assistant Prosecutor Avery Weiswasser never called any of the black witnesses. When I asked Mr. Weiswasser about this during one of the breaks, he told me, "I didn't call them because their testimony would be irrelevant." Needless to say, the killers were released on the basis on insufficient evidence to charge them.

Four of what we believed to be plainclothes officers attempted to shoot Lonnie and me on Euclid or Philadelphia Street near Grand River Street. We were running so low to the ground that I had to push dirt and sand out of my pocket to maintain my balance. We survived. We also believed that the police had set our friend Ed Vaughn's bookstore on fire during the week of July 26. We knew that hosting the tribunal was risky.

A planning committee for the tribunal was organized, consisting of Lonnie Peek, Dorothy Dewberry, Richard Henry, Milton Henry, Madelyn Cheeks, our stenographer Carolyn Cheeks (later Congresswoman Carolyn Cheeks Kilpatrick), Ron Pugh, Selina Howard, Edward Howard, Ed Vaughn, myself, and a number of other people who were members of the Shrine of the Black Madonna. We approached Rev. Cleage, the pastor, asking for permission to host the tribunal at the church, and he enthusiastically gave his support and encouragement.

Milton Henry advised the committee on how to hold a tribunal. Attorney Justin Ravitz presided as the judge, attorney Andrew Purdue served as the defense attorney for officers August, Paille, and Senak. Attorneys Milton Henry and Ken Cockrel served as prosecuting attorneys for the black community. The jury consisted of Mrs. Rosa Parks, People Against Racism director Frank Joyce, novelist John O. Killens, entrepreneur Ed Vaughn, and eight other people whom I cannot remember at the moment. The charges were three counts of first-degree murder, among other charges. Special seating was arranged and set aside for members of the press, including the *Michigan Chronicle*, the *Detroit Free Press*, the *Detroit News*, and international press from as far away as Sweden.

Officers August, Paille, and Senak were invited to participate in the event, as were assistant prosecutors Weiswasser and James Garber, Wayne County Prosecutor William L. Cahalan, the families of the slain youths, an attorney for the Detroit Police Officers Association named Norman Lippitt, and witnesses from the Algiers Motel—Michael Clark, Lee Forsythe, James Sorter, and Charles Brown. After a presentation of the evidence, the three officers were convicted of first-degree murder, with sentencing to be handed down in the future by the community.

The church was filled beyond capacity, with people standing in the balcony, every aisle, and the basement and spilling out to cover both sides of Linwood Avenue, in front of the church and across the street. The Rev. Cleage estimated that the crowd was easily more than two thousand, but the *Detroit Free Press* and the *Detroit News*, both of which had only a few words to say about the event, estimated the attendance at a couple of hundred, even though there were more than two hundred people standing outside who couldn't get in. Loudspeakers were placed outside for their benefit.

14. *Report of the National Advisory Commission on Civil Disorders* (New York: Bantam, 1968), 1–29.

In another account by Bill McGraw, a longtime reporter for the *Detroit Free Press*, he discloses that William Scott threw the bottle that set off the rebellion. See: http://www.bridgemi.com /detroit-bankruptcy-and-beyond/he-started-detroit-riot-his -son-wrestles-carnage

15. Ibid.

16. Joe T. Darden and Richard W. Thomas, *Detroit: Race Riots, Racial Conflicts, and Efforts to Bridge the Racial Divide* (East Lansing: Michigan State University Press, 2013), 13.

17. Joann Castle, from her unpublished manuscript, Nov. 29, 2014. She further noted, "Another was the early strength of the Communist Party in Detroit and the class analysis portrayed in its slogan 'Black and white, unite and fight.' Black workers in the plants understood the real enemy. WCO's mission of self-determination was consistent with this class analysis that perceived race to be a distraction in the real fight against injustice. In the summer of 1969, Tony and I were encouraged by Sheila to share the information we had secretly replicated at the Chancery office on the misuse of poverty program funds with representatives of The Black Manifesto. I knew a little about the Manifesto from what I had read in the newspaper."

18. Sidney Fine, *Violence in the Model City: The Cavanagh Administration, Race Relations, and the Detroit Riot of 1967* (Ann Arbor: University of Michigan Press, 1969), 375.

19. Paul Lee, *Michigan Citizen*, June 22, 2008, http://michianciti zen.com/prophet-of-possibility-pt-ii.

20. Interview with Ron Lockett, June 4, 2014.

21. Georgakas, op. cit., 43.

22. Interview with Gene Cunningham, June 12, 2014.

23. Nick Medvecky, e-mail, Oct. 8, 2014.

Chapter 19: Our Thing Is DRUM!

1. Dan Georgakas and Marvin Surkin, *Detroit: I Do Mind Dying—a Study in Urban Revolution* (New York: Viking, 1994), 21.

2. Michael Hamlin and Michele Gibbs, *A Black Revolutionary's Life in Labor: Black Workers' Power in Detroit* (Detroit: Against the Tide Books, 2013), 125.

3. Ibid., 19.

4. Ibid., 34.

5. Dick Cluster, ed., *They Should Have Served That Cup of Coffee: 7 Radicals Remember the 60s* (Boston: South End Press, 1979), 75.

6. Robert H. Mast, ed., *Detroit Lives* (Philadelphia: Temple University Press, 1994), 309. The Black Panther Party never gained much traction in Detroit, but they did have several serious encounters with the police, including some that resulted in the shooting deaths of officers. Dr. Ahmad A. Rahman's essay on the party's brief existence in the city provides an understanding of what happened and why. "Detroit's insurrection of 1967 bequeathed complicated political dynamics for those who established a Panther presence in that city," Professor Rahman concluded. "The Panthers' simplistic 'off the pig' rhetoric did not meet the political challenge of the day. Youthful idealism and courageous dedication proved insufficient to the tasks of survival for a Panther underground. Without expertise in covert warfare, the Black Panthers' overt warfare headed for inevitable defeat from the start. They were, in fact, an army marching blind." Ahman A Rahman, "Marching Blind: The Rise and Fall of the Black Panther Party in Detroit, 1942–1971," in *Liberated Territory: Untold Perspectives on the Black Panther Party* (Durham, NC: Duke University Press, 2008).

7. Cluster, op. cit., 78.

8. James Forman, *The Making of Black Revolutionaries* (Washington, DC: Open Hand Publishing, 1985), 545.

9. Gayraud S. Wilmore and James H. Cone, eds., *Black Theology: A Documentary History, 1966–1979* (Maryknoll, NY: Orbis Books, 1982), 84.

10. Forman, op. cit., 549.

11. Cluster, op. cit., 100.

12. Nick Medvecky, e-mail, Oct. 8, 2014.

13. Patricia Bosworth, *Jane Fonda: The Private Life of a Public Woman* (Boston: Houghton Mifflin Harcourt, 2011), 336.

14. Kenneth and Sheila Cockrel Collection, Reuther Library, Accession 1379, Box 1. The letter from Fonda was dated April 26, 1972. Cockrel's reply was written on May 8, 1972. And after hoping to meet her someday to discuss further any projects, he concluded the letter by congratulating her on winning an Oscar for her role in *Klute* and her acceptance speech, which he said "was handled most 'correctly' given the expectations of the vipers."

15. Mast, op. cit., 310.

Chapter 20: Under Duress from STRESS

1. David Ritz, *Divided Soul: The Life of Marvin Gaye* (New York: Da Capo Press, 1985), 148.
2. Dan Georgakas and Marvin Surkin, *Detroit: I Do Mind Dying—a Study in Urban Revolution* (Nre York: Viking, 1994), 168.
3. Ibid.
4. See http://rdpffa.org/main-files/pdf/unity/unity0112rev.pdf.
5. *Toledo Blade*, Mar. 9, 1972, p. 1.
6. Interview with Sadiq Bey, Mar. 28, 2014. Dr. Melba Joyce Boyd has a more personal account of this incident in her essay devoted to the memory of Chokwe Lumumba in *Free The Land!* ed. Charles Ezra Ferrell (Southfield, MI: Liberation Voice, 2015), 182.
7. *Sault Sainte Marie Evening News*, Dec. 15, 1972, p. 11.
8. See www.odmp.org/officer/reflections/2144-police-officer-robert-p-bradford-jr.
9. Socialists Workers Party *Militant*, May 28, 1973, p. 3.
10. Coleman Young with Lonnie Wheeler, *Hard Stuff: The Autobiography of Mayor Coleman Young* (New York: Viking Penguin, 1994), 200.
11. Ibid., 200.
12. *Detroit Black Journal* with Trudy Gallant, 1989, http://abj.matrix.msu.edu/videofull.php?id=29-DF-1F.
13. Al Stark, *Detroit News Sunday Magazine*, Mar. 18, 1973, p. 21.
14. Dan Fisher, *Los Angeles Times*, Apr. 15, 1971, p. 2.
15. Young, op. cit., 219.

Chapter 21: Muses and Music

1. Naomi Long Madgett, "Dudley Randall's Life and Career," Modern American Poetry, www.english.illinois.edu/maps/poets/m_r/randall/life.htm.
2. Melba Joyce Boyd, *Wrestling with the Muse: Dudley Randall and the Broadside Press* (New York: Columbia University Press, 2003), 3. Boyd also produced and directed a fifty-four-minute documentary on Randall's life entitled *Black Unicorn: Dudley Randall and the Broadside Press* (1995).
3. William J. Maxwell, *F.B. Eyes: How J. Edgar Hoover's Ghostreaders Framed African American Literature* (Princeton, NJ: Princeton University Press, 2014), 168. Randall's FBI file was relatively

thin compared to those of other writers, such as Claude McKay, Langston Hughes, James Baldwin, and Amiri Baraka, even when covering only the three years from 1966 to 1969.

4. James Edward Smethurst, *The Black Arts Movement: Literary Nationalism in the 1960s and 1970s* (Chapel Hill: University of North Carolina Press, 2005), 76.

5. Harold Bloom, *African-American Poets*, vol. 1 (New York: Info-base Publishing, 2009), 32.

6. Haki R. Madhubuti, *Liberation Narratives: New and Collected Poems, 1966–2009* (Chicago: Third World Press, 2009), xxi.

7. Betty DeRamus, "On Dudley Randall," *Detroit News*, Aug. 15, 2000, www.english.illinois.edu/maps/poets/m_r/randall/life.htm.

8. Smethurst, op. cit., 227.

9. See www.english.illinois.edu/maps/poets/m_r/randall/life.htm.

10. Martha Reeves, and Mark Bego, *Dancing in the Street: Confessions of a Motown Diva* (New York: Hyperion, 1994), 201.

11. Cited from the brochure "A Salute to Paul Robeson" dispensed that evening at the concert, which was co-published by the Paul Robeson Archives and the Afro-American Museum of Detroit.

12. Nick Sousanis, "The Art of Seeing Art," *Detroit Metro Times*, Jan. 4, 2006, www.metrotimes.com/detroit/the-art-of-seeing-art/Content?oid=2183585.

13. Barbara Weinberg and Herb Boyd, *Jazz Space Detroit* (Detroit: Jazz Research Institute, 1980), 17.

14. *Black World*, Mar. 1975, 81.

Chapter 22: Coleman and Cockrel

1. "By the summer of 1975, now a year and a half into new Mayor Coleman Young's first term, the city was about to nose dive into even deeper and yet more troubled waters. On a sweltering July day in 1975, Bolton's Bar off Livernois was busy keeping its white clientele cool. With the continual racial fallout from the '67 riot 8 years previous still spreading like a cancer, most of the old mom and pop stores had long since pulled out and re-anchored in the suburbs. But not Andrew Chinarian, the bar's owner, who had ignored the tidal wave of white flight over the depressive decade of the 70s to man the last stand of whites in Old Detroit.

"On July 28th, Chinarian exited the bar, only to find several black youths tampering with a car in the parking lot. Chinarian fired a shot at 18 year old Obie Wynn, striking him in the back of the head. Wynn died 9 hrs later.

"Chinarian claimed he was only attempting to fire a warning shot over Wynn's head. The triggering point came when Chinarian was taken into custody and then released on a paltry $500 bond. The neighborhood at Livernois & 7 Mile exploded. Bolton's Bar was ransacked and set on fire."

See www.detroits-great-rebellion.com/Post-Riot-Detroit.html.

2. Coleman Young with Lonnie Wheeler, *Hard Stuff: The Autobiography of Coleman Young* (New York: Viking, 1994), 232.

3. Rev. Charles Butler, *Detroit Lives*, ed. Robert Mast (Philadelphia: Temple University Press, 1994), 193.

4. Ibid., 196.

5. Thomas J. Sugrue, *The Origins of the Urban Crisis: Race and Inequality in Postwar Detroit* (Princeton, NJ: Princeton University Press, 1996), 113; and *Detroit Free Press*, Nov. 7, 1977.

6. Jeanie Wylie, *Poletown (Community Betrayed)* (Urbana: University of Illinois Press, Urbana, 1990), xiv.

7. Herb Boyd, "Last Hired, First Fired," *Detroit Metro Times*, Oct. 16–30, 1980, p. 1.

8. Nick Salvatore, *Singing in a Strange Land: C. L. Franklin, the Black Church, and the Transformation of America* (Urbana: University of Illinois Press, 2006), 309.

9. Ibid., 316.

10. Wylie, op. cit., 139.

11. Bill McGraw, *The Quotations of Mayor Coleman A. Young* (Detroit: Wayne State University Press, 2005), 8.

12. Interview with Moten, Sept. 17, 2014.

13. Tom Lawton, *Michigan Journal*, Oct. 3, 1979, p. 2.

14. Dan Georgakas and Marvin Surkin, *Detroit: I Do Mind Dying—a Study in Urban Revolution* (Boston: South End Press, 1994), 211.

Chapter 23: Postindustrial Blues

1. See www.metrolyrics.com/detroit-city-blues-lyrics-fats-domino.html.

2. Ron Chepesiuk, *The War on Drugs: An International Encyclopedia* (Santa Barbara, CA: ABC-Clio, 1999), 269. An inside view of the gang is disclosed in Raymond Canty's *Autobiography of Butch Jones Y.B.I Young Boys Inc.* (H Publications, 1996).

3. Interview with George Gaines, June 13, 2014. A similar account of this experience can be found on YouTube, https://www.you tube.com/watch?v=f9hp07cQ8hA.

4. Dudley Randall, *Rose and Revolutions—The Selected Writings of Dudley Randall*, (Detroit: Wayne State University Press, 2009), 208.

5. Interview with Emmett Moten, September 17, 2014.

6. Herb Boyd, *Detroit Metro Times*, Apr. 2–16, 1981, p. 10.

7. Ibid., 11.

8. Steve Babson, *Working Detroit: The Making of a Union Town* (Detroit: Wayne State University Press/Adama Books, 1984), 215.

9. *Owosso* [MI] *Argus-Press*, Nov. 3, 1986, p. 20.

10. James Barron, "Judge Is Critical of Detroit Mayor," *Detroit Free Press*, Sept. 2, 1984, www.nytimes.com/1984/09/02/us/judge-is-critical-of-detroit-mayor.html.

11. Judge Feikens also incurred the wrath of Anna Diggs-Taylor, who wrote him a letter released to the press in which she chastised him for his insensitive remarks about the inability of African Americans to run a city. In 1997 she became the first chief judge to receive the baton from a previous black chief judge.

12. Ze'ev Chafets, *Devil's Night and Other True Tales of Detroit* (New York: Vintage e-book, Oct. 1991), 1.

13. Stephen Ward, ed., *Pages from a Black Radical's Notebook: A James Boggs Reader* (Detroit: Wayne State University Press, 2011), 322.

14. Dianne Hudson, producer, and Ed Gordon, host, "Teen Gang Violence," *American Black Journal*, 1985, http://abj.matrix.msu.edu/videofull.php?id=29-DF-1D.

15. Coleman Young and Lonnie Wheeler, *Hard Stuff: The Autobiography of Mayor Coleman Young* (New York: Viking, 1994), 287.

16. Stephen Franklin, "Murders Torment Detroit," *Chicago Tribune*, Jan. 13, 1987, http://articles.chicagotribune.com/1987-01-13/news/8701040022_1_highest-murder-rate-mayor-coleman-young-suburbs.

17. Peter Gavrilovich and Bill McGraw, eds., *The Detroit Almanac: 300 Years of Life in the Motor City* (Detroit: Detroit Free Press, 2001), 501.

18. Woodie King Jr., ed., *New Plays for the Black Theatre* (Chicago: Third World Press, 1989), 165.

19. Ward, op. cit., 327.

20. Christopher J. Singleton, "Auto Industry Jobs in the 1980s: A

Decade of Transition," *Monthly Labor Review*, Feb. 1992, www
.bls.gov/mlr/1992/02/art2full.pdf, p. 22.

21. Several conversations with Ms. Coley over the years.

22. Denise Crittendon and Charlie Cain, *Detroit News*, Apr. 30,
1989, p. 1. Jesse delivered these words during his testimony at
his brother's memorial service.

23. See www.johnsinclair.us/columns-and-reviews/20-features/861-
in-memory-of-kenneth-v-cockrel.html.

24. Michael Hamlin and Michele Gibbs, *A Black Revolutionary's Life
in Labor: Black Workers' Power in Detroit* (Detroit: Against the
Tide Books, 2012), 16.

25. Dan Georgakas and Marvin Surkin, *Detroit: I Do Mind Dying:
A Study in Urban Revolution* (Boston: South End Press, 1998),
211.

26. Jeanne Theoharis, *The Rebellious Life of Mrs. Rosa Parks* (Boston:
Beacon Press, 2013), 231. At Parks's birthday salute, Lou Rawls,
Dick Gregory, Sister Sledge, Dionne Warwick, Cicely Tyson, and
Melissa Manchester were among the performers.

27. "Flashback: 18 Hours in 1990 when Mandela Charmed Detroit," *Detroit Free Press*, Dec. 5, 2013, www.freep.com/arti
cle/20131205/NEWS05/312050141/1990-flashback-Nelson-
Mandela-s-18-hour-fund-raising-visit-Detroit.

28. Peter J. Hammer and Trevor W. Coleman, *Crusader for Justice:
Federal Judge Damon J. Keith* (Detroit: Wayne State University
Press, 2014), 234.

29. Arthur Johnson, *Race and Remembrance: A Memoir* (Detroit:
Wayne State University Press, 2008), 225.

Chapter 24: A Mayor and Malice

1. Coleman Young and Lonnie Wheeler, *Hard Stuff: The Autobiography of Mayor Coleman Young* (New York: Viking, 1994), 294.

2. *Michigan Chronicle*, editorial, Jan. 13, 1990, p. 6a.

3. Bill Harris, *Riffs & Coda: Two Plays* (Detroit: Broadside Press,
1990), 131.

4. Dennis Bowles, *Dr. Beans Bowles "Fingertips": The Untold Story*
(Ferndale, MI: Sho-nuff Productions, 2003), 171.

5. Jill Day-Foley, "Merchants' Steps to Economic Freedom," *Michigan Chronicle*, Feb. 10, 1990, p. 6. Vaughn observed that every
ethnic group in the country "takes care of themselves. We on the

other hand, love everyone else but ourselves first, give to everyone but ourselves."

6. See http://hbcuconnect.com/colleges/52/lewis-college-of-business.

7. "Toughing It Out," *Black Enterprise*, June 1991, p. 100.

8. "Malice Green Beating Death Trials: 1993–2000," http://law.jrank.org/pages/3568/Malice-Green-Beating-Death-Trials-1993-2000.html.

9. Ibid., 2.

10. "Medical Technical Tells Detroit Trial About Gruesome Beating of Motorist," *Baltimore Sun*, July 15, 1993, http://articles.baltimoresun.com/1993–07–15/news/1993196176_1_walsh-malice-green-blood.

11. "Malice Green Beating Death Trials: 1993–2000," http://law.jrank.org/pages/3568/Malice-Green-Beating-Death-Trials-1993-2000.html.

12. Sue Ellen Christian, *Chicago Tribune*, Feb. 10, 1998, http://articles.chicagotribune.com/1998–02–10/news/9802100262_1_malice-green-retrial-detroit-police-officer.

13. Joe T. Darden and Richard W. Thomas, *Detroit: Race Riots, Racial Conflicts and Efforts to Bridge the Racial Divide* (East Lansing: Michigan State University Press, 2013), 121.

14. Young, op. cit., 320.

15. Darden, op. cit., 125. This is a quote from urbanologist W.J.V. Neill, though it's unclear which source is used, because the date cited is different from the one listed in their bibliography. Even so, Neill's indictment of the Young administration is consistent with his article "Lipstick on the Gorilla: The Failure of Image-Led Planning in Coleman Young's Detroit," *International Journal of Urban and Regional Research* 19, no 4, (Dec. 1, 1995), 639–53.

16. Thomas J. Sugrue, *The Origins of the Urban Crisis: Race and Inequality in Postwar Detroit* (Princeton, NJ: Princeton University Press, 1996), 270.

17. Jeanne Theoharis, *The Rebellious Life of Mrs. Rosa Parks* (Boston: Beacon Press, 2013), 233.

18. Ibid.

19. Khaalid Walls, *African Americans on Wheels* magazine, 1998, National Automotive History Collection, Detroit Public Library.

20. Arthur L. Johnson, *Race and Remembrance: A Memoir* (Detroit: Wayne State University Press, 2008), 226.

21. Amy J. Schultz, David R. Williams, Barbara A. Israel, and Lora

Bex Lempert, "Racial and Spatial Relations as Fundamental Determinants of Health in Detroit," *Milbank Quarterly* 80, no. 4 (Dec. 2002), 677–707.

22. *Michigan Chronicle*, Apr. 23–29, 1997, p. C-6.

23. Cassandra Spratling, *Detroit Free Press*, Dec. 24, 2013.

24. Dr. Roberta Hughes Wright, *The Man & The Museum: The Charles H. Wright Museum of African American History and Charles H. Wright* (Detroit: Harlo Printing and Publishing, 2014), 232.

25. *Detroit Free Press*, Oct. 20, 1999; see also Carol Brennan, *Contemporary Black Biography*, 2000.

26. See http://history.house.gov/People/Detail?id=12254.

27. Ibid.

28. Walter Gilbert and Lina Jones, "Detroit Schools Takeover Approved by Michigan Legislature," *World Socialist*, Apr. 6, 1999, www.wsws.org/en/articles/1999/04/det-a06.html.

29. Ibid.

30. John Telford, "Fascism & Classism in Detroit and Lansing," *Detroiter Resisting Emergency Management*, Dec. 22, 2013.

31. CNN.com, Sept. 6, 1999, http://edition.cnn.com/US/9909/06/detroit.schools.01.

32. Rich Gibson, "The Theory and Practice of Constructing Hope: The Detroit Teachers' Wildcat Strike 1999," http://clogic.eserver.org/2-2/gibson.html.

33. Alex P. Kellogg, "Black Flight Hits Detroit," *Wall Street Journal*, June 5, 2010, http://datadrivendetroit.org/wp-content/uploads/2010/04/WSJ-article.pdf.

34. Melissa Maynard, "Michigan and Detroit: A Troubled Relationship," *USA Today*, July 31, 2013.

Chapter 25: Emergency, Resurgency

1. *Michigan Chronicle*, Jan. 5–11, 2000, p. 3.

2. See http://www.encyclopedia.com/doc/1G2-3057100023.html.

3. See http://www.heidelberg.org.

4. Myron Wade Curenton, *Plowshares Theatre Company: The First Twenty Years* (Ann Arbor, MI: ProQuest, 2008), 88.

5. Susan Whitall, *Women of Motown: An Oral History* (New York: Avon Books, 1998), https://groups.google.com/forum/#!topic/alt.music.soul/2262MWeT0FI.

6.   Maxine Powell, "When I Think of Gwen," *Michigan Chronicle*, Jan. 5–11, 2000, p. D-2.

7.   Larry Gabriel, *Detroit Metro Times*, Sept. 27, 2000.

8.   *Michigan Chronicle*, Jan. 5–11, 2000, p. A-8.

9.   Ibid., A-9.

10.   Detroit City Council Proceedings and Minutes, Nov. 29, 2000, p. 3050, http://www.detroitmi.gov/Portals/0/docs/city-clerk/2000%20Council.pdf.

11.   Curt Guyette, "Points of Doubt," *Detroit Metro Times*, Dec. 6, 2000.

12.   "Police Secrets," *Detroit Metro Times*, Mar. 21, 2001; and Diane Bukowski, "Detroit Family Wins $2.5 Million in Police Lawsuit," *Chicago Final Call*, Aug. 17, 2010.

13.   Jack Lessenberry, "Detroit's Mayoral Primary Turned Upside Down," *Toledo Blade*, Sept. 29, 2001.

Chapter 26: Kwame Time!

1.   M. L. Elrick, Fox 2 News, WJBK Detroit, Oct. 19, 2012.

2.   Bill McGraw, "The Rise and Fall of Kwame Kilpatrick, *Detroit Free Press*, Sept. 5, 2008.

3.   Tim Jones, "Motor City Mayor Racing to Improve City," *Chicago Tribune*, June 16, 2002.

4.   Kevin Chappell, *Ebony*, Apr. 2003, p. 160.

5.   Ibid.

6.   Carmen Regalado and Ron Lare, "The Detroit Teachers' Strike," *Solidarity*, Jan.–Feb. 2007, www.solidarity-us.org/node/308.

7.   "Records: Detroit Mayor Charged $210K for Wining, Dining," Associated Press, May 3, 2005.

8.   Desiree Cooper, "Kilpatrick's Win Was Not Really a Surprise," *Detroit Free Press*, Nov. 10, 2005, p. B-1.

9.   Carlos Osario, "Thousands Attend Rosa Parks' Funeral in Detroit," Associated Press, Nov. 2, 2005.

10.   John Corvino, "Uninspiring Campaign," *Detroit Free Press*, Nov. 21, 2005, p. 8.

11.   See www.c-span.org/video/?190593–1/detroit-mayoral-inauguration.

12.   Desiree Cooper, "Super Bowl Event Also a Chance to Honor King," *Detroit Free Press*, Jan., 26, 2006.

Chapter 27: A Spark of Redevelopment

1. Angel Cecil, "Performers Get Freedom Honors," *Detroit Free Press*, May 16, 2006, p. B-2.
2. See http://nonprofit.umich.edu/students/minicase/cccminicase_content.pdf.
3. Jeff Karoub, "Wall That Once Divided Races in Detroit Remains, Teaches," Associated Press, May 1, 2015.
4. Alejandro Bodipo-Memba, "4 Black Business Groups Join Forces to Lift Economy," *Detroit Free Press*, Oct. 17, 2006, p. E-1.
5. See www.hungercenter.org/wp-content/uploads/2014/02/Co-op-Grocery-Stores-Clark.pdf.
6. See www.detroitblackfoodsecurity.org.
7. Cassandra Spratling, "Bert's Marketplace," *Detroit Free Press*, June 14, 2007.
8. See www.blackenterprise.com/mag/desperate-in-detroit/2.
9. Howard Bossen and John Beck, eds., *Detroit Resurgent* (East Lansing: Michigan State University Press, 2014), 152.
10. Mark Lee, "N'Namdi Center for Contemporary Art Grows to Offer Broader Services in Detroit's Creative Sector," *Crain's Detroit*, Nov. 19, 2014, http://www.crainsdetroit.com/article/20141119/BLOG106/141119755/nnamdi-center-for-contemporary-art-grows-to-offer-broader-servicesN'Namdi.
11. Interview with Ron Lockett, July 12, 2016.

Chapter 28: Dhaka in Detroit

1. Courtney Flynn, Michigan Department of Community Health; and www.detroitkidsdata.org/dkdquickfacts.htm.
2. U.S. Census Bureau, https:www.census.gov/newsroom.
3. Kurt Badenhausen, "America's Most Miserable Cities," *Crain's*, Jan. 30, 2008.
4. Mitt Romney, "Let Detroit Go Bankrupt," *New York Times*, op-ed, Nov. 18, 2008.
5. Herb Boyd, "Ovations for Obama in Motown," *Amsterdam News*, June 16, 2008.
6. Interview with Addie Thompson, Jan. 2014.
7. Trevor Calero, *Michigan Daily*, Nov. 5, 2008, www.michigandaily.com/content/2008–11–05/michigan-democratic-watch-party.

8. Susan Saulny and Nick Bunkley, "Detroit's Mayor Will Leave Office and Go to Jail," *New York Times*, Sept. 3, 2008.

9. Ibid.

10. Drew Sharp, *Dave Bing: A Life of Challenge* (Champaign, IL: Human Kinetics, 2013), 227.

11. Ibid., 228.

12. Corey Williams and Ed White, "Aiyana Jones, 7-Year-Old Shot and Killed by Detroit Police, Was Sleeping, According to Family," Associated Press, May 17, 2010.

13. Bridgette Outten, Politics365, July 11, 2010, http://politic365 .com/2010/06/11/exclusive-detroit-mayor-bing-talks-budget-aiyana-jones-and-more.

14. Sharp, op. cit., 256.

15. See http://robertbobbgroup.com/about-us/robert-c-bobb.

16. Nick Anderson, "Former D.C. Official Robert Bobb Making Waves in Troubled Detroit School System," *Washington Post*, Dec. 24, 2010.

17. Ibid.

18. Sharp, op. cit. 258.

19. Jim McFarlin, "Mayor Bing's Ousted Chief Communicator, Karen Dumas, Speaks," *Hour Detroit*, Aug. 16, 2011. See: Drew Sharp, *Dave Bing—A Life of Challenge* (Human Kinetics, Champaign, Il, 2013), 268–270

20. Dave Bing, "The Community Celebrates Michigan Chronicle Publisher Sam Logan's Leadership and Life," *Michigan Chronicle*, Dec. 29, 2011.

21. Interview with Dave Bing, June 15, 2014.

Chapter 29: A Looming Chimera

1. Jennifer Chambers, "Detroiters' Optimism Captivates Ford Foundation Head," *Detroit News*, June 16, 2015.

2. Donald James, "New York–Based Capital Management Firm to Open Detroit Office," *Michigan Chronicle*, Sept. 10–16, 2014, section C. Rhea could have talked about another far more romantic coalition with his wife, Tiffany Hall, a former Detroiter. They were married in the spring of 2014 and, coincidentally, their fathers, Walter Rhea and Elliott Hall, both attended Chadsey High School.

3. "Thousands Line Up For 500 Jobs Available at Quicken Loans," CBS Detroit, Apr. 20, 2013.

4. Monica Davey and Mary Williams Walsh, "Plan to Exit Bankruptcy Approved for Detroit," *New York Times*, Nov. 7, 2014.

5. See www.crainsdetroit.com/article/20160210/BLOG009/160219986/shinola-launches-national-ad-campaign-focused-on-employees-job.

6. See https://www.glassdoor.com/Overview/Working-at-Shinola-EI_IE678762.11,18.htm.

7. Interview with Councilman James Tate, June 17, 2014.

8. Interview with jessica Care moore, June 24, 2014.

INDEX

ABOUT THE AUTHOR

HERB BOYD is a journalist, activist, teacher, and author or editor of twenty-three books, including his latest, *The Diary of Malcolm X*, edited with Ilyasah Al- Shabazz, Malcolm X's daughter. His articles have been published in the *Black Scholar, Final Call*, the *Amsterdam News, Cineaste, Downbeat*, the *Network Journal*, and the *Daily Beast*. A scholar for more than forty years, he teaches African American history and culture at the City College of New York in Harlem, where he lives.

ALSO BY **HERB BOYD**

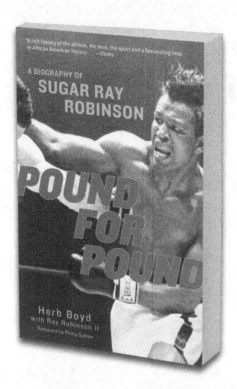

POUND FOR POUND
A Biography of Sugar Ray Robinson
Available in Paperback and eBook

"A rich history of the athlete, the man, the sport, and a fascinating
time in African American history." —*Ebony*

Hailed by critics as a long overdue portrait of Sugar Ray Robinson, a man who
was as elusive out of the ring as he was magisterial in it, *Pound for Pound* is a lively
and nuanced profile of an athlete who is arguably the best boxer the sport has ever
known. Exposing Robinson's flaws as well as putting his career in the context
of his life and times, renowned journalist and bestselling author Herb Boyd,
with Ray Robinson II, tells for the first time the full story of a complex
man and sport-altering athlete.